THE FUJIMORI LEGACY

THE FUJIMORI LEGACY

THE RISE OF ELECTORAL AUTHORITARIANISM IN PERU

EDITED BY JULIO F. CARRIÓN

THE PENNSYLVANIA STATE UNIVERSITY PRESS
UNIVERSITY PARK, PENNSYLVANIA

Publication of this book has been supported by a grant from the Department of Political Science and International Relations, University of Delaware.

Library of Congress Cataloging-in-Publication Data

The Fujimori legacy : the rise of electoral authoritarianism in Peru / edited by Julio F. Carrión
     p.   cm.
Includes bibliographical references and index.
ISBN 0-271-02747-9 (cloth : alk. paper)
ISBN 0-271-02748-7 (pbk. : alk. paper)
1. Fujimori, Alberto.
2. Authoritarianism—Peru—History.
3. Political corruption—Peru—History.
4. Populism—Peru—History.
5. Peru—Politics and government–1980– .
I. Carrión, Julio.

F3448.2.F86   2006
985.06'43'092—dc22
2005024058

25935003

Poder Ejecutivo
El que consiga
En el Perú ocupar puesto tan alto,
Jefe es legal, si sube por intriga;
Usurpador si sube por asalto;
Pero diga la Carta lo que diga,
Bien con legalidad, bien de ella falto,
Con tal que diestro asegurarse pueda,
El que logró subir, arriba queda.
. . . .
Y ¿qué hace la Nación? Modesta y blanda,
Encuentra más holgado y más ligero
A los pies prosternarse del que manda

—FELIPE PARDO Y ALIAGA,
CONSTITUCIÓN POLÍTICA: POEMA SATÍRICO, 1869

CONTENTS

Acknowledgments   ix

List of Abbreviations   xi

Introduction   1
   Julio F. Carrión

1   The Rise and Decline of Fujimori's Neopopulist Leadership   13
   Kurt Weyland

2   An Authoritarian Presidency: How and Why Did Presidential
Power Run Amok in Fujimori's Peru?   39
   Philip Mauceri

3   Fujimori and the Mayors of Lima, 1990–2001: The Impact
and Legacy of Neopopulist Rule   61
   Robert R. Barr and Henry Dietz

4   Do Parties Matter? Lessons from the Fujimori Experience   81
   Kenneth M. Roberts

5   The Immoral Economy of Fujimorismo   102
   Catherine M. Conaghan

6   Public Opinion, Market Reforms, and Democracy in
Fujimori's Peru   126
   Julio F. Carrión

7   All the President's Women: Fujimori and Gender Equity in
Peruvian Politics   150
   Gregory D. Schmidt

8   Redirection of Peruvian Economic Strategy in the 1990s:
Gains, Losses, and Clues for the Future   178
   John Sheahan

9   Against the Odds: The Paradoxes of Peru's Economic
Recovery in the 1990s   201
   Carol Wise

10   The Often Surprising Outcomes of Asymmetry in
International Affairs: United States–Peru Relations in the
1990s   227
   David Scott Palmer

11   Electoral Authoritarian Versus Partially Democratic Regimes:
The Case of the Fujimori Government and the 2000 Elections   242
   Cynthia McClintock

12 Endogenous Regime Breakdown: The Vladivideo and the Fall
    of Peru's Fujimori   268
        Maxwell A. Cameron
    Conclusion: The Rise and Fall of Electoral Authoritarianism
    in Peru   294
        Julio F. Carrión

    Bibliography   319
    Appendix. Peru, 1990–2000: A Basic Chronology   341
    List of Contributors   345
    Index   349

ACKNOWLEDGMENTS

This book would not have been possible without the generosity and support of many people. The international conference that led to this publication, held in 2002 in Washington, D.C., was funded by the University of Delaware and the Dante B. Fascell North-South Center at the University of Miami. At Delaware, the Department of Political Science and International Relations, the Center for International Studies, and the College of Arts and Sciences at the University of Delaware provided much needed funds for this effort. Joe Pika, Suzanne Austin, David Pong, Tom Dilorenzo, and Mark Huddleston were instrumental in launching this project by providing support and encouragement.

In 2002, I was appointed adjunct senior research associate of the North-South Center. In that capacity, I organized the conference and began working on the book manuscript. Thanks to Ambler Moss, director of the center at the time, and Antonio Garrastazú, former program director of its Washington office, for their encouragement and support. Antonio carried out all the logistic arrangements that made this conference possible. The Peruvian Embassy in Washington, D.C., also collaborated in this endeavor. Ambassador Allan Wagner opened the conference and held a lovely reception for all participants in the embassy's elegant residence.

Other people in the Dante B. Fascell North-South Center were also instrumental in shaping this book. Jeff Stark, former director of research and studies, and Kathy Hamman, former editorial director, enthusiastically supported the idea of turning the conference proceedings into a book. Unfortunate circumstances that led to the shutdown of the center by the University of Miami prevented this project from being completed at the center's press.

The enthusiasm and professionalism of the book contributors, who found time in their busy schedules to work on the multiple revisions that a project of this nature entails, have made this book possible. I am greatly indebted to all of them, and in particular to Cathy Conaghan, who enthusiastically supported the idea when it was in its formative stage and offered valuable advice throughout the project. I also want to thank

Jo-Marie Burt and John Carey for their participation in the conference. Other commitments prevented them from being part of this book. Charles Kenney read the whole manuscript and offered valuable suggestions. The comments of three anonymous reviewers were also extremely useful and helped to improve the final version. Sara Parker, a graduate student at my department, helped prepare the final manuscript. I am also grateful to Sandy Thatcher for his great editorial advice. It goes without saying that none of the above individuals or institutions should be held responsible for the shortcomings or errors that may remain in the book.

Doriz, my wife of almost twenty years, was the source of much help and support when this project started. Her unsuccessful fight against cancer did not allow her to see its culmination. But she lives in all of us who knew and loved her. I dedicate this book to her loving memory. During this difficult period, my kids, Doris, Antonio, and Alicia, demonstrated a resilience that was both heartwarming and inspirational. I'm forever indebted to them for showing me the meaning of strength. And thanks again to Doris for improving her dad's prose.

LIST OF ABBREVIATIONS

AP	Acción Popular
	Popular Action
APEC	Asia-Pacific Economic Cooperation
APRA	Alianza Popular Revolucionaria Americana
	American Popular Revolutionary Alliance
ATV	Andina de Radiodifusión
	Andean Broadcasting
BCRP	Banco Central de Reserva del Perú
	Central Bank of Peru
CADE	Conferencia Anual de Ejecutivos
	Annual Conference of Business Executives
CCD	Congreso Constituyente Democrático
	Democratic Constituent Congress
CEPAL	*See* CEPAL/ECLAC
CEPAL/ECLAC	Comisión Económica para América Latina y el Caribe (CEPAL)
	Economic Commission for Latin America and the Caribbean (ECLAC)
CIA	Central Intelligence Agency
C90-NM	Cambio 90/Nueva Mayoría
	Change 90/New Majority
CONFIEP	Confederación Nacional de Instituciones Empresariales Privadas
	National Confederation of Private Business Institutions
COPRI	Comisión de Promoción de la Inversión Privada
	Commission for Promotion of Private Investment
CTAR	Consejo Transitorio de Administración Regional
	Regional Administration Transitory Council
DD	Delegative democracy
EA	Electoral authoritarianism
ECLAC	*See* CEPAL/ECLAC
FARC	Fuerzas Armadas Revolucionarias de Colombia
	Revolutionary Armed Forces of Colombia

FDI	Foreign direct investment
FIM	Frente Independiente Moralizador
	Independent Moralizing Front
FONAVI	Fondo Nacional de Vivienda
	National Housing Fund
FONCODES	Fondo Nacional de Compensación y Desarrollo Social
	National Fund for Social Compensation and Development
FONCOMUN	Fondo de Compensación Municipal
	Municipal Compensation Fund
FREDEMO	Frente Democrático
	Democratic Front
FREPASO	Frente País Solidario
	Front for a Country in Solidarity
FSLN	Frente Sandinista de Liberación Nacional
	Sandinista National Liberation Front
GEIN	Grupo Especial de Inteligencia
	Special Intelligence Group
IFI	Internacional financial institution
INDECOPI	Instituto Nacional de la Defensa de la Competencia y Protección de la Propiedad Intelectual
	National Institute for the Defense of Competition and Intellectual Property
INEI	Instituto Nacional de Estadística e Informática
	National Institute of Statistics and Informatics
INFES	Instituto Nacional de Infraestructura Educativa y de Salud
	National Institute of Educational and Health Infrastructure
INVERMET	Fondo Metropolitano de Inversión
	Metropolitan Investment Fund
IPC	International Petroleum Company
IU	Izquierda Unida
	United Left
JNE	Jurado Nacional de Elecciones
	National Election Board
LASA	Latin American Studies Association
MIBANCO	Banco de la Micro-Empresa
	Microenterprise Bank

MRTA	Movimiento Revolucionario Tupac Amaru
	Tupac Amaru Revolutionary Movement
NAFTA	North American Free Trade Agreement
NDI	National Democratic Institute
OAS	Organización de Estados Americanos
	Organization of American States
OCMA	Oficina de Control de la Magistratura
	Office of Judicial Oversight
ONPE	Organización Nacional de Procesos Electorales
	National Organization of Electoral Processes
PETROPERU	Petróleos del Perú
	Petroleum of Peru
PP	Perú Posible
	Possible Peru
PPC	Partido Popular Cristiano
	Popular Christian Party
PROFAM	Programa de Lotes Familiares
	Program of Family Lots
PROMUDEH	Ministerio de Promoción de la Mujer y del Desarrollo Humano
	Ministry for the Promotion of Women and Human Development
PRONAA	Programa Nacional de Asistencia Alimentaria
	National Program of Food Assistance
SBS	Superintendencia de Banca y Seguros
	Superintendency of Banks and Insurance
SIN	Servicio de Inteligencia Nacional
	National Intelligence Service
SOE	State-owned enterprise
SUNAT	Superintendencia Nacional de Administración Tributaria
	National Superintendency of Revenue Administration
TC	Tribunal Constitucional
	Constitutional Tribunal
UPP	Unión por el Perú
	Union for Peru
WLCA	Women's Leadership Conference of the Americas
WOLA	Washington Office for Latin America

Introduction

JULIO F. CARRIÓN

The collapse of the presidency of Alberto Fujimori in November 2000 brought an end to one of the most controversial periods in the contemporary political history of Peru. After a decade in power and a contested reelection in 2000, President Fujimori was removed from office on the ground of "moral incapacity" by a vote of Congress. Thus far, Fujimori remains in exile in Japan and has refused to return to Peru to face the myriad investigations about his conduct in office.

Fujimori's longtime national security advisor, Vladimiro Montesinos, also fled but was later detained in Venezuela and returned to Peru to face justice. In the course of the investigation of his activities, hundreds of videotapes and audiotapes were discovered that recorded the meetings held by Montesinos with an array of public officials and media and business executives. Congressional investigators examined this evidence and made the recordings public. Montesinos is currently on trial, and other members of the regime have been either convicted or are also being tried.[1] The videos provide extraordinary new insights and evidence about the inner workings of the Fujimori regime. The tapes document how the government corrupted the media, manipulated the judiciary, subordinated Congress, and constructed elaborate campaigns to control public opinion and harass political opponents. With the Fujimori era concluded and with a new cache of evidence available, scholars are now in a position to write the definitive history of the Fujimori presidency, reflect on the legacy of Fujimorismo for Peru and for the region as a whole, and draw the necessary lessons.

The Authoritarian Project

Fujimori depicted his political project as one of "reengineering Peru." This reengineering involved stabilizing the economy through the implementation of neoliberal policies and engaging in a successful fight to end leftist guerrilla insurgencies. But Fujimori's remaking of Peru also included the 1992 *autogolpe* (autocoup) that suspended the constitution and shut down Congress.[2] The autogolpe was followed by eight years of governance that frequently failed to live up to the standards and practices normally associated with a democracy, even in a region such as Latin America.

Very few observers doubted that Fujimori was embracing the authoritarian path when, on April 5, 1992, he decided to dissolve Congress, dismiss the judiciary, and rule by decree. International pressure forced him to call for a new election (for a new congress in charge of drafting a new constitution) but the organization and implementation of this election was left in the hands of Fujimori, the one who had broken Peru's democratic continuity in the first place. Not surprisingly, Fujimori significantly altered the existing rules in order to enhance his electoral chances (Rospigliosi 1994). Even though Fujimori had promised the Organization of American States (OAS) that electoral rules would be coordinated with all political parties, his unwillingness to incorporate differing views forced many parties to abandon negotiations with the government. Moreover, the Fujimori-appointed Supreme Court named new members to the Jurado Nacional de Elecciones (National Election Board [JNE]), including its chair, thus preventing the success of any legal challenges from the opposition. Ultimately, the regime enacted a 147-article decree that arbitrarily set new electoral rules. Elections were to be held for a unicameral chamber containing only eighty members, elected from a single national district. Those elected would be ineligible to run for the next congress. This radical departure from existing constitutional arrangements was set *before* the people's representatives had any opportunity to debate them. Most of the traditional parties rejected these new rules and refused to participate in the election, but those who participated—along with the new organizations created for that purpose—lent a false legitimacy to the electoral process. In the meantime, the press was subjected to harassment. *Caretas*, Peru's most important political weekly, was ordered by the new Supreme Court to refrain from mentioning the name Vladimiro Montesinos in print, while its editor faced additional governmental harassment. Other journalists were subjected to investigations for their role in uncovering human rights abuses. The new constitution produced by the defective 1992 electoral process allowed Fujimori to run for immediate reelection in 1995. The 1995 presidential election results themselves are not disputed (although the congressional results are; see Chapter 11), but it is not difficult to conclude that the process that led to Fujimori's reelection was seriously flawed. The 1992 legislative election, the 1993 referendum to ratify the new constitution, and the subsequent 1995 reelection were events that legitimized an authoritarian regime. They played the functional role of "plebiscitary moments" that Fish (2001) describes as part of authoritarian reversals in some postcommunist regimes.

After the 1995 elections, Fujimori engaged in a behavioral pattern aimed at securing his grip on power by all means necessary. In this effort, no representative institution was spared. Fujimori and his chief security advisor, Vladimiro Montesinos, corrupted members of the judiciary and the JNE in order to secure favorable rulings that would allow Fujimori to run again for reelection in 2000. Furthermore, the regime sheltered the military from investigations into human rights violations. Fujimori and Montesinos colluded with prominent members of the establishment and the media to silence the opposition, and Fujimori used his majority in Congress to enact "midnight" laws that paved the way for his second reelection.

Throughout the life of the Fujimori presidency, scholars searched for a term to adequately characterize the regime. To many observers, it appeared to be a new hybrid that combined the formal appearance of a democracy with nondemocratic practices. Elections and institutions were reinstalled after the 1992 autogolpe and there were no formal controls over the press. Yet there were effectively no checks and balances in the system and no real oversight of the conduct of the executive branch. In the view of some observers, the regime was part of a new breed of "delegative democracy" (a term first developed by political scientist Guillermo O'Donnell), although with some special characteristics that made the label "neopopulist" more appropriate (Roberts 1995; Weyland 1996). Cynthia McClintock and most Peruvian scholars argued that the Fujimori regime deserved to be characterized as authoritarian (for a summary of these characterizations, see McClintock 1999), even though many policymakers in the international community resisted the idea of placing Peru in this category because of its obvious implications for multilateral and bilateral relations. As I argue in the Conclusion in this volume, while the term *neopopulism* can be applied to describe Fujimori's political strategy, it does not describe the regime's nature. For this reason, after the 1992 autogolpe, the regime should not be characterized as a democracy—even with *delegative* or some other adjective used to qualify it—but as a type of authoritarianism quite prevalent in our time, namely electoral authoritarianism. Even under Przeworski and coauthors' (2000, 16) rather "minimalist" definition of democracy, the Fujimori regime could not be considered democratic, because it failed to provide for full contestation. This regime severely restricted political competition for higher office by failing to provide a level playing field to the opposition and by establishing a secretive and conspiratorial government whose overarching goal became remaining in office and looting the public treasury.

Fujimori and his administration officials, of course, always maintained that the regime was democratic. They insisted, however, that they were developing a new type of democracy—one that privileged results (the delivery of material goods) over abstract procedures.

The arguments about how to characterize the Fujimori regime reflect the ongoing concerns about the future of democratic development in the region, especially the threats posed by popularly elected presidents who interpret their victories as a mandate to ride roughshod over constitutions. The elections of President Hugo Chávez of Venezuela and Lucio Gutierrez of Ecuador, both former coup plotters, and the continuing popularity of Lino Oviedo of Paraguay, another coup plotter, are examples of this trend. Chávez has embarked on an exercise similar in some ways to that of Fujimori, and its consequences have been deleterious for democratic development in Venezuela. Before he was forced to resign in April 2005, Gutierrez had dismissed all members of the Supreme Court, the Electoral Tribunal, and the Constitutional Court in order to replace them with loyalists. These examples, as well as Peru's experience under Fujimori, certainly underscore that the "authoritarian temptation" still persists and, further, demonstrate how it can be acted on under the guise of elected leadership.

The debate concerning the nature of Fujimori's regime also highlights the significant policy consequences that a regime characterization entails. The United States government and the international community at large have developed a set of mechanisms aimed at punishing governments that violate democracy in the region. "Delegative" democracies may escape the probing eyes of the international community, but authoritarian regimes will certainly not. The Fujimori administration was intensely aware of this distinction and thus carefully cloaked its authoritarian behavior in democratic forms. "Keeping democratic appearances" was crucial to this project for at least two reasons: first, it allowed the international community, including the United States government, to continue its flow of economic and developmental support to buttress a government that was perceived as being the least of a choice of evils in a country ravaged by domestic insurgency and drug trafficking. In addition, the facade provided a convenient alibi to those members of the Peruvian political and economic elite who wanted to support Fujimori without being accused of consorting with an authoritarian government.

Analytical Perspectives and Themes

This book joins the growing number of recent works in both English and Spanish that examine this controversial presidency.[3] All are valuable contributions; some, however, examine only particular periods or aspects of this regime, while others are written primarily for a Peruvian audience. *The Fujimori Legacy* is an effort to provide a comprehensive assessment of this controversial presidency. The authors in this book discuss the circumstances that favored Fujimori's sudden rise to power as well as chronicle the development and fall of the authoritarian presidency. We also examine the regime's efforts to reduce political competition as well as analyze the runaway corruption of its later years. In addition, we examine Fujimori's sources of political support, his economic policies, and the regime's relations with the United States. By offering an in-depth look at this controversial presidency, *The Fujimori Legacy* illuminates the persistent obstacles that Latin American countries face in establishing democracy.

This much discussed and much debated regime is analyzed from two different yet complementary analytical perspectives. One perspective focuses on the analysis of the regime's interaction with outside forces such as public opinion, political parties, women, Lima's mayors, and the U.S. government. The other perspective privileges the examination of the regime's inner workings and logic, namely, concentration of power in the presidential office, the governing coalitions determining economic policies, the corruption networks underpinning the regime, and the unsavory relationship between Fujimori and his de facto security advisor, Vladimiro Montesinos. This dual approach provides us with a more nuanced understanding of the regime's evolution, policy choices, and downfall than could an analytical strategy that relied exclusively on one single approach.

In addition to evaluating the impact of the Fujimori presidency on Peru's political development, the contributors to *The Fujimori Legacy* raise some broader comparative questions. Why and how was this government, elected with impeccable democratic credentials in 1990, able to evolve into an authoritarian project? Why was the regime able to endure for a decade? What were the regime's weaknesses that prevented its consolidation? How did Fujimori manage to secure public support as well as collaboration from various media executives and business elites? What can we learn from Peru's economic policies during this controversial period? What should the United States policy be toward this new breed of authoritarian governments? Are the international mechanisms that have been developed to protect democracy in the region applicable to this type of regime, and are they sufficient to prevent the emergence of new ones?

Contributors were asked to write on their specific fields of expertise, and thus the chapters cover a wide variety of issues related to this controversial presidency and address the questions posed above. Despite this diversity, a set of common themes can be identified. One of the main themes of *The Fujimori Legacy* is the analysis of presidential leadership in Peru and how it was used to subvert the institutions of democracy. This analysis is, of course, related to the more general theme of how political power is won and exercised in unconsolidated democracies. Although Fujimori catapulted to the peak of the political scene almost overnight—a development few could have predicted—his election and subsequent behavior followed recognizable patterns. His surprising election was a function of the wave of "outsiders" who came to high office in the wake of Latin America's "lost decade." Similarly, Fujimori's governing style, up to the 1992 autogolpe, was consistent with what O'Donnell (1994) describes as delegative democracy. After the autogolpe his regime came to resemble the type of electoral-based authoritarianism found in other developing and transitional societies.

Another theme of the book is the analysis of political support, broadly defined. As is widely acknowledged, Fujimori's efforts to establish an authoritarian regime could have been unsuccessful if not for the substantial support he elicited from wide swaths of Peruvian society. Broad-based support was required not only to validate his regime in the eyes of the international community but also to keep the opposition subdued.

Fujimori could not use the mobilizing power of a political party, because he not only lacked one but also consistently avoided the creation of one, lest his power be constrained. To compensate, he took advantage of the regular release of polling figures that showed sustained (although declining in later years) support for most of his policies, a development made possible by the growth of the polling industry in Peru. Fujimori also adopted specific policies aimed at increasing his support among key constituencies such as the poor, women, business elites, and media executives. Clientelism, corruption, and targeted legislation (such as that stipulating, female quotas for municipal and congressional lists) were some of the instruments used for this purpose.

The final theme of the book revolves around the uneasy relationship between governance and democratization in Latin America. Governance, defined broadly as the capacity to formulate and implement policies in an effective manner, can sometimes clash with the demands of democratization. Governance usually requires resolute leadership; democratization might be better served by consensus-seeking leaders. Governance may require swift institutional and economic reforms; democratization may require slow-moving consultation and compromise. The goals of governance might put a premium on securing domestic tranquillity at all costs; the goals of democratization might be better achieved by a strict adherence to constitutional regulations. Situations of extreme crisis, such as that experienced by Peru in the late 1980s and early 1990s, may exacerbate this uneasy relationship by persuading many to accept the claims of aspiring dictators that the country "cannot afford" democracy. Many of the chapters in this book illustrate how Fujimori's successful efforts in introducing institutional reform, liberalizing the economy, and pacifying the country—thus strengthening governance—were amply rewarded, both domestically and abroad, despite his penchant for authoritarianism.

Organization of the Book

In Chapter 1, Kurt Weyland analyzes the emergence of neopopulist leadership in Peru. He argues that this type of leadership emerges in contexts of severe crises and that, because of this, neopopulist leaders must attain considerable performance success if they are to establish and extend their political preeminence. The paradox is that when they become successful, as was the case for Fujimori, they then remove the very conditions that made their own ascendance possible. Weyland suggests that regimes such as Fujimori's are structurally unstable because their institutional precariousness leads to a diminishing capacity to sustain performance and therefore prevents them from routinizing their charisma and institutionalizing their leadership.

In Chapter 2, Philip Mauceri discusses the institutional factors that enabled the establishment of electoral authoritarianism in Peru. He shows how Fujimori took advantage of the strong powers traditionally given by the constitution to presidents and used them to undermine Peru's democracy. Mauceri describes in detail the manner in which, during the 1990s, institutional and societal checks on presidential power in Peru were weakened to such a degree that an unrestrained, authoritarian presidency emerged under Fujimori's leadership.

To sustain his authoritarian presidency, Fujimori needed to subdue political competition. This placed him on a collision course with Lima's mayors, who usually seek higher office. As Robert Barr and Henry Dietz argue in Chapter 3, Fujimori's determination to dominate the political arena led to a number of obstructionist policies that were aimed at reducing the powers of Peru's mayors, particularly those of Lima. Barr and Dietz document the different ways in which the regime sought to control or subdue the mayors, including media manipulation, public attacks, and more important, legal maneuvers to shift both resources and responsibilities from the municipalities to the central government.

Kenneth Roberts analyzes in Chapter 4 how the extreme fragility of the party system led to the emergence of independent political personalities in Peru. He identifies three types of independent figures that rose to fill the political vacuum left by the parties: the "defectors," the "frontperson," and the "populist outsiders" (of which Fujimori was the most successful example). According to Roberts, neopopulist leaders have short time-horizons and an "all or nothing" mentality because they know that, once voted out of office, they are unlikely to return to enjoy the spoils. Neopopulist leaders, he writes, usually get trapped in a vicious circle because of their fear of displacement, a situation that leads them to adopt a "profit while one can" mentality that in turn undermines their legitimacy.

In Chapter 5, Catherine Conaghan shows the extremes to which this mentality can lead. She presents a mesmerizing account of the corruption and clientelistic networks that supported the regime and details how the regime's "immoral economy" grew to include significant members of Peru's elite. Conaghan discusses a number of "greed rings" that have been identified in the criminal investigations of this regime. These rings included (besides Montesinos and Fujimori) high-ranking public officials, top commanders of the armed forces and their family members, owners of major media outlets, judges, prosecutors, members of the JNE, top judicial officials, top managers of private banks, and perhaps even narco-traffickers.

While Conaghan describes how significant members of the Peruvian elite collaborated with the regime, my own analysis of public opinion, in Chapter 6, offers a discussion of why the mass public, while critical of some of Fujimori's policies, was largely supportive of the regime. Aside from examining the determinants of this strong (albeit declining) support, I chronicle the increasing public dissatisfaction with the regime's market reforms and with its efforts to secure reelection in 2000. I conclude by arguing that, politically speaking, public opinion played a contradictory role during the Fujimori regime. It was highly influential to the extent that it helped legitimize the authoritarian regime, but powerless in that citizens were completely unable to influence governmental policy in those areas in which their views clashed with those of the regime.

Further examining Fujimorismo's bases of political support, Gregory Schmidt considers in Chapter 7 the unprecedented role that women played in this regime. As part of his efforts to solidify electoral support, Fujimori strongly supported gender-equity legislation, entailing measures that included the adoption of gender quotas in municipal and congressional slates. Schmidt argues that, although it may look paradoxical, the fact that an authoritarian government adopts progressive policies toward women is not unusual in the Peruvian or wider Latin American context. He correctly notes that many of the gains made my women in Peru (divorce, right to vote, equal rights to common-law marriage) were granted under military regimes. He also mentions that although Fujimori's leadership was crucial to progress toward gender equity in the 1990s, it was not the only factor that explains those gains.

The book then turns to the analysis of two important policy issues: market reforms and U.S.-Peru relations. In Chapter 8, John Sheahan examines Fujimori's economic policy, discussing its weaknesses and strengths. Yet his argument goes beyond offering us a balance sheet of the policy. He identifies the structural factors that made it difficult to sustain equitable economic growth in the 1990s, factors that included the unequal educational system, the oversupply of low-skill labor, and the limited competitive capacity of both modern services and the industrial sector. Sheahan also finds that the Peruvian program made some significant gains in terms of gross domestic product, but observes that the gains would have been greater had the regime better managed the exchange rate. Sheahan's general conclusion is that the potential advantages of economic liberalization can be lost to an exchange rate policy that makes imports too cheap and reduces incentives to enter export markets. As he notes, the regime's decision to keep an overvalued currency was driven by politics, since this policy translated into lower inflationary levels.

How was it possible to have this combination of relatively successful economic performance with authoritarianism and rampant corruption? Part of the answer has to do with the timing of these events. The bulk of market reforms were implemented during Fujimori's first administration, whereas the most egregious corruption developed after the 1995 reelection. Carol Wise argues in Chapter 9 that Fujimori's electoral survivability during his first administration hinged on his ability to deliver good economic performance. This need provided him with strong incentives to overhaul state institutions that were crucial to economic recovery. Relying on an unexpected coalition with Peru's business class and the military, Fujimori moved quickly to do so. But at the same time, Wise argues, his excessive reliance on the military and the security apparatus, along with a lack of accountability and legislative oversight, prevented the deepening of the economic program or the adoption of much needed "second phase" reforms. As Wise notes, the president's appetite for reform was greatly diminished after the 1995 reelection as the worst corruption excesses began to occur and Fujimori and his clique established full control of all governmental branches.

One would imagine that a government that gave such ample examples of its authoritarian predilections would have been subjected to public criticism, if not outright condemnation, by the United States. Although U.S.-Peru relations were in general problematic throughout the 1990s, Fujimori—argues David Scott Palmer in Chapter 10—was able to use in his favor the eagerness of many U.S. agencies to support Peru's efforts to liberalize the economy and stem drug production despite the increasing evidence of his corruption and authoritarianism. Moreover, rarely was the United States in a position to ensure outcomes that it favored in Peru. Palmer contends that the United States' overriding policy concern in Peru was to maintain order. Even during the regime's final moments, the United States tried to keep Fujimori in charge.

While the United States may have acted favorably toward Fujimori out of an excessive preoccupation with order and continuity and a mistaken hierarchy of policy goals (stressing market liberation and drug interdiction over democratic governance), it is more difficult to understand the reluctance of the international community in condemning elections sponsored by authoritarian regimes (although it should be acknowledged that Eduardo Stein, head of the OAS electoral mission in Peru, adopted a very principled position). In Chapter 11, Cynthia McClintock argues that, in classifying regimes, analysts should assess not only electoral processes but also the regime's overall record. Despite the compelling evidence of Fujimori's prior authoritarianism, claims McClintock, the 2000 elections became a critical test of whether Peru would continue to be classified as partially democratic or would slip under the authoritarian label. She then examines this election in detail to show how close international electoral observers came to accepting it as legitimate because of their failure to examine the regime's intentions and capabilities. She also discusses the difficult challenges that opposition forces face under electoral authoritarianism, since there are both costs and benefits associated with a decision to boycott elections.

Many of the previously cited authors discuss the changing environment that Fujimori faced in the wake of the 2000 elections. Although his popularity was still impressive by Peruvian standards (as I show in my chapter on public opinion), it had certainly declined in relation to previous years (as Weyland notes in his chapter). After years of relatively complacency, both the United States and the international community were less willing to grant Fujimori complete freedom of action. Although the OAS did reject demands to declare the 2000 elections invalid, it sent a mission to Peru to "strengthen democracy," effectively introducing a degree of oversight that had previously been absent. In addition, despite the failure of the opposition and civil society forces to dislodge the regime through social mobilization, they were much more active and successful than in the previous years. Finally, although Fujimori had been able to eke out an electoral victory in 2000, a vast segment of the population (significantly larger than in 1995, as I demonstrate in Chapter 6) questioned the legitimacy of the result.

If we rely exclusively on an "outside" approach to analyze the regime's demise, we may conclude that these factors were crucial in determining the regime's final collapse. Our understanding of this collapse is greatly enhanced, however, if we examine the regime's inner logic and evaluate how it affected the final outcome. This is what Maxwell Cameron does in Chapter 12. He asserts that the disintegration of the regime was not primarily the result of societal mobilization or external pressure but was instead the product of forces endogenous to the regime itself. He argues that the release of the videotape showing Montesinos's bribery of an elected opposition politician was as damaging as it was because it exposed the regime's many facades. The release created an unsolvable situation because Fujimori was unable to keep governing with Montesinos but, at the same time, was unable to govern without him. The only way out of this dilemma, argues Cameron, was for Fujimori to announce his decision to cut his term short. Once he did so, the regime fell apart.

In the Conclusion, I place the Fujimori regime in a historical and theoretical perspective. I discuss the theoretical connections between delegative democracy, neopopulism, and electoral authoritarianism. In addition, I offer a discussion—drawing on the book's contributions—of the factors that favored the emergence of electoral authoritarianism in Peru and of those that prevented its consolidation. Finally, I reflect on the most important legacies of this controversial regime for Peru's democracy.

NOTES

1. The transcripts of the videos and audiotapes have been recently published by the Peruvian congress. See Congreso del Perú 2004.

2. An autogolpe is defined as the illegal usurpation of power by an elected president who typically suspends the constitution and rules by decree.

3. See, for instance, Bowen and Holligan 2003; Conaghan 2005; Cotler and Grompone 2000; Dammert Ego Aguirre 2001; Degregori 2000; Durand 2003; Kenney 2004; McClintock and Vallas 2003; Marcus-Delgado and Tanaka 2001; Pease García 2003; Wise 2003b.

ONE

The Rise and Decline of Fujimori's Neopopulist Leadership

KURT WEYLAND

The government of Alberto Fujimori is a prototypical case of neopopulist leadership (Roberts 1995; Weyland 1996, 2001) and "delegative democracy" (O'Donnell 1994). In this type of government, a personalistic, plebiscitarian leader rules based on a quasi-direct, largely unmediated relationship to a heterogeneous, mostly unorganized mass of people.[1] Neopopulism embodies a majoritarian conception of political rule: "the will of the people"—as interpreted by a predominant chief executive—reigns supreme, largely unconstrained by parliament and the courts. Checks and balances are weak and horizontal accountability is low, but the vertical relationship between a personalistic leader and "the masses" sustains neopopulism.

Like charismatic authority (Weber 1976, 654, 657), with which it often overlaps, neopopulist, delegative-democratic leadership arises from deep, acute crises (O'Donnell 1994; Roberts 1995; Weyland 2001). While institutional weaknesses, especially inchoate, fragmented party systems, provide important permissive conditions for the emergence of personalistic leaders, grave, urgent problems confronting a country trig-

The present chapter draws heavily on Weyland 2002, chaps. 5, 7, with the permission of Princeton University Press. I thank Julio Carrión, Charles Kenney, and three anonymous reviewers for many useful comments on earlier versions of this chapter.

ger their often dramatic rise to prominence and power. For instance, Argentina's Carlos Menem (1989–99) and Brazil's Fernando Collor de Mello (1990–92) won large-scale support because they promised to overcome the serious economic difficulties facing their nations, which were soon to experience painful hyperinflationary episodes. Most notably, Fujimori unexpectedly emerged out of total obscurity in a country that had suffered from hyperinflation as well as brutal insurrectionary violence and equally brutal military repression. Thus, crises bring forth neopopulist leadership: they delegitimate the established "political class" and pave the way for outsiders; weaken intermediary organizations, especially parties and interest groups, and thus open up opportunities for personalistic leaders; and induce many citizens to run considerable risks by supporting untested newcomers who lack a promising track record and whose promises of salvation are therefore shrouded in uncertainty.

Given the importance of crisis conditions—a conjunctural factor—for the rise of neopopulist leadership, what are the chances for neopopulism's "consolidation"? To establish and extend their political preeminence, personalistic chief executives must, first of all, succeed in overcoming acute problems, such as hyperinflation. Given neopopulism's precarious, unorganized base, unsuccessful leaders tend to face powerful challenges and see their tenure in office cut short, as suggested by the ignominious removal of Abdalá Bucaram in Ecuador (1996–97), Collor in Brazil, and Carlos Andrés Pérez in Venezuela (1989–93) as well as the recurring difficulties of Hugo Chávez in Venezuela (1999–present). Thus, personalistic chief executives must demonstrate special performance or prove their charisma (see Weber 1976, 140, 655–56) by combating effectively the difficulties assailing their country. Without considerable success, they cannot maintain mass support, the most important—but fickle—foundation of their rule.

Can successful neopopulist leaders translate their policy accomplishments or proven charisma into lasting political predominance? Can they use crises as "critical junctures" to reshape the country's institutional framework and assemble a support coalition that backs their personalistic leadership over the long run? Thus, can they "routinize" their charisma (Weber 1976, 142–48, 681–87) and institutionalize their rule?

This chapter suggests a negative answer. President Fujimori was, arguably, the most successful neopopulist leader in contemporary Latin America. Despite his lack of governmental experience and organized support, he rescued Peru from imminent collapse, restored economic stability, and defeated one of the most powerful and dangerous guerrilla movements in Latin American history. What other leader managed to parlay equally limited assets into such tremendous accomplishments? No wonder that from 1993 until 1996, Fujimori maintained stratospheric approval ratings and won democratic reelection in a landslide in 1995, obliterating the meager remnants of the old party system. Thus, Fujimori constitutes a "most likely case" for neopopulism's consolidation: if personalistic, plebiscitarian rule does not attain longevity despite such success, it is unlikely to do so anywhere.

But typical of neopopulism, Fujimori's predominance rested on precarious foundations. Based on unorganized mass support, his government declined in approval ratings during 1997 as quickly as it had risen in 1990 and 1991–92. His growing weakness induced the president and his top aides to resort to ever more questionable means to extend his tenure further. This heavy-handed manipulation and attendant large-scale bribery undermined the government's legitimacy, weakened the feeble institutional framework created by Fujimori himself, and exacerbated the regime's personalistic nature. These shady tactics also made the president ever more dependent on his scheming intelligence advisor, Vladimiro Montesinos, who in the end challenged Fujimori's authority itself. When glaring evidence of Montesinos's misdeeds and pressure from the United States forced the president to try to reassert his primacy by dismissing this longtime aide, personal loyalties to the two protagonists were so divided among the political and military leadership that a stalemate resulted and the government quickly imploded. In a denouement resembling that of a soap opera, Fujimori's neopopulist leadership collapsed as both protagonists fled the country. Thus, the president stumbled over the personalism and lack of institutionalization that had for years allowed him to govern the country at will. Neopopulism self-destructed.

After a brief discussion of Fujimori's rise, in this chapter I examine his successful efforts to extend his rule to a second term. Thereafter, I investigate the decline of Fujimori's neopopulism and the tragicomic end of the administration. Finally, I assess the likelihood of a resurgence of neopopulism.

Strengths and Weaknesses of Neopopulist Leadership

Before analyzing Fujimori's case, it is useful to clarify the opportunities and constraints facing neopopulist leaders. Most remarkably, their political fortunes vary dramatically. They often arise virtually out of no-where—but then can fall from power as quickly. One year, they are world record holder in popularity ratings, only to see their mass support evaporate the following year. What drives these striking fluctuations?

The crucial permissive cause for the volatility of personalistic leadership is the uninstitutionalized nature and antiorganizational tendency of neopopulism. In this respect, neopopulism diverges from the classical populism of the 1930s to 1950s. Whereas leaders such as Argentina's Juan Perón, Peru's Víctor Raúl Haya de la Torre, Mexico's Lázaro Cárdenas, and Brazil's Getúlio Vargas created new organizations to promote the initial incorporation of mass sectors (but kept these organizations under their own personal control), neopopulists such as Collor and Fujimori bypassed these established organizations and created loose movements and diffuse electoral vehicles. To stand apart from the "corrupt" political class and well-organized "special interests," they deliberately avoided forming typical parties. New means for reaching their followers and demonstrating public support, especially television and opinion polls, respectively, allowed them to forego powerful collective mobilization, which classical populists needed as a means to prove and use their mass backing. Also, neopopulist appeals primarily targeted the informal sector and rural poor, whose members are difficult to organize at the national level, whereas classical populists courted the working class, which can form strong unions and parties.[2] Thus, while sharing crucial features of political strategy and style with classical populists, neopopulist leaders did not build collective organizations, but bypassed, overpowered, weakened, or destroyed them.

The uninstitutionalized nature and antiorganizational tendency of neopopulism underlie both the sudden emergence of personalistic, plebiscitarian leaders and their often spectacular downfall. On the one hand, the weakness or dramatic weakening of intermediary organizations, especially political parties, allows for the rise of neopopulist leaders out of obscurity. As established organizations are discredited, personalistic politicians can attain prominence and quickly gain massive support. Therefore, dark-horse candidates such as Collor and Fujimori can suddenly emerge during election campaigns and attain tremendous success. After reaching office, neopopulist leaders maintain their personalistic strategy. This deliberate lack of institutionalization gives them a wide margin of discretion, enhancing their power and autonomy. They really govern the country "as they see fit" (O'Donnell 1994). Popular aversion to parties—widely seen as vehicles of a self-seeking "political class"—reinforces neopopulists' tendency to avoid creating firm party organizations of their own. Where they arose as complete outsiders, as did Fujimori in Peru, they ensure that their electoral vehicles remain loose, heterogeneous, unorganized movements; where they arose by taking over an old populist movement party, as did Argentina's Menem, they accentuate their personal discretion over the party and deinstitutionalize it (McGuire 1997). This lack of firm institutionalization allows neopopulist leaders—especially complete outsiders—to have unchallenged predominance over their supporters. They see efforts at institutionalization as a threat to their unlimited discretion, autonomy, and power. Therefore, neopopulism has a clear antiorganizational character: its leaders both refuse to create their own firm institutions and systematically undermine competing organizations.

On the other hand, this pronounced personalism and anti-institutional tendency, which allow for the meteoric rise of neopopulist leaders and give them enormous power while they command massive support, also create risks. In particular, they make neopopulist leaders vulnerable to challenges when their performance sags. The lack of institutionalization deprives neopopulism of the cushion of lasting loyalty that firm organizations provide. The mass support these leaders gain remains fickle. As quickly as many citizens flock to back neopopulists, just as quickly they may abandon self-proclaimed saviors who cannot fulfill their promises and fail to prove their charisma.

Notably, the drastic fluctuations in support are driven primarily by the prospective and actual performance of neopopulist leaders. They rise on the basis of ambitious promises and hopes, especially the expectation that they could turn the crisis-ridden country around. Thus, they gain legitimacy and support as prospective saviors. Since they can blame their predecessors from the corrupt, discredited "political class" for the problems afflicting the nation, they obtain an important credit of trust at the beginning of their tenure. Where the "political class" used to be particularly well entrenched and the crisis was especially long and painful, as in contemporary Venezuela, this honeymoon can last for more than a year, as Chávez's sky-high popularity ratings in 1999 and 2000 show. But eventually, citizens demand concrete success, namely, actual improvements in their life circumstances, and real evidence of the leader's charisma. If leaders fail to perform, their popularity drops and their mass support fades, as Chávez noticed in 2001. In fact, the frustration of popular hopes can rapidly erode a neopopulist's support base, as Alan García Pérez found out: his approval ratings hovered around 75 percent in 1986, but fell to below 10 percent in January 1989. Such dramatic abandonment by mass supporters exposes a neopopulist leader to serious threats, as Collor realized during the corruption scandal in 1992 that led to his impeachment and resignation.

Thus, neopopulism's lack of institutionalization makes personalistic leaders highly dependent on performance legitimacy. Citizens let them govern as they see fit—as long as they govern effectively, resolve urgent problems, and produce improvements for the citizenry. People support the concentration of power in a neopopulist leader if that leader uses this concentrated power to attain concrete accomplishments. They are willing to extend a credit of trust to a charismatic politician—but see this credit as an investment, not a gift, and therefore demand payback sooner or later (on Fujimori, see Balbi 1996).

Neopopulist leaders' dependence on performance legitimacy raises the question, Under what conditions can they achieve good performance? Essentially, neopopulist leaders "need" deep, open crises, which give their promises of salvation resonance among the population and allow them to prove their performance and give their rule sustainability. These leaders can best produce improvements by helping to overcome crises. Specifically, problems that quickly afflict and seriously affect large numbers of people, but that can be effectively combated with a few bold countermeasures, provide the best opportunities for the rise and perpetuation of neopopulist leadership. The prototype of such a catastrophic problem is hyperinflation, which quickly threatens to impoverish much of the population, but which can be resolved with determined stabilization plans. Such a catastrophic problem permits leaders to prove their charisma by averting an impending meltdown and turning the country around with a seeming stroke of magic. Fujimori rose out of nowhere precisely because he faced two catastrophic problems: hyperinflation and large-scale insurrectionary violence. And he established political predominance by wielding these problems as weapons against his adversaries—especially in justifying his autogolpe—and by then making great progress toward resolving these problems.

But paradoxically, this very success threatens to remove neopopulist leaders' main raison d'être: it resolves the resolvable problems that neopopulists "need" to justify their predominance, and leaves unresolved other difficulties that are much more intractable, especially un- and underemployment, poverty, and low incomes. Through this "problem shift," neopopulists' very success makes further success less likely. Thus, in performing the tasks that citizens expect, they become ever less capable of fulfilling citizens' subsequent set of expectations. For instance, while Fujimori managed to end hyperinflation with a drastic (and painful) adjustment plan and his police succeeded in decapitating the Shining Path (Sendero Luminoso), the government found it extremely difficult to make a dent in important remaining problems such as unemployment. Fujimori merely created the temporary illusion of fulfilling these hopes, through artificial economic expansion and an unsustainable extension of social benefits, timed right before the 1995 election. But this illusion of success in tackling these intractable problems came at a heavy price: the preelectoral spending increase required adjustment afterward, one that caused a recession and exacerbated the above-mentioned problems (see Chapter 8, this volume). Fujimori's popularity plummeted as a result, and he felt compelled to use more openly authoritarian and manipulative means to maintain his political predominance and prepare for a second reelection, in 2000. His incapacity to resolve the intractable problems left over after his initial policy successes set in motion the above-mentioned processes, which eventually caused his neopopulist rule to implode.

Neopopulist leaders thus face a paradox. They "need" serious problems to defeat the established political class, to rise as outsiders, and to attain unprecedented power. But then, after winning power, they need to resolve those problems. That very success, however, weakens the rationale for their continued preeminence and leaves behind problems that are much more difficult to resolve, especially in the efficacious, speedy fashion with which a catastrophic crisis such as hyperinflation can be ended. Neopopulist leaders thus face a "paradox of success" (Weyland 2000): they need to achieve success to prove their leadership, but that success ends up undermining the precondition of their very leadership.

Personalistic, plebiscitarian leaders are particularly exposed to this paradox of success—much more so than presidents sustained by well-organized political parties. Given the precarious institutional nature of neopopulism, which does not entail the organization building performed by classical populists, these leaders depend mostly on performance legitimacy. Their systematically diminishing capacity to attain the necessary level of performance prevents them from routinizing their charisma and institutionalizing their leadership. Consequently, neopopulist leadership is by nature a temporary phenomenon—difficult to extend beyond the medium run. Certainly, however, the decline and eventual fall of one neopopulist leader may pave the way for another's emergence. Thus, individual neopopulist leaders have a limited political life span, but neopopulism—as a strategy of rule—can be a recurring phenomenon.

The Rise of Fujimori's Neopopulist Leadership

The emergence of Fujimori and his surprising election victory in 1990 would be unimaginable without the grave dual crisis afflicting Peru at that time, namely incipient hyperinflation and massive insurrectionary violence. Peru's serious economic problems during the 1980s and the seemingly unstoppable advance of the violent Shining Path guerrilla movement discredited the established "political class," which had obviously failed to fulfill minimal performance expectations. Because established politicians were widely seen as bickering among themselves rather than resolving Peru's urgent difficulties, outsiders managed to rise, while existing parties saw their support melt away. In the presidential contest of 1990, the incumbent Alianza Popular Revolucionaria Americana (American Popular Revolutionary Alliance [APRA]) candidate was eliminated in the first round. Anticipating defeat, the two center-right parties that had governed from 1980 to 1985 decided not to field a candidate, but back an independent—world-famous novelist and political novice Mario Vargas Llosa. Thus, Peru's "political class" was defeated by two newcomers, Fujimori and Vargas Llosa.

The eventual winner of the 1990 election was an outsider whose vague campaign rhetoric and obscure track record provided little indication of his future course of action, but who promised to "save" the country (O'Donnell 1994, 65; Degregori and Grompone 1991, 34–36, 125–28; Rospigliosi 1992, 353–55; Fujimori 1991, 97). As a candidate, the unknown Fujimori was more unpredictable than Vargas Llosa, who was allied with two mainstays of the political establishment. In fact, Vargas Llosa's coalition with these parties made voters question his outsider status and prefer Fujimori "because he hadn't done anything yet," as a street vendor expressed the prevailing popular sentiment (quoted in Guillermoprieto 1990, 124; see Boggio, Romero, and Ansión 1991, 19–20, 34, 51, 99–102). Similarly, Fujimori's simplistic slogan "Honesty, technology, and work," his failure to present a campaign program until right before the second round (Loayza Galván 1998, 24–26, 69–73), and the vague generalities that his movement finally published (Cambio 90 1990) embodied greater uncertainty than Vargas Llosa's clearly defined proposals. In fact, Fujimori's rejection of Vargas Llosa's bold shock plan of economic stabilization (see Vargas Llosa and Fujimori 1990) had much less influence on vote choices than his political independence and outsider status (Degregori and Grompone 1991; Dietz 1998, 218–19,

280). Assailed by dramatic economic and security problems, citizens preferred a newcomer. Peru's dramatic crisis was crucial for Fujimori's rise.

Fujimori's Establishment of Political Predominance

When Fujimori took office in July 1990, his government's viability seemed questionable. Facing tremendous problems, he lacked a coherent cabinet, a firm support coalition, and a majority in Congress. How could he—virtually on his own—confront such tough challenges? But the new president skillfully turned problems into assets: he took advantage of the country's very difficulties to demonstrate his courage, prove his performance and charisma, and attain clear political supremacy. By allowing him to attack his adversaries and win new supporters, the crisis served as a springboard for his neopopulist leadership. It also enabled him to disregard procedural constraints and claim unprecedented discretion. To rein in challenges, he reigned supreme.

Fujimori attained his first success by quickly ending hyperinflation with his brutal shock plan of August 1990. As prices rose again after December 1990, he appointed as economy minister doctrinaire neoliberal Carlos Boloña, who forced down inflation with unrelenting austerity and ambitious neoliberal reforms. While imposing tremendous additional pain, these tough measures restored economic stability by late 1991. Accordingly, Fujimori's approval ratings, which had been quite high in 1990 but had dropped in early 1991, recovered. Thus, the president first secured his rule by combating the single most urgent problem: hyperinflation. In fact, his popularity ratings—crucial for neopopulist leadership—closely tracked economic policy approval during his first fifteen months in office (see Julio Carrión's analysis in Chapter 6).

After reestablishing minimal control over the economy and tightening his personal grip over the military, Fujimori turned his attention to the second catastrophic problem, the insurrectionary violence of the Shining Path. He advanced a bold, tough, and comprehensive strategy for combating this challenge in the ambitious package of 126 legislative decrees that he submitted to Congress in September 1991. Much of the suffering population eagerly supported a determined attack on the enemies of the state, who had caused tremendous damage and made daily life a game of Russian roulette. Thus, Fujimori's courageous strategy for taking on the brutal guerrilla insurgents boosted his support, as the rise of his popularity above the levels of economic policy approval in late 1991 show.

Yet while most citizens longed for an end to the virtual civil war and backed the government's antiterrorism measures, congressional politicians raised procedural and constitutional objections. While invoking important liberal-democratic principles, these criticisms looked to much of the desperate population as the typical bickering of established politicians intent upon attaining partisan advantages at the price of undermining governmental efficacy. The fact that at that time, the party opposition—led by Fujimori's predecessor Alan García—indeed sought to regroup and oppose the government more effectively reinforced this impression, and as a result, the president's tough attacks on his adversaries, including Congress itself, reinforced his popularity. Thus, the dangerous guerrilla challenge, which profoundly affected most citizens, allowed Fujimori to enhance his neopopulist leadership: his planned countermeasures garnered strong support, and his adversaries further discredited themselves by appearing to be obstructionist.

Fujimori used these two effects to his greatest advantage in his coup of April 1992. With the need to combat insurgency effectively and overcome the obstacles posed by Congress and the judiciary (Fujimori 1992, 43–47) put forth as justification, the autogolpe elicited tremendous popular support. Approval ratings of the self-coup and its protagonist reached up to 82 percent in polls (Conaghan 1995, 227, 236). Important sociopolitical groups, especially the private sector, also offered firm backing; two prominent business leaders entered the government.[3]

Even on the international front, the crisis plaguing Peru gave Fujimori protection from stronger pressures for immediate redemocratization. Certainly, the more consistent international commitment to democracy prevailing after the end of the Cold War led to widespread foreign opposition to Fujimori's assumption of dictatorial powers. The United States, Japan, and a number of European countries suspended aid and threatened Peru with additional sanctions. Economy Minister Boloña feared that the negative international reaction would keep Peru excluded from international financial markets and jeopardize the precarious stabilization that had been achieved through painful adjustment measures. Threatening to resign, Fujimori's top economic aide helped to persuade the reluctant president to cede to foreign demands.[4] Therefore, Fujimori begrudgingly announced a gradual return to democracy.

Yet while strong international pressure thwarted Fujimori's openly authoritarian project and compelled him to restore the basic mechanisms of democracy, powerful external forces, especially the U.S. government and international financial institutions, were careful not to undermine the president's hold on power. As described by Palmer (Chapter 10, this volume), they eagerly cooperated with Fujimori, a trusted ally against leftist insurgents and drug traffickers and the most reliable guarantor of market reform in Peru. In this way, the economic and safety problems that continued to afflict the country helped this neopopulist leader garner significant external support and maintain his political predominance.

While presidential popularity slowly diminished after the coup, the capture of the Shining Path leadership in September 1992, which brought about the strategic defeat of this dangerous guerrilla movement, boosted Fujimori's approval ratings again, to 65–75 percent. Thus, the president's bold removal of obstacles to his leadership via the autogolpe and the proof of his government's efficacy with the decapitation of the Shining Path elicited enormous popular support. For a large majority of people, the quest for substantive performance—especially, determined efforts to end Peru's dual crisis—took precedence over formal democratic procedures and liberal principles of checks and balances. Many Peruvians—desperate for effective results—wanted to boost governmental power and supported the elimination of procedural limitations and political counterweights that could hinder Fujimori's proven efficacy. They thus backed the majoritarian, nonliberal concept of democracy underlying neopopulism.

By late 1992, Fujimori had established political predominance as a neopopulist leader. Counting on massive popular support and backing from important "powers-that-be," especially among the military and private business, he enjoyed unchallenged leadership. He had demonstrated his performance by decisively containing the two main problems afflicting the country. The restoration of price stability, reintegration into the international financial community, and enactment of wide-ranging market reforms reignited economic growth, which reached 7 percent in 1993. And the capture of Shining Path leaders greatly diminished guerrilla violence, restoring the basic safety that people seek in their daily lives. Fujimori had attained stunning success, after assuming power with barely any political assets.

The Extension of Fujimori's Neopopulist Leadership

Fujimori used his policy success and the resulting political predominance to prepare for his immediate reelection. Personalistic leaders typically seek to prolong their tenure. In Peru, the decay of intermediary organizations and the resulting personalization of rule allowed Fujimori to depict himself as indispensable to guaranteeing the recently won economic stability and political order, which continued to face threats.

To extend his tenure, Fujimori needed to modify the constitution, which prohibited immediate reelection. The autogolpe allowed the incumbent to change the rules of the game in his favor. Facing international pressure for redemocratization, he convoked a Constituent Assembly to prepare for the return to competitive rule. The partisan opposition disagreed on whether to participate in this contest and thus legitimate Fujimori's institutional restructuring. Persistent popular rejection of the old political class, Fujimori's policy successes, and adroit institutional engineering gave his movement a clear plurality of votes and an absolute majority of seats.

The new unicameral body elaborated a charter that enshrined many of the government's proposals. Above all, it allowed for immediate presidential reelection. It also strengthened the presidency's institutional powers, albeit less than the opposition had feared (Schmidt 1998, 113–14). Based on Fujimori's majoritarian concept of democracy, the new constitution abolished the Senate, providing for a unicameral congress. Under this arrangement, a governmental majority would encounter fewer "veto points" and could more easily attain political predominance. Furthermore, the restructuring of the judiciary weakened institutional protections for judges, many of whom held only "provisional" appointments in subsequent years. As demonstrated by Mauceri (Chapter 2, this volume), all these restrictions of liberal-democratic "checks and balances" gave the incumbent, who tightly controlled his supporters in Congress, greater autonomy and power. Thus, the new constitution augmented the institutional instruments for Fujimori's neopopulist leadership and allowed for its perpetuation.

The Struggle for Reelection

With the reelection provision in place, Fujimori prepared his campaign, for which he commanded important assets. First of all, his track record was impressive. Determined adjustment had restored economic stability and fueled growth. By ending the economic crisis and decapitating the Shining Path, the president had also managed to resurrect the authority of the state and give the population a renewed sense of normality and order (Mauceri 1995). Fujimori's successes instilled optimism and induced many people to favor the incumbent. They preferred "the devil they knew" to the untested opposition. To maintain his support, the president deliberately kept the memory of the initial crises alive and reminded citizens of his accomplishments (see, for example, Fujimori 1994).

But Fujimori could not rest on his laurels. He faced the danger that citizens would take the restored normality for granted and regard his continued stewardship as no longer necessary. People commonly assimilate gains quickly, seeing the improved situation as normal, while their earlier predicament fades into oblivion. This tendency seems to be particularly pronounced where people earlier faced problems that appear as departures from normality, such as hyperinflation or insurrectionary violence. Resolving these problems simply restores the status quo, that is, the situation that should always have prevailed and that people feel entitled to.

People's quick adjustment to gains thus exposed Fujimori to a paradox of success (Weyland 2000). By overcoming problems and restoring normality, the president diminished the motivation for people to appreciate these successes. His very achievements in combating crises lowered the salience of these problems and redirected voters' attention to other, persisting problems. The accomplishments had ever lower weight in shaping citizens' assessment of and support for the incumbent.

Fujimori was rudely alerted to this paradox of success when his government won the 1993 plebiscite on the new constitution with a surprisingly narrow margin—or, as some observers suspect, only by resorting to fraud.[5] Especially in outlying provinces where poverty was deep and widespread, a majority of voters rejected the new charter and, by implication, the incumbent. Only one year after the Shining Path's decapitation and the recuperation of economic stability, these accomplishments no longer swayed a substantial sector of the population. Rather than displaying lasting gratitude, many people expected and demanded further improvements. As the salience of terrorism and inflation declined, citizens redirected their concerns to such issues as poverty, low wages, and employment problems (see Carrión's analysis in Chapter 6, this volume).

These problems, however, unlike hyperinflation and guerrilla violence, are impossible to resolve in a striking, visible manner. Whereas a determined government can end hyperinflation from one day to the next, it cannot create millions of jobs by fiat. In fact, Fujimori's market reforms made it especially difficult for him to respond to popular demands for quick socioeconomic improvements. For instance, large-scale employment programs or government-decreed wage raises were out of the question.[6] Thus, Fujimori was shown to be unable to resolve the problems that Peruvians saw as their highest priorities from the mid-1990s onward (see Chapter 8).

Facing fiscal constraints, the government confined itself to instituting targeted social-assistance programs, which sought to benefit many people at relatively low cost. The external enforcers of financial discipline, especially the World Bank, recommended such programs and provided generous loans to enhance popular acceptance of neoliberalism (Graham 1994). The Fujimori government subsequently allocated hundreds of millions of dollars to targeted antipoverty schemes, especially a demand-driven social-investment fund (Fondo Nacional de Compensación y Desarrollo Social , or National Fund for Social Compensation and Development [FONCODES]), which spent a total of $285 million until April 1995, the date of the presidential election (Schady 2000, 292); an education and health fund that engaged mostly in school building (Instituto Nacional de Infraestructura Educativa y de Salud, or National Institute of Educational and Health Infrastructure [INFES]) and that committed a total of $334 million until April 1995 (Graham and Kane 1998, 95); and a nutrition program (Programa Nacional de Asistencia Alimentaria, or National Program of Food Assistance [PRONAA]).[7] In response to the near defeat in the constitutional plebiscite and in preparation for the 1995 election, expenditures were especially high in 1994 and early 1995 (Graham and Kane 1998, 95; Roberts and Arce 1998, 233; Schady 2000, 293–94). The new discretionary programs were coordinated and directed by the Ministry of the Presidency, an organizational arrangement that strengthened presidential powers and allowed for the political manipulation of expenditure decisions.

These programs' focus on very poor people suited both neoliberal experts and the neopopulist leader. From the neoliberal perspective, targeting guarantees a high "marginal return" because a few dollars can make a significant difference to the destitute. Large numbers of citizens receive visible benefits, but at limited cost to the public budget. The new social programs therefore did not undermine economic adjustment. At the same time, targeting allowed the neopopulist Fujimori to use social programs for his political purposes. Whereas universalist policies provide benefits indiscriminately to friends and enemies, targeted programs give the government discretion over whom to favor and whom to exclude. Incumbents can thus reward their followers, hurt opponents, and win over the undecided (see Schady 2000, 298–302). Since the government has this discretion, anticipated reaction often induces aspiring beneficiaries to offer obedience and support and refrain from backing the opposition. Targeting also permitted Fujimori to dole out goodies in a visible manner that had substantial political payoffs. For instance, festive donation or inauguration ceremonies gave the president direct contact with common citizens and reinforced his image as a "man of the people." For these reasons, targeted antipoverty schemes were attractive to both neoliberal experts and the neopopulist president.

These new social programs reinforced popular support for Fujimori. His approval rating, which declined gradually in 1993, rose again after early 1994, when social spending expanded considerably. When asked in opinion surveys why they backed the incumbent, 28.9 percent of the poorest respondents in Lima pointed to his "public works" and his "support for education," probably referring to his high-profile school-building program.[8] Popular appreciation for Fujimori's antipoverty and public-works programs helped the president win an overwhelming reelection victory in April 1995, as interviews and focus groups with poorer people suggest (Salcedo 1995, 67, 73, 80–81, 95) and statistical analyses confirm (Roberts and Arce 1998, 233–38; Weyland 1998b, 557–58; Graham and Kane 1998, 85–97; Balbi 1996, 207–14).

In conclusion, targeted social programs that distributed some of the fruits of recovery boosted Fujimori's electoral chances, helped him counteract the political fallout from the paradox of success, and win a landslide reelection victory that extended his neopopulist leadership by five more years.

Renewed Economic Problems and the Decline in Fujimori's Popularity

The very means that Fujimori had used to prolong his political predominance soon began to weaken his leadership, however. After stimulating the economy and expanding social programs to guarantee his reelection, the president had to shift course after the contest. In late 1995, he adopted restrictive measures to prevent a serious overheating of the economy and imbalances in Peru's external accounts. As a result, growth slowed to a meager 2.6 percent in 1996 (Gonzales de Olarte 1998, 14) and employment problems worsened further (see Chapter 8, this volume).

This new round of belt-tightening disappointed popular hopes that painful neoliberal adjustment would usher in sustained prosperity—a hope that the recovery of 1993 to 1995 had reinforced. It now became obvious that the new market model was also subject to conjunctural problems, like its predecessor. In fact, the greater openness to the world economy and the restrictions imposed by neoliberal principles of budget austerity and balance in external accounts made growth more vulnerable to exogenous shocks and ruled out determined countercyclical policies.

These renewed economic problems suggested to many citizens that Fujimori would face much greater difficulty in combating the problems left over after the restoration of economic stability and the defeat of the Shining Path. As mentioned above, the paradox of success caused a shift in issue salience: many Peruvians now saw unemployment and poverty as the main problems facing their country. They wanted their president to produce significant results on those fronts; recurring economic difficulties, however, greatly weakened governmental performance in these areas. Contrary to his earlier successes, Fujimori proved unable to resolve these problems; in fact, renewed adjustment worsened them. The incumbent began to lose his image of efficacy.

These economic problems were reflected in Peruvians' subjective evaluations. From February 1996 onward, negative retrospective assessments of people's economic situation were measured consistently and significantly higher among Lima residents than were perceptions of recent gains.[9] After October 1996, perceptions of recent losses rarely fell below 40 percent and reached almost 50 percent on several occasions in 1997 and early 1998. Another round of adjustment in 1998 further raised these negative assessments, which hovered around the 50 percent mark from mid-1998 to mid-1999.[10]

As a result of the frustrated hopes for socioeconomic improvements, support for the incumbent diminished considerably at the beginning of his second term, while approval for the opposition rose. After reaching 75 percent in January 1996, Fujimori's popularity rating dropped to around 60 percent by midyear and 45 percent in December. From mid-1997 onward, it generally fell between 35–45 percent, whereas disapproval reached 50–63 percent.[11] Survey respondents attributed their diminishing support for the incumbent to the economic deterioration. When those who disapproved of Fujimori were asked for the most important reason, 69 percent named "the economic situation."[12] Fujimori's incapacity to produce continuing socioeconomic improvements, which his earlier success in combating catastrophic problems had pushed to the center of people's attention, began to weaken his neopopulist leadership.

The Disappearance of Opportune Issues for Neopopulist Leadership

The new round of adjustments that Fujimori had to institute to compensate for his preelectoral spending spree exacerbated the political difficulties emerging from the general "problem shift" from resolvable to intractable issues that resulted from the paradox of success. The president's very achievements in combating the catastrophic crises that he faced upon taking office kept him from finding important issues that he could resolve in similarly quick and striking ways. During his second term, he lacked opportune problems for justifying and boosting his neopopulist leadership. The difficulties that Peru continued to confront could not be resolved with the bold countermeasures that neopopulist leaders are best prepared to take. And by resolving catastrophic problems and restoring normality, Fujimori made his own courageous leadership appear superfluous. As the grave crisis of the late 1980s receded into the past, this daring neopopulist appeared ever more dispensable to many citizens and interest groups. His special strengths became less appropriate and well suited for alleviating Peru's remaining difficulties. They even threatened to become counterproductive for the patient institutional rebuilding and systematic development policies that held the greatest promise. Whereas Fujimori's willingness to concentrate power and bend or break institutional constraints had been crucial for combating catastrophic problems and pushing through bold neoliberal reform, it became an obstacle to the institutionalization of the new market model and the flourishing of a high-quality democracy. As the salience of different issues changed, neopopulism, in the minds of many, was changed from a solution to problems into a problem itself. The very qualities that had made Fujimori so successful in the beginning—his courage, cunning, and ruthlessness—became less useful and even dysfunctional.

Given the paradox of success, Fujimori faced great difficulties in identifying problems that he could successfully address through the bold measures that befitted a neopopulist leader. As mentioned, the main concerns of Peruvians after 1995—poverty, precarious employment, and low wages—cannot be resolved by political fiat. Further, Fujimori could not find other opportune issues that might have boosted his neopopulist leadership. Stressing the persistence of the terrorist threat was a double-edged sword because it diminished one of the main accomplishments of his first term. The president therefore emphasized a new security issue, namely growing common crime, which he combated with some of the tough measures used against the Shining Path (Toche 1998). In addition, he took advantage of natural catastrophes, especially the extensive floods caused by El Niño in 1998, touring the affected regions and promising quick relief.[13] But these new issues lacked the intensity and salience of hyperinflation and massive insurgency.

The absence of catastrophic problems that hurt vast numbers of people yet could be resolved quickly with bold countermeasures prevented Fujimori from enhancing his standing in public opinion during the second half of the 1990s. Even the brilliant rescue of the hostages held by the Movimiento Revolucionario Tupac Amaru (Tupac Amaru Revolutionary Movement [MRTA]) in the Japanese ambassador's residence gave his approval rating only a fleeting boost. All told, Fujimori did not manage to stem the decline in his popularity that the renewed round of adjustments had helped to produce.

This decline in Fujimori's standing also had political causes. In particular, more and more sectors criticized his neopopulist leadership as such, especially the frequent violations of liberal-democratic principles, norms, and procedures that he and his supporters committed. While large portions of the population had accepted these transgressions as necessary for combating the catastrophic problems confronting Peru during the early 1990s, Fujimori's very success in restoring normality made his continuing transgressions appear ever more unnecessary. As the strengths of this neopopulist leader—his courage and willingness to run risks and override constraints—became less important, his weaknesses, that is, unrestrained discretion and concentration of power, became less acceptable to many citizens. Fujimori's autocratic tendencies appeared increasingly as an *un*necessary evil.

For all these reasons, this neopopulist leader was unable to maintain the massive backing that he had garnered during his first term in office. His diminishing support hindered pursuit of his most important goal, namely, a second immediate reelection. The first reelection drive was endorsed by many citizens and powerful interest groups, especially big business, which saw a second term for Fujimori as crucial for cementing economic and political stability. But the further consolidation of stability made the incumbent dispensable, and his desire to perpetuate himself in office was viewed by many citizens as an illegitimate, dangerous hunger for power. In fact, continued dependence on personalistic leadership, which would keep institutional structures fluid and weak, came to be seen as a source of future instability. Important sectors—including business—perceived a change in top leadership as important for institutionalizing the new market model and for improving the quality and stability of Peruvian democracy.[14]

The Effort to Impose the Continuation of Neopopulist Leadership

Although Fujimori's past accomplishments and continuing social programs targeted at the poorest sectors guaranteed the president a solid base of support among 30–40 percent of the population, his neopopulist leadership faced growing challenges. The incumbent responded in a distinctly autocratic fashion, trying to impose his will against opposition. In particular, he sought through all possible means to pave the way for a second consecutive reelection in the 2000 contest. For this purpose, he had to bend or break his own 1993 constitution, which prohibited such a move. While the majority that he controlled in Congress allowed him to obtain formal approval for this democratically questionable strategy, his manipulative efforts delegitimated the precarious political and institutional order created by the charter that he himself had engineered. Also, these problematic moves reinforced the widespread popular impression that Fujimori was an autocrat who did not hesitate to trample on formal rules and democratic principles to get his way. As a result, discontent intensified, especially among the middle class. This opposition in turn induced the president and his spymaster Montesinos to resort to even more questionable tactics, including large-scale bribery. This systematic usage of corruption (analyzed in Chapter 5) eventually triggered the government's collapse. Thus, while the Fujimori government long remained tremendously powerful and used all the power at its disposal, it became ever more brittle and precarious. The samurai was marching into dangerous quicksand.

The distinctive nature of Peru's political trajectory during Fujimori's second term becomes more obvious through a comparison with Argentina, where another neoliberal neopopulist—Carlos Menem—faced similar challenges. While the Argentine president failed to override these constraints and therefore could not run for a second consecutive reelection, his Peruvian counterpart combated these challenges head-on and did win a third term—but the questionable means by which he accomplished this feat soon ended up also bringing him down. Yet whereas Argentina then elected an antineopopulist, Fernando de la Rúa—a leader who was incapable of leading—Peru had to choose between two neopopulists in the second round of the 2001 contest, namely, eventual winner Alejandro Toledo, the personalistic head of an amorphous, unorganized mass movement, and veteran neopopulist Alan García, who despite his disastrous government performance (1985–90) pulled off a stunning political resurrection. Thus, while both countries have relieved themselves of their incumbent neopopulist leaders, neopopulism has remained the predominant political strategy in Peru, but not in Argentina.

These differences arose from institutional, political, and societal factors. Constitutional reform left less space for personalistic leadership in Argentina than in Peru. Whereas Menem negotiated the reelection provision in a functioning democracy and therefore had to accept significant constitutional limitations on presidential powers, Fujimori imposed the reelection rule after suspending democracy. In this way, the latter succeeded in fortifying the presidency. In line with populist notions of democracy, his supporters also strengthened the majoritarian elements of Peru's constitution, especially by instituting a unicameral legislature with extensive powers.[15] For these reasons, Peru's new constitution provides a more propitious institutional setting for neopopulism than does the reformed Argentine charter.

In addition, the constellation of political forces has been highly favorable to neopopulist leadership in Peru because the old parties have remained virtually destroyed and because new opposition movements have failed to acquire organizational strength and programmatic coherence. In Argentina, by contrast, a new center-left party—Frente País Solidario (Front for a Country in Solidarity [FREPASO])—emerged; the old, seemingly moribund Unión Cívica Radical (Radical Civic Union [UCR]) rebounded in the second half of the 1990s; and above all, the Peronist Party retained sufficient organizational strength to hem in Menem's personalistic leadership and allow for the emergence of internal rivals, especially Buenos Aires provincial governor Eduardo Duhalde, who managed to wrest the party's presidential candidacy for 1999 away from Menem.

By contrast, Fujimori deliberately kept his own support base institutionally weak. This lack of organization gave the president virtually unlimited authority inside his movement. Except for spymaster Montesinos, anybody who held a position of power in the government or its electoral vehicle Cambio 90/Nueva Mayoría (Change 90/New Majority [C90-NM]) owed his or her rise—and fall—exclusively to presidential discretion. Fujimori used this predominance to prevent any internal rival from emerging. Jealously guarding his power, he systematically undermined potential challengers, such as former minister of the presidency Jaime Yoshiyama (Mauceri 1997a, 907–8). In this way, Fujimori made himself indispensable to his own supporters, who lacked an alternative for the presidential contest of 2000 and therefore had to back his second reelection.

Peru's other political forces—too unorganized to deserve the label *party*—remained weak and fragmented, as leading opposition politicians admitted.[16] The variegated groups in civil society that opposed Fujimori and supported his adversaries lacked organizational cohesion. For years, Fujimori thus dared and managed to defy the growing opposition and pushed very hard for the opportunity to run again in the 2000 election. The majority in Congress that Fujimori controlled "reinterpreted" the constitution in 1996 to pave the way for his renewed candidacy; in 1997, it undermined the Constitutional Tribunal, which struck down this distortion of the 1993 charter; and in another act of questionable legality, in 1998 it virtually prohibited a plebiscite that the opposition called in order to take advantage of the aversion in public opinion against another reelection. These paraconstitutional and undemocratic measures further discredited Fujimori and reinforced his autocratic image among middle-class groups. But they did not undermine his support among poorer sectors that were dependent on government social programs, which actually grew from late 1998 onward, pushing his approval ratings steadily higher and making a second reelection appear ever more unavoidable. In addition, the opposition did not manage to develop an organized, programmatic alternative to Fujimori. Instead, the only serious rivals of the incumbent were themselves personalistic leaders, namely, first Lima mayor Alberto Andrade; then Luis Castañeda Lossio, a former official of the Fujimori government; and—at the very end of the 2000 campaign— Alejandro Toledo (Carrión 2000, 6–14).[17] While Toledo managed to pose a surprisingly strong challenge to the incumbent, his meteoric rise bore striking resemblance to Fujimori's own emergence from obscurity in 1990 and demonstrated the tremendous fluidity of political alignments and loyalties in Peru. In particular, Toledo also lacked organized backing and therefore used a populist political strategy to garner support.

The Collapse of Fujimori's Neopopulist Leadership—and the Likely Recurrence of Neopopulism

With his controversial reelection victory in mid-2000, guaranteed by means of numerous irregularities, Fujimori seemed bound to prevail in

Peruvian politics for years to come. But his legitimacy, both domestic and international, was greatly weakened by all the infractions of democratic principles and procedures that he and his supporters had felt compelled to commit in order to ensure his victory despite the shrinking of his support base after 1995, which resulted from the paradox of success. Thus, Fujimori's neopopulist leadership had been hollowed out as procedural tricks and autocratic imposition compensated for diminishing plebiscitarian support. The caudillo was standing on feet of clay.

As a personalistic strategy that lacks institutionalization, neopopulism is vulnerable and can collapse quickly once its mass support weakens. In fact, a severe power struggle between the autocratic president and his shady, unscrupulous, utterly corrupt advisor, Montesinos, surprisingly imploded the government in the fall of 2000, prompting the ignominious flight of both protagonists (Balbi and Palmer 2001). This collapse was triggered by a bribery scandal, resulting from Montesinos's effort to buy Fujimori the congressional majority that the electorate had denied the president. Thus, a particularly blatant effort to compensate for the decline of neopopulist leadership backfired; under domestic and international pressure, Fujimori sought to dismiss his discredited right-hand man, but Montesinos had become so powerful and had established so many connections to core regime supporters—especially in the military—that he managed to block the president's effort. As a result of this stalemate, Fujimori called new elections and promised to step down. With the end in sight, more and more of his erstwhile supporters defected, inducing him to flee in order to avoid prosecution. The unorganized nature of his political support coalition now came to haunt the president as, so to speak, the rats jumped the sinking ship. The lack of institutionalization that had brought about Fujimori's meteoric rise in 1990 and allowed him to attain unprecedented discretion and power during the following decade contributed greatly to his dramatic downfall in late 2000 (see Chapter 12).

After this stunning collapse, Peru's civil and political society, reacting to the widespread abuse, manipulation, and corruption under Fujimori's neopopulist leadership, put a particularly high premium on the restoration of democratic principles and republican values. The transition administration of Valentín Paniagua indeed took important steps toward reinstituting the rule of law, guaranteeing greater accountability, and subordinating the military to civilian control; it also held clean elections in mid-2001.

Despite these efforts to deemphasize personalism and build democratic institutions, the door remains wide open for neopopulism. Current president Toledo heads a very loose, heterogeneous movement that cannot guarantee firm, cohesive backing for his government. Since he lacks organized support and a congressional majority, he needs to maintain mass backing in order to promote his political initiatives. Given that he cannot draw on firm loyalties, he is resorting to typically populist tactics. In fact, with his special appeal to poorer, rural sectors and his heavy use of indigenous symbols, his governing style has striking resemblances to Fujimori's neopopulism. But the absence of opportune issues for proving charisma, which eroded Fujimori's leadership, has also kept Toledo's support limited in extension and intensity. Thus, the new president faces a dilemma: he needs to—but cannot—become a successful neopopulist (Barr 2003). His notorious failings as a leader further diminish his chances of success. In fact, his popularity ratings plummeted quickly during his first few months in office and have hovered at dangerously low levels ever since, raising questions about his capacity to serve out his five-year term.

Given the organizational weakness of Peru's political society, Toledo's persistent political difficulties will not produce organized alternatives, however, but strengthen other populist leaders, especially Alan García. Peru will find it difficult to escape from personalistic, plebiscitarian leadership and institutionalize democracy. In fact, neopopulism seems to be the only feasible political strategy at present. Peru's system of intermediary organizations—especially political parties—is tremendously weak; party organization has virtually ceased to exist. Even García's stunning political resurrection in the 2001 contest derived mostly from his charismatic personality and skillful neopopulist tactics, not from APRA's organizational strength. The very fact that vote intentions for the ex-president hovered around 5 percent in January of 2001 yet increased dramatically in the following months suggests that he owed this surprising success to his personal charisma and renewed quasi-direct contact with voters, which he managed to reestablish after his return to Peru. Long-standing party loyalties would have guaranteed García stronger support immediately upon his entering the campaign. The rapid growth of his following resulted from personalistic, plebiscitarian—that is, populist—tactics.

Since Peru's political society remains organizationally weak (see Chapter 4), any leaders intent upon founding their government on organized support would not find much of a base to stand on. The only glue that is left for building electoral and governing coalitions is personalistic attraction and, potentially, charisma. This organizational weakness turns neopopulist leadership into the default option for Peruvian politics. Given the inherent challenges that neopopulism poses to the quality of democracy, Peru's prospects are not bright. In fact, the dilemmas and limitations of neopopulism that the preceding analysis of the Fujimori administration has demonstrated and that the rapid decline of Toledo's political standing confirms could soon jeopardize the very survival of democracy.

Conclusion

In this chapter I have advanced a crisis argument to account for the dramatic rise and equally stunning fall of the neopopulist Fujimori. The catastrophic problems plaguing Peru in the late 1980s allowed this complete outsider to rise to prominence and surprisingly win the chief executive office. The new president's impressive success in combating these problems and restoring normality initially boosted his power and helped him extend his rule, especially with the autogolpe, the new constitution, and his first reelection. But this very success soon came to limit Fujimori's neopopulist leadership as the salience of issues that he managed to resolve diminished, while people placed increasing priority on other, more intractable problems. This paradox of success induced the president to resort to increasingly questionable means, which bolstered his leadership in the short run, but turned it ever more precarious. In this vein, the preelectoral spending spree of 1994–95 required renewed adjustment in 1996, which drastically diminished presidential popularity. In order to nevertheless extend his grip on power further, Fujimori and his cronies infringed on the spirit and letter of the constitution that they themselves had engineered, thus undermining the domestic and international legitimacy of his rule. A particularly blatant infraction, designed to compensate for a lack of votes by literally buying seats in Congress, finally brought the president down by imploding the personalistic core of his regime.

The present analysis suggests that neopopulist leadership is a strategy of political rule that by nature has only temporary effectiveness; its "routinization" and institutionalization seem unlikely. Whereas many—though by no means all—of Latin America's "classical populists" of the 1930s to 1950s managed to create (personalistically dominated) organizations that often survived their founders' fall from power or even their death, the neopopulists of the 1980s and 1990s are applying more anti-institutional tactics. First, mass political organizations, especially parties and trade unions, have become highly discredited in many countries, and neopopulists, who arise as outsiders opposed to the established "political class," have little incentive to build similar institutions. Second, given that existing organizations retain the allegiance of some sectors, especially from the middle and organized working class, neopopulists have focused their appeals on the poorer, less educated strata, especially in the informal sector. Given their tremendous heterogeneity, these sectors would be difficult to organize. Therefore, neopopulism embodies a much clearer contrast between a largely unorganized mass supporting a personalistic leader and organized civil society than classical populism did. Third, modern means of mass communication, especially television, enable neopopulist leaders to reach their supporters in a seemingly direct fashion, diminishing the need for constructing organizational networks. Finally, personalistic leaders are by nature skeptical of organizations, which hem in their discretion, autonomy, and power. The diminished political need for institution building allows neopopulists to indulge this desire for unconstrained personalistic predominance more than classical populists could afford. For all these reasons, neopopulists do not construct firm organizations that could consolidate their support and gradually transform their personalistic leadership into a more organized form of rule. Rejecting institutionalization, they do not routinize their charisma. Their tenure in office thus remains dependent exclusively on performance, and the paradox of success inherently limits their capacity to achieve such performance. Therefore, neopopulist leadership is by nature a temporary phenomenon.

Ironically, however, where the anti-institutional tactics of neopopulist leaders are effective and further weaken intermediary organizations, the downfall of one neopopulist leader does not usher in a systematic effort at institutionalization; rather, it paves the way for the next neopopulist to emerge. Thus, whereas each neopopulist leader is transitory, neopopulism may well be recurrent. Rather than immunizing the body politic, the experience of neopopulist leadership, which further undermines intermediary organizations, may make it more susceptible to a relapse. Whether democracy will survive this infection remains to be seen.

NOTES

1. For an extended conceptual discussion, see Weyland 2001, esp. 12–16; for a response to critics, see Weyland 2003, 1101–6. This definition focuses on

neopopulists' central political strategy and excludes economic and social characteristics as logically accidental. In particular, since personalistic, plebiscitarian leaders are nonideological and opportunistic, neopopulism cannot be defined by the content of its policies. For instance, Fujimori enacted an ambitious neoliberal program, whereas Venezuela's Hugo Chávez is charting a heterodox economic course. Despite these substantive differences, both these personalistic, plebiscitarian leaders qualify as neopopulists because they base their government on largely unorganized mass support.

2. On these differences, see Weyland 2001, 15–16.

3. Confidential interviews by the author with two top figures from the business community, Lima, February 1995 and July 1999.

4. Interviews with Carlos Boloña, former minister of economy and finance (1991–93), Lima, August 14, 1996, and Hernando de Soto, former special advisor to President Fujimori (1990–92), Lima, August 20, 1996.

5. Former president Fernando Belaúnde Terry, interview by the author, Lima, August 2, 1996.

6. The increase in public-sector employment during the late 1990s was too limited to make a significant dent in Peru's employment problems.

7. On the scandalous political utilization of PRONAA in Fujimori's re-reelection campaign of 1999–2000, see "Mecánica Naranja," Caretas, June 24, 1999, 33–36. In the present volume, all figures in dollars are in U.S. dollars.

8. Poll conducted by Imasen, September 1994.

9. Apoyo, November 1996, 28.

10. Apoyo, various issues.

11. Apoyo, September 1997, 7; June 1999, 6; see also Carrión's analysis in Chapter 6, this volume.

12. Apoyo, December 1998, 7–8.

13. Apoyo, February 1998, 19; Grompone 1998, 36.

14. Important business representative, confidential interview by the author, Lima, August 1996; Guido Pennano, former minister of industry and commerce (1990–91), interview by the author, Lima, August 7, 1996; Grompone 1998, 28.

15. Most transgressions of democratic rules and principles after 1995 were indeed carried out by the legislature, not the presidency (though clearly on behalf of the president).

16. Lourdes Flores Nano, leader of the PPC, interview by the author, Lima, July 3, 1999; Henry Pease, leader of UPP, interview by the author, Lima, July 6 July, 1999; Anel Townsend, congresswoman and opposition leader, interview by the author, Lima, June 30, 1999.

17. On Fujimori's determined efforts to undermine Andrade, see Chapter 3; on the 2000 elections in general, see Chapter 11.

TWO

An Authoritarian Presidency:
How and Why Did Presidential Power Run Amok in Fujimori's Peru?

PHILIP MAUCERI

Since first being elected president in 1990, Alberto Fujimori dominated the politics of Peru by defining the policy agenda, redesigning the country's institutional framework and maintaining almost consistently high public-approval ratings. No other institution within the state structure appeared to check presidential power, and until the very end of the regime in 2000 no organizations in civil or political society effectively challenged what at times appeared to be an almost inevitable concentration of political power in the presidency. These trends raise important questions about the role of presidents in Peru and in Latin America in general, as well as how we understand regimes and regime change. Were the sources of Fujimori's power and legitimacy in the 1990s the result of a particular conjunction or indications of structural or institutional conditions that are likely to influence the course of Peruvian politics in the coming decades? What made the Fujimori presidency qualitatively different from its predecessors was the use of executive powers to substantially change the regime, from a democratic to an authoritarian one. This transformation grew out of the effective neutralization of institutional and societal checks on executive power, seriously compromising key compo-

The author would like to thank Julio Carrión, Charles Kenney, Maxwell Cameron, and the anonymous reviewers for their helpful comments. Any errors are the author's sole responsibility.

nents of liberal democracy: limitations on governmental power, due process, and civil liberties.

The purpose of this chapter is to examine the process by which institutional and societal checks on executive power were undermined, creating a situation of arbitrary rule. I argue that even though the administration undermined many checks through purposeful policies, there is no question that the country's social structure and the prior weakness of many institutional factors laid the basis for an extension of presidential power.

Checks on Presidential Power in Liberal Democracies: The Role of Institutions and Society

Unchecked power has long been a concern of democratic theorists and provoked the fear expressed by James Madison in Federalist Paper 47: "The accumulation of powers [in the same hands] . . . whether hereditary, self-appointed or elective may be justly pronounced the very definition of tyranny." Such a system forces participants to negotiate, bargain, and compromise in order to achieve their objectives, inhibiting "winner take all" scenarios, whereby oppositions, minority groups, or both have no ability to shape or influence policymaking. We can delineate four institutional and societal checks in modern presidential liberal democracies.

Mutual Checks Under Separation of Powers

The most important element in the Madisonian scheme was the separation of executive, legislative, and judicial branches of the national government. While the specific mechanisms will vary, the purpose of formal checks on the presidency is to provide the other branches of government with legal restraints on the policymaking and implementation powers of the executive. Nonetheless, the mere existence of formal/legal checks on presidential power does not in itself guarantee their effectiveness, particularly where there is not the political will to enforce the authority of those checks. The unwillingness to exercise that authority might result from a variety of factors, from partisan closeness to the president to outright corruption. A good example of this dynamic is the legislative power given to presidents. In a number of systems, including Peru's, the congress can cede legislative authority to the executive. Under most circumstances that authority is limited to specific issues within a set time limit (Mainwaring and Shugart 1997). Although legislative-decree powers, if used sparingly, would not necessarily result in excessive presidential power, the unwillingness of legislatures to set specific limits or timetables or enforce those limits, often for partisan reasons, usually contribute to concentrated presidential power. Thus it is not the formal/legal mechanism but the abdication of legislative authority that neutralizes the check on power.

Decentralized Power/Federalism

Beyond formal/legal checks by other branches of government on the president, the Madisonian approach to checks and balances also creates multiple sources of legitimacy and authority, namely, the division between national and local power in a federal system. The justification is found in Federalist Paper 51, where Madison argues, "The different governments will control each other." The impact of federalism or other forms of decentralization is to carve out a series of policy arenas and jurisdictions over which presidents have little effective power. Moreover, the alternative governing figures limit the ability of presidents to proclaim themselves the embodiment of the national will by establishing other actors with a legitimate claim to represent the people's will.

Party Organizations and Party Systems

Our understanding of checks and balances has largely been shaped by the Madisonian tradition, which focuses on specific constitutional mechanisms to divide and check power. Although these remain the primary checks on presidential power in modern liberal democracies, there are clearly other societal checks worth considering, one of them involving parties. Parties as organizations function as "interest aggregators" linking the state and society, but they also provide important links between branches of government as well as between national and local governments. Shared party membership can increase common political interests among officials in these different institutions.[1] Moreover, the autonomous political and institutional interests of parties create a level of accountability between the "executive as politician" and members of party elites and masses who are interested in their own future electoral prospects.

In short, parties as organizations have a broad range of interests—ideological, electoral, financial, membership—which they are likely to enforce when dealing with political actors, including a president. The consequences of policies on party interests over the long term will inevitably be an important part of presidential decision making and is likely to act as a constraint. Since executives in presidential systems are likely to come from the party machinery, there is a sense of mutual obligation between party leaders and the president to advance each others interests and avoid policies that might be costly to each other.[2]

The existence of a party system, understood as "the system of interactions resulting from inter-party competition" (Sartori 1976, 44) also serves to check presidential power. The existence of organized alternatives found in opposition parties limits the possibility of presidents' claiming a monopoly on governmental legitimacy. The institutionalization of interparty competition ensures that an electoral check on presidential power is effective, by offering an alternative not only in the executive branch, but also in the legislature as well as at other governmental levels.

Civil Society Organization

A dynamic and free civil society is a fundamental precondition for democracy. What makes civil society—understood as self-organizing groups and individuals that are autonomous from the state and that articulate values and identities to advance their interests (Linz and Stepan 1996, 7)—so critical in democracy is the role it plays in fostering individual and group identities that can contest state power and policies. More than a permanent opposition, however, a strong civil society acts as a counterbalance to the enormous power and resources of the modern state apparatus, limiting the state from imposing values, identities, and policies on social actors and individuals alike.

The implications for presidential power are obvious. In a context of strong civil societies, presidential power and authority are likely to be highly scrutinized, analyzed, and criticized by many groups. The organizational resources of civil society can be mobilized not only for protest in the streets but also for lobbying other institutions of the political system and swaying public opinion against the president.

The Historic Basis for Presidential Powers in Peru

Several factors have generally favored strong presidential powers in Peru. First, the colonial legacy of a highly centralized and autocratic viceroyal system laid the basis for a view of the executive as not only the primary source of authority and decision making, but also one that should largely remain unencumbered by other institutions. Viewing the president as "a natural heir to the viceroy" Peruvian philosopher José Pareja Paz-Soldán could suggest in the early twentieth century that the existing presidential system was a natural extension of this model (Loveman 1993, 55). The Madisonian framework had little relevance where the idea of restraint on power was moral rather than procedural (Dealy 1982, 168). Disputes and shifts in presidential power in nineteenth-century Peruvian constitutions (1823, 1826, 1827, 1834, 1837, 1839, 1856, 1860, 1867) reflected the ongoing struggle between rival caudillos, particularly those who had achieved national power and thus favored strong centralized presidential systems and those who remained strong at a regional level and were most interested in reducing central authority.

Second, a generally weak civil society with a very limited conception of citizenship made it difficult for societal groups to organize, let alone demand accountability from the president. The country's large indigenous population, whose rights have been historically restricted by discrimination, social exclusion and racist practices, were largely excluded from the political system until the middle of the twentieth century. In addition to the lack of effective citizenship rights for the indigenous, the dominant form of social organization has traditionally been corporatist, impeding the development of a clear concept of individual rights and a culture of accountability. Individual autonomy in both the political and economic spheres in corporatism was subordinated by defining and legitimizing the social or functional group as the primary agent of participation, allowing authorities enormous control and leverage.

This leads to a third factor fostering strong presidential powers, namely, a weak party system, understood as a system composed of parties with little capacity to mobilize voters, few affective ties, a weak national organization, and few representational capacities. For most of Peru's twentieth-century history, only one party, the Alianza Popular Revolucionaria Americana (American Popular Revolutionary Alliance [APRA]), could meet the criteria for being a "strong" party, with other parties and electoral coalitions either disbanding in less than a decade, lacking most of the components of party strength, or both. Many of Peru's twentieth-century parties were either regionally based (in Lima or elsewhere) or directly linked to the popularity of a local caudillo, lacking both the organizational and electoral staying power that would allow them to survive the declining power of their founders. Peru's twentieth-century civilian presidents therefore rarely felt the constraints, outlined above, that normally come with strong party organizations and systems.[3]

Finally, and perhaps most important, Peru has a long history of authoritarianism in the form of both military rule and civilian oligarchy, which has made the presidency the primary focus of political power in the country. In the twentieth century, Peru's longest uninterrupted experience with civilian democratic rule was twelve years (1980–92), prior to which it had been five years (1963–68). During the long periods of authoritarianism, constitutions have generally been suspended, manipulated, or rewritten to meet the needs of authoritarian rulers (Klarén 2000; McClintock 1994; Werlich 1978; Cotler 1978).

With Peru's return to democracy in 1980, a new constitution was inaugurated. In general, the 1979 constitution ushered in a period of growing presidential power and influence. In part this resulted from the substantial majorities Presidents Fernando Belaúnde Terry (1980–85) and Alan García Pérez (1985–90) enjoyed in Congress. Partisan powers were used to assert and expand constitutional powers. Both presidents extensively used their legislative-decree powers, duly granted to them by Congress. More than 50 percent of the laws passed during the Belaúnde administration and 60 percent of those passed during that of García were legislative decrees issued by the executive (Planas 1999, 120). In addition, no ministers were censured and few were called by Congress for interrogation. Important policies were usually initiated by the executive, without prior communication or coordination with party officials or congressional allies. The most egregious example of this dynamic was the 1987 bank nationalization by President García, a plan that was developed by a small circle of advisors and launched with little outside input— which dominated the political agenda of the country for two years.[4] Both presidents were known for their highly personalistic style of governance.

Additional factors in the trend of the 1980s toward greater presidential power were the growing threats from the severest economic crisis in a half century and the rapid expansion of the Maoist Sendero Luminoso (Shining Path) insurgency. Both exigencies turned the presidents into "crisis managers," willing and able not only to use their existing constitutional powers to their fullest, but also to claim for themselves ever more resources and powers to meet the extraordinary circumstances of these challenges. Insurgency in particular lent itself to this dynamic, as emergency powers were granted to the armed forces in most parts of the country, so much so that by the end of the decade nearly 70 percent of the population was effectively living under military rule, with severe restrictions on civil and political rights (Americas Watch 1992; Palmer, 1992).

Toward the Authoritarian Presidency, 1990–2000

At one level, the Fujimori presidency merely built on the historic tradition of strong centralized presidencies while accelerating the trend of presidents in the 1980s to use and extend their institutional powers to the fullest while relying on partisan support and favorable public opinion to undermine checks on the use of that power. At the same time, however, I argue in this chapter that a real qualitative shift occurred, as the scope and range of presidential power was extended to such a degree that few practical institutional or societal restraints on the exercise of that power remained. There is a clear differentiation therefore between the governments of the 1980s, as discussed above, and the Fujimori administration. By the mid-1990s it was clear that the extension and use of executive powers were so vast and unchecked that Peru had undergone a regime change. The classification of regime types has been of growing interest to political scientists, as the number of regimes meeting at least one of the criteria for consideration as a democracy has increased. The mixing of democratic and authoritarian characteristics has resulted in the emergence of new types of regimes, such as "delegative democracy" and "hybrid regimes." Given the fluidity with which many regimes combine these characteristics, and the inherent difficulties in pinning down a regime type, it is still incumbent on comparative analysts to assess the degree to which the core characteristics of a regime are present.[5] Although it is beyond the scope of this chapter to review all the characteristics of the Fujimori administrations, the remainder of the chapter will focus on one key characteristic—limited, as opposed to arbitrary, government—to provide an insight into the change of regime.

The most direct challenge to democratic institutionalism during Fujimori's administration came in April 1992, when the president used the armed forces to forcibly shut down Congress and the judiciary. Largely as a result of international pressure, the administration was forced to hold Constituent Assembly elections, and ultimately a new constitution was approved by voters in a 1993 plebiscite. Under the 1993 constitution, both Congress and the judiciary saw their formal powers reduced. During the remainder of the regime, neither Congress nor the judiciary, which were dominated by Fujimori appointees and loyalists, impeded the adoption or implementation of a major policy initiative of the president. Where the threat of such an event occurred, as in the Constitutional Tribunal's decision regarding presidential reelection, institutional rules and personnel were arbitrarily changed.

Institutional Checks I: Checkmating Mutual Checks

The effort to reshape the relation between governmental institutions began in earnest with the 1992 autogolpe. The president's decision to suspend the 1979 constitution had a notable impact in executive-legislative relations and set the pattern of executive dominance over the legislature for the remainder of the decade.[6] Under the new 1993 constitution, Congress became smaller, had even fewer clear checks on presidential power than was allowed in the 1979 constitution, and was more vulnerable to the threat of dissolution. The 1993 constitution created a unicameral legislature of 120 members, compared to the 240-member bicameral legislature under the 1979 constitution. As Fernando Tuesta Soldevilla (1996b, 137) has pointed out, the Peruvian congress was one of the smallest in the world and only comparable to those of much smaller countries.

The smaller size and thus reduced representativeness of Congress was accompanied by new limitations in checks on the president. Among the most important policy checks on executives in a presidential system are legislative approval for international treaties and high-level diplomatic and military promotions. Although the wide majorities enjoyed by the García and Belaúnde governments meant that no significant treaties or promotions were rejected, the process allowed Congress to question candidates and provided opposition parties the opportunity to expound their alternatives. The 1993 constitution eliminated this requirement, freeing the president to make and ratify treaties in a series of policy arenas (Article 56) and to designate ambassadorial and military appointments without congressional approval.

The presidential veto, and congressional ability to override it, is a classic type of mutual check in presidential systems. Article 108 of the 1993 constitution maintains the right of presidents to *observar* (put on hold) congressional laws, a veto mechanism that existed in the 1979 constitution. If the president does not promulgate a law within fifteen days of congressional passage, the law expires. Congress may then promulgate it with the votes of 51 percent of its members. The only difference in this regard between the 1979 and 1993 constitutions is that the latter allowed the president to partially promulgate a law, in what amounts to a rough equivalent of a "line-item veto" in the U.S. system (Chirinos Soto 1995, 187–91). As legal observers in the United States have noted, such partial vetoes enhance the power of executives, allowing them to pick and choose which aspects of the law they find palatable. In the Peruvian context, the majorities favorable to the president and the fact that most laws originated in presidential decrees, made the use of presidential *observaciones* rare. Nonetheless, a new line-item veto was yet another concession to presidential power.

In the area of economic policymaking, the new constitution retained the limited role of Congress in developing and administering the nation's finances and budget. Article 211 of the 1979 constitution clearly gave this authority to the president. Congress may discuss, debate, and finally vote on the budget, but it cannot substantially alter spending proposals, the initiation of which remains an executive prerogative. The 1993 constitution continued this tradition. If anything, the restriction is reinforced in Article 79 by requiring the prior approval of all tax laws by the Ministry of Economics and Finance. A persistent problem facing Congress in this area was the lack of independent economic or budgetary information. Congress did not have its own budgetary research staff and as a result, members received their information from the executive branch, the media, or private research institutes, clearly putting Congress at disadvantage.

Congress did not have any specific investigatory powers, and its ability to remove officials is similarly limited. Ministers can be interrogated by Congress on policy and, as mentioned earlier, cabinet censure is a prerogative of Congress. In some ways censure appears to be a legislative "check" on presidential power. However, the censure of a minister or even of an entire cabinet did not affect the president, whose extensive policymaking and implementing powers remain unaffected. Moreover, censure carries inherent dangers for Congress. Under the 1979 constitution three cabinet censures by Congress allowed the president to close down that body for new elections. Under the 1993 constitution, the president can dissolve Congress after only two cabinet censures. Moreover, unlike the older censure mechanism, which restricted the president to proceeding with only one congressional dissolution per term, the 1993 constitution allows the president to dissolve Congress an unlimited number of times and provides that the president can govern through "decrees of urgency" until a new Congress is elected, creating an incentive for presidents to provoke crises should an uncooperative Congress emerge.

Despite limited investigatory powers and few resources, Peru's Congress in the 1980s did appoint a number of multiparty investigative commissions, primarily in the area of human rights violations that resulted from public pressure and were critical of executive actions. These included investigations of paramilitary activities and the 1986 prison massacre. The 1990s witnessed no significant investigations, despite calls from the media and opposition legislators to appoint such commissions to examine accusations of corruption, drug trafficking, and human rights violations carried out by executive branch officials. In dealing with abuses of power or accusations of malfeasance, Peru's constitution does not have an "impeachment" clause. The closest mechanism is the *antejuicio* (literally, a pretrial) in which officials from all three branches can be stripped of their immunity from prosecution if they are found to have committed wrongdoing in office. Unlike impeachment in the United States, an *antejuicio* does not cover violations of the constitution or abuse of power, but is restricted to specific criminal conduct (Paniagua 1995, 127–29).

A final area where legislative authority was limited further was in the area of legislative decree power. The 1979 constitution gave Congress the power to cede to the president law-making authority on specific issues for a set time period, a power that Belaúnde and García used extensively. Article 104 of the 1993 constitution continued this tradition and only required that the president inform Congress of such decrees when they are issued. The new constitution also created a new category of decrees that are considered "urgent" and can thus be put into place without prior congressional authorization (Fernandez Segado 1994, 38–40; Schmidt 1998).

The judiciary in Peru has historically been the branch most susceptible to political manipulation and domination by the president and, as a result, has offered few effective checks on presidential power. After dismissing most of the country's judges, including members of the Supreme Court during the 1992 autogolpe, President Fujimori promised wide-ranging reforms to deal with a judiciary that was largely viewed as corrupt and inefficient. Many of these reforms, such as the introduction of elected justices of the peace and a new Defensoría del Pueblo (Ombudsman's Office) were promising; however, their development remained highly vulnerable to executive manipulation.

During this period, two important bodies within the judicial system that had the potential to check presidential power were the Consejo Nacional de la Magistratura (National Council of Magistrates), which directs the selection of judges, and the Tribunal Constitutional (Constitutional Tribunal [TC]), which reviews the constitutionality of laws. Both institutions were subject to political pressures by the executive, seriously compromising the idea of judicial independence. Up to four of the seven members of the National Council can be from outside the judicial system and even the field of law, opening the way for purely political appointments, which had been the practice of the administration (Fernandez Segado 1994, 53). Moreover, the appointment of an executive "reorganization" commission in 1996, headed by former admiral Jose Dellepiane, effectively took control of the National Council's functions, by purging and appointing a new series of justices throughout the system. Executive intervention in the Constitutional Tribunal was even more egregious. Members of the tribunal are elected by Congress and can also be removed by Congress. In 1997 three members of the tribunal were removed by Congress, at the behest of pro-Fujimori legislators, for having voted against the possibility of a presidential reelection. With only four Fujimori loyalists remaining on the tribunal after this removal, the body issued rulings that were consistently on the side of the executive (Planas 1999, 215).

Executive efforts to influence judicial decision making and thus undermine judicial independence occurred largely where either administration officials were accused of corruption or where investigations of human rights abuses threatened to undermine the administration's counterinsurgency campaign. Judges and prosecutors were pressured to end investigations, and the outright dismissal of investigators was a common occurrence. When serious allegations of corruption involving drug trafficking against presidential advisor Vladimiro Montesinos surfaced during the trial of one of Peru's most notorious drug kingpins, prosecutors suppressed possible evidence and refused to allow further questioning. Clearly, such pressures were not unique to the Fujimori administration. What was unusual was how widespread and routine they became.

The most notable intervention in judicial processes involved human rights abuses. As evidence mounted in 1995 that security forces were involved in the killing of students and professors at the National University of Education (informally known as La Cantuta), Congress at the behest of the president, passed a blanket amnesty law for all military officers involved in human rights abuses. In a further limit on judicial independence, trials of terrorist suspects were carried out by special military tribunals, over which no civilian court had jurisdiction. During these trials, cross-examinations were not allowed, evidence was not shared with defense attorneys, and sentences could only be appealed once to a higher military court. Most trials lasted only a few minutes, the minimum guilty sentence was thirty years, and the conviction rate of those accused was an astounding 97 percent (Gamarra 1995). Needless to say, these procedures were a fundamental violation of due process. Although most of the laws allowing these trials were suspended by 1998, their use demonstrated the vulnerability of judicial independence to arbitrary executive authority.

A final element in highlighting the lack of checks and balances within the governmental structure of Peru in the 1990s was the growing power and authority of the executive itself. As noted earlier, the presidency has traditionally dominated the policy process, particularly through the use of legislative decrees. During the Fujimori administration, this dominance was enhanced by an expansion in the size and scope of the executive bureaucracy. In 1992 the administration created the Ministry of the Presidency, which concentrated previously scattered executive offices under one cabinet-level ministry. From its creation until 1995, its budget expanded ninefold (Kay 1996, 83). The ministry concentrated control over all spending on infrastructure projects, from road building to school construction, as well as on most social programs. A significant part of the ministry's budget went to the latter, particularly a series of new programs designed and implemented during Fujimori's first term in office. These included the Fondo Nacional de Compensación y Desarrollo Social (National Fund for Social Compensation and Development [FONCODES]), the Fondo Nacional de Vivienda (National Housing Fund [FONAVI]), and the Programa Nacional de Asistencia Alimentaria (National Program of Food Assistance [PRONAA]). In addition, the ministry took control of previously existing programs, most notably the Vaso de Leche (Glass of Milk) program, which was created and run by municipalities until 1996. Funding for these programs initially came from profits derived from privatization efforts and had the support of international aid agencies. Nonetheless, the implementation of these programs were carried out in ways that advanced the president's political interests. Not surprisingly, billboards announcing the benefits of the programs were painted in bright orange, the same color used by Fujimori's electoral vehicle Cambio 90.

Institutional Checks II: Reversing Decentralization, Curtailing Local Autonomy

Centralization was a key feature of Peru's political system throughout the nineteenth and twentieth centuries, although local *caciques* (strongmen) had considerable autonomy and used their economic and social dominance not only to perpetuate themselves in power, but also on occasion to resist efforts by national actors to impose their authority (Manrique 1988; de la Cadena 1999). Without a system of local governments, Peru historically lacked an important check on executive power: a legitimate set of regional institutions that could initiate and implement policies independent of the national executive. One of the most promising features of the 1979 constitution was the promise of regionalization. For the first time in Peru's history, the constitution mandated a federal-like system of regional governments with control of local development issues, extending the first steps toward local autonomy taken in the 1960s with the election of mayors. Although the Belaúnde administration did not actively develop plans to implement this mandate, the García administration put into place a scheme that divided the country into twelve regions, each with a regional assembly that would have substantial powers to legislate and control local finances (McClintock 1994, 293).

The movement toward decentralization was to prove short-lived, as the Fujimori administration moved quickly to end regionalization. As a result of the 1992 autogolpe, the regional assemblies were closed down. In their place, President Fujimori established Consejo Transitorio de Administración Regional (Transitional Councils of Regional Administration [CTAR]), whose members were designated by the president and which were dependent on the Ministry of the Presidency. The CTARs were meant to be transitional bodies leading to the creation of permanent and locally elected councils. The promise of such councils was held out in Articles 188–90 of the 1993 constitution, but never implemented. Instead, the CTARs and presidentially designated "regional presidents" remained the only form of local governance. The limits to any future development of regional autonomy were made clear in the constitution's Article 199, which explicitly stated that both regions and municipalities "must report their budgets to the Controlaria General de la República (National Comptroller's Office). They are regulated by law" (my translation). The effect of this article was to make all local governments responsible to the central government, specifically the executive branch.

Municipal initiatives, which allowed the opposition an important organizational as well as policy forum, became a major target of the Fujimori administration's effort to define and dominate the country's political agenda. During the first six years of the administration, a number of decrees were issued by the presidency that were intended to eliminate or curtail municipal powers, from tax powers to regulation of bus routes (see Chapter 3). Decree Law 776, issued in 1993, eliminated the ability of municipalities to raise revenue by taxation and provided that all municipal revenue come from a Fondo de Compensación Municipal (Municipal Compensation Fund [FONCOMUN]), whose criteria regarding the distribution of funds is determined by executive decree laws and the Ministry of Economy and Finance, in effect making municipalities fiscally dependent on the executive branch (Planas 1999, 311). Continuing with the trend of reducing municipal prerogatives, an executive decree was issued in 1996 transferring authority over the Glass of Milk program from municipalities to the Ministry of the Presidency and thus effectively eliminating the possibility of municipalities to initiate social-welfare policies. During the 1990s, as many countries in Latin America were moving toward greater decentralization (Colombia, Mexico, El Salvador) as part of a broadening democratization, Peru was moving decisively in the opposite direction.

Societal Checks I: The Collapse of the Party System

From the 1960s through the 1980s, Peru had a weak multiparty system. Parties mixed ideology and strong class identity with the charisma of a founding leader. However, few parties outlasted the passing of their founders, and the system remained highly unstable; as new parties emerged, some were combined in electoral alliances and others disappeared in the wake of poor electoral performance. Party organizations and party system dynamics capable of exercising checks on presidential power, as outlined earlier, have thus historically been highly limited in Peru. During 1989–95, that party system virtually collapsed, as Roberts notes in Chapter 4.

Viewed from a historical perspective, Fujimori's highly personalistic style of governance was certainly not unprecedented in either Peru or the region. Fujimori was very successful in appealing to the different social classes and groups that make up modern Peru, by creating a discourse that linked his own person with the needs, interests and even culture of these disparate sectors. Like the populists of the past, Fujimori demonstrated enormous political skill, mixed with demagoguery, in convincing people with such divergent interests that loyalty to him personally was the best way to achieve their goals within the political system. Fujimori's ability to maintain such personal loyalty even while implementing policies that created high economic costs for these constituencies was one of the most surprising aspects of his administration and also the source of much academic attention (Roberts 1995; S. Stokes 1996a).

What is perhaps most astonishing is that this support persisted well into the decade of the 1990s despite the administration's complete disinterest in political organization and mobilization. Unlike classic populist politicians such as former president Alan García, Fujimori was uninterested in mobilizing support from lower-class groups and avoided using class-oriented appeals or redistributive policies to gain support. While the administration cultivated approval in opinion polls and elections, there were no significant progovernment organizations designed to channel support for its policies. From the start of the administration, Fujimori consistently attacked the concept of parties as well as the existing parties in Peru. The four "parties" developed by Fujimori and his supporters—Cambio 90 (Change 90), Nueva Mayoría (New Majority), Perú 2000, and Vamos Vecino (Let's Go, Neighbor)—were little more than electoral vehicles: all lacked national organizational structure, independent leaderships, and programmatic agendas and were largely viewed as mere electoral labels for pro-Fujimori candidates.

In order to accomplish many of the tasks that a formal party structure might provide, President Fujimori was astute in creating a web of personalistic networks throughout the administration made up of people loyal to his person and occupying formal and informal roles in the government. These networks provided the president with a staff of loyal followers within the state bureaucracy; in the case of other presidents, such a staff would often be recruited from a political party. Fujimori's staff helped him manage and ultimately aggregate the demands coming from different sectors of society. Unlike party officials, however, they did not have an independent power base of their own and were thus unable to provide a check on presidential activities. During both the García and Belaúnde administrations, members of the ruling party, including ministers, opposed executive policies and, in such cases as the García bank nationalizations, worked to undermine the president's initiative. In the case of Fujimori, the extreme dependence on the president meant that their positions were tied to their ability to loyally serve the interests and needs of the president. If they were perceived as threatening, they could be easily removed, and in contrast to the dismissal of party officials who might have organizational interests of their own, there would likely be few if any repercussions for the president. The extension of personalistic networks throughout the entire state apparatus provided the basis for what Conaghan terms "greed rings" (Chapter 5, this volume). Executive power was used not only to politically dominate and manipulate the state apparatus but also to extend the influence of key actors who were involved in corruption without oversight.

There were two primary networks that Fujimori developed from the start of his administration, admittedly with some overlap: social/familial and technocratic. Lacking a formal political party, it was almost inevitable that once elected, Fujimori would turn to friends and family to staff his administration. Although many in the developing family/social network were highly trained and competent, others had little more than their ties to Fujimori as qualifications. Santiago Fujimori, the new president's brother, became de facto chief of staff, overseeing appointments and promotions within the executive branch, and until their separation, Fujimori's wife, Susana Higuchi, also played a role, as informal advisor. Víctor Joy Way, a successful Chinese-Peruvian businessman from the Andean department of Huánuco and friend of the president, had at various points been prime minister and president of Congress. The administration recruited heavily among the Japanese-Peruvian community, which had traditionally not been politically active or mobilized. During the 1990s, several prominent ministers and vice-ministers came from this community, including Daniel Hokama, former minister of energy and mines; Alejandro Afuso Higa, director of the social program FONCODES; and Víctor Kobashigawa, vice-minister of education. The most prominent figure from this community and one of the most influential officials of the first Fujimori administration was Jaime Yoshiyama, who first as minister of energy and mines and later as director of the Ministry of the Presidency oversaw much of the economic and governmental restructuring that took place between 1990 and 1995. Yoshiyama was often mentioned as a possible successor of Fujimori and became the administration's candidate for mayor of Lima in November 1995 but narrowly lost. Yoshiyama's growing prominence, ambitions, and semipublic efforts to build an independent political base were important factors behind his summary dismissal as governmental minister at the end of 1996.

The penetration of the state bureaucracy by this social network, although providing a loyal staff for the president, often led to charges of corruption (as with Santiago Fujimori) and the erosion of professionalism. Nowhere is the latter more clear than in the security forces. By far the most powerful of the informal advisors to the president was the shadowy figure Vladimiro Montesinos, a former army captain who had been Fujimori's attorney during the 1990 presidential campaign. Montesinos was instrumental in using his contacts in the security forces to help purge the armed forces and establish the new president's control over them. Although he occupied no formal position within the governmental structure, he had effective control over both the armed forces and the intelligence agency, Servicio de Inteligencia Nacional (National Intelligence Service [SIN]). Promotions, retirements, and assignments were heavily influenced by Montesinos, and his power and influence were long the source of resentment within the security apparatus (Obando 1996; Rospigliosi 2000).

A second type of personalistic network that was used extensively during the 1990s was the technocratic one. Technocrats are highly trained and specialized functionaries. Most have advanced degrees from foreign universities, particularly in the United States, with a focus on economics or finance. Throughout Latin America in the 1990s, technocrats developed extraordinary influence in state policymaking, and Peru has not been an exception. Technocrats played a central role in reorganizing the state structure and implementing economic reforms. Their ability to forge links between government politicians, international economic actors (both financial organizations and multinational corporations), and the domestic business sector played a critical part in the successful implementation of the administration's structural-reform package.

Where party systems exist, the party organization can provide the core of trained personnel beyond that which exists in the civil service. Such a cadre of party technocrats is likely to have constituencies and support within the party apparatus, as well as interests that likely transcend those of the sitting president. As Geddes (1994) has shown, in her examination of forty-four Latin American presidential administrations, presidents who emerge from strong party organizations are likely to concentrate on appointing their partisan loyalists in bureaucratic positions. Those presidents who are independent or have weak party ties are likely to rely on outside technocrats. The recruitment of technical personnel outside a party structure accentuates the already strong links that exist between technocracy and the executive branch, since technocrats are generally found in the executive branch bureaucracy. The potential for a virtual monopoly by the executive on technical expertise is a very real danger that puts other governmental branches as well as political society at a disadvantage. Unable to acquire the expertise needed to evaluate presidential policies, these last two groups must either rely on the executive to provide this information or acquiesce in the presidential monopoly on technical information. In Peru, as in most of Latin America, the legislative and judicial branches have few resources and have traditionally not developed an independent technical staff that could serve their institutions in the way the executive is served by its bureaucracy. An "information gap" between these institutions then contributes to an increase in presidential power and influence.

The Fujimori administration relied heavily on technocrats for both developing and implementing its economic-reform project. Technocrats occupied all levels of the executive, from ministers to agency staff, and were especially important in restructuring agencies that were seen as having a strategic role in the liberalization of the economy. Not surprisingly, two agencies stand out: the Superintendencia Nacional de Administración Tributaria (National Superintendency of Revenue Administration [SUNAT]), the tax-collecting agency, whose priority was to increase tax collections and thus strengthen governmental revenue, and the Comisión de Promoción de la Inversión Privada (Commission for Promotion of Private Investment [COPRI]), the agency charged with overseeing the privatization of state enterprises. Staff and managers at both agencies were notable for being highly trained professionals, predominately lawyers, accountants, and economists, many with foreign degrees. In addition to providing valuable technical advice, they played a key role in forging links between the executive; international financial institutions, including multinational corporations; and the domestic business sector. This was especially true in the first (and for economic reforms, the most critical) Fujimori administrations, with figures such as former minister of economy Carlos Boloña and informal advisor Hernando de Soto providing important international contacts and also attracting a cadre of technocratic advisors to work in the administration. The reliance by the president on technocratic networks that were directly responsible to the executive to design and implement economic restructuring effectively marginalized other institutions in the policymaking process and in fact contributed to the perception that legal or legislative deliberation was merely an obstacle to overcome rather than an integral part of the process. The acceleration of privatization efforts in the immediate aftermath of the autogolpe highlights the virtual disdain that some technocrats had toward the process of democratic deliberation (M. Centeno 1994).

Societal Checks II: Weakening Civil Society

The link between strong civil societies and democracy has long been established, even though the precise mechanisms by which this is accomplished have not always been clear. While some argue that civil society relationships foster democracy through the promotion of civil and associative values, others suggest that civil society associations as autonomous organizations function as a counterweight to state power and therefore limit abuses of power (Foley and Edwards 1996, 38–39). It is this latter interpretation that is most relevant to the discussion of presidential power. Strong civil society associations capable of challenging presidential abuses through voting power at the ballot box, influence/persuasion over public opinion through the media, and protests and demonstrations in the streets provide an important incentive for presidents in a democratic context to not abuse or overextend their powers.

Although Peru historically had a relatively "weak" civil society, the 1970s and 1980s in particular suggested a growing level of organization and sophistication among a variety of social interests, especially those that had been excluded from social and political power. New labor and peasant unions, along with neighborhood associations, human rights groups and church-related organizations, all witnessed dramatic growth in these decades (Tovar 1985; Mauceri 1996). These entities became increasingly influential in the 1980s, representing a new electoral base for parties of the Left and Center Left and also playing an active role in protesting governmental policies during that decade. A parallel development occurred on the right, as conservative think tanks, business associations, and church-related groups emerged in the 1980s, playing an important role in challenging state policies during the García administration, such as the 1987 bank nationalization (Durand 1997).

The early 1990s witnessed a clear reversal of this trend. To a large degree, the economic crisis of the 1980s and the violence carried out by both the military and the Shining Path weakened civil society and benefited Fujimori by reducing societal pressures to conform to the democratic process. Fujimori thus confronted a very different situation from that of either Belaúnde or García. Nonetheless, independent associations, particularly on the left, were viewed warily by the administration as potential sources opposition, and sustained steps were taken to restrict and control the autonomy of civil society groups. As referred to earlier, neighborhood organizations, such as the Glass of Milk and Popular Kitchen Committees, were either repressed or co-opted into new governmental agencies. Changes introduced into the Labor Code in the early 1990s weakened the collective bargaining and strike powers of labor unions, while the new agrarian law that eliminated cooperative ventures made it more difficult for peasants to organize.

An additional element in the demobilization of civil society during the 1990s was the manipulation and intimidation of press freedoms. Peru's press has had a long tradition of vigorous investigative reporting, representing the full range of ideological positions in the country. As such, it has always been a terrain upon which political and social groups could mobilize public opinion. Not surprisingly, the Fujimori administration viewed the press with distrust, seeing it as a potential source of opposition, and actively engaged in a pattern of harassment and manipulation, using supposed tax code violations to prosecute journalists and other members of the media; extorting money from and bribing media owners, such as those of the daily *Expreso*; wiretapping journalists; and, in the most extreme case, that of Channel 2 owner Baruch Ivcher, using trumped-up charges of treason to persecute opponents. In combination with intimidation moreover, the Fujimori administration created a virtually "alternative" press, supported by the intelligence services and the military, in the form of the *prensa chicha,* the sensationalistic tabloids that served as a vehicle for pro-Fujimori propaganda and scandalmongering carried out against opposition figures (Conaghan 2002; Fowks 2000). While many media outlets were able to resist government pressure and combat efforts at intimidation, there is no question that Fujimori's media policy certainly made it more difficult both to investigate and publicize government abuses and corruption, as well as to mobilize and coordinate opposition in civil society.

Unlike the party system, civil society organizations reemerged in the late 1990s to present a major challenge to the Fujimori regime, reaffirming the fundamental role they play as a check on presidential power. Beginning with student protests in 1996, and at a time when political society was largely quiescent, new social movements joined with some preexisting associations to challenge regime efforts to push for a third presidential term. Likewise, civil society organizations played a crucial role in the protests and demonstrations against the electoral fraud that took place in the 2000 presidential campaign, helping to delegitimize the Fujimori regime and focusing international attention.

The Presidency Under Fujimori and Beyond

In this chapter I have outlined the impediments to the effective implementation of institutional and societal checks on presidential power in Peru during the 1990s. After reviewing these checks and their development in Peru prior to 1990, I suggested that through a combination of contextual variables and purposeful policies, presidential power during the Fujimori period went largely unrestrained, laying the ground for a regime change that took Peru into its first authoritarian experience since the 1970s. A review of the operation of institutional and societal checks on presidential power in Peru in the 1990s suggests that they either are not part of the institutional structure of Peru's political system or had been rendered inoperable by the political practices of President Fujimori and his followers. Although President Fujimori played a significant part in limiting such institutional checks, it is clear that political elites in Peru also bear some responsibility.

Democratization cannot take place without an institutional structure that provides incentives for political actors to engage in democratic behaviors. However, institutional structures are themselves the result of complex historical and cultural legacies, not all of which may be compatible with democratic norms. In the case of Peru, such legacies include racism, economic inequality, political and economic centralization, authoritarian and clientelistic behaviors by elites, the lack of a culture of accountability, and the belief in concentrated political power as the ultimate agent of social change. The dilemma for those interested in deepening democratization lies in not only recognizing the importance of institutional structures in shaping behavior, but also developing creative institutional arrangements that can overcome, or at least minimize, past choices and legacies that have impeded democratization thus far. This is clearly not an easily accomplished task.

The lessons of the Peruvian case also point to the importance of context and leadership in the task of democratic consolidation. The deep economic crisis, growing insurgency, and political polarization in a weak party system that existed in Peru in the late 1980s allowed President Fujimori to make the argument that concentrated power in the executive was needed to tackle these difficulties. The strong public support that Fujimori enjoyed almost until the end of the decade suggested that many, if not most, Peruvians shared this belief. The general political and economic decay of the 1980s thus paved the way for the authoritarianism of the 1990s. By the same token, the willingness of Fujimori to adopt methods of leadership that prioritized the arbitrary and personalistic exercise of power also contributed to the development of an authoritarian presidency. The reluctance to compromise, to adhere to democratic rules, and to ultimately give up power after two constitutional terms made it impossible for either institutions or societal groups to check presidential power in any effective way.

NOTES

1. While partisan ties generally facilitate cooperation between different branches and levels of government in the United States, different interests and constituencies often result in intraparty conflicts. See Fisher 1987; Poole and Daniels 1985. Comparatively, Mainwaring and Shugart (1997, 395) note that although disciplined parties can facilitate executive-legislative relations, undisciplined parties can actually be destructive, particularly where presidents do not enjoy a legislative majority.

2. Mexico provides an interesting example of this dynamic. Although the *presidencialismo* of the Mexican system was highly authoritarian and paternalistic, it was far from a model of personal and arbitrary rule. Mexican presidents were traditionally constrained by party elites and interests both those within the party organization and those entrenched in the state apparatus. See Camp 1999, chap. 6.

3. Prior to Fujimori, three presidents saw their agendas blocked by congressional opposition, ending in coups: Guillermo Billinghurst in 1914, José Luis Bustamante y Rivero in 1948 and Belaúnde in 1968. In the last two cases, APRA was the opposition party.

4. The nationalization was ultimately modified by the Senate.

5. Diamond (2002, 32) refers to the Fujimori regime as "electoral authoritarian." See also Carrión's discussion in the Conclusion.

6. This dominance remained in place until the various scandals of 2000 effectively resulted in the breakdown of discipline among pro-Fujimori's congresspersons. For a convincing explanation of this dynamic that relies on the importance of recorded voting in the Congress, see Carey 2003.

THREE

Fujimori and the Mayors of Lima, 1990–2001: The Impact and Legacy of Neopopulist Rule

ROBERT R. BARR AND HENRY DIETZ

Alberto Fujimori's tenure as Peruvian president serves as an exemplar of neopopulist rule, with its exaggerated levels of personalism, anti-institutionalism, and heavy reliance on support from the marginalized masses (Roberts 1995; Weyland 1996). Significant bodies of research compare and contrast the nature of neopopulism with that of classic populism, as well as document many of the features of Fujimori's prototypical case (Crabtree 1998; Ellner 2003; Kay 1996; Roberts 2003; Weyland 2001). This literature, however, overlooks an important aspect of both neopopulism in general and Fujimori's rule in particular—the relationship between the neopopulist executive and subnational officials, namely, the mayors of Lima. Lima is home to roughly 30 percent of Peru's entire population, not to mention the bulk of the country's economic activity. The city's dominant position makes its mayor the most important elected official after the president. And this point, in turn, allows us to address the questions of whether and how neopopulism affects executive-municipal relations.

Two individuals served as Lima's mayor during Fujimori's ten years in office. Ricardo Belmont Casinelli first took office in 1989, marking the first major triumph for a political independent since the transition to democracy, and was elected for a second term in 1993. Following Belmont in 1995 was Alberto Andrade Carmona, who was reelected in 1998. These two men had several characteristics in common: each was elected for two terms; each defeated Fujimori's chosen candidates; and each was a political independent while mayor.[1] In addition, each harbored, at least for a time, presidential aspirations. Finally, and more important for our purposes, each found himself constantly opposed and harried by Fujimori.

We argue that Fujimori's acrimonious dealings with the mayors of Lima can be understood in relation to his neopopulist form of rule. More so than the classic populist variant, neopopulism relies on unmediated, unorganized connections between leader and followers. This explicit lack of institutionalization makes neopopulist leaders more dependent on (and vulnerable to) popular approval than those who can rely on more stable organizational backing. It follows that neopopulists have a heightened sensitivity to independent hubs of public support and therefore are more likely to take extreme steps to prevent them from developing. Hence, these leaders are concerned not only with the "positive" aspect of building their own sociopolitical coalition, but also with the "negative" aspect of denying others from doing the same thing.

This logic led Fujimori to direct a whole range of obstructionist policies at Peru's larger subnational units, and especially at Lima's mayors. As a result, many local initiatives were frequently stymied by Fujimori-led presidential and congressional actions aimed at blocking Belmont and Andrade from developing independent bases of public support. Our chapter is thus not concerned with how Belmont or Andrade won office or with presenting a narrative account of their terms in office. Rather, by examining the contentious nature of national executive–capital city mayor relations in the 1990s, we may be able to highlight the lengths to which Fujimori was willing to go in undercutting potential rivals and to offer a few generalizations about the nature of neopopulist rule and its seemingly inevitable tendency to centralize power at any and all costs. Before reaching those generalizations, we first discuss neopopulism and its "negative" political incentives. This allows us to develop our expectations of how a neopopulist president might deal with subnational officials and thus to explain why Fujimori had such acrimonious relations with the Lima mayors. We then consider Lima and its place in Peruvian politics and offer illustrative examples of Fujimori's behavior toward both Belmont and Andrade.

Neopopulism: Implications and Expectations

A full discussion of the concept of neopopulism is beyond the scope of this chapter, but a few comments are in order to frame our empirical analysis. We consider the core of both populism and neopopulism to be the mobilization of a mass following behind a personalistic, plebiscitarian leader (see Chapter 1). Importantly, authority relations in populism, as opposed to other forms of political organizations or movements, are not only vertical or top down but also have nonmediated linkages between leader and followers (Mouzelis 1985). The more recent variant, nevertheless, in three principal ways is distinct from the classic populism that had its heyday in the 1940s.[2] First, its primary constituency is composed of members of the informal economy as opposed to labor unions. Second, neopopulists are associated with the implementation of neoliberal or market-oriented economic policies, as opposed to the universalistic and expansive policies of their predecessors. Third, as Weyland discusses in Chapter 1 in this volume, neopopulism is an even less organized phenomenon than classic populism, to the point that it seeks to deinstitutionalize politics. Even in cases where neopopulists rise through existing party apparatuses (for example, Menem and Salinas), they undermine the party establishment to secure their *personal* control (Weyland 2001, 15). These factors, moreover, are interrelated and reinforcing. As Roberts (1995, 113) explains: "The theoretical nexus between populism and neoliberalism, then, is grounded in their reciprocal tendency to exploit—and exacerbate—the de-institutionalization of political representation."

Together, these factors highlight the antiorganizational bias of neopopulism and, consequently, the reliance upon broad public support. Neopopulists' primary basis of political strength, that is, does not come from a well-organized party, which could provide legislative support as well as the loyalty of its core activists. Similarly, ties to the nation's oligarchy or support from the military are secondary, not primary, sources of strength. As Weyland (2001, 12) describes, this characteristic is revealed in critical moments: "When pushed to the wall, they invoke and thus reveal the *ultima ratio* of populism: broad mass support." It is not simply with respect to the election or reelection of the populist president that public support matters; it is also important during congressional or subnational contests to elect supporters of the leader, plebiscites or referenda to enact policies or even constitutions that enhance the leader's power, and mass rallies and opinion polls that boost his influence over political opponents and grant him some measure of legitimacy to rule in a delegative manner.

An important implication of these factors is the extent to which neopopulists are vulnerable to the fluctuations of public opinion. High levels of mass support can provide the leader with significant political strength, but because this support is uninstitutionalized, it can quickly erode. Personal charisma has been an important tool enabling many populists to maintain support in the absence of organized linkages such as patron-client networks. Not all populists are charismatic, of course, and charisma alone may be insufficient to maintain support over long periods. Likewise, national crises provide opportunities to demonstrate their leadership, yet resolution can eliminate the "need" for citizens to continue supporting the populist leader (Weyland 2000). This fragility inherent in their principal source of strength helps explain the often humiliating and dramatic collapse of populist or neopopulist presidencies. For instance, Abdalá Bucaram, Fernando Collor de Mello, and Carlos Andés Pérez were removed from office, while Carlos Salinas de Gortari and Fujimori wound up in exile.

Because neopopulists rely more *directly* on mass support than do many other politicians and because this reliance makes them politically vulnerable, the realm of public opinion becomes comparable to a zero-sum game. Naturally, during elections public support can usually be considered zero sum, but this point applies to interim periods as well; public backing shapes the prospects of governance. To the extent that a political figure views any support gained by others as a loss of his or her own power, it becomes imperative that he or she block the construction of independent bases of public support. Based on this logic, one might expect a neopopulist to engage in especially aggressive efforts to block potential opponents.[3] It goes without saying that neopopulists, like other politicians, rely on a range of collective and selective incentives to develop and maintain their followings. What we wish to emphasize here, however, is not those "positive" means of securing one's power, but the "negative" means entailed in obstructing one's opponents. Further, despite their relative neglect in the literature, likely opponents are not limited to national-level political actors but include those at the subnational level as well.

What we might expect from a neopopulist president, then, are various measures designed to undercut the potential for subnational political officials to build their own followings. The more likely targets of such efforts would be those responsible to large population centers. Hence, neopopulists might design policies to reduce the discretion of mayors (and others) over public resources while enhancing their own control. Where possible, they might modify the institutions of government to facilitate these ends (Barr 2002). And where direct control over resources is not feasible, they might seek to disperse discretion among more actors.

Such a "divide and conquer" strategy would minimize the threat from any single person. Further, should these means prove insufficient, we might expect more heavy-handed tactics, quasi-legal methods, or perhaps even illegal means of maintaining support and undercutting the opposition. While neopopulism should not be automatically associated with corruption (or its absence with nonpopulists), given the stakes they face regarding popular support, the incentives to use any means whatsoever may be relatively high.

Yet doing any or all of these requires the maintenance of a democratic veneer. The foremost reason concerns the legitimacy gained through the electoral process: winning the vote in apparently open contests may be the best way to demonstrate one's popular support.[4] Fujimori's dramatic defeat of Mario Vargas Llosa in 1990 with 62 percent of the national vote in the second round (his share was a more modest 53 percent in Lima) spoke volumes regarding his new role in Peruvian political life. His first-round victory in 1995 over Javier Pérez de Cuéllar with 64 percent of the national vote reconfirmed Fujimori's position. The nuisance of elections, of course, is the possibility of losing. As is discussed below, Fujimori used the resources at his disposal—both legal and extralegal—to limit the electoral potency of his challengers. While some of Fujimori's actions were blatantly authoritarian in nature—the autogolpe being the most obvious, but not only, instance—throughout his tenure he continued to uphold the formal trappings of democracy.

Having thus laid out the implications and expectations of neopopulist rule, we can now turn to the case at hand: Fujimori and the mayors of the city of Lima as an instance of how neopopulist leadership can affect subnational leaders and urban politics.

Lima: Its Place in Peru and Its Mayors

Lima is the quintessential Latin American primate capital city.[5] It has been dominant in Peru since its founding in the 1530s, when it was created as the capital of what was to become one of the wealthiest viceroyalties of New Spain. It has been Peru's largest city since that time and through most of the twentieth century was anywhere from eight to almost ten times larger than the nation's second-largest city. But its dominance is much more than demographic. It has been and continues to be the financial, economic, banking, social, cultural, and political capital of the nation, and today, at the start of the twenty-first century, it shows no sign of losing its strength.

Partly as a result of its overwhelming importance, it has been for the past half century a magnet for rural-origin migrants, and its growth has been vertiginous by almost any standards. For example, its population was slightly more than six hundred thousand people in 1940 (about 10 percent of the country's total), but rose by 1993 to more than eight million (about a quarter of the total). Any city that grows more than thirteenfold in fifty years obviously exerts an extraordinary if not unhealthy influence over the rest of the country.

But such growth also means extreme difficulties. Maintaining (let alone getting ahead in) basic infrastructure (water, sewerage, electricity, roads, housing, police protection, jobs) has proved to be an enormous challenge for whoever was in control of the city, especially since much of the city's growth has resulted from the influx of vast numbers of low-income residents. For the past fifty years, all observers as well as practitioners would agree, Lima's fundamental problems have included widespread poverty, extreme inequality, inadequate transportation, environmental degradation, and a massive informal economy.

The task of coping with these problems has been formally placed in the hands of Lima's mayors, who until well after World War II were appointed by the president, whether elected or military. This status changed briefly in the 1960s, when then president Fernando Belaúnde Terry allowed national local elections (1963 and 1966). In 1968, however, Belaúnde was overthrown by the military, which returned to the practice of appointing mayors. When the military gave up power in 1980, Peru's new constitution mandated the nationwide election of all local officials.[6] This new political reality rapidly came to mean that the mayor of Lima held probably the second most important electoral position in the country after the president, and that anyone who occupied that post would doubtless be at least looked upon as a potential presidential candidate. And since no one could be elected president without a strong showing in Lima (the city contained more than a quarter of the nation's electorate), a whole new set of political realities and tensions between the president and the mayor were created. For example, no longer can a civilian president count on Lima's mayor being from the same party as that president; just as important, no longer can a Lima mayor count on the automatic support of the president. The president and the mayor have different constituencies with different needs; what might be a successful campaign in Lima for a presidential candidate might not work at all for a mayoral candidate. For all that, what might make a Lima mayor successful might not translate at all into national popularity, given the centuries-long tension between Lima as the capital and the rest of the country, viewed (often arrogantly) as "the provinces."

In the city's races for mayor, a variety of parties and candidates took turns winning. In 1980, Eduardo Orrego of the center-right Acción Popular (Popular Action [AP]) won with 34.7 percent of the popular vote. The same year brought Fernando Belaúnde Terry, founder of AP, to the national presidency. Alfonso Barrantes, leader of a leftist coalition, followed Orrego in the 1983 elections, winning with 36.5 percent of the vote. He was later defeated in a bid for reelection in 1986 by Jorge del Castillo of the center-left Alianza Popular Revolucionaria Americana (American Popular Revolutionary Alliance [APRA]) (37.6 percent). APRA's Alan García Pérez was Peru's president at this time. As mentioned earlier, the independent Ricardo Belmont took the mayoral elections of 1989 and 1993. Following him was Alberto Andrade of Somos Lima in 1995 and 1998. Most recently, Luis Castañeda Lossio of Unidad Nacional defeated Andrade's effort at securing a third term in the 2002 contest.

A bit of clarity is needed here in terms of nomenclature. *Lima* refers to three specific geographic and legal entities. In the first place, Lima is the name of one of Peru's twenty-five *departamentos* (equivalent to a state in the United States). Within the department of Lima is the *provincia* of Lima, one of ten provinces that make up the department. And finally, within the province of Lima is the *distrito* of Lima, one of the forty-three districts that make up the metropolitan area. Lima's districts vary enormously in size and in character; for example, San Juan de Lurigancho in 1993 had close to 600,000 inhabitants, while Santa María del Mar, an outlying coastal resort area, had 181. Likewise, some districts are quite wealthy (Miraflores, San Isidro), while others are uniformly poor (El Agustino, Villa El Salvador).

For all practical purposes, the province of Lima today constitutes metropolitan Lima. The mayor of Lima is the mayor of the province as well as of the district of Lima (officially known as Lima Cercado); each of the other forty-two districts has its own mayor. To say precisely what the division of power is across these various levels of government is difficult. Basically, the president of the nation is preeminent; much power (de facto as well as de jure) is concentrated in his office, and he has the capacity to make life for Lima's mayor difficult or easy, especially when it comes to financial resources, a matter we discuss in some detail below. In more or less parallel form, the mayor of Lima is preeminent within the city. District mayors have the responsibility for matters such as garbage collection and other strictly local affairs, but they are limited by what revenue they can collect within their districts. Some wealthy-district mayors thus have a good deal to work with, but the mayors of Lima's poor districts have very little, especially when the magnitude of their many problems is considered. Regardless of the specific district they may govern, the mayor of metropolitan Lima has far greater say about the city as a whole and about interdistrict policymaking than anyone else.

As mentioned earlier, the creation of elected local officials in the 1980 constitution has meant a much richer and much more complex political life for Peru's cities. Tensions, bargaining and all other such political considerations are now part of Peruvian local politics, whether they occur between the president and the mayor or between the metropolitan mayor and the district mayors.

The President and the Mayors

In 2000, Fujimori ran for a legally questionable third term in office. After accusations of electoral fraud and the release of the "Vladivideos," his government fell apart amid the corruption scandal, which Cameron details in Chapter 12.[7] Despite his dramatic fall from grace, Fujimori had maintained significant levels of public support for much of his tenure. His average approval rating for his entire time in office—including the period of quadruple-digit inflation and when his government was collapsing—was 54.3 percent. As Carrión explains in Chapter 6, Fujimori used this public opinion to legitimate his rule.

Nevertheless, there were limitations to this support, as the Lima elections revealed and as is discussed below. With the defeat of his chosen candidates, the Lima elections conferred significant popular support to individuals not beholden to Fujimori. Belmont and Andrade posed strong threats to Fujimori's support base. Plus, these men could mount national-level challenges against Fujimori and both held presidential aspirations. As a neopopulist, Fujimori had as one of his overriding goals, in addition to forming his own sociopolitical coalition, to undermine any and all possible sources of opposition. Given the need to maintain a democratic veneer (for reasons noted earlier), he was willing to allow such defeats to go uncontested. Yet he also had alternative means of stunting the political influence and rise of subnational figures who might pose a threat. Indeed, largely as the result of his ability to control or frustrate the policies and initiatives of Lima's mayors, he quashed the challenges of Belmont (Schmidt 1999, 103; Degregori 2000, 51) and Andrade. It is to these measures that we now turn.

In 1989, the year prior to Fujimori's political debut, Ricardo Belmont, a television personality and a politically independent novice, won a significant plurality (43.4 percent) and took the Lima mayoral race. His electoral strength was consistent; he did somewhat better in upper- and middle-class districts (47.7 percent and 45.6 percent, respectively) than in upper-income districts (36 percent), but he did well throughout the city. Belmont was thus serving as mayor when Fujimori won his first election.

Their relations were civil at first. Belmont, as an independent, was spared Fujimori's harsh and continual rhetorical harangue directed against the political establishment. Moreover, during Fujimori's first two years in office his primary efforts were directed at battling Sendero Luminoso (Shining Path) and getting inflation under control. His handling of these crises, along with the closure of Congress, generated very impressive approval ratings. Save for 1995, his highest annual average approval rating came in 1992. He took advantage of this support by calling for a Constituent Assembly, which he was able to pack with his supporters. The assembly produced a document that substantially enhanced the power of the president and allowed for his reelection.

Two events during 1993, however, demonstrated the limits of Fujimori's public support. His candidate for mayor of Lima, Pablo Gutiérrez, withdrew from the race prior to the vote because he had virtually no chance of winning (Tanaka 1999, 16). Similarly, although the public approved the new constitution in a referendum, the margin of victory was unexpectedly narrow. Apparently his approval ratings in the 60 to 70 percent range did not necessarily translate into political domination or the automatic approval of his measures. It was from this point that his means of generating public support turned from leadership in solving crises and lambasting the political elite to offering selective incentives to supporters in the form of targeted benefits. It was after this time that his treatment of subnational officials became more hostile.

In advance of the municipal elections of 1993, Fujimori reduced the number of signatures required to get on the municipal ballot (O'Neill 1999, 61), apparently in hopes of proliferating the number of candidates and thus dispersing popular support among them. As a result, thirty-eight candidates ran for mayor in Lima, although Belmont still emerged with a strong plurality. Nationwide, some fifteen thousand independent candidates ran in municipal races that year (Roberts 1995, 101). Fujimori made a similar move with respect to Congress, when he replaced all the congressional districts across the country with a single, nationwide district. While this move significantly enhanced Lima's representation in Congress, it limited the possibility that any single representative would be able to build a widespread following in the city. That is, metropolitan Lima's representation was now divided among most of the 120 members of Congress as well as the mayor.

Belmont was easily reelected in the 1993 elections. He took a slightly better vote total (44.6 percent) and showed remarkably even strength right across the board, with virtually no variation regardless of district profile (45 percent, 45.1 percent and 43.7 percent poor, medium, and wealthy, respectively). Although the relationship between Fujimori and Belmont had been reasonably warm during the elections, they quickly deteriorated afterward. Around that time, opinion polls showed Belmont to be more popular than the president,[8] suggesting that an independent politician was developing his own base of support and thus could pose a threat to Fujimori's neopopulist rule.

In response, Fujimori vastly increased the level of spending on educational infrastructure. Of the $112 million spent on school construction nationally in 1994, 61 percent was dedicated to Lima and Callao (Graham and Kane 1998, 95). He, rather than Belmont, could claim credit for the highly visible projects. Indeed, polls in 1994 indicate that the public considered school construction one of Fujimori's most important accomplishments, closely following that of defeating Sendero Luminoso (El Comercio, cited in Graham and Kane 1998, 95). Belmont repeatedly protested Fujimori's educational investment in Lima, arguing that municipal governments should control public investment within their jurisdictions. For instance, Belmont sarcastically remarked on the program Buenos Días on August 27, 1993, that Lima had two mayors: one who had money (Fujimori) and another who was poor (himself). Fujimori, in one response to Belmont's protestations, simply noted that if municipalities had resources, they should use them. The view that Fujimori was taking over the responsibilities of the mayor was repeated in newspaper opinion pages. Fujimori in turn suggested that mayors should be appointed, rather than elected, as such appointments could save the country the $10 million spent on local electoral campaigns.

Belmont then ratcheted up the rhetoric with demands for financial assistance from the Bank of the Nation. He threatened to resign his post if the national government continued to deny his repeated requests for a

$30 million loan. Escalating the conflict, Belmont demanded to meet with the president in order to discuss the financial needs of Lima. Fujimori responded by saying that if Belmont wanted a loan from the Bank of the Nation, he should speak to the bank's president, and if he wanted credit from the Ministry of the Economy, he should speak to the head of the ministry. In so doing, Fujimori cut off any hopes of dialogue that the mayor had. Mirko Lauer of *La República* commented that Fujimori wanted Belmont's resignation because, among other factors, his popularity had exceeded that of the president; Lauer further noted that Fujimori was willing to use all means at his disposal against possible electoral rivals.[9]

Having heard enough, Fujimori issued Decree 776, a devastating initiative for Lima. With this decree, issued December 31, 1993, Fujimori dramatically altered the financial landscape of Peru's municipalities, and especially that of Lima. Although this measure benefited the smallest communities, it severely restricted the larger ones. AMPE, the national association of Peruvian mayors, denounced the reform as an unconstitutional usurpation of municipal authority (Kay 1996, 14). As one observer explains, the decree "was a political offensive."[10] The decree had two major components: a restructuring of local taxes and a new mechanism for municipal disbursements. First, the decree simplified local tax systems by reducing the number of municipal taxes from twenty to six. Despite the inherent appeal of streamlining complex systems, this decree shrank the resource pool available to local governments. They retained the authority to set tax rates for the remaining taxes, but could not establish others. Hence, actual and potential sources of municipal funding were eliminated.

Decree 776 also created the Fondo de Compensación Municipal (Municipal Compensation Fund [FONCOMUN]) to manage transfers from the central government to local governments. Although the total amount transferred to municipalities did not change as a percentage of government revenues (it hovered between 3.5 and 4 percent during Fujimori's administration), it radically changed the allocation structure. Under the law, transfers were distributed according to population and infant mortality, with rural areas receiving greater weight than urban ones. The exception to this rule concerns Lima, where the distribution to district governments was made according to housing quality and illiteracy, thereby benefiting the poorer areas. Although the amount of transfers was to be determined according to a formula, analysts have pointed out inconsistencies in the distributions. The department of Huánuco, for instance, lost 76 percent of its transfers as a result of the decree, a disproportionate share given its midlevel per capita income and very high rate of infant mortality (Graham and Kane 1998).

Prior to the law, central-government transfers went to provincial governments, which were charged with distributing shares to the district governments under their purview. This proviso made provincial mayors powerful, as the district mayors were beholden to them for resources. With Decree 776, Fujimori undermined provincial power by making district governments the direct recipients of central-government transfers. As such, the means of exerting provincial influence were sharply curtailed. In other words, Fujimori broke the local-level system of clientelism and thereby reduced the power of provincial leaders.[11] He may have also sought to weaken the regional power of the traditional parties by curtailing the resources of the larger provincial cities (Graham and Kane 1998, 92).

The losers from the law were the urban provincial governments. In addition to losing their influence over districts, they saw their resources were substantially reduced. In 1992, Lima received 54 percent of all funds transferred to provinces; two years later it received only 17.4 percent (Graham and Kane 1998, 91). The Fondo Metropolitano de Inversión (Metropolitan Investment Fund [INVERMET]), the investment fund for Lima, lost between 60 and 70 percent of its resources as a result of the decree (Alvarado 1994, 121). Combined with the changes in the taxing structure, Lima witnessed a single-year decline in revenues of 85 percent.[12] While Decree 776 was primarily directed against the mayor of Lima, it also reflected a broader strategy of preventing alternative centers of power from appearing in population centers around the country.

Districts were the relative winners from the law. Although the districts have the same taxing authorities as their provincial counterparts, the vast majority of their resources come from central-government transfers. Most districts lack a sufficient income base to support significant taxing revenues, and roughly half of all districts get all their revenues from the FONCOMUN and the sustenance program Vaso de Leche (Glass of Milk) (Ortiz de Zevallos and Pollarolo 2000, 20). As such, Decree 776 did little to alleviate the financial dependency of district governments. Indeed, it merely changed the locus of that dependence from the provincial mayors to the president. While in principle the decree helped correct an imbalance in the distribution of municipal resources, in practice it did not. By some estimates, half the nation's district governments were bankrupt by the year 2000.[13]

The war of words between Belmont and Fujimori escalated in response to this decree. Lima's mayor said the central government was responsible for having "assassinated" Peru's local governments and especially the capital city. *La República* opined that Belmont was correct in his complaints; he had been "the object of an outrageous policy of strangulation."[14] He also announced that the city would take legal action against the decree. Lima's city council then responded by voting, 35 to 4, to declare Fujimori persona non grata in the capital city. These recriminations continued with a suspension of payments to the Lima municipal government, a lawsuit against the central government, the closure of Belmont-owned Channel 11 in Lima, and legal actions against Belmont for fraud. Belmont also announced a campaign for president in 1995, but he had been too crippled by Fujimori's actions to mount an effective campaign. As Henry Pease García remarked, "Belmont [was a] victim of excessive power in a single hand."[15] After his loss Belmont retired from political life (Dietz and Tanaka 2002).

Belmont was followed in 1995 by Alberto Andrade, who won a slim majority of the popular vote (52.5 percent). His strength clearly lay in the city's upper-income districts, but he pulled enough votes in poorer areas to win. During the campaign he competed against Jaime Yoshiyama, Fujimori's handpicked successor. In order to avoid a direct confrontation with Fujimori himself, Andrade softened his criticism of Decree 776.[16] His victory over Yoshiyama again revealed the limits of Fujimori's popular support. Not long before, Fujimori had received an overwhelming mandate in the presidential elections, capturing more than 60 percent of the vote. However, his public support did not translate into backing for Yoshiyama in the November municipal elections. As a result of the elections, Fujimori considered Andrade to be a direct threat.

In response, Fujimori issued eighteen laws and decrees between June 1995 and the end of 1996 alone that curtailed mayors' ability to build support. Ley (Law) 23637, for instance, stripped the authority of the Lima and Callao governments—but of no other municipalities—to manage the Vaso de Leche program, one of Peru's chief sources of social spending. In addition to such decrees, a variety of regulations eliminated municipal business licensing, reduced the amount of the national sales tax dedicated to municipalities, eliminated the commercial exploitation of certain local resources, and manipulated local taxing authority. Andrade claimed that these measures cost Lima more than $1 billion over the decade.[17] The logic behind the government's policies, succinctly stated, was that "[w]hatever *obra* [work] he did was one less for Fujimori."[18] Another response to this loss was the creation of Vamos Vecino. This was another of Fujimori's electoral mechanisms (like Cambio 90 and Nueva Mayoría), but directed toward supporting municipal candidates. Specifically, the party, under the control of Absalon Vásquez, sought out leaders of local-level popular movements. The idea was to co-opt popular groups as well as undercut the opportunities for his opponents to rise to prominence. The party, then, was not created to help Fujimori govern, manage public works, or channel interests of citizens. Rather, it was a way to "to help him perpetuate his power."[19] Interestingly, Fujimori and Montesinos became wary of Vásquez's growing support, which resulted from his control over the party and its local candidates. Because public support for anyone other than Fujimori represented a threat or potential threat, Fujimori kicked Vásquez out of his inner circle, and Vamos Vecino was left to rot.

In spite of Fujimori's measures, in 1998 Andrade once again won the Lima municipal contests. He took 58.8 percent of the popular vote, winning majorities in wealthy areas and significant blocks (pluralities, strong seconds) in others. As in 1995, he defeated Fujimori's choice for mayor, who this time was Fujimori's first prime minister, Juan Carlos Hurtado Miller. This victory placed him in a good position to mount an effective challenge to Fujimori's planned 2000 presidential campaign. Again Fujimori responded, although this time with a number of informal and even illicit moves. In one instance, he refused to support Andrade's attempt to secure credit for Lima from the World Bank.[20]

In another instance, Montesinos asked Callao (Lima's port) mayor, Alex Kouri, to run against Andrade in the 1998 Lima race. Concerned about Andrade's strength, Fujimori sought Kouri's help in dividing Andrade's support by splitting the vote. Although Kouri refused the request, he offered to help undermine Andrade's reelection as Lima's mayor and his pursuit of the presidency in exchange for $4 million to pay off Callao's municipal debt.[21]

In addition, Fujimori's influence over the press resulted in a virtual blackout of television ads for Andrade.[22] Just before the elections, the watchdog group Transparencia found that Fujimori received 99 percent of electoral publicity in broadcast television (Transparencia 2000). Indeed, when Andrade announced his candidacy for president, none of the three major Lima television channels would air his paid campaign ads (Youngers 2000b, 10).

Among the newspapers, the daily tabloids, or *prensa chicha*, were the most compliant with Fujimori (Felch 2004). They regularly and virulently criticized Fujimori's political opponents, while lionizing him. For instance, the tabloids lambasted Andrade's stewardship of Lima while calling him the puppet of the discredited Alan García. Also, and in keeping with Fujimori's antiestablishment rhetoric, they referred to Andrade as a member of the *pituco* (snob) upper class of the city (Degregori 2000, 150–64). The mayor was also harshly criticized for attempting to clean up central Lima by removing thousands of street vendors. The *prensa chicha* saw this as evidence of his indifference to common Limeños and of his caring more for tourists than for locals. Meanwhile, the tabloids treated Fujimori according to a different standard, calling him "un presidente como tú" (a president like you) and highlighting his successes. These moves took their toll on Andrade's future political prospects. After being one of the two leading front-runners against Fujimori early in the 2000 presidential campaign, Andrade received less than 3 percent of the valid votes cast. He then lost to Luis Castañeda Lossio in the 2002 Lima elections, taking just under 30 percent of the vote.

Through roughly fifty decrees and laws, Fujimori eroded the powers and financial independence of mayors.[23] As a municipal official explained, "What changed under Fujimori was the autonomy of municipalities to manage local affairs and generate revenues."[24] He restricted mayors' financial autonomy by eliminating their ability to issue business licenses, reducing the amount of the national sales tax dedicated to municipalities, eliminating the commercial exploitation of mineral and thermal waters, and taking other, similar measures. He also consistently attacked the decision-making authority of municipalities, restricting their power over issues such as urban planning, public transportation, civil registration, property rights, and so forth. Consider that in Lima, the local government had such diminished authority that the central government took over the responsibility for traffic management, the location of street vendors, and the protection of parks (Degregori, Coronel, and del Pino 1998, 245). By reducing their autonomous sources of revenues, Fujimori increased the dependence of local governments on central-government spending, such as through the Fondo Nacional de Compensación y Desarrollo Social (National Fund for Social Compensation and Development [FONCODES]) or the Instituto Nacional de Infraestructura Educativa y de Salud (National Institute of Educational and Health Infrastructure [INFES]). And by restricting their discretion over what resources they had, he blocked the ability of civic leaders to build their own followings. While most of these applied to all municipal level governments, the primary target was Lima's mayor, who held the one subnational position powerful enough for the incumbent to mount a significant political threat.

Moreover, despite the need for maintaining a democratic veneer, Fujimori was more than willing to use a variety of tools (legal and illegal) in his neopopulist arsenal. As became especially clear after the release of the Vladivideos, Fujimori's regime relied heavily on the illicit manipulation of politicians, political institutions, and the press. As the hundreds of videos demonstrate, and as Conaghan explains in Chapter 5, many politicians sold their support to him, ensuring a compliant Congress and a subdued opposition. He and his intelligence service also used strong-arm tactics, such as wiretapping, targeted tax audits, and even threats of violence, against all his major political opponents (Youngers 2000a, 6–10). The electoral process was also subject to manipulation. The 2000 presidential elections constituted the most obvious case, but there were also widespread concerns about the municipal races in 1998. And as the democratic veneer began to thin with the increased role of Vladimir Montesinos and more obvious electoral manipulations, Fujimori had increasing difficulty maintaining public support. In 1997, for example, a majority of Peruvians believed that Montesinos was more powerful than Fujimori; and whereas in 1990 only 32 percent of Limeños thought the elections were fraudulent, in 1998 that figure was 64 percent (*Debate* 1997, cited in McClintock 1999, 79, 94).

The Fujimori Legacy and the Future

Fujimori's actions obviously were not calculated to foster good relations between the president and the mayors, and they did not do so. In fact, in his ten years in office, Fujimori never once set foot in the mayor's office, despite the importance of Lima to Peru and the fact that the presidential palace sits next to city hall. Nevertheless, Fujimori's measures effectively secured his public support for a sustained period of time: his approval ratings averaged a remarkable 61 percent for his entire first term (see Chapter 6). Importantly, Fujimori also held support for his opponents to low levels. For instance, confidence in parties floundered at an average of 14.3 percent from 1990 to 1995 and never climbed above 19 percent before Fujimori resigned in 2000.[25] Soon after Fujimori faxed his resignation from Tokyo at the end of 2000, relations between the mayor of Lima and the executive office improved. During Lima's 466th anniversary of its founding in January 2001, interim president Valentín Paniagua showed up for the ceremony in the Lima city hall, the first time in a decade that a president had done so. Paniagua also pledged to begin removing the restrictions that had been placed on Lima's mayor under Fujimori. The 2001 elections brought Alejandro Toledo to office, along with some rhetoric for decentralization and even a new regionalization program. Yet the extent to which Toledo and his successors will dismantle Fujimori's highly concentrated system of governance remains to be seen. On the one hand, the current political context is promising for undoing the institutional legacies of neopopulism, including the concentrated power in the executive office and enfeebled representative institutions. Because Fujimori has been so fully discredited by the revelations of corruption, it may be politically advantageous to pursue policies contrary to those of the prior administration. During the 2001 campaign there was some jockeying to be the most anti-Fujimori of the candidates. This same logic could apply to intergovernmental policies: if curtailing municipal authority is associated with Fujimori, then enhancing it may now be politically propitious.

On the other hand, Fujimori's impact on Peru's party system could pose a significant obstacle to the process of reversing the neopopulist system of government. Although the traditional political parties went a long way toward discrediting themselves during the 1980s, Fujimori contributed heavily to their downfall. The continued poor confidence levels in political parties confirm the point. By contrast, popular support for "independents" rose dramatically. In contests throughout Peru, both local and national, the parties of Peru's old political class were replaced by innumerable personalistic electoral vehicles and single-issue movements (Sabatini 2001). In 1995, for instance, independents collectively took 96 percent of the popular vote in Peru's municipal contests. Curiously, though, former president Alan García of the APRA party went to the second round of the 2001 presidential contest, and the party took almost 20 percent of the congressional vote. This could be indicative of a turnaround in the fortunes of the traditional parties, but the instability of Peruvian politics means, of course, that no single trajectory is a certainty. At best, the parties face huge obstacles in rebuilding their organizations, not to mention their credibility. At worst, it may be correct to argue that Peru is in an age of postparty politics (Levitsky 1999).

In either case, to the extent that Peru's political parties have been deinstitutionalized and replaced by personalistic electoral mechanisms, the opportunities and incentives for neopopulist behavior remain strong (see Chapter 1). Lacking any organizational backing, politicians find their fortunes more directly connected with mass public support. They themselves must establish ties with the electorate; they have no party mechanism to distribute patronage, support them in Congress, and so forth. In such circumstances, leaders like Fujimori may find it in their interest to use the resources of their offices to prevent their opponents from developing independent sources of popular support.

Conclusions

Should populists or neopopulists persist in the presidency of Peru, Lima and its mayors may continue to pose a special political problem. As a primate city, it contains the plurality of the country's electorate and is of particular political importance. Its elected mayors, for the same reasons, are automatically important political players in national politics and have the potential to be significant presidential contenders. As such, their popular support may play foil to that of populist presidents.

This same logic highlights a broader point from the Peruvian case for populism or neopopulism more generally: the role of subnational and particularly capital-city opposition to national-level politics. If populism is primarily a political concept, then blocking the growth of opponents' public support is by definition a central part of the populist strategy. Support given to the opposition is support a populist does not have (to put the matter as a zero-sum game). To understand the behavior of any given populist requires paying attention to the most likely arenas of political opposition.

In the Peruvian case, among the most significant institutional changes that Fujimori implemented were directed against municipal governments in general and Lima in particular. Populist leaders may have an incentive to engage in similar behavior in other primate cities. Of course, the extent to which mayors present genuine political challenges depends on a number of factors, the most fundamental of which is whether the position is elected. In addition, in federal systems, provincial leaders (for example, state governors) may have greater power or potential to develop public support than does the mayor of a primate city (or any other city, for that matter). For instance, in the case of Argentina under Menem, many of his measures to concentrate power came at the expense of the provinces. In his first eighteen months (when he can most accurately be described a neopopulist), he expended significant political capital to reduce federal revenue transfers to provinces and increase his discretion over spending at the expense of the provincial governors. During this time the mayoralty of Buenos Aires was not an elected position. Hugo Chávez in Venezuela, similarly, curtailed the power of regional governments as well as of local ones.

The spread of subnational elections throughout Latin America with the third wave of democratic transitions has appropriately prompted the study of subnational politics. Yet very little attention has explicitly been paid to the politics of subnational-central government relations. The mayors of primate cities may always be important political figures, but they and other subnational politicians may take on greater importance when populists occupy the presidency. And as recent events have demonstrated, populism is far from dead in the region, despite the spread of neoliberal economic policies. Indeed, just as neoliberalism has added new wrinkles to the populist agenda, subnational elections may have done the same. Understanding neopopulist behavior has always necessitated paying attention to potential sources of political opposition; today, with all countries having elected subnational actors, it is more important than it has ever been in Latin American history.

NOTES

1. Andrade had been a member of the PPC while mayor of Miraflores.

2. By our definition, classic populism is not strictly limited to the first part of the twentieth century. Rather, it was simply a more common phenomenon during that era. More recent examples of classic populists would include Peru's Alan García Pérez of the APRA party, who resisted the structural adjustment of the economy. Ellner (2003) argues that Venezuela's Hugo Chávez is also better considered a classic populist than a neopopulist.

3. We are not suggesting that nonpopulists never have incentives to block their opponents or that they never act aggressively to do so. Rather, we are suggesting that the incentives for such behavior may be stronger in neopopulism than in less personalistic forms of rule.

4. International pressure and economic factors are additional reasons to maintain the democratic veneer. The United States, Spain, and Germany, for instance, immediately suspended aid to Peru after the autogolpe. Access to international credit, however, was critical for Fujimori's strategy of building support, in part through public works. Not until he agreed to hold new elections, however, was such support a possibility.

5. Primate cities are those that have primacy within a country, in terms of population, economic activity, and influence. A city that is at least twice as large as the second-largest city can be considered primate.

6. Peruvian electoral history since 1980 has been, by the country's standards, unprecedented in its success and continuity. Prior to 1985, only once since

World War I had one constitutionally elected president turned power over to an elected successor (1945, Manuel Prado to José Luis Bustamante), and local elections (as already noted) had been little more than a brief experiment in the 1960s. But presidential elections were held as constitutionally mandated in 1980, 1985, 1990, 1995, 2000, and 2001. Likewise, local elections occurred in 1980, 1983, 1986, 1989, 1993, 1995, 1998, and 2002. In addition, the Peruvian military showed no interest in intervening in the electoral process, of seizing power, or of overturning any results that might have run against their own wishes.

7. These were the hundreds of videos in Vladimiro Montesinos's collection that exposed the extent of corruption in Peru, and thus erased what was left of Fujimori's democratic veneer.

8. *Gestión*, March 16, 1993.

9. *La República*, August 27, 1993.

10. Carlos Barrenechea, ESAN decentralization expert, interview by Barr, Lima, April 12, 2001.

11. Alberto Alva, general secretary of the provincial municipality of Huaraz, interview by Barr, Huaraz, April 24, 2001; Enrique Juscamaita Aranguena, director of development and management projects at the Ministry of the Presidency, interview by Barr, Lima, March 27, 2001.

12. *Quehacer*, January–February 1994.

13. Ricardo de la Flor Bedoya, director of INICAM, interview by Barr, Lima, March 2, 2001.

14. *La República*, March 31, 1994.

15. *Expreso*, February 15, 1996.

16. *Caretas*, January 18, 1996.

17. *La República*, January 19, 2001.

18. Alva, interview.

19. María Mendez Gastelmundi, former official in Fujimori's Council of Ministers, interview by Barr, Lima, March 2, 2001.

20. This position changed following Fujimori's resignation from office. On December 12, 2001, President Toledo announced that municipal governments could apply directly for international credits.

21. *La República*, March 1, 2001.

22. Although he never took over the media, Fujimori repeatedly used strong-arm tactics to ensure their loyalty. In one well-known instance, he closed down the popular Lima-based television program hosted by César Hildebrant for its criticism of the government. In other cases, he used SUNAT (Peru's taxing authority) to coerce the press into compliance.

23. Concurrent with the limitations on the financial autonomy and discretion of municipal governments was an increase in the discretion of funds controlled by Fujimori himself. In 1991 he created the Ministry of the Presidency to gain greater control over government spending. By the middle of his time in office, this ministry managed more than 22 percent of the total government budget (Webb and Fernández Baca 2000, 1127).

24. Alva, interview.

25. Kay (1996, 24) argues that one reason for the continued disintegration of political parties was Fujimori's strategy of continually attacking, discrediting, and undermining the influence of the traditional parties.

FOUR

Do Parties Matter?
Lessons from the Fujimori Experience

KENNETH M. ROBERTS

Political parties have performed such a diverse array of representative and governing functions that it is difficult to conceive of democratic politics in their absence. Indeed, even many authoritarian regimes have used parties to mobilize popular support, penetrate and control civil society, staff the government with political loyalists, coordinate the policymaking process, and implement public policies. Under the autocratic rule of Alberto Fujimori, however, the Peruvian electorate and political entrepreneurs alike dispensed with party organizations to a degree that is virtually without parallel among modern, competitive political systems. Despite the retention of a competitive (though not fully democratic) regime in the 1990s, neither government officials nor opposition leaders were able to secure political support by resurrecting or constructing party organizations, and many did not even bother to try. At the presidential level, the electoral arena was reduced to a battle between contending personalities, and the nation's political fate hinged on their strategic whims and the ebb and flow of their popular appeal. Traditional parties were relegated to the margins of the national legislature, while a bewildering variety of independents, regional fronts, and ad hoc coalitions or groups won elections to municipal governments and the Chamber of Deputies (Cotler 1995; Levitsky and Cameron 2003; Planas 2000; Lynch 1999b; Tanaka 1998; Kenney 2003).

The result was a political landscape that was almost entirely devoid of national representative institutions. Although parties—minimally defined, following Sartori (1976, 64), as "any political group that presents at elections, and is capable of placing through elections, candidates for public office"—existed in the legal sense, the reality was that established parties had been rendered electorally insignificant, and the new "parties" winning elections represented little more than registration labels for independent candidates and their coterie of collaborators. The organizational development of these parties was minimal, informal, and ephemeral, as they lacked the central features associated with modern political parties. Most made little or no effort to register members; establish local branches or offices; develop a national bureaucracy or leadership structure; formulate organizational bylaws and operating procedures; articulate an identifiable ideological position; or create affiliated organizations for workers, women, students, or other social groups.[1] As Tanaka (2003, 227) says of the Fujimori regime, "Its anti-institutional nature lay in the fact that there was not, properly speaking, any political movement behind it. The various incarnations of this movement . . . were only electoral vehicles, not authentic representational organizations." The same could be said of most of the other new pseudoparties that contested the electoral arena in the 1990s. In short, Peruvian "parties" were electoral labels rather than political organizations, and their empty shells served as little more than vehicles for dominant personalities.

The Peruvian experience is rife with lessons about the centrality—or lack thereof—of party organizations in contemporary political life. At one level, it provides compelling evidence of the growing dispensability of party organizations for electoral contestation in an era of independent electorates, fragmented civil societies, truncated ideological spectrums, and pervasive forms of mass-media communication. Mass party organizations developed historically as a means to encapsulate voters and mobilize electoral support in response to expanded suffrage rights and the creation of large-scale secondary associations among workers (Epstein 1980). Today, however, political entrepreneurs are increasingly disinclined to invest in resource-intensive party-building tasks when densely organized social blocs are not available for electoral encapsulation and candidates can appeal to individual voters directly via television without any sort of institutional intermediation. Indeed, the Peruvian case suggests that party organizations can be so discredited by political and economic mismanagement that they may come to be viewed as electoral liabilities by aspiring public officials. In such a context, independents, outsiders, and antipoliticians may reap electoral gains from their detachment and insulation from established party organizations.

Paradoxically, however, the Fujimori experience also demonstrates how indispensable party organizations are to democratic governance. Over the course of a decade in power, the Fujimori regime resorted to a series of increasingly autocratic measures that were motivated to a significant degree by its dearth of organized support. The political scandals unleashed by these measures contributed to the erosion of Fujimori's public support, and they detonated the internal crisis that eventually caused the breakdown of the regime in 2000. Furthermore, the absence of partisan organization made it virtually impossible for voters to hold the regime accountable to its electoral and programmatic mandates, and it undermined opposition efforts to establish institutional checks and balances on the erratic and manipulative behavior of the executive.

In short, parties' electoral and governing functions became increasingly disjoined over the course of the 1990s. Whereas parties were marginal and even dispensable actors in the electoral arena, they remained vital institutional vehicles for securing democratic practices in the exercise of public authority, and their absence proved corrosive for democratic accountability. In the analysis that follows I explore this basic paradox in the political centrality of party organizations. I begin with a brief overview of the crisis and demise of Peru's party system, then trace the failure of both governing and opposition elites to reconstruct representative institutions. I proceed with an analysis of parties' electoral dispensability and explain why their absence was associated with a range of autocratic maneuvers, political scandals, and democratic deficiencies. I conclude with an assessment of the legacies of the Fujimori regime for the reconstruction of democratic institutions in a context in which parties are largely absent from both civil society and the electoral arena.

Electoral Dispensability and Party System Demise in Peru

Peru's pre-1990 party system was renowned for personalism, volatility, and a lack of institutionalization, despite the establishment of a competitive and relatively inclusive democratic regime in 1980. According to Cotler (1995, 337–39), Peruvian party elites were unaccountable and unresponsive to social demands, routinely ignoring their electoral mandates, exercising autocratic authority over their party organizations, and adopting uncompromising positions that prevented them from developing consensual solutions to the nation's deepening crisis (see also Lynch 1999b). Nevertheless, the decomposition of the party system at the beginning of the 1990s was shocking and unexpected. Whatever its faults, the party system at least boasted a number of long-standing organizations with solid networks of party identifiers and significant linkages to social actors. As Tanaka persuasively argues, the demise of Peru's party system was rooted less in a lack of representation than in a failure of governability (1998, 71–85), when a decade of recurring economic crises and spiraling political violence severed the ties between established parties and their social constituencies.

The fulcrum of the party system was the Alianza Popular Revolucionaria Americana (American Popular Revolutionary Alliance [APRA]), the nation's first and largest mass party, whose emergence in 1930 signaled the beginning of the end of the traditional oligarchic order. Despite its congenital association with the charismatic leadership of Víctor Raúl Haya de la Torre, APRA was one of Latin America's best-organized populist parties. Like many other populist parties in the region, it was flanked on the right and left by more conservative and radical competitors. Following the 1980 transition to democracy that ended twelve years of reformist military rule, the conservative side of the political spectrum was occupied by the Acción Popular (Popular Action [AP]) party, which was founded in 1956 by future two-time president Fernando Belaúnde Terry, and the Partido Popular Cristiano (Popular Christian Party [PPC]), which split off from the Christian Democratic Party in 1966. On the left, a coalition of small, militant parties formed the Izquierda Unida (United Left [IU]) in 1980 to contest APRA's historic hold over popular constituencies. Included in the IU were the Peruvian Communist Party, founded by leftist icon José Carlos Mariátegui in 1928, and an ideologically diverse collection of "New Left" and Maoist parties that emerged from the guerrilla movements and popular mobilizations of the 1960s and 1970s (Roberts 1998, 204–9).

These four actors dominated the electoral arena during the 1980s, collectively averaging 96 percent of the vote in the 1980 and 1985 presidential elections and 91.9 percent of the vote in the lower house of Congress (Tuesta Soldevilla 1994).[2] Electoral volatility was very high during this period, with aggregate vote shifts of 38.5 percent and 50.4 percent of the electorate in the 1985 presidential and legislative elections, respectively, but this fluidity was largely intrasystemic; that is, it entailed large vote shifts from one systemic party (primarily AP) to others (primarily APRA and the IU). This volatility continued through the 1990s, but with a fundamental change in character: vote shifts became predominantly extra-systemic in the 1990s, reflecting vote swings away from all the systemic parties to a series of independent and "outsider" candidates. Consequently, whereas electoral volatility in the 1980s led to democratic alternation in office, with voters choosing to replace one governing party with another, volatility in the 1990s produced more far-reaching systemic change—namely, a decomposition of the established party system and the emergence of ephemeral electoral movements that were essentially personal vehicles of new (and occasionally old) political entrepreneurs (Lynch 1999b; Tanaka 1998; Planas 2000; Kenney 2003).

Party organizations thus became highly dispensable instruments of electoral mobilization in the 1990s. Indeed, it appears that they were seen by politicians and voters alike as electoral liabilities. As expressed by a member of the Political Commission of Alberto Andrade's Somos Perú, the traditional parties weighed down their potential candidates and prevented them from attracting support among a growing mass of independent voters.[3] This perception is troubling for modern theories of democracy and political representation, which assume that parties are privileged agents of mass political representation under conditions of universal suffrage (Sartori 1976; Mainwaring and Scully 1995). Although parties first emerged in the United States and western Europe to coordinate legislative activities under restrictive democracies, they developed important electoral functions and strong societal linkages once suffrage was expanded and mass labor movements emerged. For political elites, parties were the chosen vehicles by which to reach mass electorates, providing dedicated cadres and organizational resources that made it possible to overcome collective action problems in the process of electoral mobilization (Aldrich 1995, 23). Political entrepreneurs thus built parties to penetrate and encapsulate civil society, aggregate interests, broaden their appeal, and turn out the vote. Once established, parties provided aspiring politicians with organized, predefined electoral constituencies that were bound together by collective identities and political loyalties, thus obviating the need to build constituencies from scratch during every electoral cycle. In short, parties institutionalized linkages between political entrepreneurs and mass constituencies, providing elites with a foundation of relatively secure baseline loyalties and networks of affiliates through which to mobilize adherents and sway the uncommitted.

Despite their origins in elite political entrepreneurship, parties are also assumed to perform a number of important services for voters and citizens. As part of their representative function, parties frequently articulate societal demands and channel them into public institutions, where they seek to influence the policymaking process. Such interest articulation is a primary mechanism through which parties secure political loyalties, especially among organized social blocs, whose political integration is often contingent on partisan ties (R. B. Collier and Collier 1991). Parties also help to define programmatic alternatives, as they are one of the few institutions capable of transforming myriad and conflicting individual preferences into coherent policy packages (Aldrich 1995, 22–23). As such, parties can simplify the vote choice for citizens; they create "brand name" loyalties and information shortcuts that allow voters to support a common platform without learning the positions and idiosyncrasies of every candidate running for public office (Aldrich 1995, 49; Dalton and Wattenberg 2000, 6).

Clearly, these varied political functions had become inoperative in Peru by the 1990s at both the elite and mass levels. For political entrepreneurs, a party label was required for candidate registration, but beyond this, a party membership, a program, branch units, a leadership structure, and organizational rules were superfluous. A candidate and a small, trusted circle of acquaintances were sufficient to manage a campaign, communicate personality-based appeals in the political marketplace, and turn out the vote on election day.[4] The mass media and informal social networks largely displaced grassroots party organs, labor unions, and other secondary associations as solutions to the collective action problems that are inherent in electoral mobilization (Tanaka 1998, 52). In a context in which established parties had presided over a series of human-made calamities—including a brutal guerrilla insurgency, a repressive counterinsurgency campaign, sustained hyperinflation, and the worst recession since the 1930s—political entrepreneurs calculated that the mobilizing potential of party organizations was more than offset by the political liabilities they bore as embodiments of a tainted status quo. Likewise, voters whose expectations had repeatedly been raised and then dashed by a string of elected officials lost confidence in the ability of parties to carry out alternative collective projects. Instead, they delegated authority to individuals who translated their inexperience and independence into political assets by running against established institutions, which they held accountable for the national crisis.

There was not, however, a uniform model of political independence that congealed over the course of the 1990s. In fact, three quite different types of independent figures emerged to fill the political void as the party system decomposed. The first type, which might be called the "defector model," emerged when leaders who had previously been affiliated with one of the established parties broke away to chart a more independent course. These leaders calculated that party sponsorship had become an electoral liability, either by restricting their base of support to party loyalists or by burdening the candidate with the political failures of the past. The pathbreaker for this pattern of independent leadership was Alfonso Barrantes, the former mayor of Lima from the IU who clashed with the leftist coalition's larger, more militant parties and subsequently abandoned the alliance for an independent bid at the presidency in 1990.[5] Barrantes feared that the radical discourse and sectarian organizational tendencies of the leftist parties would narrow his potential electoral constituency by alienating centrist and independent voters. Consequently, he opted for the strategic autonomy and flexibility that an independent candidacy provided, although this ultimately failed to yield the anticipated electoral payoffs.

From the opposite end of the political spectrum, prominent defectors included Alberto Andrade, Lourdes Flores Nano, and Luis Castañeda Lossio. With the established parties in evident crisis, Andrade abandoned the PPC to run a successful independent campaign for the mayorship of Lima in 1995, only to fail in a bid for the presidency as the candidate of Somos Perú in 2000. Likewise, Flores Nano of the PPC ran unsuccessfully for the presidency on an ad hoc label in 2001, while Castañeda Lossio left AP to enter the 2000 race. Although numerous other defectors have been elected to the national legislature, the defection strategy has proved deficient at the presidential level. The candidacies of Andrade and Barrantes, in particular, were spectacular failures, falling well short of expectations in the voting booth despite their solid records as municipal authorities and their apparent strengths in public opinion surveys at the outset of their respective campaigns.[6]

A second type of independent leader who appeared on the Peruvian political stage might be labeled the "frontperson." The frontperson is the obverse of the defector; rather than a political entrepreneur who abandons a party that is perceived as an electoral liability, the frontperson is an outsider "free agent" who has attained distinction in nonpartisan spheres of activity and is thus supported as a candidate by parties that are too weak or discredited to field viable candidates from their own ranks. This model is typified by Mario Vargas Llosa, the world-renowned literary figure who spearheaded elite opposition to Alan García Pérez's bank nationalization scheme in 1987, founded a conservative political movement, and then ran for president in 1990 with the backing of AP and the PPC. Vargas Llosa was the overwhelming favorite to win the presidency until his campaign was derailed by the last-minute surge of Fujimorismo. Another prominent example of the frontperson phenomenon is Javier Pérez de Cuéllar, the former United Nations secretary-general who ran against Fujimori for the presidency in 1995 with the support of several opposition parties and leaders. Despite his international diplomatic credentials, Pérez de Cuellar stood little chance in an election held at the apex of Fujimori's political and economic power.

Finally, a third—and ultimately the most electorally successful—type of independent leader to emerge was the "populist outsider." These figures lacked partisan ties and political experience, which allowed them to pose as representatives of the common people. This also insulated them from responsibility for existing political and economic problems, which they inevitably attributed to the venality, incompetence, and corruption of established parties and political elites. The populist outsiders thus ran independent campaigns sponsored by ephemeral electoral movements that were little more than personal political vehicles of the candidate. The contemporary rise of this phenomenon began in 1989, when television personality Ricardo Belmont swept to victory in Lima's mayoral race, providing the first clear evidence that nearly a decade of economic crisis and political violence were taking their toll on the party system. The following year witnessed the stunning presidential victory of Fujimori, an obscure university rector who capitalized on his outsider status and common touch to launch a meteoric rise in the polls in the final weeks before the first round of the election. And in 2001, Alejandro Toledo employed a similar formula to win the presidency after the fall of Fujimori, emphasizing his humble origins and indigenous roots, the perseverance that underlay his academic achievements, and his independence from the incumbent political establishment. The "parties" that accompanied all three of these leaders were highly personalistic and organizationally fragile movements cobbled together during electoral conjunctures, and none of these leaders showed significant interest in building them into anything more durable. Belmont's Obras (Works) was formed in anticipation of the 1989 municipal elections and then laid down after Belmont left the mayoralty in 1995. Fujimori routinely established a new party organ for each electoral cycle, thus running on behalf of four different parties or electoral fronts during his decade in politics. His primary electoral vehicle, Cambio 90/Nueva Mayoría (Change 90/New Majority), was only capable of garnering 3 of the 120 seats in Congress in the 2001 elections that followed his ignominious exodus from power. Toledo's party, Perú Posible, was founded (under a different name) for the 1995 presidential campaign, then allowed to lie dormant until it was revived and rebaptized prior to the 2000 race. Its organizational bonds were so tenuous that nearly a third of its congressional deputies elected in 2000 accepted bribes from intelligence chief Vladimiro Montesinos to switch sides and support Fujimori (Levitsky and Cameron 2003, 19).

The populist outsiders were clearly the most independent of these three types of leaders, as they did not have significant ties, either in the past or the present, to the established parties of the pre-1990 period.[7] Likewise, the "parties" that sponsored their candidacies were little more than registration labels; without a party bureaucracy or organized constituencies to hold them accountable, these leaders possessed exceptionally high levels of strategic autonomy and flexibility as they adopted (or changed) policy positions, electoral tactics, and coalition partners (see Kitschelt 1994). Likewise, lacking any sort of organized constituency, populist outsiders were uniquely unbeholden to group interests in civil and political society. Despite the absence of encapsulated voters or social blocs, however, they were formidable contenders in the electoral arena; indeed, populist outsiders were the most successful of the three types of independent leaders in presidential campaigns. The electorate repeatedly opted for leaders who were the most detached from, and thus the least tainted by, established parties and political elites.[8] Voters did not need party organizations to identify attractive candidates, and neither were the candidates dependent on parties to finance and manage their campaigns or provide foot soldiers to mobilize support and turn out the vote.

Such independent modes of campaigning are widely attributed to the impact of television (Epstein 1980; Mancini and Swanson 1996), which played an instrumental role in the rise of outsider figures such as Ricardo Belmont in Lima and Fernando Collor in Brazil. It is important to recognize, however, that neither Fujimori nor Toledo relied heavily on the mass broadcast media to appeal to voters during their initial campaign surge. When Fujimori first ran for office in 1990, the airwaves were dominated by Vargas Llosa and his coalition, the Frente Democrático (Democratic Front [FREDEMO]), which had the financial resources and media backing necessary to mount an expensive (and arguably counterproductive) advertising blitz. Fujimori, by contrast, relied on billboards, fliers, personal appearances in poor communities, and direct contact with the masses, along with informal social networks linked to evangelical churches and small-business groups. Although he spoke regularly on evangelical radio broadcasts, he could only afford one amateurish television spot during the first round of the election (Bowen 2000, 19). In a context in which established parties were decomposing and a large percentage of the electorate was prone to support whichever candidate emerged as the most viable alternative to Vargas Llosa and his proposed economic "shock" measures, such informal social networks (along with the clandestine support of President García) were adequate to place Fujimori on the political radar screen. Once he emerged from the pack as Vargas Llosa's most formidable competitor, the dynamics of electoral polarization and tactical voting swelled his support far beyond the reach of his primary social and political networks.

Likewise, Toledo's campaign ten years later had to contend with broadcast media that had been largely taken over or cowed into submission by the Fujimori regime, along with numerous tabloid publications set up to support the president. Television news devoted most of its coverage to Fujimori and his activities, largely neglecting the political opposition, while proregime tabloids oriented toward popular audiences launched scurrilous campaigns against Fujimori's competitors (Conaghan 2001, 8–10). Limited access to the media forced Toledo to mobilize support through public meetings and rallies, yet he still devoted little energy to party-building activities. After running a distant fourth in the 1995 presidential race, he largely disappeared from the political scene, only to reemerge as Fujimori's primary competitor (with a new party label) in 2000 after the early opposition favorites, Andrade and Castañeda Lossio, sank in the polls (at least in part because of the media campaigns against them). Toledo was thus positioned to capture a large bloc of independent, anti-Fujimori voters who were willing to support whichever opposition figure emerged from the pack at the end of the campaign, much as Fujimori had earlier capitalized on the political polarization engendered by Vargas Llosa.

The shallowness of Toledo's support was evident when the Fujimori regime crumbled after the 2000 election and Toledo was hard-pressed to defeat a resurgent García in the 2001 presidential race. Despite the complete electoral eclipse of Fujimorismo, Toledo's first-round vote declined by almost 5 percent between 2000 and 2001, and he struggled in the runoff against a candidate (García) who had been thoroughly discredited by his first term in office and whose party (APRA) had received a minuscule 1.3 percent of the vote the year before. García's remarkable comeback demonstrated that the demise of traditional parties was neither complete nor necessarily permanent; indeed, some scholars have suggested that it augurs a rebirth of the Peruvian party system (Kenney 2003). Nevertheless, the large gap (nearly 25 percentage points) between APRA's 2000 vote and García's first-round 2001 vote raises questions about whether the latter's strong showing was more of a personal comeback than a partisan revival.

Although APRA undoubtedly stands to gain from García's political resurrection, the 2001 election and the reinstallation of democracy did little to alter the most notable features of political representation in post-1990 Peru: the almost complete absence of representative institutions and the occupation of the institutional void by a series of competing personalities. Indeed, Peru appears to be mired in a pattern of iterated or "serial populism" marked by a sequence of dominant personalities, a pattern that is reinforced rather than altered by García's populist resurrection. The post-Fujimori interim government led by Valentín Paniagua took major strides to restore the rule of law and uphold democratic checks and balances by respecting the institutional autonomy of Congress, the courts, the electoral machinery, and the media, and Toledo has been more inclined to exercise personal leadership within the confines of such instruments of accountability than Fujimori ever was. Nevertheless, the protest movement that helped drive Fujimori from power was not channeled by opposition parties, and neither did it leave organizational residues behind to launch a process of party system recomposition. Likewise, neither the post-Fujimori electoral campaign nor the responsibilities of governance induced Toledo to devote significant energy to organization building. Instead, his government has been plagued by disorganization, isolation, social protests, and plummeting public-approval ratings, leaving serious doubts about the capacity of the president to complete his term in office. The restoration of democratic governing institutions, therefore, has not been paralleled by a serious revival of representative institutions in either civil society or the partisan arena, with the partial exception of APRA. This is troubling, as Peru's recent experience suggests that such representative institutions are vital to the healthy functioning of democratic checks and balances. As explained below, there was an integral connection between the Fujimori regime's dearth of partisan organization and its increasingly corrupt and authoritarian mode of governance. Despite the superfluous role of party organizations in the electoral arena, they are indispensable agents of democratic accountability, whose absence sealed the fate of Fujimorismo.

The Partisan Void and Political Autocracy Under Fujimori

Although the populist outsider strategy can be electorally formidable, especially under crisis conditions, it is intrinsically problematic as a mode of democratic governance. Indeed, it has a built-in tendency toward self-negation, as the Fujimori experience suggests. A candidate can run for office as an outsider by attacking the political establishment, but once victory is obtained and public office is assumed, incumbency eventually transforms the outsider into the new establishment (Roberts 1995, 115). A primary mechanism of legitimation thus tends to dissipate over time, leaving the government inordinately dependent on performance criteria to sustain its popularity. But as Weyland (2000) convincingly shows, the payoffs derived from even the most extraordinary political successes—such as Fujimori's early 1990s defeat of hyperinflation and of the Shining Path (Sendero Luminoso) insurgency—are subject to a law of diminishing returns. Incumbents may reap large short-term political dividends from such achievements, but over time this halo effect diminishes as the saliency of vanquished demons subsides and new issues displace them on the political agenda.

When performance falters, as it generally does in a context of economic dependence and volatility, personal appeal alone is a weak foundation for political legitimacy. Leadership that is undergirded by party organization has a number of built-in advantages for muddling through such hard times, as it is less prone to volatile positive or negative bandwagon effects. Responsibility for policy failure can be shared (and thus diffused), policymakers can be rotated, and leaders can draw upon reservoirs of organizational loyalty to limit defections.[9] Executives with legislative support that is bound by organizational ties are more capable of governance in hard times than those with legislative support that is contingent on personal appeal. Furthermore, party government lengthens the time horizons of incumbent officials, as second-tier leaders, at least, can absorb an electoral defeat of their party and return to compete in subsequent electoral cycles on the party label. As such, they have incentives to play according to the democratic rules of the game and safeguard their party's public image.

In contrast, government by personalistic cliques has more of an all-or-nothing character that encourages short time horizons. Once voted out of office, such cliques are unlikely to return, and they generally lack mechanisms to carry out a leadership succession. Indeed, Fujimori failed miserably to translate his own personal popularity into electoral success for his favored candidates in municipal elections. In short, there could be no Fujimorismo without Fujimori. Lacking institutionalized protection, personalistic cliques are unusually vulnerable to political retaliation or legal prosecution when they relinquish state power, especially if they can be plausibly linked to political corruption or violations of democratic norms. The Fujimori/Montesinos experience shows that personalistic regimes can easily get trapped in a vicious cycle: conscious of their institutional fragility, they have a fear of displacement that leads to a "profit while one can" mentality and a desperate manipulation of democratic procedures, which in turn undermine the legitimacy of the regime and stoke its opposition. Furthermore, bereft of organized support in civil society, personalistic cliques are prone to seek institutional sustenance from the state—in this case, the armed forces and the intelligence service (Grompone 2000). This transforms these public, unelected institutions into personal instruments of power, with pernicious consequences for democratic accountability.

These dynamics can be observed at several intervals within the Fujimori regime, and they ultimately led to its implosion after ten years in office. Initially, antidemocratic methods were linked to Fujimori's dearth of partisan support, but they met with popular approval rather than derision, as they played into Fujimori's outsider attack on the political establishment. Despite winning the presidency in a second-round landslide against Vargas Llosa, Fujimori took office with only 32 of the 180 seats in the lower house of Congress and seventeen of the sixty-two senators belonging to his Cambio 90 party, which had been hastily assembled by Fujimori and his collaborators in the months preceding the election. The leadership of Cambio 90 was so weak and inexperienced that Fujimori did not include a single member of the party in his first cabinet (Bowen 2000, 41).[10] Indeed, following his election, Fujimori quickly demobilized Cambio 90 and his civic support groups, and the small-business and evangelical groups that had supported his election soon found themselves excluded from effective influence. Fujimori clashed with other Cambio 90 leaders and congressional representatives over his economic shock program, his reluctance to prosecute García on corruption and human rights charges, and the method for selecting parliamentary candidates. In response, Fujimori sacked the party's secretary-general, closed its central office, and resisted policy input from Cambio 90's parliamentary bloc (Planas 2000, 347–51). Cambio 90 congressional leader Luz Salgado conceded that it was difficult for many supporters to accept Fujimori's about-face on economic policies, while acknowledging that the president's lack of ties to organized social and political groups gave him a high level of policy autonomy. Salgado insisted that Cambio 90 was a "political movement" rather than a party, and admitted that it never developed a procedure to register party members.[11]

Congress initially acquiesced to Fujimori's strong-arm rule, as AP and the PPC embraced his unexpected turn to neoliberal economics. Opposition from the congressional majority began to mount in late 1991 and early 1992, however, as legislators balked at an ambitious wave of security decrees proposed by Fujimori. This resistance undoubtedly contributed to the April 1992 autogolpe (see Kenney 1996). Fujimori justified the coup as an attempt to sweep away the corrupt *partidocracia* ("party-archy") that had brought the country to the brink of economic collapse and millenarian revolution, and the public bought it, as the president's approval ratings soared to the 80 percent level (Conaghan 1995a).

If the weakness of Fujimori's partisan support in Congress contributed to the autogolpe, the postcoup political reconstruction temporarily corrected the problem. In preparation for Constituent Assembly elections, the president created a new "party," known as Nueva Mayoría (New Majority), among sympathetic technocrats to ally with Cambio 90, which had been largely dismantled. With the opposition in disarray, and much of it abstaining from electoral participation, the pro-Fujimori coalition won a narrow majority in the one-hundred-seat assembly, which subsequently served as the legislative branch of the government. Riding the coattails of Fujimori's landslide 1995 reelection, his two-party coalition then replenished its majority in the new Congress. Despite the organizational fragility of its constituent parties, the Cambio 90/Nueva Mayoría (C90-NM) bloc in Congress governed as a disciplined majority, as its legislators—virtually all political novices handpicked by Fujimori and his confidants—had no independent political base of their own and were thus highly dependent on Fujimori and his intelligence chief, Montesinos. According to Carey (2003, 994–96), members of the C90-NM congressional delegation were instructed how to vote by the administration, and legislative resources such as office space and staff assistance were contingent on personal loyalty to Fujimori. Congress thus supported Fujimori at every turn, reinterpreting the new constitution to allow him to run for a third presidential term, passing a blanket amnesty to cover up human rights violations, and rejecting an opposition petition with 1,441,535 signatures that called for a referendum on the constitutionality of Fujimori's second reelection (Conaghan 2001, 6).

The postcoup political order, then, was highly autocratic, as there were no effective institutional checks on the power of Fujimori and Montesinos. Congress was supine; the judiciary had been purged and handpicked; and loyalists were placed in command of the armed forces, which was firmly allied with the regime's authoritarian project. Even the means of mass communication were transformed into instruments of executive control as the regime used political and economic pressure to induce sympathetic television and newspaper coverage (8–10).

The only available mechanism of accountability was the ballot box, where Fujimorismo ultimately proved to be vulnerable, in part because of the absence of party organization in the electorate. In essence, Fujimori built his party organs from above, without meaningful grassroots structures that would allow them to penetrate society. Nueva Mayoría, in particular, had scarcely any organizational presence outside the national Congress. According to its leader and congressional president, Ricardo Marcenaro, Nueva Mayoría was not a party but "a group of independents who collaborate with President Fujimori." Nueva Mayoría did not register members or form local offices, and it rejected institutionalization, claiming that "it would be our weakness, not strength."[12]

Given the dearth of local branches and organized social constituencies, Fujimori was unable to translate his own popularity or his formidable command of state resources into electoral success for his followers at the subnational level. Both the 1994 and the 1998 municipal elections produced disappointing results for Fujimori, as his favored candidates were defeated by a series of upstart independents, local caudillos, and defectors from traditional parties. The grassroots structures of C90-NM were so tenuous that Fujimori chose not to sponsor a nationwide list of candidates for the 1995 municipal elections.

Fujimori created a third party vehicle, Vamos Vecino (Let's Go, Neighbor), for the 1998 municipal elections, and he placed his former minister of agriculture, an ex-APRA member named Absalón Vásquez, in charge of the party-building effort. Offers of state support brought many of the independent mayors onto the Fujimori bandwagon, and Vásquez turned his political connections and state patronage networks into the beginnings of a grassroots political machine. Nevertheless, his party-building project clashed with the interests and technocratic vision of some of the old-guard Fujimoristas from C90-NM (Burgos 2000; M. Paredes 2000), and Fujimori downplayed the nascent party when he began preparing for the 2000 general elections. Running well ahead of his competitors in the polls, he opted to create his fourth electoral movement (known as the Frente Independiente Perú 2000 [Independent Front Peru 2000]) for these elections, a fateful decision that backfired on the regime. Lacking the grassroots mobilizational structures needed to register a new party in short order, Fujimori's handlers forged more than a million signatures to get the new "party" on the ballot. When details of this blatant fraud leaked out to the public, the resulting scandal hit Fujimori in one of his most vulnerable spots—on the issue of respect for democratic procedures and the rule of law. Domestic and international critics assailed the manipulation of the electoral process, questioning the validity of the entire exercise. Meanwhile, Alejandro Toledo began his ascent, separating himself from the pack of Fujimori opponents and establishing himself as the most viable contender to an increasingly manipulative autocrat.

Fujimori ultimately prevailed in the second round of a heavily tainted electoral process that witnessed Toledo's withdrawal from the race. Nevertheless, Fujimori's partisan supporters were unable to provide him with the congressional majority that he had enjoyed since the postautogolpe political reconstruction. Unwilling to govern under the constraints of legislative checks and balances, the regime resorted to yet another blatant manipulation of the democratic process, bribing opposition congressional deputies to support the ruling coalition. Intelligence agency videotapes of Montesinos offering bribes were leaked to an opposition member of Congress, triggering a firestorm of criticism that ultimately led to a schism between Fujimori and Montesinos. Montesinos became a fugitive and was eventually arrested in Venezuela, while Fujimori submitted a faxed resignation during a visit to Japan. Congress stripped Fujimori of his office, and the self-exiled former president subsequently devoted his energies to fighting the extradition efforts of his successors. Pro-Fujimori parties won only 3 of 120 seats in new congressional elections, and by 2002 they had dissolved entirely (Carey 2003, 988). Thus ended one of the most unlikely and enigmatic regimes in modern Latin American history.

In retrospect, it can be seen that the dearth of partisan organization was, paradoxically, Fujimori's greatest asset and his most vexing liability, and it left its imprimatur on his regime in myriad ways. The lack of a party apparatus solidified Fujimori's outsider status and lent credibility to his attacks on the political establishment. It also enhanced his strategic autonomy, which he used to realign his bases of political support after taking office and to implement the kind of harsh structural adjustment policies that he had campaigned against when they were advocated by Vargas Llosa. However, the lack of party organization at times left Fujimori politically isolated and dependent on the security forces for institutional support. At the beginning and end of his regime he lacked a legislative majority, and he consistently had difficulty electing supporters to local government positions. His mass constituencies were never organizationally encapsulated, leaving their political loyalties contingent on performance criteria and a continuous stream of targeted state patronage. By the end of the 1990s the threat of hyperinflation and insurgency had receded, while the economic boom of the mid-1990s had ground to a halt, eroding support for Fujimori and placing his second reelection in jeopardy.

With no successor waiting in the wings, the regime engaged in blatant manipulation of the democratic process and the rule of law in order to circumvent the 1993 constitutional ban on multiple reelections and then ensure victory at the voting booth. The C90-NM bloc in Congress passed a law in 1996 reinterpreting the constitution to exclude Fujimori's first term in office and thus allow him to stand for reelection in 2000.[13] Congress subsequently removed three magistrates from the Constitutional Tribunal who had voted against the constitutionality of this law, reconfigured the National Election Board to restrict its political autonomy, and blocked a popular referendum drive on Fujimori's candidacy. Once the legal path for Fujimori's candidacy was cleared, the regime used various forms of political and economic pressure to silence critical voices on television, harassed and planted scurrilous stories on opposition candidates in the tabloid press, manipulated social-assistance programs for electoral support, and forged more than a million signatures to register Fujimori's new party label (Conaghan 2001, 4–12). And when the highly tainted electoral process returned Fujimori to office without a congressional majority, the stage was set for the Montesinos bribery scandal that ultimately sealed the regime's fate.

Clearly, these machinations destroyed whatever democratic credentials the Fujimori-Montesinos regime might have retained. Although the autocratic proclivities of these two leaders might have undermined democracy under any set of institutional circumstances, the lack of partisan organization exacerbated their authoritarian tendencies by eroding democratic accountability and encouraging blatant manipulation of democratic procedural norms. Indeed, the partisan vacuum was itself an expression of the preference for autocracy; despite the potential organiza-tion-building opportunities provided by state power and resources, the two leaders eschewed any sort of institutionalization that might limit their strategic autonomy, hold them accountable, or spawn future com-petitors.

If the dearth of progovernment partisan organization exacerbated the authoritarian inclinations of Fujimorismo, the partisan void on the side of the opposition also undermined efforts to check abuses of power and hold the regime accountable. The delegitimation of established parties made them easy targets for Fujimori's political attacks during the early years of his administration, and it rendered them virtually defenseless against the presidential coup that ruptured the democratic regime in 1992. When international pressure left Fujimori little choice but to re-store a democratic facade, the debility of the opposition parties and the electoral abstention of several of them allowed the president to capture a servile congressional majority despite the absence of a well-organized partisan vehicle of his own. And when economic stagnation and political manipulation began to erode his popular support, causing him to lose his congressional majority in 2000, the opposition parties were far too frag-ile to shift the balance of power to their advantage. Indeed, the political loyalties of their elected congressional deputies were so shallow and con-tingent that Montesinos quickly bribed his way to a congressional major-ity (Grompone 2000, 151). Weak and fragile opposition parties were unable to provide a significant check on executive power, which became increasingly centralized, arbitrary, and corrupt over the course of the Fujimori decade.[14]

The demise of opposition parties might not have mattered had civil society proved strong enough to mobilize on its own to defend demo-cratic norms and procedures, but this also failed to occur. The Peruvian case does not fit the pattern observed in some neighboring countries, where the revival of traditional parties during periods of democratic tran-sition contributed to the demobilization of social actors and protest movements (Oxhorn 1994; Canel 1992). In Peru, there was no clear in-verse relationship between social and political mobilization. Parties were negligible actors throughout the 1990s, yet social mobilization and pro-test were also highly sporadic. Social mobilization peaked during the 1997–98 signature campaign for a referendum on reelection and the pro-test movement against electoral fraud after Fujimori's "victory" in 2000, but in general it was anemic and unsustained. In fact, what remained of civil society became increasingly dependent on state social-assistance programs in the 1990s, enveloping its leaders in a web of politically compromising clientelistic exchanges that dampened oppositional social mobilization and robbed many popular organizations of the political autonomy they had previously cherished (Grompone 2000, 135–37). Given the absence of strong opposition parties and the fiscal and political weaknesses of local governments, popular organizations had few places to turn to other than the state, which blatantly manipulated social-assistance programs to generate political support and dependency (Graham and Kane 1998; Schady 2000; Roberts and Arce 1998).

Ultimately, although the role of opposition parties and civil society in the downfall of Fujimori should not be ignored, it would be a mistake to attribute the regime transition to their political pressure or activities. The Fujimori-Montesinos regime was not so much defeated by its opponents as it was torn apart by its own internal contradictions. In essence, the regime imploded while trying to reproduce itself, and even then the opposition found it difficult to fill Peru's chronic institutional void in political representation. The best evidence of this, perhaps, was the stunning resurrection of Alan García in 2001. Utterly discredited following his own term in office, politically detached after riding out the Fujimori decade in exile, and still anchored to a historic party whose vote had dropped below the 2 percent mark in 2000, García was nonetheless able to make a serious bid for the presidency in 2001. Following gains by APRA in 2002 municipal and regional elections, there is little doubt that García will make a serious bid to complete his political comeback during the next electoral cycle. Thus continues Peru's pattern of serial populism, in which public support flows from one personalistic leader to another, with minimal channeling by partisan loyalties or organizational bonds.

Conclusion

In this chapter I have argued that political parties are vital to democratic governance, even if they have become dispensable as instruments of electoral mobilization. As a consequence of this dispensability, parties' representative and governing functions have become detached, with potentially dire ramifications for democratic rule. If this argument is correct, it is clear that Peruvian democracy will confront a number of significant challenges in the years to come. In the decade and a half since Peru's party system began to decompose, neither governing nor opposition political elites have succeeded in partisan reconstruction, and most have invested few resources or energy in the endeavor. Even if García's personalistic leadership helps to revive APRA, Peru will remain a considerable distance from a recomposition of the party system. Although democratic institutions have been restored, the regime transition did not engender sustained sociopolitical mobilization or extensive organizational efforts, and neither did it generate a new foundational cleavage to structure partisan competition and political identities in the years to come. As such, political representation remains fluid, informal, and non-institutionalized—precisely the conditions that incubate autocratic leadership patterns (McClintock 1996).

The interim Paniagua administration demonstrated that responsible, democratic leadership is still possible under such treacherous conditions. Nevertheless, Peruvian democracy cannot be left to hinge on the goodwill of a select group of incumbents, and the social protests and declining popularity that plagued the initial years of the Toledo government are indicative of the fragility of the new regime. Democratic stability requires institutional grounding, including not only horizontal checks on executive authority, but also vertical linkages between parties and diverse social constituencies. These linkages have never been especially strong in Peru, and those that existed were sundered during the crisis of the 1980s and early 1990s. They have yet to be reconstituted under the new democratic regime. Until they are, Peruvian democracy is likely to lead a precarious and tumultuous existence.

NOTES

1. Among the new "parties," Alberto Andrade's Somos Perú made the most serious attempt to construct organizational bases, but it ultimately failed to consolidate at the end of the 1990s.

2. The average includes the votes received in the 1980 elections by the individual leftist parties that subsequently founded the IU.

3. Nora Bonifás, interview by the author, Lima, March 11, 1999.

4. Even where party organizations were not formed, however, control of the state apparatus was still advantageous for electoral candidates. It should be recognized that Fujimori's candidacy in 1990 received covert support from the García administration, and once in office he drew heavily upon state resources in his reelection campaigns. I am indebted to Charles Kenney for making this point.

5. Barrantes was actually an "independent" within the IU, as he did not belong to any of its constituent party organizations. Initially, this independence made him a consensus figure in the leadership of the Left, allowing Barrantes to serve as president of the IU and mayor of Lima as well as to be the presidential

candidate of the coalition in 1985. Internal conflicts, however, caused Barrantes to step down as IU president in 1987 and abandon the coalition in 1989 when he and a number of small parties that supported him failed in their bid to gain recognition of his candidacy on the IU label.

6. Clearly, a politician may defect from an established party and chart a more independent course, cobbling together a network of adherents under a new "party" registration label. The candidacy should still be considered independent, however, until and unless this new party consolidates an electoral presence at different levels of contestation over a series of election cycles.

7. In contrast, defectors previously belonged to an established party, while frontpeople received their backing.

8. This did not mean that voters insisted on an outsider in every election cycle; leaders such as Fujimori and Belmont were able to achieve reelection. As explained below, outsiders who become incumbents are invariably transformed into a new establishment, although it is difficult to establish at what point such a transformation occurs.

9. For example, APRA's organizational strength and second-tier leadership probably contributed to the party's respectable electoral showing in 1990 despite the debacle of García's final years. In contrast, the AP had little organizational identity beyond that of its founder, Belaúnde, and no clear successor, leaving the party vulnerable to widespread voter backlash in 1985 against the more moderate crisis that occurred under Belaúnde's watch.

10. Fujimori's first cabinet included six independents, five military or retired military officers, and five individuals from parties other than Cambio 90 (Tuesta Soldevilla 1994, 52–63).

11. Luz Salgado, interview by the author, Lima, March 18, 1999.

12. Ricardo Marcenaro, interview by the author, Lima, March 12, 1999.

13. The "Law of Authentic Interpretation of the Constitution" ruled that since Fujimori's 1990 election took place before the constitution came into effect, his first term in office did not count against the two-term constitutional limit.

14. As Carey (2003) points out, however, electronic recording of individual congressional votes was established toward the end of the Fujimori regime, which created greater legislative transparency and encouraged legislators to be more responsive to public opinion (and thus less responsive to hierarchical party discipline).

FIVE

The Immoral Economy of Fujimorismo

CATHERINE M. CONAGHAN

Historians will forever thank Vladimiro Montesinos for his devotion to documentation in the video age. Since the fall of the government of President Alberto Fujimori in November 2000, hundreds of videotapes and audio recordings chronicling the abuses and corruption of the regime have been made public. Most of the videos released to date feature the clandestine meetings that Fujimori's national security advisor, Vladimiro Montesinos, held in his office at the Servicio de Inteligencia Nacional (National Intelligence Service [SIN]) with notables and would-be notables from every walk of Peruvian life. The tapes, along with the numerous investigations that ensued, confirmed what many Peruvians had long suspected: the Fujimori administration was not just a government; it was also a vast criminal conspiracy.

Just as the Nixon tapes opened a window on the darkest vistas of American politics during the Watergate scandal, the Montesinos videos provided Peruvians with an unprecedented look at the backstage behavior of a ruling elite. The videos (later followed by testimony from Montesinos and other principals) showed how systemic the deceit, hypocrisy, and cynicism was and how integral these practices were to the reproduction of the regime. In pursuit of Fujimori's reelection in 2000, no part of the state or society was left untouched by corruption as Montesinos reached out to ensure complete control over the political landscape. He found willing accomplices. Professionals from every field—media execu-

tives, consultants, businesspeople, public officials, judges, and congressional deputies—lined up for the hefty bribes that Montesinos patiently
doled out. As he handed over envelopes or briefcases full of cash, Montesinos gave his associates their marching orders, spelling out their political obligations to the president.

There is no doubt that democratic institutions were eviscerated during
the Fujimori era, but it would be a mistake to view the period as bereft
of any institutionalization. The denaturation of democratic institutions
went hand in hand with the routinization of other behavior meant to
perpetuate the regime. As Guillermo O'Donnell (1996, 40) argues, the
apparent weakness of the formal institutions of democracy in Latin
America should not blind us "from seeing an extremely influential, informal, and sometimes concealed institution: clientelism, and more generally particularlism." During the Fujimori era in Peru, this other
"institutionalization" was in full gear; the governing clique developed an
elaborate system of corruption and clientelism, one with its own code of
conduct and culture.

In postarrest ruminations, Montesinos acknowledged his own culpability and that of his clients, the ones he found in the boardrooms and
newsrooms and among the "best and brightest" technocrats. Fujimori
and Montesinos counted on collusion and complicity at the highest levels
of Peruvian society to maintain the regime. Members of the Peruvian elite
were active participants in an immoral economy that revolved around
untold opportunities for illicit economic gains made possible by the official culture of impunity. In contrast to a moral economy, in which economic justice is defined as access to a tolerable minimum standard of
living, the Fujimorista elite constructed its own immoral economy, one
based on maximizing the economic spoils of power and structured deceit.[1]

In the Fujimori era, corruption was not simply an unhappy by-product
or a symptom of an incompetent or inefficient regime. Rather, corruption
was a primary constitutive feature of the regime, the "cartilage and collagen" that held it together and ensured its reproduction.[2] Fujimori's autogolpe of 1992 laid the essential groundwork for a government steeped
in crime and cover-ups. By effectively eradicating any oversight of the
executive branch by the legislature or the judiciary, Fujimori and his
inner circle were free from scrutiny and could act with impunity. They
did so, and the result was a system in which corruption flourished. Corruption became both a means and an end—a way to retain power and
the reason to stay in power.[3]

Unpacking the Crimes: The Investigations

The investigations undertaken after Fujimori's removal by the Peruvian congress in November 2000 were unprecedented in their number and scope. Both Congress and the judicial branch have played an active role in the Herculean task of documenting the crimes of the Fujimori era. Congressman David Waisman led the original congressional commission on Montesinos's corruption rings. Waisman's commission concluded work in June 2001, but Congress created a new set of commissions on specialized topics that continued through 2002. Congresswoman Anel Townsend chaired a wide-ranging investigation that examined the financial dealings of Fujimori and Montesinos. Congressman Fausto Alvarado led a commission on corruption in the judicial system. A commission headed by Congressman Mauricio Mulder focused on press corruption, electoral fraud, and human rights abuses. Congressman Javier Diez Canseco spearheaded an investigation into the mismanagement of public-sector firms and privatization.[4] At the same time, inquiries by the Procuraduria Ad Hoc (Special Prosecutor's Office) and the Fiscalía de la Nación (Office of the Attorney General) continued. Oficina de Control de la Magistratura (The Office of Judicial Oversight [OCMA]) produced its own findings on judicial corruption in January 2002. Military courts opened proceedings in regard to individual cases of officers.

To date, many criminal prosecutions remain pending. Montesinos, incarcerated since his arrest in June 2001, has been found guilty of criminal charges in four separate court cases as of July 2003. He faces scores of charges in at least seventy more criminal cases.[5] Other high-ranking military and civilian officials are in jail or under house arrest or remain at large. From the comfort of exile in Japan, Fujimori has repeatedly ignored summonses to appear before Peruvian courts and Congress. In July 2003, the Peruvian government formally requested Fujimori's extradition from Japan.[6]

Although the legal investigations of Fujimori and his officials are far from over, the inquiries to date have produced a substantial amount of information about how corruption was organized, thanks in great part to the incriminating evidence in the Vladivideos and the subsequent testimony offered by participants. As this chapter shows, a picture of the "other institutionalization" that took place in Peru during the Fujimori era is now emerging, although it is likely that we will discover much more as the trials continue.

As traditionally defined, *corruption* refers to the use of public office for private gain; it encompasses a broad range of practices.[7] Personal greed animates corruption, but so does power seeking and desires for self-aggrandizement (Manzetti 2000, 140). In the case of the Fujimori administration, corruption spread out across different arenas, involved different rings of participants, and served a variety of personal and political purposes.

Taking Care of Business: The Greed Rings

Corruption animated by immediate personal greed involved cliques of high-ranking public officials and shadowy brokers who worked with Vladimiro Montesinos and facilitated the illicit deals and participated in the profits. Top commanders in the Peruvian armed forces were active in the rings. The major scams involving military officers were the massive frauds in the management of the Caja Militar (military pension fund) and in arms purchases, most notably the acquisition of aircraft from Belarus and Russia.

In the case of the pension fund, the Waisman Commission report concluded that Montesinos's cronies concocted phantom companies to do business with the pension fund; real estate, services, and stocks were purchased with pension funds at wildly inflated prices. The Caja Militar lost an estimated $300 million on the operations. Among the military officers named in investigations of the fraud were former minister of interior General Juan Briones Dávila and former minister of defense General Víctor Malca Villanueva, who is still at large.[8]

Similarly, in the case of the purchase of the Belarusian aircraft, companies set up by Montesinos's protégés—Víctor Venero, Juan Valencia, and Luis Duthurburu—brokered the deals and pocketed astronomical fees. The Waisman Commission estimated that Montesinos made as much as $17 million on the deal, with an additional $32 million distributed to other conspirators in the purchase, including former head of the armed forces high command General Nicolás de Bari Hermoza Ríos.[9]

The arms deals, however, ultimately may prove to be just the tip of the iceberg. The Waisman Commission found evidence linking Montesinos and military figures to narcotrafficking and money laundering of a such magnitude that the commission was led to conclude that Peru became a "narcostate" during the Fujimori era.[10] The commission alleged that Montesinos, along with General Hermoza, received regular payoffs from drug trafficking organizations. These operations involved rings inside the military as well as the brokers who worked on the money-laundering side. The subsequent Townsend Commission concurred with the findings of the Waisman Commission. Witnesses told the Townsend Commission that narcotraffickers paid Montesinos protection money and that Montesinos used his influence in the judiciary to fix cases for drug dealers.[11] Both Montesinos and Hermoza confessed to wrongdoing on other charges, but they vehemently continue to deny all charges related to narcotrafficking.[12] Montesinos also denies involvement in arms trafficking with guerrillas in Colombia.

As the investigations by Peruvian officials unfolded, revelations of the staggering amounts of money stashed in national and foreign banks made clear how sophisticated and far-reaching the corruption was. The sheer amount of money discovered in foreign bank accounts only fueled the suspicions that narcotrafficking was part of the mix of the crimes committed. In charges issued on June 22, 2001, the Attorney General's Office accused Montesinos and twelve accomplices of the crime of "illegal enrichment," yielding profits totaling a little more than $264 million in bank accounts and property; these caches of money had been discovered with the cooperation of Swiss authorities. Montesinos's personal bank accounts, totaling nearly $33 million, were frozen. Six Swiss accounts in the name of General Hermoza held a little more than $20 million.

Military officers were not the only officials who were caught up in illegal money-making schemes. Civilian policymakers had their own rings. Officials in the Ministry of the Economy and other agencies involved in economic matters traded favors with businesspeople who used their access to information for profit. Francisco Durand (2003) identified Jorge Camet, minister of the economy from 1993 to 1998, as the head of a "white mafia" composed of economic technocrats and businessmen that manipulated economic and fiscal policy for their private gain. From the privatization of public enterprises to government procurements, official transactions opened up untold opportunities for profiteering. Former congressmen and finance minister Víctor Joy Way was discovered to have close to $11 million in Swiss accounts under his name and that of his wife. Investigators alleged that the money came from kickbacks from Chinese companies doing business with the Peruvian government.

As the Joy Way case illustrates, participants in the greed rings readily involved their own family members in a style typical of neopatrimonial systems. Family members shared in the booty—perhaps to facilitate spreading the money across multiple bank accounts. Investigators uncovered multimillion-dollar bank accounts in the names of Montesinos's ex-wife, lover, daughters, sister, brother-in-law, nieces, and nephew. General Víctor Malca complemented his savings with millions in accounts in the names of his sons and daughters, as did General Hermoza and General José Villanueva.

Fujimori's relation to Montesinos's greed rings—the extent to which he had knowledge of, or profited from, the illicit deals, especially the arms purchases—remains to be clarified. The Waisman Commission charged that, at a minimum, Fujimori had knowledge of the narcotrafficking protection rackets and therefore is necessarily implicated in the cover-up of these activities because he did nothing to stop it. The initial report issued by the Procuraduría Ad Hoc in August 2001 hypothesized that corruption was "compartamentalized," that not all the participants in the greed rings necessarily had knowledge of all the deals going on in the different arenas in which corruption was taking place. Montesinos lent credence to the compartmentalization thesis in his testimony to congressional investigators. He noted that Fujimori always kept him in the dark when it came to certain matters, especially transactions surrounding the privatization of public enterprises and the finances of the big budget ministry, the Ministerio de la Presidencia (Ministry of the Presidency). He also speculated that president's relatives might have been playing key roles in moving cash out of the country during their frequent visits to Japan.

Since his flight to Japan in 2000, Fujimori has continued to deny actual knowledge of wrongdoing in his administration. Yet Fujimori did concede to harboring suspicions about Montesinos, particularly in one case in which Montesinos fabricated false charges of narcotrafficking against a businessman and his family in 1999.[13] If Fujimori admits to doubts about Montesinos in at least one case, it stands to reason that he may have (or at least should have) wondered about the slew of accusations that constantly appeared in Peru's independent press about his closest advisor. If Fujimori did not know about the Montesinos-led corruption, it makes sense that it was because he did not want to find out, hoping to hang onto a modicum of "plausible deniability."

Current investigations into Fujimori's own personal finances and that of his family indicate that the Fujimori clan may have been involved in its own private greed ring, just as Montesinos told investigators. Montesinos revealed that he routinely sent suitcases of cash to the presidential palace. Montesinos's assistant Matilde Pinchi Pinchi corroborated the transfers. The payments were made at Fujimori's request, in monthly installments ranging from $400,000 to $700,000. The money came from the SIN's slush fund. How the president used the cash remains a mystery. It is one of the many unsolved mysteries surrounding the president and his finances, including how he managed to pay close to one-half million dollars worth of U.S. university education for his four children on his modest presidential salary (Coordinadora Nacional de Derechos Humanos 2003, 30–31).

There is no doubt that the cash flows in and out of the presidential palace were unusual. Susana Higuchi, the president's former wife, reported that in 1993 she was astounded to find in the safe in the private quarters of the palace the sum of $110,000, an amount clearly in excess of the family budget as she knew it.[14] The president's unusual proclivity for irregular cash transactions was in evidence at the end of the administration when he ponied up $15 million in cash, supposedly to pay Montesinos a "bonus" in September 2000 prior to Montesinos's departure to Panama.

Investigators have set their sights on the president's relatives, especially his sister Rosa Fujimori and his brother-in-law Víctor Aritomi, who served as Peru's ambassador to Japan. Both were directly involved in managing the multimillion-dollar accounts of two nonprofit foundations originally founded by Fujimori in 1990–91. The two foundations, Apenkai and Aken, were created ostensibly to raise money in Japan for philanthropic projects in Peru. An estimated $42 million flowed through a complicated maze of domestic and foreign banks set up by the president's relatives to manage the foundations' finances. The haphazard bookkeeping documented transactions in and out of the personal bank accounts of family members and included checks in the president's name. As of this writing, investigators are still combing through the labyrinthine financial transactions, trying to figure out how foundation monies may have been misappropriated by the Fujimori family.[15] One government investigation puts the amount misappropriated as high as $11.3 million.[16] In 2004, Peru's Comptroller's Office issued a report on the Fujimori clan's finances and foundations showing bookkeeping inconsistencies amounting to $274 million.[17]

Without any effective oversight or threat of punishment, public officials enjoyed enormous opportunities for personal enrichment during the Fujimori administration. It is not difficult to imagine why Fujimori, Montesinos, and the people around them would want to perpetuate a system in which they would never be forced to account for murky finances, whether public or private. But staying in power was no easy task, especially given the international constraints on how the regime could develop. Fujimori's initial attempt to strip all constitutional trappings through the autogolpe in April 1992 was condemned by the international community. Under pressure from the Organization of American States (OAS), Fujimori was forced to restore "democratic institutionality" with legislative elections in 1992 and the enactment of a new constitution in 1993. While the 1993 constitution removed the traditional ban on immediate presidential reelection, the two-term limit remained. The effort to maneuver around the limit and secure Fujimori's third term in 2000 intensified the corruption.

All the President's Clients: Politically Motivated Corruption

The crimes documented on the now famous Vladivideos (corroborated by Montesinos and his staff) show another dimension of the immoral economy—corruption that was expressly political in motive. This comprised the criminal transactions undertaken to manage the government's political problems and maintain power. Fujimori's problematic bid for a third consecutive reelection in 2000 animated much of the corruption in this category. Among the clients drawn into the politically motivated schemes were individuals who controlled key institutions, the sites where any resistance to the reelection project had to be preempted.

As a score of the Vladivideos confirmed, owners of major media outlets, especially television, were key collaborators in the reelection project and received lucrative payments in return. Montesinos spent lots of time with television owners plotting the reelection strategy and dictating how they should manage political coverage to favor the president and smear his opponents. The executives seen taking cash payments from Montesinos on the videos were José and Francisco Crousillat (América Televisión [Channel 4]), Samuel and Méndel Winter (Frecuencia Latina [Channel 2]), Ernesto Schutz (Panamericana Televisión [Channel 5]), and Julio Vera Abad (Andina de Televisión [ATV] [Channel 9]).

Television was important, but it was not the only media that was corrupted. Montesinos also struck deals with the owners of Peru's tabloid press (known as the *prensa chicha*). The tabloid owners took huge payoffs in exchange for planting headlines and stories provided by government sources. Montesinos named publicist Augusto Bresani as the go-between who made the payments and passed on the instructions on what stories to print, even to the point of specifying the language to be used in the headlines. The mainstream newspaper *Expreso* also became part of Montesinos's media stable. Eduardo Calmell del Solar, the director and major stockholder of the newspaper, was caught on videotape accepting two cash payments of $500,000 from Montesinos, ostensibly to buy enough stocks to assume complete control of the newspaper. Calmell was also witness to a clandestine deal in which in November 1999 $2 million in Ministry of Defense funds was channeled to fellow *Expreso* stockholder Manuel Ulloa in return for his shares in the newly founded cable-television company Cable Canal de Noticias.[18]

Trading favors with businesspeople was another key component of Montesinos's overall operations, and he put these relationships to a wide variety of uses. Enrique Bertini, director of Banco Wiese, one of Peru's largest banks, was a frequent visitor at the SIN. Banco Wiese's business was tied to the regime in several ways. Not only was the bank a recipient of a government-subsidized bail-out package, but also the institution served as a conduit for Montesinos's own labyrinthine financial transactions. In turn, Montesinos passed on requests to Bertini to facilitate loans for his other business clients, including media executives. Among the other major business figures making an appearance in the Vladivideos was Dionisio Romero, head of Peru's leading business conglomerate. He strategized with Montesinos on the reelection and agreed to break with his low-profile image and go public with his support for the president in carefully programmed pronouncements to the media. Romero's support, however, like that of so many others, was not disinterested. He too sought Montesinos's help, in his case on matters related to an international bank loan (Dammert Ego Aguirre 2001, 338).

The legal and electoral system was another important site of corruption in the system. The manipulation of judges and prosecutors was multifunctional: it allowed the personal greed rings to operate with impunity, and it ensured that the courts would not become a venue for putting the brakes on the reelection project. The makeup of the governing body of the Jurado Nacional de Elecciones (National Election Board [JNE]) was manipulated to put Montesinos's handpicked allies in charge. As in the case of media executives, Montesinos developed a system of cash payoffs to top officials in the system. An investigation by the top judicial governing board (Oficina de Control de la Magistratura, or Office of Judicial Oversight [OCMA]) traced the corruption of the judicial branch back to the creation of the Comisión Ejecutiva del Poder Judicial (Executive Judiciary Commission) in 1994. According to the OCMA investigation, judges received monthly payoffs; in some cases, the judges picked up the money in person at the SIN office while others had payments delivered to their homes. Receipts uncovered in the investigation revealed that the payoffs were for several thousand dollars a month.[19]

Fujimori's Cambio 90/Nueva Mayoría (Change 90/New Majority [C90-NM]) caucus turned Congress into a battering ram for the reelection project in the period 1995–2000. It also made sure that no congressional investigation would be allowed to unmask official corruption. When Fujimori lost his absolute majority in the tumultuous first round of the 2000 election, Montesinos immediately began what was named Operation Recruitment. The mission was to entice newly elected members of Congress to desert their political organizations and affiliate with the government caucus. Some recruits balked at the idea of publicly switching sides and becoming *tránsfugas* (turncoats), but agreed, instead, to act as spies (*topos*) and keep Montesinos informed of the activities of the opposition in Congress.

Cash was the principal inducement in Operation Recruitment, but some of the recruits also sought fixes in pending legal cases. Montesinos negotiated substantial payoffs to congresspeople, with the promise that payments would continue on a monthly basis during the congressional term of 2000–2005. Payoffs went as high as $15,000–20,000 a month and included "sign up" bonuses such as the cost of a new car.[20]

Bribing so many public officials and private citizens to insure the reproduction of the regime was a costly business. To finance the system, resources were culled from public sources. Congressional investigators uncovered accounting practices that transferred funds from the Ministry of Defense, the Ministry of the Interior, and the armed forces on a regular basis from 1992 to 2000, with a hefty spike in transfers during the years 1999 and 2000.[21] Estimates are that as much as $50.5 million was diverted clandestinely over the period 1992–2000 on Fujimori's orders.[22]

Montesinos confirmed that he used SIN funds not only to pay the bribes, but also to finance Fujimori's reelection campaign generally. Montesinos claimed, for example, that at least $2 million was spent on focus groups for the 2000 election. A state-of-the-art "war room" was set up in the SIN to manage the reelection campaign to the tune of $100,000. Montesinos also described how funds were used to support expenditures on congressional campaigns, from purchasing promotional giveaways such as calendars and T-shirts to making cash payments to a selected group of Fujimori's favorite candidates, which allegedly included Martha Chávez and Luz Salgado.

When it came to holding on to power, money was no object. In his comfortably furnished office at the SIN, Montesinos stood at the helm of a network that was carefully assembled with the goal of perpetuating the regime. Montesinos and his staff organized, then routinized, the corruption. Montesinos frequently made the payoffs, counting out the cash himself. He also insisted that his clients sign receipts for all cash transactions and that the meetings be videotaped. He trusted his inner circle of staff, notably Matilde Pinchi Pinchi, to take care of the bank withdrawals and keep files of the receipts.

In testimony to congressional investigators, Montesinos underscored Fujimori's responsibility and the political ends of the system that he administered:

> I followed orders and in every case there was a "coauthorship" because he [Fujimori] gave me orders and I carried them out. . . . So I say [to Fujimori], come and let's both answer to the country. . . . I handed out money and handed out money. . . . everything was so that *el señor* was reelected president, so that the presidency would not be declared "vacant," so that he would have a parliamentary majority, so that there was control over the judiciary, of the Public Ministry, of the Constitutional Tribunal, of the Jurado Nacional de Elecciones [National Election Board], to have a harmonious relation with the armed forces, the police, with the intelligence community. All those efforts weren't for my benefit, they were for the benefit of *el señor,* and he was the president. I never went to ceremonies. I never went to embassies or cocktail parties or anyplace. I kept myself under wraps.[23]

Like many other former officials who are facing criminal charges, Montesinos has opted for a "just following orders" defense strategy. As morally unpersuasive as his position is, he makes an important point about Fujimori's culpability. No matter how much Montesinos's own personal interests were served by his maneuvers to keep the president in power, Fujimori was, undoubtedly, the beneficiary of all the machinations that went into his 2000 reelection. Corruption served various purposes in the regime, and its connection to the reelection project was primal. Even if one were to entertain Fujimori's assertions that he was unaware of the abuses throughout the course of his reelection campaign (as he currently claims), then he must be judged as incompetent and derelict in his duties. If he ordered, or had knowledge of, the crimes being committed in pursuit of the reelection and did nothing, then he is a felon.

The consensus among prosecutors and congressional investigators in Peru is that he is the latter. Fujimori currently stands accused of various counts of conspiracy, illegal enrichment, embezzlement, and treason in relation to the misappropriation and misuse of public monies.

The Culture and Choreography of Cover-Up

Incessant wrongdoing and corruption demanded a corollary institutionalization; an official culture of cover-up was required to maintain the system. Because any real investigation would threaten to expose the systemic nature of the corruption and the involvement of the highest-ranking government officials, scandals had to be stifled at all costs. The cover-ups, in turn, demanded even more control over state and society, and more corruption.

From the start of his political career as a presidential candidate in 1990, Fujimori portrayed himself as an austere, efficient, and honest technocrat. This was an attempt to differentiate himself from the outgoing president, Alan García Pérez, whose administration was dogged by charges of corruption.[24] In his inaugural speech in 1990, Fujimori identified the fight against corruption as one of the primary goals of his government. He pledged a "relentless" effort, even proposing the creation of a new presidential commission to deal with the issue. Fujimori promised that, under his government, "moralization" would cease to be mere rhetoric and become the "great lever" of a "real change."[25]

Fujimori described his appointees as cut from the same cloth as he. They were hardworking, incorruptible technocrats whom he referred to as Peru's "management team." He constantly juxtaposed his upright leadership to that of *políticos tradicionales* (traditional politicians). In Fujimori's Manichean rhetoric, rival politicians and functionaries were self-serving, deceitful, and lazy. Sanctimonious posturing and fixation on the corruption of *others* (namely, everyone outside the ranks of his officials and supporters) became a staple in the discourse of Fujimorismo, an integral element in the legitimating formula of the regime. In his speech to the nation announcing the autogolpe in 1992, Fujimori cited the corruption of officials as one of the principal reasons for closing Congress and firing the judiciary.[26]

With anticorruption defined as the hallmark of his administration, Fujimori could neither entertain criticism on the matter, nor worse yet, real scrutiny. The promised anticorruption commission never materialized. Fujimori was at his most aggressive whenever accusations of corruption surfaced, setting the tone for how other administration officials confronted allegations. Fujimori not only denied corruption; he sought to discredit his accusers by throwing charges of corruption back at them. As the armed forces contended with narcotrafficking scandals in 1996, Fujimori used his annual address to Congress to question critics as self-serving "false moralizers" (*falsos moralizadores*).[27] Similarly, in the midst of the 1997 controversy over government interference in the operation of Frecuencia Latina television, Fujimori blasted journalists for taking bribes and serving as the "shield of corruption."[28] The "accuse the accuser" gambit became part of the stock-in-trade for all administration officials.

Fujimori's hostility to critics extended to his wife, Susana Higuchi, who became the first notable whistle-blower in the regime when she accused Rosa Fujimori, the president's sister, of profiteering from the charitable donations of clothes from Japan in 1992. The controversy generated by Higuchi's charges of the *ropa donada* (donated clothes) scandal was abruptly ended by the coup of April 1992, which cut off plans for a congressional inquiry.

After an enforced sabbatical from public life, Higuchi reemerged in 1994, accusing two cabinet ministers of taking bribes.[29] Amid the new accusations, the marriage dissolved, and Fujimori dismissed his wife as emotionally unstable and as a political pawn of his rivals. Nonetheless, a majority of the Peruvian public found Higuchi's charges to be credible; an August Apoyo poll showed that 67 percent of Peruvians believed Higuchi's charges regarding ministerial corruption.[30]

A law enacted by Congress and rulings by election authorities banned Higuchi from running for the presidency and for Congress in 1995, demonstrating how far the government was willing to go to stop the former first lady from ventilating her views about what was going on behind the scenes. As evidenced in the Higuchi case, the government's most potent weapons in its war against whistle-blowers and watchdogs were its pliant congressional majority and the public officials co-opted by Montesinos. When the JNE barred Higuchi from running for political office, she accused JNE board member Rómulo Muñoz of being at the service of Montesinos. Muñoz virulently denied the accusations at the time; videotapes later confirmed that Muñoz conspired with Montesinos to fix outcomes at the JNE.

The C90-NM majority in Congress ensured that none of the demands for investigations on corruption-related issues got off the ground. During

Martha Chávez's term as president of Congress in 1995–96, a raft of brewing scandals were buried as the C90-NM majority voted down almost every opposition motion to constitute special investigative commissions. The issues buried included requests for investigations into an incident involving the discovery of a cache of drugs on the president's plane, the privatization of public enterprises, military purchases from Belarus, and influence trafficking by Minister Manuel Vara Ochoa.[31]

Víctor Joy Way, congressional president in 1996–97, carried on in the tradition of his predecessor and buried controversial issues. This included incidents related to the operation of the greed rings. Under Joy Way's leadership, the C90-NM majority rejected six motions to form congressional commissions to investigate suspected links between narcotraffickers and public officials, including the relationship between narcotics kingpin Demetrio Chávez Peñaherrera ("El Vaticano") and Montesinos. Other motions related to investigations of arms purchases were similarly shelved.[32]

With Montesinos at the commanding heights of the whole apparatus of corruption, protecting him became an absolute priority. Any threat to Montesinos was a threat to his numerous clients and co-conspirators, who feared that they would go down with him. High-ranking public officials consistently lined up to defend Montesinos whenever necessary.

During his trial in 1996, drug boss Demetrio Chávez triggered a major scandal when he alleged that he made payoffs of $50,000 a month to Montesinos in exchange for the protection of his operations. Administration officials rallied to Montesinos's defense. Among his staunch defenders was Attorney General Blanca Nélida Colán, the top-ranking justice official. Prior to any official investigation of the charges, Colán went on television to characterize the allegations as a "tall story . . . beyond belief."[33] Other officials who joined in immediately dismissing Chávez were Finance Minister Jorge Camet, president of the High Command General Nicolás Hermoza, Minister of Justice Carlos Hermoza and Interior Minister General Juan Briones.[34] Even Bishop Luis Cipriani jumped on the bandwagon to discredit the reports, deriding the media for propagating the "violence of lies."[35]

Official attempts to discredit the story notwithstanding, the Peruvian public was not convinced. Polls showed an overwhelming majority—from 88 to 97 percent of those surveyed—in favor of an investigation of Montesinos. An Apoyo poll showed a substantial 71 percent of the public convinced of Montesinos's involvement in crimes.[36] As in so many other instances during the Fujimori regime, public opinion in this case was sim-

ply ignored. The U.S. State Department took considerable pressure off
the government when it issued a statement saying there was no proof
that Peruvian officials had links to narcotrafficking.[37] In an appearance
before Congress to answer questions on the Montesinos matter, the president of the Council of Ministers, Adolfo Pandolfi, dismissed the allegations, refusing to answer legislators' questions on the grounds that
Montesinos's specific duties in the SIN were a secret.[38]

Government officials stonewalled whenever questions about Montesinos surfaced. In April 1997, a Channel 2 television report revealed that
Montesinos's income tax declarations showed income well in excess of
the scales set for public servants. The report triggered an official congressional question period with a mandatory appearance of the president of
Council of Ministers, Adolfo Pandolfi. Pandolfi refused to answer any
of the queries regarding Montesinos's income. He covered every base in
justifying the secrecy—citing the confidential status of tax returns; the
rules stipulating confidentiality for employees of the intelligence service;
and even the professional secrecy accorded lawyers, priests, and physi-
cians.[39] In the same session, Pandolfi closed the book on the investigation
into more than one million dollars in irregular financial transactions between the army and insurance company Popular y Porvenir, owned by
the president's friend Augusto Miyagusuku.

As he did with Congress, Montesinos programmed the justice system
to ensure that the myriad scandals brought to light by the independent
news media would never culminate in prosecutions. After the flurry of
controversy over Montesinos's income and Pandolfi's congressional appearance, Attorney General Miguel Aljovín closed the legal investigation
of the matter on the ground that no proof of a crime existed.[40] After
the fall of the Fujimori government, Aljovín was arrested, as was former
attorney general Colán for being part of Montesinos's "mafia" in the
judicial branch.

Prior to the regime's breakdown in September 2000, Fujimori rarely
hesitated in his defense of Montesinos.[41] He regularly lauded his accomplishments as an architect of the government's successes in counterinsurgency and counternarcotics. In a bizarre television interview in April
1999, Fujimori and Montesinos appeared together, even sporting similar
suits and ties. They reminisced about their roles in planning the spectacular rescue mission that freed hostages held by Marxist guerrillas at the
Japanese ambassador's residence in Lima in April 1997. Apart from the
staged camaraderie, the interview was notable for Montesinos's admission that he had lived full time at the SIN headquarters for nine years,

working exclusively for the government. That revelation did not appear to bother Fujimori, even though the statement flew in the face of Pandolfi's earlier references to Montesinos's law practice as a possible source of his unexplained income.[42]

Throughout the life of the administration, Fujimori chose to ignore the public's profound unease about the role of Montesinos and the ever present speculation about his involvement in corruption. While the government was successful in shutting down official inquiries that threatened Montesinos and armed forces officials, the independent print media—the newspapers *La República* and *Liberación* and the newsmagazine *Caretas*—kept up the scrutiny. As much as the administration denied corruption, the subject was never removed from public view. The regime cranked out the cover-ups, but as opinion polls frequently showed, public cynicism never ceased. What was missing was a "smoking gun"—incontrovertible proof—to confirm the suspicions. That finally came in September 2000 with the leak of the video showing Vladimiro Montesinos bribing Congressman-elect Alberto Kouri. Scores of other videotapes eventually followed, revealing the depth of official corruption and deceit.

Explaining Corruption: When Smart People Do Illicit Things

In a candid admission, Montesinos observed that he had "crossed the porous border from legality into illegality" while at the helm of the SIN. But his willingness to concede to illegal conduct came with a clear insistence that he was one of many who were guilty of crimes. Indeed, Montesinos openly mocked the denials of wrongdoing by key figures such as Congresswoman Martha Chávez. Just by coming to the SIN to discuss political machinations and plan the reelection, Montesinos argued, government officials knowingly broke the law.

Montesinos's insistent claim that everyone involved was cognizant of breaking the law leads us back to the question of why they did it. Why did so many savvy professionals and executives (that is, people who should have known better) become enmeshed in the greed rings and the political corruption? Why did the protagonists and the participants believe that they could get away with it indefinitely, especially when other countries in the region were making demonstrable headway in prosecuting official wrongdoing?

Many of the individuals involved in these cases still await trial and many maintain their innocence. So far, we have few firsthand explanations of the rationales that motivated individuals to participate. Montesinos has offered little insight into his own motives, except to claim that keeping Fujimori in power served the greater goals of combating terrorism and political instability. In the absence of more detailed information about the motivations of individual participants, any attempt to grapple with the issues raised above is, necessarily, tentative and speculative. Nonetheless, at least some elements of broader explanation can be pieced together from relevant facts and the insights provided by the comparative research on corruption.

In his model of political corruption in Latin America, Luigi Manzetti (2000) identifies corruption as an intersection between "willingness" and "opportunity." In the case of Peru, the enormous, unchecked powers accrued by the Fujimori administration and the unscrupulousness of those in power opened up a landscape full of opportunities to engage in corrupt practices. Willingness, according to Manzetti, is rooted in three behavioral imperatives: personal greed, power seeking, and a "get it while you can" attitude. So why was the "willingness" to engage in corrupt practices so widespread during the Fujimori era?

Economic stress, uncertainty, and the precariousness of the labor market affected Peruvians from all social strata during the 1990s, including the middle and upper class. Notwithstanding the success of Fujimori's neoliberal economic reforms in reducing hyperinflation and restarting economic growth, the business climate and the job market remained problematic throughout the period. Anxiety about the economy was a pervasive fact of life even in the most comfortable neighborhoods of Lima during the 1990s and no doubt added to the temptations offered up by Montesinos.

For many media outlets, suffering from economic woes, corruption was a godsend. Among the most indebted and mismanaged businesses in Peru were television stations. Station owners were up to their ears in debt, estimated to be as much as $150 million in 1999.[43] Adding to the financial headaches were legal problems as nearly every station found itself embroiled in bitter disputes between stockholders contesting for control. The combined legal and financial problems made television station owners open to transacting with Montesinos. As the videotapes revealed, Montesinos not only proffered direct cash payments to television owners, but also offered help in the adjudication of legal cases and in loan negotiations with banks.

In the case of Congress, it was no secret that legislative seats were highly sought after prizes—not just as sources of status and power, but also for the lucrative, guaranteed five-year income, and the other benefits (such as travel) that attached to the job. Given the debilitated state of parties and electoral vehicles, congressional candidates were frequently recruited from the ranks of those with political ambitions, but with the understanding that they foot their own campaign bills. These political entrepreneurs accepted the costs as an investment made with the hope of recouping the loss once in Congress. For some legislators, the decision to run for Congress was fueled more by economics than by politics. In his study of corruption in Italy, Alessandro Pizzorno noted the phenomenon of the emergence of the businessman-politician—an individual, who views politics as a business, a means to acquire wealth. Pizzorno observed that such actors are more likely to surface in situations in which party organizations and ideological attachments are weak—a situation that prevailed in Peru in the 1990s.[44]

For a good number of legislators, the advantages of doing business with Montesinos seemed to outweigh the risks. In his testimony to congressional legislators, Montesinos recounted providing living expenses and car and apartment purchases to those he recruited. He also intervened on behalf of legislators and their family members in legal matters. Legislators also sought compensation from Montesinos for their campaign expenses. In the now famous video with Alberto Kouri, Montesinos chided Kouri for excessive campaign expenses as he counted out Kouri's payoff. Montesinos recalled one reimbursement of $40,000 for campaign expenses to another *tránsfuga* legislator. Montesinos claimed payments of $3,000 per month were made to minister and congressman Joy Way, who explained that he used the money for his "journalists" (implying that he used the cash to influence reporters).

Why were greed and ambition not tempered by fear that the transgressions might be revealed and even eventually prosecuted? Once again, Pizzorno's work on Italy is suggestive of the dynamics of how such fear is overcome as a system of corruption develops and matures. According to Pizzorno, the display of arbitrary power is a key element in the system; those who would corrupt others need to display their ability to act with impunity. By doing so, they not only demonstrate their own power (and thus make potential clients fearful of them), but also show that the risks of participating in the system are minimal. The more the laws are flaunted without any apparent costs, the more legitimate or acceptable participation in the system becomes. As the system becomes entrenched, it generates its own norms for those inside that system. Moreover, as della Porta and Vannucci (1999) describe, an atmosphere of inevitability can develop—that is, corruption appears to be a permanent, inescapable fact of life.

The Fujimori administration was masterful in projecting and using its arbitrary power. Every denial and every crime that was covered up demonstrated how unbeatable the regime was, just as the obsession with reelection showed the regime's dedication to reproducing itself. Montesinos may have "kept himself under wraps," as he put it, but the cult of secrecy that surrounded him also reinforced the image of sinister, uncontrolled power. The secrecy that he cultivated only fed the public's fear of and fascination with him. Thus, a trip to the SIN headquarters to talk with Montesinos was an exciting confirmation of celebrity and status for some visitors. For others, it must have been unsettling and, in all likelihood, enormously intimidating.

Whether or not Montesinos believed his own pronouncements about Peru's political future, the videos show him as a tireless political operative, someone who constantly impressed upon visitors that the regime would continue in power. In conversations leading up to the 2000 election, Montesinos underscored that there was no alternative to a Fujimori victory. In discussing the election with businessman Dionisio Romero in June 1999, Montesinos flatly stated: "We are going to win anyway. In other words, it's a point of no return."[45] Montesinos had even begun to plan for the 2005 presidential election, sounding out both economist Carlos Boloña and Callao mayor Alex Kouri on the possibility of becoming the handpicked successor to Fujimori. Montesinos clearly aspired to continuing on at the center of the system, with or without Fujimori at the helm.

With no end of the regime in sight and no accountability in evidence, many visitors to the SIN decided to take advantage of the considerable privileges and perks offered up by Montesinos. As the reelection juggernaut rolled on from 1995 through 2000, it was hard to imagine that anything lie ahead but more of the same.

Clearing Corruption's Remains

It was no small irony that an immoral economy in Peru was burgeoning even as the international community mobilized for a global program to combat corruption. Both the World Bank and the Inter-American Development Bank crafted new anticorruption programs in the mid-1990s, as did the United States Agency for International Development (USAID). In one of the many deceitful moments of his tenure, President Fujimori inaugurated a special international meeting on corruption that was organized by the World Bank in Lima in September 1997.

The hypocrisy and impunity came to end with the collapse of the regime in 2000. But the legacy of the era lives on, burdening subsequent governments with the costly and enervating process of documenting the crimes and meting out justice. The interim government led by President Valetín Paniagua (2000–2001) and the subsequent government of President Alejandro Toledo (2001–present) wrestled with the expensive and time-consuming task.

The mind-boggling tangle of congressional and judicial investigations into the hundreds of crimes committed by hundreds of individuals remains ongoing, with no legal closure in sight. To date, Montesinos has been tried and convicted on a number of lesser crimes, including bribing media executives. His combined sentences so far amount to fifteen years in jail. If convicted on drug- or arms-trafficking charges, Montesinos would face decades in prison. Like Montesinos, many other former luminaries are serving sentences, including former attorney general Colán, former army commander General Hermoza and former congressman Joy Way. Scores of criminal charges have been filed against Fujimori in Peru's courts. The charges include conspiracy and embezzlement along with twenty-five counts of homicide stemming from his alleged role in approving the operations of the clandestine death squad the Grupo Colina (Colina Group).

As the legal process grinds on, the public has tired of corruption investigations. In a nationwide Apoyo poll taken in February 2002, 47 percent of respondents identified investigations of the Fujimori-Montesinos government as being the top priority of the Toledo administration. In the same poll, only 2 percent agreed that the investigations should be prioritized; 49 percent listed investment and employment as the objectives that should be pursued by Toledo.[46] For the Toledo administration, the task of dealing definitely with Peru's past has been complicated by the public's desire for substantive new achievements, particularly in alleviating Peru's economic problems. Moreover, public confidence in Toledo progressively collapsed as his own administration became mired in charges of corruption and incompetence. To the deep disappointment of many Peruvians, President Toledo lost the moral high ground and failed to create a new climate of accountability in the post-Fujimori era.

As Peruvians continued to be dogged by corruption from the past and the present, the international community can benefit by reflecting on the track record of the Fujimori administration and what it reveals about the dynamics of corruption. Recent World Bank–sponsored research on the problem of corruption has produced important insights into the problems of "state capture"—the corruption of public officials by representatives of private sector firms seeking special privileges from governments.[47] While state capture does undoubtedly constitute one of the important dimensions of the problem of corruption, the Fujimori record highlights another equally important locus—the misappropriation of state resources by public officials for use in financing political campaigns. Millions of dollars were routed clandestinely to the SIN to underwrite Fujimori's political campaigns and those of his allies. Fujimori and Montesinos looted the state in pursuit of political ends. The corruption that served political ends went hand in had with the practices that served the ends of personal greed. In Peru, public officials, unrestrained by any of the normal mechanisms of accountability, became predators, corrupting the state and society in the process.

The political corruption in Peru is not unique in the recent annals of Latin America. Campaign finance scandals dogged the presidencies of Ernesto Samper in Colombia, Jamil Mahuad in Ecuador, and Carlos Salinas in Mexico.[48] All this suggests that, as intractable as the issue may appear to be, campaign finance reform needs to move to the top of the list of priorities in internationally sponsored battles against corruption in the developing world.

Finally, to close the chapter on corruption in Peru and advance the anticorruption cause throughout the region, Fujimori must be held accountable for his actions and what happened under his watch in Peru. Both Peruvians and the international community have a role to play in demanding a definitive accounting. Human rights groups in Peru have joined with international organizations and the Peruvian government in a campaign demanding that the Japanese government extradite Fujimori to Peru to stand trial. In the meantime, the evidence that corruption reached a historic zenith in Peru under Fujimori continues to accumulate, making the ex-president's denials of responsibility, issued comfortably from Tokyo, seem ever more ludicrous.

NOTES

1. The notion of moral economy is taken from Scott 1976.
2. In his analysis of PRI-led corruption in Mexico, Alan Knight (1996, 231)

noted that corruption was "less a sickly deviation from Weberian health, than the cartilage and collagen which holds a sprawling body politic together."

3. Peru's Truth and Reconciliation Commission noted the "functional relationship" between political power and criminality during the Fujimori government and how the relationship paved the way for human rights abuses and corruption. See Comisión de la Verdad y Reconciliación 2003, 59.

4. For summary reports on the findings of these and other investigative commissions, see Congreso de la República, *Diario de Debates,* Segunda legislatura ordinaria del 2001, 20 sesión, Viernes 28 de junio de 2002, http://www.con greso.gob.pe.

5. *La República,* June 4, 2003.

6. The extradition petition was based on Fujimori's alleged involvement in the "crimes against humanity," including homicide. It is alleged that Fujimori authorized the operation of a clandestine security force, the Grupo Colina, which committed crimes during his presidency. Corruption charges were not included in the original petition, but may be added on.

7. The classic definition of corruption was formulated by Joseph Nye (1967) as "behavior which deviates from the formal duties of a public role (elective or appointive) because of private-regarding (personal, close family, private clique) wealth or status gains."

8. *La República,* June 13, 2001.

9. Ibid.

10. *La República,* June 14, 2001.

11. For the full report, see Congreso de la República, Comisión Investigadora sobre la actuación, el origen, movimiento y destino de los recursos financieros de Vladimiro Montesinos y su evidente relación con el Ex-Presidente Alberto Fujimori Fujimori 2002, Informe Final, http://www.gwu.edu/nsarchiv/NSAEBB/ NSAEBB72/final.doc.

12. The narcotrafficking charges carry a penalty of twenty-five years or more in prison. Special Prosecutor Luis Valdivia recently confirmed that investigations have turned up enough evidence to indict Montesinos in at least two separate cases. In both cases, it is alleged that Montesinos demanded protection money from traffickers. See EFE World News Services, July 24, 2003. For a review of the evidence linking Montesinos to drug trafficking, see Washington Office on Latin America, "Drug War Paradoxes: The U.S. Government and Peru's Vladimiro Montesinos," *Drug War Monitor,* July, 2004.

13. EFE World News Services, August 9, 2003.

14. *La República,* September 11, 2003. Fearing that the money was illicit, Higuchi turned over the cash to a military official in the palace. The official said he later returned the money to Fujimori, who seemed untroubled by the incident. According to the official, Fujimori did not press him for any paperwork recording the hand-off of the money.

15. *La República,* October 19, 2003.

16. EFE World News Services, October 24, 2003.

17. *El Comercio,* October 3, 2004.

18. For further discussion of media corruption in this period, see Conaghan 2002.

19. "La Planilla Negra," *Caretas,* January 17, 2002.

20. For the full report by the congressional committee that discovered these facts, see Congreso de la República, Comisión Permanente del Congreso de la República, Subcomisión de la Denuncia Constitucional Número 6. 2002. Informe Final, January 14.

21. Disaggregated figures on the transfers were appended in the final report of the Subcomisión Investigadora de la Denuncia Constitucional Número 6, Comisión Permanente del Congreso de La República, January 14, 2002.

22. EFE World News Services, October 24, 2003

23. For Montesinos's testimony, see the transcript of Congreso de la República, Primera Legislatura Ordinaria de 2001, Subcomisión de la Comisión Permanente del Congreso de la República, Encargada de Investigar La Denuncia Constitucional Número 06, Presentada Contra La Congresista Martha Chávez Cossió de Ocampo y Otros por supuesto elito de receptación y otros en agravio del estado, December 20, 2001.

24. After his tenure as president, Alan García faced corruption charges, but was never prosecuted. Because of the statute of limitations, the charges expired while García was in exile in Paris after the 1992 coup.

25. The quotations are taken from the full text of the inaugural speech, "Mensaje del Presidente Alberto Fujimori," published in *La Crónica,* July 30, 1990.

26. For the text of the speech, see "Mensaje a la Nación del Presidente del Perú, Ingeniero Alberto Fujimori Fujimori, el 5 de abril de 1992," http://www .congreso.gob.pe/museo/mensajes/Mensaje-1992-91.pdf.

27. "Mensaje de Realidades y Futuro," *El Peruano,* July 30, 1996.

28. Fujimori's attack came during his speech at a Lima meeting of the OAS, eliciting whistles and howls from the gathered journalists. The speech was reported in *El Peruano,* June 2, 1997.

29. Congressional investigations confirmed that Higuchi was effectively kidnapped and imprisoned at SIN headquarters for a time after her first whistle-blowing incident. Xinhua News Agency, October 23, 2003.

30. *La República,* August 18, 1994.

31. *La República,* March 19, 1999.

32. *La República,* March 19, 1999.

33. *La República,* August 19, 1996.

34. *Resumen Semanal,* no. 833, August 14–20, 1996.

35. *La República,* August 26,1996.

36. *Resumen Semanal,* no. 877, September 11–17, 1996.

37. *Gestión,* August 19, 1996.

38. *La República,* September 6, 1996.

39. *La República,* May 9, 1997.

40. *Caretas,* June 5, 1997.

41. During the 1996 narcotrafficking episode, Fujimori was somewhat guarded in his remarks on Montesinos, noting that he could not assume the defense of Montesinos because he was not an attorney and that he would not "put his hands in fire" for anyone other than his children (*La República,* September 2, 1996). That led to considerable speculation in the press that Fujimori might be

preparing to distance himself from his advisor. But Montesinos's high-profile presence at an October meeting in the presidential palace with U.S. drug czar Barry McCaffrey appeared to reconfirm his standing in the administration.

42. For further analysis of the interview, see "Película del sordo y el sapo," *Caretas*, April 19, 1999, 16; Fernando Rospigliosi, "Limpieza técnica," *Caretas*, April 29, 1999, 18.

43. "Pressure on the Press," *Peru Monitor* 1 (July–August) 2000, 52–68.

44. The extensive work by Donatella della Porta and Alberto Vannucci (1999) on corruption in Italy draws on the concepts laid out by Alessandro Pizzorno.

45. For the entire transcript of the conversation, see Congreso de la República, Segunda Legislatura Ordinario de 2000, "Transcripción de los videos números 1574 y 1575. Reunión del Señor Vladimiro Montesinos Torres con Dionisio Romero Seminario, El General EP Saucedo Sánchez, General PNP Fernando Dianderas Ottone, Almirante Ibárcena Amico, General EP Villanueva Ruesta y General EP Bello Vásquez, 14 de junio de 1999.

46. *El Comercio*, February 18, 2002.

47. Research on state capture can be found on the Web site of the World Bank Institute. For an example, see Hellman, Jones, and Kaufman 2000.

48. Weyland (1998) has posited a relationship between the rise of neopopulist politicians and corruption.

SIX

Public Opinion, Market Reforms, and Democracy in Fujimori's Peru

JULIO F. CARRIÓN

A defining feature of the regime of Alberto Fujimori was its sustained level of approval in public opinion polls.[1] Although this support declined after 1997, it remained significantly high (in comparison with that for previous administrations) despite Fujimori's frequent and egregious abuses of power. More surprisingly, even after the public became highly critical of Fujimori's economic policy, the annual average approval rating during his second term never dropped below 40 percent. As Fujimori inaugurated his controversial third term in the wake of an electoral process marred by accusations of fraud and heavy-handed tactics, he still enjoyed a popularity rating of above 45 percent.[2] Fujimori's remarkable performance in opinion polls is even more surprising when one considers that in terms of employment and income levels, Peruvians were no better off in 2000 than in 1990. It is true that inflation was under control by 1995, but neither employment nor average income showed a dramatic recovery during the 1990s. In 2000, the unemployment rate in metropolitan Lima was 7.9 percent, only slightly better than the 8.3 percent registered in 1990 (INEI 2001a). Moreover, the average blue-collar salary only increased by a total of 5 percent between 1990 and March 2000 (INEI 2001b). Given Fujimori's penchant for authoritarianism and his rather

For their thoughtful comments and suggestions, I would like to thank Francisco Durand, Charles Kenney, Carol Wise, and the anonymous reviewers.

weak record in terms of job creation and income improvement, one wonders why almost up to the very end the public was so fond of this regime. This is one of the questions that I seek to answer in this chapter.

Another question to be asked here is related to the relationship between market reforms and presidential popularity. The Peruvian public reacted particularly well to an extremely harsh fiscal shock implemented during Fujimori's first month in office. Even though the social effects of this shock were traumatic (income and employment fell steadily in the 1990–93 period), Peru was able to avoid the deep social upheaval that plagued other Latin American nations when milder versions of market reforms were attempted. Despite the economic shock, Fujimori's popularity rose in 1990 and, after a brief decline in 1991, continued to grow in the wake of Peru's "liberal revolution" and the subsequent April 1992 autogolpe.[3]

There is no doubt that Fujimori made the most of his significant popular approval. Making virtue of necessity and given his lack of an organized and solid political party, he used public opinion polls to fight his opponents in Congress and gain political momentum. Confronted with figures that clearly indicated public approval for the president's overall performance in office, the opposition had a difficult time devising an effective strategy. In the context in which politics was becoming more media oriented (in part because of the demise of traditional parties), Fujimori's relative success in opinion polls served him particularly well. This was evident in the wake of his autogolpe. Strong public support for this authoritarian act enabled Fujimori to resort to elections to calm international concerns and legitimize his rule.

It would be erroneous, however, to conclude that Fujimori was completely in step with the public mood. Public opinion was in many instances highly critical of his actions or policies. For instance, although the public was quite willing to grant him significant freedom in the fight against domestic insurgency and even to accept some violations of due process for those accused of terrorism, Peruvians were not willing to support egregious human rights violations. In a similar vein, citizens rejected some of his economic policies regardless of their support for his overall performance in office. In almost all instances in which Fujimori found himself on the opposite side of public opinion, he chose to disregard it. Alberto Fujimori used public opinion to legitimize his authoritarian project; he was not bound by it.

Fujimori's sustained popularity raises some interesting questions about the relationship between public opinion, market reforms, and democracy in Peru. Why did the public tolerate a regime that systemically violated democratic standards? Why did the public initially support a radical program of market reforms even though these reforms were generating negative consequences in terms of income and employment generation? Why did the public remain generally supportive of Fujimori's performance in office even after it had become quite critical of his economic policy? What was the role of this continued public support in the evolution of the electoral authoritarian project? In what follows, I address these questions by examining Peru's public opinion concerning four central themes: Fujimori's overall performance in office, domestic insurgency and military abuses, market reforms, and the 2000 reelection effort.[4] In the concluding section I reflect on the role that public opinion played during the Fujimori regime.

Mass Support for Fujimori

As mentioned at the outset, Fujimori remained a relatively popular president for the majority of his ten years in office. The popularity he enjoyed during his first administration (1990–95) was particularly impressive, especially by Peruvian standards. His average approval rating during his first term reached 61.1 percent, significantly higher than Fernando Belaúnde Terry's 37.9 percent and Alan García Pérez's 52.3 percent.[5] Although Fujimori's popularity dropped during his second administration, he still finished it with approval ratings hovering around 50 percent (Figure 1).[6]

One cannot overstate the political significance of this strong popular support. Fujimori was elected president in 1990 without a majority in Congress. After a brief interlude in which he was willing to build alliances with other political forces in order to achieve a working majority in Congress, he ultimately decided to govern alone. Given his lack of a solid political organization, his most important political capital was his standing in public opinion polls. As Figure 1 shows, his popularity rating was not particularly high during the first 18 months of his 1990–95 administration and was, in fact, lower than both Belaúnde's and García's at similar points in their administrations. However, after a year and a half in office Fujimori saw his approval rating begin to climb. His popularity jumped from 32 to 54 percent between September and October 1991 and climbed steadily to reach 60 percent in December of that year.

Somewhat surprisingly, the Fujigolpe—as his April 5, 1992, decision

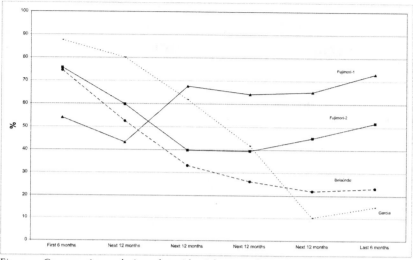

Figure 1 Comparative evolution of presidential approval ratings, 1980–2000
SOURCE: Apoyo; Datum.

to rule by decree was soon labeled—cemented Fujimori's popularity among the public (his approval rating surged from 53 to 81 percent). More significantly, his support continued to remain strong for a number of months after the coup; approval ratings did not fall below 60 percent until May 1996 (with the sole exception of February 1994 when it dipped to 58 percent). Breaking with the pattern set by the two preceding presidents, Fujimori ended his first administration more popular than when he started. In the last six months of his first term, his average popularity was twenty points *higher* than what it had been during his first six months in office.

What was really notable was Fujimori's ability to expand his political base of support. When he took office in July 1990, the bulk of his votes came from the provinces and the lower classes (Degregori and Grompone 1991). This controversial president managed to attract political support from all social classes by the end of his first term, a significant political accomplishment. In 1995, Fujimori's approval rating among the upper class was virtually identical to the one he enjoyed among the very poor.[7] Over time, however, this coalition dissolved as the upper and middle classes turned against him. Up to 1998, support for Fujimori was evenly distributed among all social classes. In the last two years of his second administration, however, the gap between support from the very poor and support from the upper-middle classes widened (see Figure 2). Fuji-

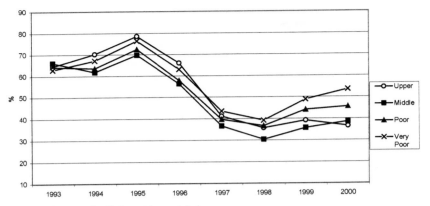

Figure 2 Support for Fujimori by social class, 1993–2000
SOURCE: Apoyo.

mori's average approval rating among the very poor in 2000 was 17 points higher than his rating among the upper class (53 and 36 percent, respectively).

Fujimori's success in attracting an initially reticent upper and middle class was clearly rooted in his embrace of market reforms and later cemented by his successful handling of domestic insurgency. Influential newspapers such as *El Comercio* and *Expreso,* with a mostly middle- and upper-class readership, strongly supported Fujimori's market reforms (Carrión 1998). It is interesting to note that this pattern of gaining the support of an initially reluctant upper and middle class was also identified in another country that adopted a similarly radical program of market reforms. In Argentina, as Levitsky (2000) shows, a significant faction of the upper- and middle-class voters rallied in support of Carlos Menem mostly out of support for his economic program.

After the adoption of his market reforms, Fujimori lost the support of his initial center-left backers (most notably the Alianza Popular Revolucionaria Americana [American Popular Revolutionary Alliance (APRA)]) but gained the favor of his conservative opponents (Cotler 1994). This upper-class support made it easier for him to establish stronger ties with the business community and its representatives (Durand 2003), thus facilitating the implementation of his economic program. It also allowed him to avoid a situation of political polarization—like the one that affected Venezuela in 2003—that could have damaged his standing with the international community. To cater to this constituency, Fujimori created the party Nueva Mayoría (New Majority) in 1992, to run in alliance with his old electoral vehicle Cambio 90 (Change 90). Fujimori's ability to attract support from all segments of Peruvian society had significant political consequences for the evolution of the regime after the 1992 coup. By gaining the support of the middle and upper classes, Fujimori expanded his electoral coalition and prevented the emergence of any credible electoral challenges to his rule. He could thus afford to adhere to electoral politics even while securing authoritarian control of Peru's political institutions.

What was the key to Fujimori's continued support in public opinion polls? Although there is probably no single factor that can explain his high approval level, two stand out as salient. First of all, the public was very grateful for Fujimori's defeat of hyperinflation in the early 1990s. High inflation was a problem during most of the 1980s, and it reached the staggering annual rate of 7,649 percent in 1990. By 1994, the annual inflation rate had fallen to 15 percent. Second, the public was also very supportive of Fujimori's antiterror policies, especially after the capture of Abimael Guzmán, the leader of Shining Path (Sendero Luminoso). In January 1992, only 43 percent of the public approved of Fujimori's antiterror policies, but by December of that year, one month after the capture of Guzmán, approval for this policy had climbed to 66 percent. People were yearning for order and security after a decade of increasing political violence. In the aftermath of the capture and the subsequent reduction of political violence in Peru, mass support for Fujimori's antiterror policy skyrocketed. In December 1993, eight out of ten Lima residents approved of this policy. Four years later, in December 1997 (the last month Apoyo asked this question), approval for Fujimori's antiterror policy was still high, reaching up to 66 percent.

Additional survey data seem to confirm that Fujimori's support was largely driven by his successes in controlling inflation and domestic insurgency. Table 1 provides information on how people evaluated Fujimori's performance in specific issue domains. Every July for most of the decade, Apoyo asked Lima residents if, at the end of another year of Fujimori in office, the situation had got better, had got worse, or was about the same in a number of issue areas. A selection of the questions that were consistently asked throughout the decade is presented in this table.

This table shows that the public consistently gave Fujimori high marks for his performance in controlling domestic terrorism. Even after 1995, when domestic insurgency was not as much of a problem as it had been

Table 1 Evaluation of Fujimori's performance in selected issue areas (percentage reporting improvement)

At the end of	Employ- ment	Control of Inflation	Control of Terrorism	Public Education	Public Health	Freedom of Expression	Human Rights
Third year (1993)	8	49	81	28	20	21	23
Fourth year (1994)	16	64	90	41	29	30	26
Fifth year (1995)	27	62	84	46	42	32	33
Sixth year (1996)	13	43	73	36	33	28	31
Seventh year (1997)	7	27	67	34	27	10	13
Eighth year (1998)	7	20	63	31	27	15	16
Ninth year (1999)	6	28	84	40	42	18	28
Tenth year (2000)	6	23	77	31	39	16	22

SOURCE: Apoyo.

at the beginning of the decade, approval for Fujimori's performance in this area remained high. Similarly, at least until 1995, Lima residents gave Fujimori the credit for controlling inflation. After this year Fujimori was, as Weyland (2000) argues, a victim of his own success. Between 1996 and 2000, the percentage of people declaring that control of inflation had improved declined precipitously. Given that inflation was very low after 1995, it is clear that once inflation lost its political salience, the public stopped crediting Fujimori for keeping it low. The public did not forget his success in fighting Shining Path; they did tend to forget his equal success in keeping inflation under control.

The same table shows that Lima residents were highly critical of Fujimori's performance in other issue domains. They were very unhappy with his performance in the area of job creation; between 1997 and 2000, less than 8 percent of those polled declared that the job situation had improved in relation to the previous year. Similarly, criticisms in the area of human rights were high. More often than not, less than a third of those surveyed were willing to state that things had got better in the areas of freedom of expression and human rights. Evaluations of Fujimori's performance in public health and education were not as negative as the assessments of human rights, but yet were not as favorable as the evaluations of terrorism control.

Clearly, Fujimori drew significant political capital from his success in fighting domestic insurgency and, until 1995, keeping inflation at bay. Thus, in a somewhat ironic turn of events, the decision by Shining Path and the Movimiento Revolucionario Túpac Amaru (Tupac Amaru Revolutionary Movement [MRTA]) to take up arms against the Peruvian state ended up solidifying public support for the very government that they wanted to overthrow. Moreover, the domestic threat gave Fujimori the necessary political cover to withstand public disapproval in other issue domains. The degree to which people rewarded Fujimori for his successes in controlling domestic insurgency should not be underestimated. Even after he left office, Peruvians remained very grateful to Fujimori on this particular account. A poll conducted in December 2000, one month after he abandoned office, asked: "Twenty years from now, when we talk about Fujimori, what will we remember?" More than half (56 percent) said "the defeat of terrorism," and only 19 percent of the respondents mentioned "corruption/graft."[8] Recent studies (Arce 2003; Kelly 2003) confirm that Fujimori's public approval was significantly affected by the levels of political violence, Fujimori's successes in fighting Shining Path, or both.[9]

Domestic Insurgency and Military Abuses

In May 1980, a Maoist faction of the Peruvian Communist Party, better known as Sendero Luminoso (Shining Path) decided to take up arms against the Peruvian state.[10] A couple of years later, the MRTA, a Guevarist group, decided to follow suit. In its efforts to polarize Peruvian society, Shining Path carried out indiscriminate attacks against labor and community leaders who refused to follow their revolutionary call to arms, as well as against peasant communities that refused to join the armed struggle. Most Peruvians strongly rejected these actions. Unfortunately for the health of Peruvian democracy, the intensity of this rejection led the public to support policies that undermined judicial due process. For instance, the public was willing to accept anonymous and military tribunals to try terrorism cases. In May 1992, in the wake of the auto-golpe and in the absence of a functioning congress, Fujimori issued Decree (Decreto-Ley) Number 25475, also known as the Antiterrorist Law. One of its provisos was the establishment of anonymous tribunals to judge those accused of terrorism. Public support for the establishment of these tribunals was very strong: three-quarters of those interviewed that month agreed with the idea that anonymous judges should judge those accused of terrorist activities and only 18 percent rejected it (7 percent had no opinion). Four years later, a majority (51.4 percent) still believed that they should not be eliminated, according to a poll conducted in December 1996. Even after these tribunals were abolished, there was a lingering sentiment among Peruvians that they had been necessary in the fight against domestic insurgency, as a poll taken in October 1997 revealed. According to this poll, 67 percent believed that the anonymous tribunals had been necessary, while only 22 percent thought otherwise (11 percent had no opinion). Moreover, the same poll showed that the public had a very positive evaluation of the judges' performance: 58 percent declared that the performance (*gestión*) of the anonymous judges had been "positive" while only 22 percent declared otherwise.

The public was also strongly in favor of using military courts to try those accused of domestic terrorism. A June 1999 poll revealed that more than half the respondents (58 percent) supported the use of military courts, while only 32 percent preferred civilian courts (10 percent had no opinion).

It should be noted that Peru's populace did not blindly support all human rights violations. Lima residents, for instance, rejected the lenient treatment of those in the military accused of being involved in the infa-

mous La Cantuta case.[11] In February 1994, Congress passed a bill assign-
ing the investigation of this case to a military tribunal. A poll conducted
that month showed that 68 percent of the respondents believed that the
bill was unconstitutional. As soon as this law was passed, the War Room
of the Supreme Council of Military Justice found the accused guilty in a
record-breaking trial that lasted less than three days. In June 1995, when
the regime enacted a blanket amnesty law for these and other military
personnel convicted of human rights violations, the public reacted
strongly in opposition. Among those familiar with the amnesty law, 75
percent rejected it, while only 20 percent approved (5 percent had no
opinion).

These data suggest that despite significant public support for a strong-
arm approach to domestic terrorism (which encouraged Fujimori to por-
tray those who opposed his policies as being virtual terrorist accomplices), the public was not willing to condone egregious human rights
violations, or support a lenient treatment of military personnel accused
of committing these violations. Unfortunately, the regime paid little heed
to these demands for greater accountability in the fight against Shining
Path.

Public Opinion and Market Reforms

The Fujimori administration implemented what is considered one of the
most drastic economic restructuring programs in Latin America (Iguíñiz
1998; Wise 2003b). The breadth and depth of the program was indeed
impressive. It started with a concerted effort to end hyperinflation by
radically cutting state spending, unifying multitiered exchange rates, re-
voking state subsidies, lifting price controls, and adopting a floating-exchange-rate system (Wise 2003b). After the appointment of Carlos
Boloña as minister of economy and finance, Fujimori proceeded to
deepen market reforms. State enterprises began to be privatized, trade
laws were liberalized, protective labor laws were abolished, and state
spending was further curtailed (Boloña 1996). These were painful economic measures and, as Figure 3 clearly shows, had an immediate negative impact on employment and income levels. Despite the harshness of
the initial "shock" program, support for Fujimori did not decline in
1990. In fact, his popularity rating and approval for his economic policy
were, in December of 1990, 15 and 9 points higher respectively than they
were in August of that year. However, Fujimori's poll numbers began to

slip as employment and income levels continued to drop in 1991. By September 1991, less than a third of those polled declared support for either his overall performance in office or his economic policy. For reasons that will be explained next, public approval for Fujimori and his economic program then took a turn and began to climb, finally peaking in 1995 at above 60 percent.

The October 1991 Apoyo poll revealed a twenty-two-point bump in Fujimori's popularity. This unprecedented one-month surge could only be explained as the result of two developments. One was the introduction of stringent antiterror legislation. The public may have perceived that Fujimori was being more "tough" against domestic terrorism than the previous administrations. The other event was Peru's reinsertion into the international financial community. Early in September, the Inter-American Development Bank had granted Peru a loan for $425 million, Peru's first multilateral credit in five years. Some days later, the International Monetary Fund (IMF) approved Fujimori's stabilization program, thus ending the country's "ineligibility" status (Bowen 2000). Finally, a few days after receiving the IMF seal of approval, Peru rescheduled its entire $6.6 billion foreign debt with the Paris Club (Bowen 2000). These actions constituted clear indications that Fujimori's market reforms were received favorably by the international community. Perhaps the public concluded that this international acceptance would signal greater foreign investment and thus increased employment. Whatever the reasons, Fujimori's rise in the polls continued and was later cemented in the aftermath of the Fujigolpe.

However, as the advertised benefits of market reforms failed to materialize, public support for Fujimori's economic program plummeted. In 1999, the annual average approval for the economic policy was almost three times lower than it was in 1995 (23 and 61 percent, respectively).

This pattern of initial support ending in disapproval can also be identified in the evolution of attitudes toward some specific market reform policies. Take privatization, for example. The privatization of state enterprises was an issue that dominated most of the 1990s. Seeking to reduce fiscal deficits and the presence of the state in the economy, a number of Latin American governments engaged in policies of privatization during the 1980s and 1990s (Teichman 2001). The Peruvian privatization program was particularly far-reaching. Between 1991 and 2000 there were 220 privatization operations, and as a result almost 80 percent of all state enterprises were transferred into private hands (Dammert Ego Aguirre 2001).

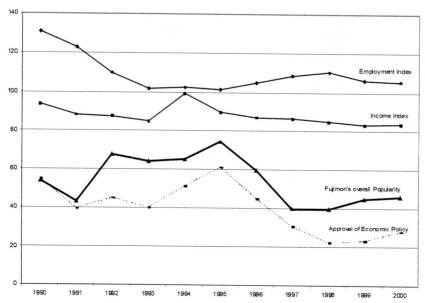

Figure 3 Evolution of two economic indicators and support for Fujimori (yearly averages)
SOURCE: Data from INEI 2001.
NOTE: Employment Index: annual average for metropolitan Lima only; baseline: January
1995. Real Wages Index: annual average for metropolitan Lima; baseline: 1994.

After a brief interlude of relatively strong support, approval for this
policy fell substantially as the decade came to an end (see Figure 4).[12]
Diminishing public approval for the sale of state enterprises can be easily
observed in this figure. While approval for privatization hovered around
60 percent between 1992 and 1994, it fell to around 40 percent between
1995 and 1997 and declined even further to around 30 percent between
1998 and 2000. Clearly, as the alleged benefits of privatization failed to
materialize, public support for this policy waned considerably.

The decline in mass support for privatization is explained by increasing concerns about the honesty with which it was being conducted and
also by the perception that it was eliminating rather than creating jobs.
Concerns for the honesty of the privatization process failed to disappear
even in the face of financially successful operations such as the privatization of the national telephone company. An October 1993 poll revealed
that about 30 percent of Lima residents were inclined to answer in the
negative when asked if the privatization process was being conducted in
an honest manner (43 percent answered in the affirmative and a signifi-

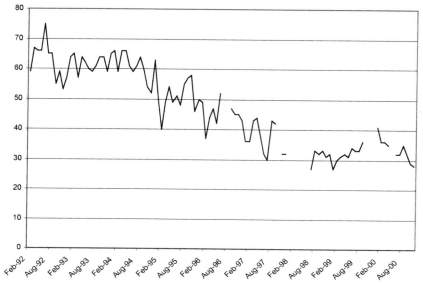

Figure 4 Approval for privatization policies, 1992–2000
SOURCE: Apoyo.

cant 27 percent gave no opinion). A few months later, right after the sale of the phone company generated more than a billion dollars in revenue for the state, a March 1994 poll disclosed that 29 percent of the sample still thought that the privatization process was not being conducted in an honest way. Doubts about the honesty of the process increased as time passed; a December 1995 poll showed that 38 percent of the respondents disagreed that the process was being implemented honestly (42 percent felt that it was and 20 percent had no opinion).

While perceptions concerning the honesty of the privatization process were more or less evenly divided, opinions on what constituted its most negative aspect were not. Despite initial enthusiasm, most respondents eventually became very concerned with the negative impact that privatization had on job creation. In November 1993, the majority (67 percent) of the people still believed that privatization would create jobs. However, by 1996 these hopes had virtually vanished; a poll taken in February that year revealed that the vast majority (81 percent) of respondents believed that the privatization policy had generated unemployment and an additional 71 percent declared that it had actually increased poverty in Peru.

As one might expect, support for the privatization policy was strongly influenced by socioeconomic status. The poor and the very poor were

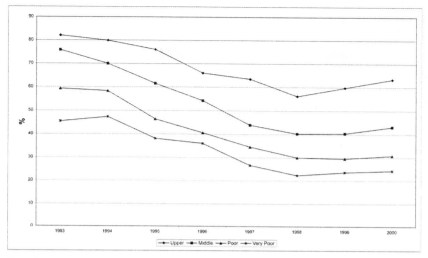

Figure 5 Support for privatization by social class (yearly average)
SOURCE: Apoyo.

significantly less likely to approve of this policy than were upper-income
citizens (see Figure 5). For instance, in 1993 about 82 percent of upper-
class Lima residents supported privatization, while only 45 percent of
very poor residents did so. Even in 2000, 63 percent of upper-income
voters continued to favor privatization, while only 24 percent of the
poorest approved. These figures show that only those placed in the upper
economic echelons of Peru's society could be described as being enthusi-
astic supporters of privatization. The working class and the middle class
were much more skeptical to begin with, and over time became increasingly more so.

The growing displeasure of the poor and the very poor toward privatization was indicative of a more general trend of disenchantment with
free-market economics. As the new millennium approached, public support for specific market-oriented policies declined significantly. Table 2
documents attitudes concerning free-market policies throughout the
1990s. The information reported in this table suggests that, first, the public approved of some free-market policies more strongly than others and,
second, overall support for free-market economics dropped over time.
For instance, there was strong public agreement with the fostering of
foreign investment and with the idea that private enterprise was benefi-
cial for the country—although support for these two ideas dropped

Table 2 Public support for free-market policies (percentage in agreement)

Free-Market Policy	Jul 1990	Aug 1991	Apr 1993	Mar 1994	Apr 1997	Sep 1998
Foreign investment should be encouraged	87	84	80	89	73	73
Private enterprise is beneficial for the country	70	80	77	75	67	62
The state should leave productive activities in the hands of the private sector	56	59	61	59	50	51
The state should be small	52	54	51	46	35	30
Most state enterprises should be sold	48	58	55	53	n.d.	25
A market economy is the most convenient system for the country	58	72	61	66	69	59

SOURCE: Apoyo.

somewhat by the end of the decade. However, the public was much more reluctant to endorse the views that the state should be small and that most public enterprises should be sold. Support for these two policies fell significantly between 1990 and 1998.

The previous discussion is not meant to imply that the public, even those placed at the lowest echelons of the socioeconomic ladder, did not come to accept some elements of the free-market paradigm. For instance, there was a growing acceptance that the market, not the state, should determine most prices. While only 27 percent of the poorest Lima residents accepted the market as the main allocator of prices in 1992, that figure had jumped to 53 percent by 1998. But even as the poor came gradually to accept the free market as the main allocator of prices, they were significantly less likely to embrace this idea as compared to Lima's wealthiest residents. By 1998 about 80 percent of those classified as upper class accepted the market as the main allocator of prices (among the very poor that figure was, as I mentioned, slightly above 50 percent). This discrepancy is yet another example of the existing chasm between the wealthiest and the poorest of Peruvian residents. A February 2000 Apoyo poll found similar responses to a question that was worded differently. Respondents were asked, "In general, which do you prefer to determine the price of goods, the government/the authorities or the market/supply and demand?" About 63 percent of the total sample chose the market and 33 percent chose the government; the market was preferred by 53 percent of the poorest residents and by 73 percent of the wealthiest ones.

Even as a majority of citizens preferred the market to determine most prices, there was a strong reluctance to endorse a small, noninterventionist state. As Table 2 indicates, by the end of the decade only a third of respondents agreed with the idea that the state should be small. Likewise, a September 1998 Apoyo poll posed the following question: "What do you think is more important, a government that actively intervenes in the life of its citizens or a government that leaves you alone?" About 56 percent of the sample preferred an active government, while only 36 percent preferred a laissez-faire government (9 percent had no opinion).

To summarize, the free-market paradigm made some inroads in Peruvian public opinion but at the same time people grew increasingly critical of some of its aspects. The public came to accept, for instance, that foreign investment should be encouraged, that private enterprise was important for Peru's development, and that the market should determine most prices. However, the public still supported the notion that the state should be actively involved in citizens' lives but rejected the idea of a reduced state and did not support the privatization of state enterprises. This reluctance to fully embrace the free-market paradigm was particularly noticeable among the poorest sectors of Peruvian society. As noted, this growing disenchantment was likely related to the rather poor performance of these reforms in terms of job creation and income growth. Given the particularly strong rejection of these reforms by the poorest sectors of Peruvian society, it is not surprising that Fujimori decided to increased state spending among the poor to shore up his poll numbers and thus enhance his reelection chances in 2000. Fujimori's microlevel populism (Roberts 1995) was necessary in order to counteract the politically negative impact of his market reforms. By contrast, the adoption of free-market reforms was very favorably received among Lima's middle- and upper-class residents, which broadened Fujimori's base of political support. However, as we will see now, this middle- and upper-class support declined as Fujimori pushed for a second reelection.

The Reelection Controversy and the 2000 Presidential Election

Not even a year had passed after Fujimori's reelection in 1995 when it became painfully clear that he was not planning to relinquish power at the end of his second term. In 1996 the regime embarked on a series of legal maneuvers aimed at securing an unconstitutional reelection bid for the 2000 elections.[13] According to the Law of Authentic Interpretation, enacted on August 23, 1996, the 1993 constitution could not be applied retroactively, and it effectively decreed that Fujimori's first administration did not count for reelection purposes. In an effort to defeat this new reelection attempt, a civil society movement was organized to push for a referendum on the issue. Not only did the public quickly rally behind the referendum initiative, but support for it was very strong across all social classes (see Table 3). Between October 1996 and August 1998, when the Fujimori-controlled Congress finally voted against holding the referendum, overall support for it was never below 60 percent and usually hovered around 70 percent.

Many Peruvians reacted angrily when Congress voted down this initiative. After years of relative calm, the streets became noisy again as thousands of demonstrators displayed their disagreement with the congressional vote. University students were particularly outspoken against the regime's successful efforts to kill the referendum initiative. These ral-

Table 3 Support for referendum on the 2000 reelection by social class (percent)

Date of Poll	Upper	Middle	Poor	Very Poor	Total Sample
October 1996	70	75	65	76	71
November 1996	73	71	75	64	71
February 1997	49	59	66	56	60
May 1997	75	71	69	72	71
June 1997	81	70	71	64	70
July 1997	76	74	74	60	69
August 1997	70	73	70	66	70
September 1997	60	58	71	59	63
November 1997	65	63	60	59	61
July 1998	84	81	75	62	74
August 1998	87	87	75	70	77
Average	71.8	71.1	70.1	64.4	68.8

SOURCE: Apoyo.

lies and mobilizations marked a turning point because, for many years, opponents to the regime were unable to provoke any such significant displays of discontent with Fujimori. Unfortunately, although these demonstrations were important and energized the opposition, they did not yet reach the massive proportions that rallies against Fujimori would eventually achieve in the wake of the 2000 elections. Public opinion polls echoed the popular dissatisfaction with the congressional vote. A September 1998 poll inquired into the respondent's feelings on learning of the unsuccessful outcome of the referendum initiative. The responses were telling: 40 percent acknowledged that they felt rage/powerlessness; 17 percent stated that they felt sadness/despair. An additional 17 percent declared that they felt indifference, and 11 percent felt tranquility/satisfaction (7 percent had mixed feelings and 9 percent had no opinion). In other words, about 60 percent of those polled manifested negative feelings against the vote that put an end to the referendum initiative.

In January 2000, three months before the presidential election, thousands of people invaded the outskirts of Lima. Opposition leaders quickly denounced these land invasions as an electoral tactic designed to boost Fujimori's standing in the polls. These accusations were confirmed when on February 13, 2000, Fujimori announced the creation of an ambitious program (Programa de Lotes Familiares [Family Lot Program (PROFAM)]) that would provide urban squatters with state-owned land. Less than two weeks after the announcement, more than a quarter of a million people had applied to obtain a free lot. Opposition leaders denounced the creation of the land program as an outright vote-buying mechanism.

Public knowledge of and support for the PROFAM initiative was extremely high even though the majority recognized it as a vote-buying tactic. A survey taken in March 2000 showed that almost 97 percent had heard of the program. More important to Fujimori's electoral purposes, a very solid majority of 77 percent was in favor of distributing the land (21 percent were against it, and 2 percent had no opinion). However, when asked if the land program was a vote-buying measure (*medida electorera*) or a good solution to a real problem, 60 percent declared that it was a vote-buying measure and only 36 percent said it was a good solution (4 percent volunteered no answer). Clearly, people were able to ascertain Fujimori's intentions but still agreed with the substance of the program. As expected, opinions on this issue were split along social class lines. For instance, a March 2000 poll showed that while 86 percent of the poorest residents supported the creation of PROFAM, only 45 percent of the wealthiest citizens shared such approval.

An additional controversy surrounding the 2000 electoral campaign was concerned with whether the process was being conducted in a just and fair manner. The opposition declared the playing field to be uneven and that the election was therefore vitiated. International observers from a variety of organizations (including the Organization of American States [OAS]) issued a communiqué after the first round of elections lamenting that the process did not conform to international standards (see Chapter 11). Similarly, the Peruvian public overwhelmingly considered the electoral process to be unfair but was split evenly on the question of whether actual electoral fraud had been committed. An April 2000 poll conducted immediately following the first round of elections asked: "Do you think that this past election was fair [*justa*] for all participants or do you think that some parties or candidates were at a disadvantage?" Only 33 percent declared that the race was fair, while 63 percent thought that some candidates were at a disadvantage (4 percent had no opinion). However, when asked, "Do you think that the ONPE [National Organization of Electoral Processes] results reflect the national vote or do you think there was a fraud?" the public split almost evenly: 43 percent believed that the results had actually reflected the popular vote, while 47 percent thought that there had been electoral fraud (10 percent had no opinion).

Citizens' evaluations of the fairness of the electoral process became even more negative after the second round of elections, in which Fujimori ran unopposed following the resignation of Alejandro Toledo. Answering to a question posed by a June 2000 poll—"Do you feel that at some point the government's candidate was given an advantage or do you think that all candidates competed in equal conditions?"—a solid 62 percent declared that the government's candidate was given an advantage, while only 34 percent said that all candidates had equal opportunities (4 percent had no answer). Again, the recognition of the process as unfair did not translate into an acknowledgment of the presence of electoral fraud. The same poll also asked if the runoff's official results reflected the popular vote or were instead the product of an electoral fraud. Only 43 percent thought that the results were fraudulent and 50 percent felt they were a valid reflection of the national vote (7 percent did not answer). In short, a clear majority agreed that Fujimori had an unfair advantage in the 2000 election but less than half of the public thought that electoral fraud was committed.

Politically, however, the fact that the public split so closely on the issue of electoral fraud was in itself extremely damaging to the continuity of the regime. Very few had contested the election's validity in 1995; in 2000 this was no longer the case. In April 1995, only 17 percent of those interviewed immediately following the presidential election believed the official results to be fraudulent. In April 2000, however, 47 percent said that the official results were fraudulent. Clearly, a significant portion of the public was now challenging both the legitimacy of the 2000 reelection and the continuation of the regime.

Although Fujimori's machinations enabled him to secure a second reelection despite the significant public outcry, it came at a high political cost. The reelection bid in 2000—while not rejected by an overwhelming majority—certainly polarized the country. Moreover, it marked the end of the electoral coalition that had sustained the regime since 1992. Although Fujimori won the plurality of votes in Lima, polls revealed that this victory was driven, as it had been back in 1990, by his electoral appeal among the very poor. A poll conducted in Lima after the April election showed that Fujimori had won 64 percent of the vote among the very poor, but only 29 and 39 percent of the middle- and upper-class votes, respectively. This was a significant change in relation to 1995, when Fujimori had won 65, 60, and 78 percent of the votes of the very poor, the middle class, and the upper class, respectively (according to an Apoyo poll conducted in April 1995 in Lima).

The country's political polarization encouraged the opposition to rally behind a single candidate for the second round of elections, and the political consequences of this unifying act should not be overlooked. After years of division and disorientation, the opposition to Fujimori finally realized that the only way to put an end to the regime was through a concerted effort. The high point of this effort came in the form of a huge popular demonstration against the reelection project, a rally known as la Marcha de los Cuatro Suyos (the March of the Four Suyos).[14] Although this rally (actually a series of rallies) failed to dislodge the regime, it inflicted a serious political blow against the administration by challenging its monopoly on public support. Not only did the Marcha de los Cuatro Suyos attract considerable public support (46 percent approved of it according to a July 2000 Apoyo poll), but it actually put hundreds of thousands of people on the streets to protest the continuation of the regime. The government was unable to assemble any similar expression of support. The international and domestic isolation that the 2000 reelection project brought about made the regime extremely vulnerable to political crisis. The regime's final demise would come just a few months later as the result of internal contradictions.

Conclusion: The Ambivalent Public and the Limits of Public Opinion

The preceding discussion shows that public opinion revealed an ambivalent attitude toward the Fujimori regime. By and large, Peruvian public opinion showed approval of Fujimori's overall performance in office, backing for his antiterror policy, initial support of his market-reform policies, and rallying behind him at reelection time in 1995. However, the public rejected some of his human rights policies, strongly opposed his legal maneuvers to orchestrate a second reelection in 2000, and eventually came to reject his economic policy and became critical of his overall performance.

It is clear that the significant public support that Fujimori enjoyed during his first term was crucial to the regime's evolution. First, it spared him the need to turn his regime into an openly repressive one after the 1992 autogolpe, which would have made its authoritarian character evident to the international community. Second, it allowed him to use elections as a legitimizing mechanism in the wake of the coup, for he was confident of his electoral appeal. It was this noticeable decline in appeal that caused him to run into serious difficulty in the 2000 elections. Unsure of an easy victory at the polls, the regime resorted to heavy-handed techniques that further polarized the country and alienated significant portions of the international community. While the regime enjoyed widespread approval, Fujimori could afford to maintain the appearance, although rarely the substance, of a democratic framework. In addition, strong popular approval had afforded him enough political momentum to withstand the criticisms of a largely divided and demoralized opposition. As public support waned, the regime felt the need to resort to more openly authoritarian practices that only further undermined its support. The public may have been willing to turn a blind eye to the abuses committed against members of the insurgency, but it was much less inclined to overlook attacks against the democratic opposition.

There is an additional factor that explains why broad-based support was crucial to the smooth continuation of the regime. In Peru, as in many other Latin American nations, the dominant political culture tends to favor the plebiscitary dimension of democracy and pays less attention to democracy's institutional and constitutional features (O'Donnell 1994). In this prevailing atmosphere, mass support (as established in opinion polls) for presidents gives them an aura of political legitimacy even as they engage in authoritarian politics.

To the extent that public opinion played this legitimizing role, it was politically influential during this controversial period of Peruvian history. However, public opinion was unable to influence Fujimori's behavior in the areas in which its views clashed with those of the regime, and in this sense, it was politically powerless. It was only when negative poll numbers were coupled with massive street demonstrations and international pressure that the regime's behavior was somewhat affected, as in the case after the 2000 elections when the regime accepted an OAS mission to monitor the condition of democracy in Peru.

The role that public opinion played during this controversial period helps shed some light on the relationship between public opinion and democracy in Peru. The Fujimori experience shows that a shrewd leader bent on aggrandizing his or her own power can use public support to legitimize authoritarian practices. Public opinion in general and opinion polls in particular can take on this role when intermediary organizations (such as political parties) are weak or unpopular. When organized voices stop being effective in their representation of people's views, unorganized voices—what we call public opinion—assume a larger political role. Unfortunately, unorganized voices are easier to manipulate to buttress a regime bent on limiting political competition. Unorganized critical voices are also easier to disregard, because they lack the political strength that comes from organization. This period of Peruvian history also suggests that while public opinion can be effectively used to legitimize electoral authoritarianism, it is generally ineffective in checking the power and affecting the behavior of the authoritarian leader. To this extent, the ability of public opinion alone to play a democratizing role is clearly limited.

If the Peruvian experience of 1990–2000 shows something, it is that in authoritarian settings (even of the electoral kind), public opinion, precisely because it is composed of disorganized voices, is usually impotent in influencing governmental behavior when these opinions are not coupled with organized activism. There existed significant and increasing dissatisfaction with key elements of the market reforms as well as growing unhappiness with the regime's persistent efforts to alter the legal framework in order to secure a third term for Fujimori. But in the absence of sustained and massive popular street demonstrations against these policies, public opinion was unable to influence the outcome of political events. It was only later—in the wake of the 2000 election—that mass mobilization reached a level that the regime could not easily disregard.

To conclude, the Peruvian case shows that given the right set of circumstances, public opinion can rally behind an authoritarian leader. This indicates that the relationship between public opinion and democratization could be problematic. In Peru, the public was so grateful for the defeat of hyperinflation and domestic political violence that it overlooked the serious democratic deficits of a manipulative leader. It was only at the turn of the new century, when the regime's machinations to remain in power had reached scandalous proportions and the effects of market reforms had proved feeble, that growing segments of the public withdrew political support. The convergence of this growing discontent as manifested through opinion polls along with street action and international condemnation would eventually undermine the legitimacy of the regime's continuation and ultimately make it vulnerable to its own internal tensions.

NOTES

1. This chapter focuses on the analysis of political views expressed in public opinion polls. The examination of other forms of political preferences, such as voting, is not included. Some question the honesty of polling agencies and thus the validity of opinion polls conducted in the 1990s, but there is no evidence to substantiate those claims in the case of trustworthy organizations such as Apoyo, Datum, Universidad de Lima, and Imasen. In fact, polls conducted by these agencies tend to show similar figures—apart from the normal differences stemming from different question wording—validating one another's results.

2. Apoyo registered an approval rate of 46 percent in August 2000. This support would drop to 23 percent in November 2000, the last month that Fujimori was in office.

3. Fujimori's average approval rating held at around the 40 percent mark. To put this number in some perspective, it should be noted that Peru's current president, Alejandro Toledo, who took office in July 2001, had only three months in which his approval rating was greater than 40 percent. Toledo's average approval rating was 22 percent in 2002, 17 percent in 2003, and 10 percent in 2004 (according to monthly polls conducted by Apoyo in Lima).

4. Strictly speaking, this is an analysis of Lima's public opinion. Lack of systematic national polls conducted at regular intervals forces us to limit our analysis to the capital city. This shortcoming is greatly compensated by the fact that we can use monthly polls that cover almost all the decade. Lima contains about 40 percent of the country's population, and thus is by far the most important city in Peru. Moreover, most polls reported by the media during this period were conducted in this city. Therefore, to a great extent, Lima's public opinion is, politically speaking, Peru's public opinion. I thank Alfredo Torres and Guillermo Loli of Apoyo for giving me access to their monthly surveys. All surveys quoted in this chapter come from this polling agency unless noted otherwise.

5. Data for the Belaúnde and García administrations are taken from *Informativo Mensual* (Lima: Datum), July1990.

6. Data for his third administration (August–November 2000) are not included in this figure. Fujimori's approval rating in his last month in office was 23 percent.

7. Apoyo stratifies its Lima samples in four different socioeconomic groups: upper, middle, low, and very low. Fujimori's average popularity among the upper and very low socioeconomic groups for the period January–July 1995 was 73 and 76 percent, respectively.

8. An additional 10 percent mentioned "the power of Montesinos," and 4 percent "dictatorship/authoritarianism." References to Fujimori's economic successes were negligible (less than 3 percent). This question allowed multiple answers; the percentages presented here refer to only the first mention.

9. Earlier analyses of Fujimori's popularity ratings did not include the effect of political violence. See, in particular, S. Stokes 1996a and Carrión 1998, 1999.

10. Many excellent books on Shining Path and political violence in Peru have been published in the past ten years or so. For an overview, see Degregori 1990; McClintock 1998; Palmer 1994; Stern 1998.

11. La Cantuta is the nickname that people use to refer to the University Enrique Guzmán y Valle. On July 18, 1992, nine students and one professor from this university were kidnapped and killed in a commando operation conducted by the army intelligence service under the direction of Major Martín Rivas.

12. The question was worded as follows: "In general, would you say that you approve or disapprove the privatization of public enterprises?" Figure 4 shows the percents that approved of this policy.

13. For a full description of the regime's strategy to ensure its continuation beyond 2000, see Conaghan 2001.

14. *Suyo* can be roughly translated as "land" or "province."

SEVEN

All the President's Women: Fujimori and Gender Equity in Peruvian Politics

GREGORY D. SCHMIDT

In the 1980s and early 1990s, women were almost invisible on the Peruvian political stage. By 2000, however, they were hard to miss. During Fujimori's *decenio* (ten-year presidency), the adoption of gender quotas for political candidates facilitated dramatic increases in the number of women elected to municipal governments and the national legislature. Indeed, at the beginning of his ill-fated third term, Fujimori handpicked an all-female steering committee (*mesa directiva*) to run Congress, an institution that he had to control in order to stay in power. By the dawn of the new millennium, women had become prominent throughout the Peruvian government, as well as in opposition politics and other realms of the public sphere. Moreover, issues of special concern to women had been added to the political agenda and, in some cases, were the subject of landmark legislation.

Was the political emergence of women and an increasingly gender-

The Center for Latino and Latin American Studies of Northern Illinois University provided financial support for this study. I also would like to thank Violeta Bermúdez, Cecilia Blondet, and Ana María Yáñez, who graciously helped a male gringo appreciate the changing roles of women in Peruvian politics. Martha Chávez, Lourdes Flores Nano, and Beatriz Merino generously shared their time and insights from beyond the glass ceiling. Charles D. Kenney's comments on the manuscript were very useful. Responsibility for the final product is, of course, mine alone.

sensitive policy agenda during the *decenio* merely a coincidence, or did Fujimori play an important role? In this chapter I argue that presidential leadership was indeed a significant factor, though hardly the only one. As shown in the first section, the political role of women had long lagged behind trends in gender relations before Fujimori's election in 1990. In the second and third sections I highlight the political breakthroughs of women under Fujimori and probe his motivations for supporting greater gender equity. The fourth section examines the adoption of gender quotas and their impacts in municipal and congressional elections. In the final sections I briefly review gender-sensitive initiatives in public policy during the decade and extrapolate some major conclusions from the study.

Social Progress and Political Marginality

The recent political emergence of women in Peru is rooted in lengthy and complex processes of social change. After World War II, the Peruvian educational system expanded rapidly and became accessible to women, while modernization and migration opened up new employment opportunities in an increasingly urbanized society. These social trends and the growing availability of modern forms of contraception began to transform traditional gender roles. Moreover, progress toward gender equality in Peru has been stimulated and reinforced by feminist movements in the advanced industrialized countries and the diffusion of new social and political norms through intergovernmental and nongovernmental organizations (NGOs).

By the time that Peru slid into a long period of economic decline in the mid-1970s, a clear trend toward greater gender equity was apparent, though it advanced unevenly across the economic and ethnic fault lines of a very stratified society (Blondet 1995, 104–6). Economic necessity and the growing acceptance of women in nontraditional roles led to a dramatic increase in the female percentage of the workforce, from 21.9 percent in 1981 to 36.5 percent in 1991.[1] Moreover, during the 1980s a new generation of female university graduates began to make its mark in professions that had been dominated by men, and female reporters attained prominence in print and broadcast journalism.[2] The feminization of the professions continued in the 1990s.[3]

Several distinct types of female activists emerged during the late 1970s and 1980s, when women became involved in social movements, feminist groups, political parties, NGOs, self-help organizations, and other associations in civil society. Although the emergence of a cohesive women's movement and a feminist policy agenda were undercut by harsh stabilization policies and the violence emanating from Sendero Luminoso (Shining Path) (Blondet 1995), the major advances of women in the public sphere became widely accepted as part of a new "common sense" regarding appropriate gender roles (Blondet and Montero 1994, 17). Nevertheless, women played only a nominal and largely symbolic role in Peruvian government before the 1990s. Only in 1955 had literate Peruvian women obtained the right to vote and hold office at the national level. During the following thirty-five years, women were elected to Congress during periods of constitutional rule, but they never constituted more than 7.2 percent of either chamber and played only token roles in the leadership of the various political parties (147–48). Women were absent from the cabinet until 1987, when President Alan García Pérez assigned the health and education portfolios to Ilda Urízar and Mercedes Cabanillas, respectively. [4] Behind the scenes, however, the new generation of female professionals was beginning to work its way up the bureaucratic ladders of the public sector. [5]

Before 1990 women enjoyed their greatest political success at the local level. The 1962–63 military junta tapped Anita Fernandini to be mayor of Lima. During the 1984–86 period, when the United Left (Izquierda Unida [IU]) governed Lima, women filled 17.9 percent of the seats on the capital's provincial council and 10 percent of its district mayorships. Women did not fare as well in the 1986 election, which was dominated by the Alianza Popular Revolucionaria Americana (American Popular Revolutionary Alliance [APRA]), but in 1989 they won 20.5 percent of the seats on the provincial council and 9.5 percent of the district mayorships (Blondet and Montero 1994, 22–23, 143).

The Feminine Face of Fujimorismo

Under Fujimori, women were appointed or elected to top government posts in unprecedented numbers. But unlike Athena springing forth from the head of Zeus, they did not suddenly gain political prominence. Instead, the growth of female political representation during the decade resembled a snowball being rolled down a hill: it was barely perceptible at the beginning but gathered momentum during the middle years and was impossible to overlook at the end.

The First Term

As a hopeless minor presidential candidate in early 1990, Fujimori had to round out the congressional lists of his Cambio 90 (Change 90 [C90]) party with many marginal figures, some of whom were women.[6] As shown in the top rows of data in Table 1, women accounted for a greater proportion of Fujimori's lists than those of the other parties that won seats in 1990. However, inspection of the middle rows of the table reveals that female candidates running on C90 lists in 1990 were significantly less likely to be elected than their male counterparts.[7] Thus, the electoral performance of C90 women was relatively weak, given that individual "preferential votes," rather than list order, determine which candidates fill the congressional seats won by each party in Peru. Nevertheless, the relatively small C90 delegations in both the Chamber of Deputies and the Senate included a notably higher percentage of women than those of the other parties, as reported in the bottom rows of Table 1.

Fujimori appointed only one female cabinet member during the twenty months of constitutional rule before the April 1992 autogolpe. Gloria Helfer won widespread public praise for combating corruption in the scandal-ridden education ministry but was soon sacrificed in order to appease APRA, Fujimori's tactical ally at the time. The president, however, often turned to female professionals, as he began to modernize Peru's public administration. During the initial months of his first term, Carmen Higaonna, a fellow Japanese-Peruvian, was appointed superintendent of customs, and Martha Chávez, a labor lawyer, entered the government as an advisor on privatization (Bowen 2000, 38–39).[8] By the end of Fujimori's first term, women accounted for 20 percent of Peru's vice-ministers, as well as 38 percent of executives and 47 percent of professionals in the Superintendencia Nacional de Administración Tributana (National Superintendency of Revenue Administration [SUNAT]), one of the vanguard agencies of bureaucratic modernization (Blondet and Montero 1994, 21–22).

A month after the autogolpe, Fujimori appointed Blanca Nélida Colán as chief public prosecutor (*fiscal de la nación*). As a pawn of spymaster Vladimiro Montesinos, Colán played a pivotal role in thwarting legal challenges to the regime and subordinating the judiciary to the executive branch. A series of laws of dubious constitutionality allowed her to wield the powers of this office on a de jure or de facto basis until shortly before Fujimori's flight from Peru in November 2000. Many of the controversial provisional appointees to the judiciary were also women.[9]

The stars of other women rose during the nine months of dictatorial

Table 1   Gender of congressional candidates, 1990–2001

| | Bicameral | | Single National District | | | Unicameral |
| | 1990[a] No Gender Quotas | | | | | Departmental Electoral Districts 30% Quota |
	Deputies	Senate	1992 (CCD)	1995	25% Quota 2000	2001
Female % of Candidates						
Fujimori's lists	10.0[b]	25.0	11.3	9.2	25.8	41.1[c]
Other lists winning seat	6.0[b]	7.0	10.3	10.7	25.9	35.6
Success Rates: Fujimori's Lists						
% Female candidates elected	0.0[b]	13.3	55.6	63.6	48.4	5.9[c]
% Male candidates elected	25.0[b]	26.7	54.9	55.0	41.6	0.0[c]
Success Rates: Lists of Other Parties Winning Seat						
% Female candidates elected	25.0[b]	9.5	2.7	3.9	4.0	4.3
% Male candidates elected	14.9[b]	15.8	5.3	3.7	7.2	12.4
Female % of All Candidates Elected						
Fujimori's lists	9.4	14.3	11.4	10.4	28.8	100.0[c]
Other lists winning seat	5.4	4.5	5.9	11.3	16.2	16.2
All lists winning seat	6.1	6.7	8.8	10.8	21.7	18.3

SOURCE: Calculated from data in Blondet and Montero 1994, 122–28; ONPE 2002; Tuesta Soldevilla 2001, 66–68, 71–73, 76–88; Villanueva Flores 1998, 31; Yáñez and Guillén 2001, 20; Webb and Fernández Baca 2000, 264.

[a] During the 1980–90 period the Chamber of Deputies was elected in the 24 departments and in special electoral districts for the Provinces of Lima and Callao, while the Senate was chosen in a single national district.

[b] Lima only. Data on the gender of lower-house candidates elsewhere is not available.

[c] Refers to Cambio 90/Nueva Mayoría lists. Some pro-Fujimori candidates also ran on the lists of Solución Popular, which did not win any seats.

rule that followed the autogolpe. Chávez became cabinet secretary, former senator Ana Kanashiro was appointed to head the agency that houses orphans and promotes the family, and former deputy Lucila Shinsato assumed the presidency of a regional government. In addition, María Herminia Drago became comptroller general, but her nomination was later rejected by the Congreso Constituyente Democrático (Democratic Constituent Congress [CCD]) after she displayed a streak of independence.

During the campaign for the unicameral CCD in late 1992, women constituted a smaller proportion of the pro-Fujimori list than in 1990, but those selected were markedly better candidates than in the former year. Indeed, female supporters of the president were slightly more likely to be elected than men running on his list (see Table 1). Five of the seven women elected to the CCD were from Fujimori's Cambio 90/Nueva Mayoría (C90-NM) alliance. The most notable female Fujimoristas in the CCD were Chávez and Luz Salgado, a former employee of the National Agrarian University, where Fujimori had been a professor and rector. Both were reelected in 1995, 2000, and 2001. As the head of the CCD's oversight committee, Chávez played a critical role in heading off attempts by the opposition to investigate allegations of corruption and abuse of power against the government. In its waning days, she sponsored legislation that quintupled the number of signatures that political parties needed for registration.

Women continued to gain political prominence during the remainder of Fujimori's first term. Ana María Arana and María Luisa Federicci both headed the Ministry of the Presidency, which oversaw most public works and social-assistance programs during the decade. Federicci supervised the massive increases in social spending that paved the way for Fujimori's first reelection and aggressively promoted women to decision-making positions.[10] Lilliana Canale, the top executive of the National Society of Exporters, became the Minister of Industry, Commerce, Tourism, and Integration in 1994. Vice-Minister Luzmila Zanabria—who would later become Peru's ambassador to China—began Peru's campaign for admission to the Asia-Pacific Economic Cooperation (APEC) forum, an effort that attained success in 1998. Outside the public sector, Susana de la Puente, a Peruvian executive with J. P. Morgan, played a critical role in restoring flows of foreign capital to her country.

The Split with Susana

The growing prominence of women in Fujimori's first administration was overshadowed by the president's increasingly public marital problems. Fujimori had been credited with numerous affairs over the years and, during the 1990 campaign, accused of sexual improprieties with his students (Bowen 2000, 25, 58, 196). His relationship with his wife, Susana Higuchi, a successful civil engineer, had long been a subject of gossip. In the late 1980s the couple reportedly lived under a Japanese arrangement, *kateinai-rikon*, by which they eschewed marital intimacy while sharing a house with their four children.[11] Participants in Fujimori's 1990 campaign reported that the candidate treated his wife "as if she were a servant" (Daeschner 1993, 229).

Higuchi assumed a high profile as first lady, and by early 1992 there was widespread speculation that she would run for mayor of Lima later that year. Thus, on the eve of Fujimori's mid-March departure for a state visit to Japan, Lima's chattering class was surprised when the presidential palace abruptly announced that a cold would prevent Higuchi from accompanying him. Shortly thereafter, the first lady publicly accused two of the president's siblings, Santiago and Rosa, as well as Santiago's wife, of corruption in the distribution of donated clothing and other aid from Japan. These allegations were more than just a personal embarrassment for Fujimori, given that Rosa and especially Santiago played important roles in his administration behind the scenes and that Rosa's husband served as Peru's ambassador to Japan. Congressional plans to investigate the scandal probably influenced the timing of the autogolpe. Higuchi subsequently disappeared from public view for several months, during which she remembers being imprisoned and tortured by army intelligence.[12] She was later "seen but not heard" at official events.

The first lady's political aspirations were not quelled by this ordeal and may have even been stoked by the conflict with her husband. In early August 1994, Higuchi's secret plans to challenge her husband in the 1995 election became public, and she moved out of the presidential palace. To the delight of the opposition, the first lady soon became an open critic of Fujimori's administration, speaking out against corruption, human rights abuses, military influence in the government, insufficient support for social programs, and constant surveillance of her activities. She even denounced Vladimiro Montesinos by name at a time when he was still unknown by most Peruvians. The president retaliated by "firing" his wife as first lady, a role that was subsequently filled by the couple's oldest daughter, Keiko Sofía, during her vacations from studies at a U.S. university. Fujimori's insinuation that his wife suffered from mental illness was parroted by the Servicio de Inteligencia Nacional (National Intelligence Service [SIN]) and his supporters. When Higuchi continued to use her office in the presidential palace, her husband had the doors to the street entrance welded shut.

Polls showed that the former first lady had virtually no chance of becoming president, but also that her candidacy threatened Fujimori's bid for reelection because Peruvians were inclined to believe her allegations, especially the charges of corruption. After the National Board of Elections (JNE) voided her candidacy for failure to collect a sufficient number of valid signatures, Higuchi accused the SIN of erasing names from the diskettes that she had presented. In January 1995 the JNE also overturned Higuchi's congressional bid because her list did not include a full contingent of candidates, a decision that provoked a brief hunger strike by the former first lady.[13] Higuchi and Fujimori were divorced in 1996.

Higuchi later ran successful campaigns for Congress, in 2000 and 2001. Although the specific allegations that she made in the used-clothing scandal and other cases have yet to be proved legally, history has shown her negative portrayal of the Fujimori regime at the height of its popularity to be largely accurate.[14] Once widely dismissed as delirious or vengeful, the former first lady has been vindicated in the minds of many Peruvians.

After the breakup of his marriage, Fujimori was romantically linked to several women, and his personal life became grist for Lima's rumor mill. The president set off a media feeding frenzy by commenting that he was thinking of remarriage and citing "good legs" as a prerequisite for a prospective bride.[15] The remark evoked criticism from feminists and countless jokes about the criteria used to select women for public office.

The Second Term

Fujimori rewarded Martha Chávez's fierce loyalty in the CCD by placing her at the top of his C90-NM congressional list for the 1995 election. As shown in Table 1, women constituted a slightly smaller percentage of the pro-Fujimori list than those of the other parties that won seats in 1995 but were considerably more likely to be elected than were the president's male supporters. Female candidates running on other lists, however, were also more likely to win office than their male counterparts. Thus, in contrast to 1992, women accounted for a slightly higher percentage of successful candidates on opposition lists.

Chávez—who had received the most preferential votes in the election—became president of Congress, thus holding the second most powerful elected position in Peru during the first year of Fujimori's second administration. She later blocked any serious investigation of government wiretapping or other abuses of power as the chair of the Committee on National Defense, Internal Order, and Intelligence and participated in a key ploy to provide a legal rationale for Fujimori's second reelection. Martha Hildebrandt—a linguist and the former head of the National Institute of Culture under the military governments of the 1970s—was the most notable addition to the ranks of female Fujimoristas. She twice served as the president of Congress. During the Fujimori administrations, the "two Marthas" were the only women to appear among the ten most powerful Peruvians in the annual polls conducted by Apoyo.[16]

Both progovernment and opposition congresswomen outshone their male colleagues. As a headline in *El Comercio* (1999) put it, "They're thirteen [congresswomen], but they seem like more." Female legislators were disproportionately represented on the congressional steering committee and among committee chairs (Blondet 1998, 12). They also played leading roles in floor debates, especially deliberations on the peace agreement with Ecuador.[17]

Gender equity quickly became a major theme of Fujimori's second administration. The president emphasized the importance of family planning in his second inaugural address in late July 1995. He reiterated this theme in mid-September as the only male head of state to address the United Nation's Fourth World Conference on Women, held in Beijing. An official Web page, Mujer en el Perú, soon displayed the president's Beijing address, and topics of special concern to women began to be featured regularly in his speeches.[18]

In 1996 Peru created the Ministry for the Ministerio de Promoción de la Mujer y del Desarrollo Humano (Ministry for the Promotion of Women and Human Development [PROMUDEH]), becoming the first and only Latin American country to have a cabinet-level agency devoted explicitly—though not exclusively—to women. The same year saw the establishment of a Committee on Women in Congress and a special women's division in the new Defensoría del Pueblo (Ombudsman's Office). As discussed later in this chapter, Fujimori played a decisive role in passing gender-quota legislation in 1997 and supported the addition of gender-sensitive topics to the political agenda. In 1998 his government founded the Banco de la Micro-Empresa (Microenterprise Bank [MIBANCO]), an institution that makes loans to microenterprise owners, a majority of whom are women.

The feminization of the public sector continued during Fujimori's second term. Elsa Carrera became the first female minister of transport and communications in 1996. Miriam Schenone—a pro-Fujimori feminist who had ties to Montesinos—served as the first minister of PROMU-DEH.[19] In 1999 she was succeeded by Luisa María Cuculiza, "a striking and tough-talking former beauty queen" who played a key role in Fujimori's 2000 reelection campaign (Bowen 2000, 335). Two other women held portfolios during Fujimori's second administration, and a third served during his short-lived last term.[20]

Also gaining power and visibility during Fujimori's second administration were two glamorous, U.S.-educated women, both named Beatriz, who had been appointed during the waning months of his first term. Former Catholic university professor Beatriz Ramacciotti, Peru's ambassador to the Organization of American States, tenaciously and quite effectively defended an increasingly controversial regime.[21] After returning to Peru from a prominent New York law firm, Beatriz Boza served as the president of the National Institute for the Defense of Competition and Intellectual Property Protection (INDECOPI), another vanguard agency in Fujimori's efforts to redefine the economic role of the state. She simultaneously headed PromPerú, a government agency that promotes tourism and foreign investment through slick public relations campaigns and frequent "road shows" abroad.[22]

Boza had exceptional star quality, but she was one of many young, well-educated, and self-assured young women in the public sector. An all-female task force led by Leoni Roca and later Cayetana Aljovín drafted a blueprint for modernizing the Peruvian state. Women also headed MI-BANCO and the women's division of the Ombudsman's Office. By 1997 female executives filled almost a third of decision-making positions in the government, with even higher proportions in some ministries (Htun 1998, 4). By 1999 almost half the vice-ministers were women (Kogan 1999, 97).

Even the police and armed forces were no longer exclusively male domains. Female police officers had long directed traffic and written tickets, and in late 1998 they joined motorcycle patrols. Hinting that female cops were less likely to be bribed—a perception shared by many Peruvians—Fujimori remarked that women can "demonstrate their ability to be assertive when it comes to making people obey traffic laws."[23] Whereas the navy and especially the air force had long accepted female volunteers in their ranks, during Fujimori's second term women gained admission to all three service academies.[24]

As shown in Table 1, there was little difference in the female shares of the official and opposition party lists in the 2000 election, due to the adoption of a 25 percent gender quota (discussed below). Fujimori, how-ever, focused more attention on women by placing them in five of the first ten and nine of the first twenty positions on his list.[25] Whereas female Fujimoristas were once again more likely to be elected than men running on the president's list, the chances of women on other lists were only about half those of their male colleagues. Consequently, the female per-centage of candidates elected on the Perú 2000 list was considerably higher than that on opposition lists.

Some Alternative Explanations

Fujimori's increasing tilt toward women, like many political phenomena, was overdetermined. In other words, a number of distinct explanations are plausible, and these are not mutually exclusive (see Blondet 1998, 19). In this section I review a series of potentially complementary factors, progressing from general, structural explanations to motives that are more specific, occasionally personal, and in some cases open to specula-tion.

A "Bull Market" for Women in Politics

As shown in the first section of this chapter, the political role of women had lagged behind changes in gender relations since at least the early 1980s. In the mid- and late 1990s several factors converged to produce a latent demand for greater female representation. The collapse of Peru's discredited and male-dominated political parties opened up new oppor-tunities for public service. Women especially stood to benefit, given their political marginality and popular stereotypes that portrayed them as being more honest and virtuous than men.[26] In addition, it became easier to place issues of special concern to women on the political agenda after the taming of hyperinflation; the capture of Abimael Guzmán, the leader of Sendero Luminoso; and the beginning of economic recovery. More-over, the feminization of the professions since the early 1980s had cre-ated a deep pool of female talent that could be tapped. Thus, both "demand" and "supply" factors worked to create a "bull market" for women in politics.[27]

Public opinion data provide evidence of this new, positive market for female representation.[28] By wide margins, both male and female respon-dents to surveys in Lima and three major provincial cities in late 1997 and early 1998 believed that women were more honest, more concerned about the poor, and better administrators than men. Women were also seen as less authoritarian. Not surprisingly, attitudes supportive of women in politics were strongest in the capital. Throughout Peru, however, respondents of both genders said that female political participation should increase and that they were more inclined to vote for a woman. Nevertheless, a "glass ceiling" mentality is also evident in the responses. Indeed, outside Lima, men were generally favored to be mayors and congressional representatives.[29]

Opposition parties were certainly aware of the burgeoning political market for women. Mercedes Cabanillas of APRA and Lourdes Flores Nano of the Partido Popular Cristiano (Popular Christian Party [PPC]) became the leaders of their respective parties.[30] Moreover, in 1995 Cabanillas became the first female presidential candidate of a major party,[31] and women constituted more than a quarter of the vice-presidential candidates on opposition tickets. In Congress, Flores Nano and Anel Townsend were among the most effective members of the opposition. Working for Mayor Alberto Andrade, Flor de María Valladolid and Patricia Díaz Velarde directed a historical restoration program that greatly improved the appearance of Lima's downtown area.

Nevertheless, Fujimori was much more adept at adjusting to the bull market for women than was the opposition. It is well known that the president was addicted to polls and focus groups, and he was the only political leader who had access to the SIN's elaborate public opinion research. Thus, Fujimori could more rapidly and fully appreciate the positive political stereotypes of women. Moreover, while the fragmented opposition was always regrouping behind new leaders, the president could build on the successes of his female candidates in 1992 and 1995. Whereas the internal dynamics of the male-dominated opposition groups still tended to work against women, Fujimori was the undisputed leader of his own personalistic movement and thus free to recruit female talent that would enhance his government's image.

In contrast to the clientelistic or haphazard recruitment of opposition lists, Fujimori used methodical screening processes to select candidates for Congress. Prospective candidates were subjected to background checks, public opinion surveys, and even psychological interviews.[32] A similar process was used to scrutinize candidates for the position of minister and for other top bureaucratic posts (Bowen 2000, 42). Although these recruitment methods may have been more appropriate for selecting corporate executives than public servants, they were more receptive to new female talent than were the old-boy networks of the established political parties and the newer opposition movements. Thus, ironically, the autocratic, "personalistic" president used relatively objective methods of political recruitment.

Loyalty, however, was the sine qua non for nomination to Fujimori's congressional lists or selection to key political positions.[33] Women in Peru are widely viewed as more loyal and less competitive or "independent" than men, and the leading female Fujimoristas were loyal to a fault.[34] However, many talented women in less sensitive positions were not necessarily Fujimori partisans. Moreover, extraordinary connections allowed a few high-profile women—Beatriz Boza, Sonia Goldenberg, and Susana de la Puente—to maintain a certain political distance from Fujimori while collaborating with him.

Although the political recruitment of women increased greatly during the regime, neither Fujimori nor the opposition came close to "cornering the market" on female talent in the public sphere.[35] The supply of able women was abundant, and their professional interests and political inclinations were as varied as those of men. Continuing trends that had begun much earlier, many women who were independents, or at least not actively involved in partisan politics, attained public prominence during these years.

Commitments to democracy, civil liberties, and human rights—rather than partisan motivations—placed some women on a collision course with the government. Female leaders such as Sofía Macher and Susana Villarán played prominent roles in the human rights movement. Cecilia Valenzuela was among Peru's most courageous and renowned independent journalists. Still other women—including Antonia Saquicuray, Ana Cecilia Magallanes, Greta Minaya, and Delia Revoredo—resisted Fujimori's efforts to subordinate the judiciary.[36] Two female agents in army intelligence, Mariella Barreto and Leonor La Rosa, were murdered and tortured, respectively, because they had been suspected of leaking information about covert operations against opposition politicians and the press. After fleeing Peru, another woman in army intelligence, Luisa Zanata, exposed telephone taps on opposition politicians and efforts to control the opposition press.

Electoral Strategy

In Table 2, postelection polls by two of Peru's most reliable survey research firms are used to break down the presidential vote by gender in Lima, which accounts for a third of the Peruvian electorate. Although

Table 2   Support for Fujimori in Lima

| | 1990 | | 1995 | 2000 | |
	First Round	Second Round		First Round	Second Round
As Reported in *Post-election Polls* (projected % of valid vote)					
Female	36.8	51.2	65.0	53.8	79.7[a]
Margin of error (+/-)	6.0	7.0	6.5	5.7	5.9
Male	35.5	55.4	61.0	46.8	67.7[a]
Margin of error (+/-)	6.0	7.1	6.3	5.7	6.0
Total	36.6	53.4	63.0	50.4	73.4[a]
Margin of error (+/-)	4.2	5.0	4.5	4.0	4.2
Official Result in Lima (% of valid vote)	34.2	53.3	63.0	50.1	78.6

SOURCE: Elaborated from Apoyo, April 1990, 23; April 1995, 12, June 2000, 21; Imasen 1990–2000; Tuesta Soldevilla 2001, 323, 333, 450, 501, 510.

[a]Respondents who interpreted their vote as pro-Fujimori, rather than against any candidate.

the gender gap for all but the last of the surveys in Table 2 is within the margins of error—a result of small samples—it is highly unlikely that the overall trend of greater female support for Fujimori is accidental. Moreover, confidence in these data is bolstered by the fact that the overall results of all but the last poll closely approximate the actual outcome of the respective election in Lima. Thus, the last survey in the table—for the 2000 runoff—stands out for having a gender gap and an overall result that are both outside the margins of error, in contrast to the other polls. We will return to this anomalous case below.

Although women were among the politically excluded sectors that Fujimori claimed to represent in 1990, he did not develop a gender-sensitive strategy during his highly improvised first campaign. The data in Table 2 suggest that women were slightly more likely than men to vote for Fujimori in the first round of the 1990 election. The same poll, however, indicates that women were also more inclined than men to support the front-runner Mario Vargas Llosa and less likely than males to vote for the Left.[37] Thus, given leftist support for Fujimori over Vargas Llosa, the former did somewhat better among men than women in the runoff.

Fujimori's marital difficulties probably provided the initial impetus for his political tilt toward women, as focus-group sessions provided evidence of a female backlash against the president for the shoddy treatment of his wife and his comment about the legs of a prospective new bride (Bowen 2000, 239). Higuchi, however, remained a largely discredited figure during the 1995 campaign, and there was little incentive for a gender-sensitive electoral strategy, given Fujimori's overwhelming popularity and the weakness of the opposition. Nevertheless, the data in Table 2 indicate that in 1995 he did better among women than men.

Sometime after the 1995 election, Fujimori's media advisors crafted a political marketing strategy directed at women that became readily apparent by the time of his 1996 Independence Day address.[38] The president was already adept at using fawning female reporters, disparagingly nicknamed "geishas," and he could later count on the aggressive support of Peru's leading talk show hostess, Laura Bozzo, who ironically had run for Congress on an opposition list in 1995.[39] The repackaging of existing social-assistance programs into PROMUDEH virtually guaranteed a female face in the cabinet but did not preclude the linkage of food aid and other assistance—on which women and children disproportionately depend—to political support. Some keen observers soon concluded that PROMUDEH was "little more than an electoral machine" for Fujimori (Htun 1998, 12). Indeed, the political manipulation of social programs became more flagrant during the 2000 campaign.

The president's efforts to woo or cajole support from women, especially among the poor, paid off in the 2000 election. As shown by the data in Table 2, Fujimori won a first-round majority of the female vote in Lima, but only a plurality among men in the capital. Interpretation of the runoff results is complicated by Alejandro Toledo's withdrawal from the race, but the gender gap is nevertheless striking. In one of the last preelection polls made public, a projection of the valid vote in Lima gave Fujimori a 66–34 percent margin among women but only a 52–48 lead among men.[40] Table 2 shows that a far higher percentage of women than men in the capital reported a pro-Fujimori ballot, as the president received an artificially inflated share of the valid vote.[41] The difference is slightly greater than the combined margins of error for the two small, gender-specific samples. Moreover, the statistically significant discrepancy between this last survey and the actual result is attributable to the male, rather than female, respondents. In marked contrast to men, women were not ashamed to report a vote for Fujimori.

Political Tactics

The recruitment of female talent and a policy agenda that addressed the concerns of women helped Fujimori to deal with critical constituencies, disarm the opposition, and paper over differences in his own coalition. As Peru became polarized over Fujimori's plans to seek a third term, the presence of women in key positions gave the government useful ammunition against foreign and domestic critics who questioned the regime's commitment to democracy and human rights. The two Beatrizes, for example, provided glitz and glamour on the international stage while also reinforcing the modern image of technocratic competence that Fujimori had cultivated. More gender-sensitive policies ingratiated Fujimori with foreign donors[42] and diverted international attention from the unsavory aspects of his administration. These policies also appeased many middle-class feminists who were generally wary of the president but willing to work with him on specific issues. Some of these feminists helped design and implement policy and mediated relations with various groups in Peru's weak civil society (Blondet 1998, 13–14, 17–20). In contrast to the uproar over Fujimori's "good legs" remark in 1995, few feminists objected in 1999 when he gave a punning endorsement of miniskirts worn by female employees in government offices.[43]

Whereas leading male Fujimoristas in Congress were often soft-spoken or colorless, the president's most passionate defenders were women. PROMUDEH minister Luisa María Cuculiza openly defended authoritarianism as "a good mode of governing."[44] Martha Chávez was even more infamous for making extreme and often outrageous statements.[45] On more than one occasion, members of the opposition expressed a reluctance to respond to the diatribes of Fujimori's female defenders out of deference to their gender.[46] Moreover, the government preempted or ameliorated opposition attacks by having women—especially Colán and Chávez—do much of its dirty work, as discussed previously.

Ironically, Fujimori never chose a woman to be one of his running mates. Open proclamations of interest by several of his prominent female supporters—most notably Chávez and Cuculiza—may have clashed with the president's secretive style of political recruitment. In any event, Fujimori's postcoup vice presidents had much less power and visibility than did his leading female supporters. The president's interest was probably better served by placing outspoken and unquestionably loyal women in more significant roles.

When male-led legislative factions competed for power at the beginning of Fujimori's third term, the president created an all-female steering committee that represented the major groups in his coalition, drawing on the popular perception (and perhaps his own belief) that women are more team oriented than men.[47] As her leader came under relentless pressure after the release of the notorious Montesinos-Kouri video, Congress president Martha Hildebrandt proclaimed, "We are four women defending the principle of loyalty—loyalty to Fujimori."[48] In the end, however, the president's congressional coalition—which was essential to his political survival—cracked under the weight of unprecedented scandal. As Congress prepared to oust Hildebrandt and her female colleagues, Fujimori fled into exile.

Policy Linkage, Prestige, and Commitment?

Fujimori may have advocated gender equity in order to pursue other policy objectives or to enhance his stature as an international leader. He also may sincerely believe in this principle.

On numerous occasions, including the speeches at his second inauguration and the Beijing conference, the president linked family planning to his efforts to alleviate poverty. There is also some evidence that he viewed the empowerment of women as essential to both objectives.[49] Even some women who were not supporters of the president became convinced of his commitment to gender equity.[50] These professed views are not necessarily inconsistent with Fujimori's own personal experience: a construction business run by Susana Higuchi accounted for most of the family income before his improbable election. Moreover, Higuchi recalled that her marriage was characterized by relative equality and affection before Fujimori became involved in academic politics (Bowen 2000, 9).

The Peruvian president also spoke out on gender issues at other international forums during his numerous trips overseas. Whatever his true feelings may be, by forcefully advocating the principle of gender equity, Fujimori gained the attention that he appeared to crave as an aspiring international leader.[51]

Gender Quotas

Peruvian feminists publicly advocated gender quotas as early as 1990. The campaign for quotas in Peru was greatly bolstered by the passage of the Argentine Ley de Cupos in 1991, the Platform for Action adopted at the 1995 Beijing conference, and a February 1997 interparliamentary meeting on gender equity in New Delhi attended by Martha Hildebrandt and Luz Salgado.[52] Soon after the New Delhi conference, Congress took up the issue during hearings on new electoral legislation. After the Constitution Committee blocked a proposal by Lourdes Flores Nano for a

30 percent quota, the newly created Committee on Women endorsed a 25 percent plan sponsored by Hildebrandt and Salgado. The fledgling committee, however, did not yet have the authority to report a bill to the floor.

At this point, Fujimori decisively intervened by publicly stating that he would send a quota bill to Congress.[53] Whereas most members of Congress had been against quotas and had even ridiculed the idea, the majority immediately reversed its position and applauded the president's initiative (Yáñez and Guillén 1998, 20). Once the passage of quotas became a foregone conclusion, only several congressmen—all from opposition parties—raised philosophical objections in a largely perfunctory floor debate.[54] Law 26859, a new basic statute on national elections passed in September 1997, stipulated that women and men must each make up at least 25 percent of party lists for Congress. Similar language was soon incorporated into the new statute on municipal elections (Law 26864) after a limited debate that once again focused on normative issues to the total neglect of practical detail.[55] Indeed, in talking to legislators, feminists, and political analysts, I found absolutely no evidence that any attention was paid to how quotas would actually work in conjunction with the very different rules that are used in municipal and congressional elections in Peru. Although public knowledge of quotas was initially limited, by February 2000 more than fourth-fifths of respondents to a national survey (82.9 percent of women and 78.9 percent of men) expressed support for the legislation (Calandria 2000, 21).

Peru was hardly alone in emulating the Argentine system of gender quotas for political candidates. By the end of the 1990s, ten other countries in Latin America had passed similar legislation. Gender quotas, however, have been considerably more successful in increasing female representation in Peru than in most other countries of the region. After the 1998 municipal elections, women constituted a higher proportion of council members in Peru than of comparable local assemblies in other Latin American countries for which data are available (see WLCA 2001, 12–15). Table 3 shows the increased presence of women on municipal councils at the district and provincial levels. Similarly, the proportion of women in the Peruvian congress doubled—from 10.8 percent in 1995 to 21.7 percent in 2000—in contrast to an average 5 percent increase in Latin American countries that have implemented gender quotas in national legislative elections (Htun and Jones 2002, 36, 41). In 2000, only Argentina and Cuba, the latter a nondemocratic polity, had higher percentages of female legislators in the region (see WLCA 2001, 12–15).

Table 3   Women elected to municipal councils before and after quotas

	Female Percentage of Councillors		Percentage Change
	1995	1998	
Provincial Councils (n = 194)	10.81	21.54	10.73
District Councils			
Lima (n = 42)	21.82	29.70	7.88
Rest of Peru[a]	6.96	23.50	16.54

SOURCE: Elaborated from data in *El Comercio* 1999; JNE 1997, 1999; and Yáñez Guillén 1998, 78-131; 1999, 7.

[a]The number of district councils outside Lima increased from 1,576 in 1996 to 1,583 in 1998.

The effectiveness of gender quotas in Peru was greatly facilitated by certain institutional features that had not been considered during the perfunctory congressional debates.[56] In the case of Peru's majoritarian, closed-list municipal elections, the mechanical application of a 25 percent *legal* quota to councils of varying sizes produced a range of *effective* quotas, which tended to be highest in rural areas, where women face the greatest discrimination. In addition, high effective quotas and the large share of seats won by the first-place party *often guaranteed female representation* (see Schmidt and Saunders 2004). However, whereas quotas had a major impact outside Lima, their apparently positive effects on the capital's district councils—where women had long enjoyed electoral success—was really an artifact of other variables, especially political mobilization by feminist organizations. Thus, paradoxically, quotas per se were ineffective in Lima, but the political mobilization of women that accompanied them was quite successful in increasing the percentage of female council members.[57]

Specific characteristics of the open-list system used to elect the unicameral Peruvian congress also facilitated the election of women, as I have shown in detail elsewhere (Schmidt 2002). Limitations of space allow only the two most important of these features to be highlighted here.

First, casting a ballot for individual candidates is optional in Peru—in contrast to Chile—and voters from lower socioeconomic strata are less willing or able to use their "preferential votes." Thus, the Peruvian congress is chosen by a more affluent and better educated subelectorate, which has more progressive attitudes toward the political participation of women than does the country as a whole. Moreover, this subelectorate disproportionately resides in Lima and the adjacent port of Callao. For example, in 2000, voters in Lima-Callao accounted for 34.2 percent of the overall electorate, but 44.9 percent of the preferential votes received by winning congressional candidates.[58]

Second, the competitiveness of female candidates was further magnified by the single national district, which was used to elect unicameral legislative bodies in 1992, 1995, and 2000. The single district allowed professional women—who are overwhelmingly based in Lima-Callao—to run for the entire universe of congressional seats. It also centralized nominations in the hands of national party leaders, who are generally more receptive to female political participation than are regional bosses.[59] Moreover, in both 1995 and 2000, congresswomen drew a majority of their preferential votes from Lima-Callao, while congressmen relied on the provinces for most of their support (see Schmidt 2002, especially Table 5).

Although there were good reasons to abolish the single national district after Fujimori's flight from Peru in 2000, this action removed one of the key factors that had facilitated the election of women during the decade. The consequences were predictable, despite a simultaneous increase in the quota to 30 percent. In Lima and Callao, women won twelve of thirty-nine seats (31 percent), exceeding the goal suggested by the new quota. In the rest of Peru, however, female candidates were elected to only ten of eighty-one seats (12 percent). Overall, women constituted only 18.3 percent of Congress (see Table 1). Thus, the female share of the Peruvian congress declined from second to third place among the legislatures of Latin American democracies, just behind Costa Rica (Htun and Jones 2002, 41).

Women might have fared even worse in 2001 had female Fujimoristas not filled C90-NM's three seats in Lima, the only ones that this list won in the country. Indeed, the top six recipients of preferential votes on the C90-NM list in the capital were women.[60] It is no accident that the most fervent supporters of the disgraced former president voted for women who were considered by friend and foe alike to be his most loyal defenders. Moreover, in contrast to 2000, women made up a notably higher proportion of C90-NM lists throughout the country, even though the other parties winning seats also exceeded the 30 percent quota (see Table 1).

A Changing Policy Agenda

From the very beginning of his presidency, Fujimori spoke out aggressively in favor of family planning, often criticizing the Catholic Church on this issue. Indeed, the president's first full year in office, 1991, was officially designated the Año de la Planificación Familiar (Year of Family Planning), and government-sponsored contraception services improved greatly during his first term. Shortly before the Beijing conference, the pro-Fujimori majority rammed a measure through Congress that legalized sterilization as a method of contraception. The scope for legal "therapeutic" abortions also was broadened considerably under Fujimori,[61] though Peru continued to have one of the highest rates of illegal abortion in Latin America.

During his second term, the president played a hands-on role in an ambitious program that sterilized more than two hundred thousand women and a much smaller number of men. Many of these sterilizations were performed without informed consent, due to pressure to meet numerical targets, insufficient monitoring, and a lack of accountability.[62] Moreover, some poor women were pressured to undergo sterilization in order to obtain access to microcredit loans and other government benefits.[63] After some hesitation, Peruvian feminists spoke out against the program and used a U.N. committee to hold the Fujimori administration accountable for its actions (Ewig 2000b, 26–29). International pressure and monitoring by the women's division of the Ombudsman's Office helped to curb abuses in the late 1990s.[64]

On some other issues, however, pro-Fujimori and opposition congresswomen worked together to initiate legislation that unequivocally benefited women. The Committee on Women provided female legislators with an institutional base from which they could hold public hearings and draft bills. The committee was largely staffed by outstanding professionals recruited from feminist NGOs.[65] Thus, there was a direct link between a cohesive female congressional caucus and the feminist movement. Nevertheless, among female Fujimoristas, loyalty to the president always trumped any sense of gender solidarity or commitment to other values. For example, as chair of the Committee on Women, Luz Salgado vehemently defended the sterilization program from charges of coercion (Ewig 2000b, 28).

Several measures stand out among some thirty statutes favoring women that were passed during the decade. Congress approved the Law for Protection from Family Violence, sponsored by Lourdes Flores Nano in 1993 and significantly strengthened this statute in 1997. Its effectiveness was enhanced by the establishment of women's police stations and one-stop centers for victims of domestic violence. In 1997 legislation sponsored by opposition Congresswoman Beatriz Merino abolished a provision in the criminal code that had allowed rapists to escape prosecution by marrying their victims, who were sometimes coerced into such unions. A subsequent modification of the criminal code in 1999 gave prosecutors the power to investigate alleged cases of rape and press charges on their own initiative, thus further protecting victims from social pressure and threats of retaliation. A change in the civil code, also passed in 1999, authorized the use of DNA in contested paternity cases. This last measure had major political repercussions in the 2000 and 2001 presidential campaigns.

Thus, most of the laws that benefited women during Fujimori's administrations were initiated by female legislators, sometimes working with feminist organizations, not by the president. To his credit, Fujimori accepted much of this new agenda, but there were limits. He especially resisted legislation that he believed would place a substantial burden on business, such as stronger measures against sexual harassment and longer maternity leaves.[66] More generally, the neoliberal 1993 constitution weakened individual and social rights, including those of women. Ironically, after his boost from poor women in the 2000 election, the president's third inaugural address featured a proposal to extend health benefits to female workers in popular self-help organizations, such as *comedores populares* (soup kitchens). The abrupt end of Fujimori's third term makes it impossible to determine whether this initiative was serious or mere demagoguery.

Conclusions

During the 1990s Fujimori placed unprecedented numbers of women in key government positions, championed gender quotas, backed other policies benefiting women, and successfully appealed to the female electorate. The pursuit of progressive policies by an increasingly authoritarian government may seem paradoxical, but it is hardly extraordinary. Indeed, an impressive cross-national study shows that the degree to which a polity is democratic has no significant impact on the success of female candidates for the legislature or the executive (Reynolds 1999, 569–70). In Peru, constitutional rule and social progress have often been incompatible, and prior to Fujimori, women made their greatest strides under authoritarian regimes.[67]

Although Fujimori's leadership was critical to progress toward gender equity during the *decenio,* it was hardly the only factor. By the end of his first term, long-standing social trends, the collapse of Peru's party system, economic recovery, and the defeat of terrorism had created a context that was favorable to political gains by women. Moreover, female members of Congress introduced the major laws that improved the rights of women, including quota legislation. Had Fujimori not championed quotas— whose impact was magnified by quirks in the Peruvian electoral system—it is highly likely that trends in gender relations and feminist political activism would have eventually produced this reform, as in other Latin American countries. Thus, the former president is best viewed as an accelerator of greater female representation, rather than its fundamental cause.

Fujimori's formidable political skills are nevertheless evident in this chapter. As various investigations continue to shed light on the seamy, authoritarian side of his presidency, we should not forget that he was extremely adept at manipulating issues in ways that built genuine popular support. It is worth noting that musings of the former president on his Web site are often directed at women, whom he apparently views as critical to plans for a political comeback. Although such a scenario is far-fetched, recent experience has shown that discredited but charismatic former presidents of Peru should not be taken lightly.

A rather surprising finding of this study is the high degree of collaboration among leading female Fujimoristas, opposition Congresswomen, and feminist NGOs in the formulation of policy. This pattern may simply be an aberration, but then again there are hardly any serious studies of policymaking during the decade. On some other significant issues, the policy process also might have been more permeable than is suggested by the caricatures of Fujimori's government in many academic writings. Not everything was decided by unannounced *carpetazos* (rubber-stamp votes) in the wee hours of the morning. Moreover, the president's tilt toward women emerged gradually, apparently as a product of political learning. The *decenio* was an extremely complex and fluid period, and readers should be wary of simplistic analyses of Fujimori's presidency.

This chapter also should be a powerful antidote to any naive notions that women are inherently imbued with political virtue. The leading female Fujimoristas were beholden to a personalistic and increasingly authoritarian government, which they defended more vehemently and more effectively than did their male colleagues. Indeed, other than gender, the key characteristic shared by most of the prominent women around Fujimori was a common blind loyalty to their leader. Some leading female

Fujimoristas are now paying a high personal price for this unconditional loyalty.

Yet there is no reason to believe that Fujimori's regime would have been any better had he relied exclusively on men. The president had an uncanny knack for spotting talented but blindly loyal followers of both genders and then using them unscrupulously. Given that the regime's glaring shortcomings were not a consequence of female leadership in some key positions and that women attained prominence in the opposition and throughout the public sphere during this decade, the feminization of Peruvian politics under Fujimori was, on balance, a very positive development.[68]

Despite widespread public repudiation of the more vehement female Fujimoristas, the political gains of women in the 1990s have not been fatally tainted by their association with the discredited president. There is broad public support for women in politics in the post-Fujimori era, as demonstrated by the passage of the 30 percent quota, Lourdes Flores Nano's strong showing in the 2001 election, and Beatriz Merino's popularity as prime minister. Just as it would be absurd to blame all men for the misdeeds of Montesinos or Fujimori, Peruvians have not generalized their disdain of certain women who supported the former president.

NOTES

1. The figures reported here are based on the 1981 national census and the 1991 national living standards survey, as reported by Blondet and Montero (1994, 30–31). I have excluded nonremunerated family workers, due to methodological differences in counting them at these two points in time.

2. For data on membership in professional guilds (colegios profesionales), see Blondet and Montero 1994, 149. An example of early gains in journalism was the founding of Caretas, Peru's leading newsmagazine, by Doris Gibson in 1950.

3. For example, by 1998, a majority (53.6 percent) of accountants and almost a third (31.5 percent) of economists were women (Webb and Fernández Baca 2000, 265).

4. In addition, María Bockos later served briefly as García's justice minister, and Luz Aúrea Sáenz became Peru's first female general comptroller during his presidency.

5. For example, in 1987–88, women constituted almost a quarter of superior directors, the fourth rung in the administrative hierarchy (Blondet and Montero 1994, 20–21, 133).

6. The most notorious case was Carmela "Madame Carmeli" Polo, a for-

tune-teller and convicted drug trafficker who ran for the Chamber of Deputies from Cuzco.

7. In contrast, Table 1 shows that female candidates from Lima running for the Chamber of Deputies on non-Fujimori lists in 1990 actually had a better chance of winning office than men.

8. Higaonna later served as comptroller general during the waning days of Fujimori's presidency.

9. Women made up 37 percent of public prosecutors (*fiscales*) by 1993 (*Caretas*, March 7, 1996, 54). By 1995 they accounted for 27.1 percent of lower court judges and 15.4 percent of circuit court judges (Webb and Fernández Baca 2000, 263).

10. *Caretas*, January 19, 1995, 23.

11. *Caretas*, March 30, 1992, 15.

12. See *Caretas*, February 28, 2002, 16. Higuchi's version has been supported by the conclusions of two congressional investigative committees.

13. In its rulings, the JNE avoided taking a position on the so-called Susana Law, a statute of dubious constitutionality that had been passed by the CCD to thwart Higuchi's candidacy.

14. Consistent with Higuchi's accusations is widespread suspicion that Fujimori used his relatives and their connections in Japan to illicitly send large sums of cash out of Peru.

15. *Caretas*, September 14, 1995, 36–37, 40.

16. *Debate*, 1990–2000.

17. Ana María Yáñez, labor lawyer, feminist scholar, and director of Manuela Ramos, a major feminist NGO in Lima, interview by the author, Lima, May 31, 1999.

18. Violeta Bermúdez, prominent feminist attorney, interview by the author, Lima, May 27, 1999.

19. While serving as vice-minister of justice, Schenone had been one of the public officials accused of corruption by Susana Higuchi. She also had headed a controversial commission charged with "reforming" the judiciary.

20. These female ministers were María Cristina Rizo Patrón (Presidency, 1999), María Carlota Valenzuela (Justice, 1999), and María Luisa Alvarado (Presidency, 2000).

21. Women also served as ambassadors to China, France, and Italy during Fujimori's second term.

22. There were persistent rumors of a romance between Fujimori and Boza, who frequently accompanied the president on his numerous foreign trips. In early 2002 two Peruvian newspapers reported secret testimony by Montesinos that a jealous Fujimori had ordered twenty-four-hour surveillance of Boza.

23. Sam Mitani, "People and Places." *Road and Track* 50, no. 3 (1998): 16.

24. One female naval cadet graduated first in her class and won a four-year scholarship to the U.S. Naval Academy.

25. While preferential votes determine which candidates are elected in Peru, candidates who are placed high on the list are seen as having more support from their respective party and are generally more successful. Ironically, candidates also covet the last position on the list—occupied by Martha Chávez in 2000—because it is highly visible.

26. Yáñez, interview, Lima, August 4, 2000.

27. I am indebted to Cecilia Blondet (interview by the author, Lima, May 25, 1999) for the market analogy.

28. Peruvian attitudes on gender issues are consistently closer to those of the more progressive Latin American countries (Brazil, Colombia, Venezuela) than those of the more traditional ones (Chile, Mexico, Paraguay). See Apoyo, November 1999, 43–44, 46.

29. The surveys were administered by Imasen and are reported in Blondet 1999. Also see Apoyo, November 1999, 45–47.

30. Ilda Urízar had briefly served as secretary general of APRA in 1986.

31. Dora Larrea de Castillo had run as the presidential candidate of a minor right-wing party in 1990. The PPC nominated Flores Nano for president in 1995, but she withdrew from the race. Susana Higuchi was disqualified in 1995, as previously discussed.

32. *Caretas,* January 26, 1995, 28–30; Martha Chávez, interview by the author, Lima, August 8, 2000.

33. Bowen (2000, 38); Chávez, interview.

34. This point about Peruvian women is often made by analysts of gender and politics in Peru. Also see survey data from Calandria reported in *Caretas,* March 7, 1996, 50.

35. For interesting typologies of women in politics during the decade, see Blondet 1998 and Kogan 1999.

36. Another independent female jurist, Elcira Vásquez Cortez, gained a seat on the Supreme Court in 1994 through the legitimate appointment process.

37. Apoyo, April 1990, 23.

38. *Caretas,* August 1, 1996, 16.

39. The term *geisha* also was used to refer to female Fujimoristas, especially those in Congress, and even to men who were obsequious to the president.

40. Apoyo, May 2000, 6.

41. Toledo's name remained on the ballot, but he urged his sympathizers to spoil their votes. Poll respondents were asked to characterize their vote as for one of the candidates, against one, or against both (Apoyo, June 2000, 21).

42. Miriam Choy, USAID liaison with other donors in Peru, interview by the author, Lima, July 9, 2001.

43. "La minifalda no afecta el decoro, sino por el contrario, decora muy bien" (The miniskirt is not a breach of decorum; on the contrary, it adds to the decor) (Ministerio de Relaciones Exteriores 1999).

44. *Caretas* May 6, 1999, 24A.

45. Among other questionable public declarations, Chávez asserted that the missing students from La Cantuta University (whose bodies were later discovered in a mass grave) must have staged their own kidnappings, suggested that the serious injuries of army intelligent agent La Rosa were self-inflicted, argued that Fujimori might have to close Congress once again if he failed to win a majority, characterized the judges of the Inter-American Court of Human Rights as leftists who sympathized with terrorists, and proclaimed that she could not rule out yet another reelection in 2005.

46. Violeta Bermúdez, interview by the author, Lima, July 9, 2001.

47. Yáñez, interview, August 4, 2000.

48. "All the President's Women Rally Behind Fujimori," CNN, http://www
.cnn.com/2000/WORLD/americas/10/20/peru.women.reut/.

49. For example, Fujimori emphasized the role of women in development in
his address to the 1998 Microcredit Summit, going beyond the sort of platitudes
that might be expected at such an international meeting (Fujimori 1998). However, family planning under Fujimori sometimes relied on coercion, as discussed
later in this chapter.

50. *Caretas,* August 17, 2000, 47.

51. Bermúdez, interview, July 9, 2001.

52. The official Peruvian delegation to the Beijing conference was composed
of three pro-Fujimori congresswomen—Martha Chávez, Martha Hildebrandt,
and Luz Salgado—and opposition Congresswoman Beatriz Merino. In addition,
opposition Congresswoman Lourdes Flores Nano attended the parallel meeting
of NGOs.

53. In the 2000 interview by the author, Chávez noted that Hildebrandt and
Salgado both lobbied Fujimori on the quota issue. Chávez believes that Salgado's
influence was decisive in winning the president's support.

54. Congreso de la República, "Transcripciones magnetofónicas," Segunda
Legislatura Ordinaria de 1996, 24ª sesión (matinal) y 24 sesión (vespertina, miércoles 1 de junio de 1997.

55. Congreso de la República, Diario de Debates, Primera Legislatura Ordinaria de 1997, 12ª sesión (matinal), y 12 sesión (vespertina), Miércoles 17 de
setiembre de 1997.

56. Any vote fraud that might have occurred in the 1998 municipal or 2000
congressional elections was marginal at the national level and thus does not affect
the ensuing analysis of the impact of quotas.

57. For further discussion, see Schmidt 2003. In the 2002 municipal elections
the share of seats filled by councilwomen rose to 23.52 percent at the provincial
level and to 26.88 percent in districts outside Lima, but fell to 25.5 percent in
districts within the capital (unpublished data from PROMUJER; compare with
Table 3).

58. Oficina Nacional de Procesos Electorales, http://www.onpe.gob.pe.

59. Yáñez, interview, August 4, 2000.

60. Two of the winning pro-Fujimori women—Luz Salgado and Carmen Lo-
zada—soon lost their seats after colleagues found them guilty of violating the
constitution. They were replaced by Martha Hildebrandt and Martha Moyano
(the sister of the martyred María Elena Moyano), who had won the fourth and
fifth highest numbers of preferential votes on the list, respectively. Martha Chávez, the other C90-NM congresswoman, was suspended from active membership
in June 2001, due to charges of corruption.

61. Bermúdez, interview, July 9, 2001.

62. Although some critics have argued that the sterilizations were carried out
under unsanitary conditions, the mortality rate was negligible in comparison to
that for maternal death in childbirth, one of the highest in Latin America. See
Ewig 2000b and Webb and Fernández Baca 2002, 259.

63. Choy, interview.

64. However, Giulia Tamayo—the feminist lawyer who first exposed the abuses of the sterilization program and later collaborated with national and international monitoring efforts—was the object of repeated harassment. Her office was mysteriously ransacked in late 1998.

65. Bermúdez, interview, July 9, 2001.

66. Yáñez, interview, May 31, 1999.

67. Divorce was legalized under the first, authoritarian government of Luis Sánchez Cerro (1930–31), literate women received the right to vote during the *ochenio* of Manuel Odría (1948–56), and Juan Velasco Alvarado's military regime (1968–75) gave equal property rights to common-law spouses.

68. I would like to thank Charles D. Kenney for helping me to clarify and emphasize this point.

EIGHT

Redirection of Peruvian Economic Strategy in the 1990s: Gains, Losses, and Clues for the Future

JOHN SHEAHAN

Of all the varied forms of economic liberalization adopted in Latin America during the 1990s, Peru's version was among the most thoroughgoing. If considered in terms of macroeconomic performance it was for some years one of the more successful: after three decades in which the growth of output per capita had been practically zero, the last two with implacably rising inflation, the growth rate in this decade outpaced the average for Latin America, while inflation came down to modest levels not seen for a generation. During the years of rapid growth, up to 1997, the incidence of poverty came down impressively too. The new economic strategy has clearly had some advantages worth preserving. But in other ways it just as clearly fell short: employment conditions remained extremely weak even through the years of expansion, the incidence of poverty went back up again in the last years of the decade, and growth stopped after 1997 when the economy proved once again to be highly vulnerable to adverse changes in external finance. The experience leaves a mixed picture: neither a disaster nor an adequate answer to the country's economic and social problems.

While these results are important in their own right, perhaps the central question to ask about a major change of economic strategy is how it affects the structural factors that underlie long-term performance. Exactly what aspects of performance and what underlying conditions matter most are, of course, open to endless debate. At least three sets of considerations are essential parts of the picture: human resources and human development, the society's institutions, and structures of production and trade.

In regard to the first, a good case can be made that human development should be seen as the main objective of economic and social policy; that "economic growth should be viewed as a contributor to it, rather than as the end product" (Ranis and Stewart 2001, 2). Human development can refer to many variables, notably education, health, nutrition, employment, and social as well as economic mobility—all essential components of life opportunity, though not normally included in the concept of economic growth. Growth can and usually does help toward such goals, though how much it helps depends on its character and on accompanying social choices.

The second set of considerations, institutional conditions and reforms, has come to be emphasized by many proponents of liberalization who recognize that its results have often been disappointing. Their interpretation is that a major cause of problems following liberalization is that it has not been accompanied by needed institutional reform (Burki and Perry 1999; World Bank 2001b). Peru in the 1990s demonstrated a striking dichotomy on these issues. With respect to administrative agencies needed to carry out government policies—tax collection, administration of social programs, supervision of the banking system, and other such specific functions—Carol Wise concludes that the Fujimori government implemented many effective reforms (2003b, 179–223). On a different plane, that government assiduously destroyed any semblance of independence of the judiciary, subverted the electoral commission, refused to implement any meaningful decentralization, and demonstrated almost unlimited disdain for any legal impediments to its own actions. This was an impressive case of increased capacity to govern accompanied by demolition of democratic constraints.

While these institutional issues are clearly central for any society, it seems doubtful that they constitute an adequate explanation of differences in the effects of liberalization programs. They leave out a third set of factors that are essential to understanding economic performance. This chapter is particularly concerned with factors that they leave out, namely, the kinds of structural problems emphasized in earlier discussions of development. They include relationships between the labor force and the availability of land and capital to work with; long-term, as distinct from cyclical, employment conditions; the competitive capacity of modern sectors; the structure of exports; dependence on external capital;

and persistent breakdowns related to external deficits. These concerns are complementary to consideration of human resources and institutions, but they lead in a somewhat different direction. Reforms in the domains of human resources and institutions are consistent with wholehearted reliance on market forces to guide investment and production, but deliberate efforts to change structures of production and trade point instead toward intervention to guide incentives of producers. They could call for modification of liberalization itself.

The first section of this chapter is focused on the nature of the structural factors that have made it difficult for Peru to establish more sustained and equitable economic growth. The second and third sections compare some of the main results of its liberalization program to those of ten other Latin American countries: the second with respect to growth and structural change; the third with respect to human development. The fourth section discusses some of the differences between liberalization programs in these countries and examines their relationships to economic performance. Finally, the fifth section reviews ways in which changes in Peru's economic program could yield most of the advantages of liberalization while going beyond that orientation to deal more effectively with persisting structural weaknesses.

Basic Structural Conditions

Whether considered in terms of economic growth, human development, or institutional coherence, the three decades prior to the 1990s were exceptionally difficult for Peru. The country achieved several short periods of good economic growth, but each time these broke down too quickly for any long-term progress. Output per capita increased barely 2 percent between 1960 and 1990, while rising 65 percent for the region (World Bank 2002). Progressively worsening employment conditions led to falling real wages of hourly paid production workers from the mid-1970s on. They went down so strongly in the last years of the 1980s that they fell below the level of 1960 (Instituto Cuánto 1990, 717; Saavedra 1997b, 28). Conflicting estimates of the incidence of poverty in the early years make it difficult to be sure of its long-term trend, but international comparisons consistently show higher levels in Peru than the averages for the region.[1] And institutional capacity, though not readily quantifiable, clearly deteriorated in many dimensions (Gonzales de Olarte and Samamé 1993).

It is not the case that Peru lacks potential for more sustained economic growth or that it has some intrinsic inability to answer its problems. Possibilities for growth have been helped by an unusually wide diversity of natural resources; by considerable success in developing new primary-product exports and a few industrial exports (notably textiles) as well; and, in recent decades by a relatively rapid expansion of access to education, including higher education extending beyond the traditional fields to engineering and basic sciences. Another significant change for the better was the elimination of the large haciendas, achieved through land reform at the end of the 1960s; this helped to raise the supply elasticity of the agricultural sector and to spread the gains of higher agricultural earnings more nearly equally than in the past. It would be difficult to find much enthusiasm about entrepreneurial capacity in the industrial sector, but it is notable that manufacturing output has responded with surprising strength in the brief periods in which economic conditions have been at all favorable, notably from 1985 to 1987 and from 1992 to 1997.

Still, against such factors supporting the potential for growth, a formidable array of structural weaknesses have limited its possibilities and shaped its character in ways unfavorable to equality. They include a highly inequitable system of education, with good-quality private schools for the minority able to attend them but extremely weak public schools for the great majority of children; a superabundance of low-skill labor relative to land and industrial capital; limited competitive capacity of the industrial sector and modern services; overdependence on primary exports and external capital; and entrenched discrimination that impedes economic and social mobility (Sheahan 1999, 10–130).

For the period 1960–90, the combination of weak education for the majority, the abundance of low-skill labor, and the near absence of economic growth practically ensured poor employment conditions. For the future, the crucial need is to improve the quality of public education and the distribution of human resources. But even that is not likely to be a sufficient answer. It needs to be backed up by progress toward the solution of a key problem that has repeatedly interrupted growth: the pattern of recurrent crises of balance of payments and foreign exchange (Iguíñiz and Muñoz 1992; Dancourt, Mendoza, and Vilcapoma 1997). That pattern could be seen as an externally imposed handicap, and in part it is. But it involves three different levels of causation.

On the most evident level, recurrent swings in external markets, for exports or for financing, can set the economy back even when domestic conditions are in good balance. That happened to Peru again in 1998–99 during the worldwide reaction to financial crises in East Asia and Russia. No country can completely escape the impacts of changes in world market conditions. But on the second level, countries that keep close to external balance under normal conditions do not suffer as frequently or as badly from financial shocks. For Peru, external breakdowns have often been provoked by fiscal deficits and excessive credit expansion. Notable examples include the deficits of the government of Juan Velasco Alvarado in the first half of the 1970s and wildly excessive credit expansion under Alan García Pérez in the 1980s. When excess spending creates rising external deficits on current account, it is only a question of time before creditors begin to draw back. Once that starts, everyone aware of the issues tries to move capital out of the country rapidly. That kind of crisis may look like an external shock but it is, fundamentally, homemade.

On the third level, the particular characteristics of Peru's structure of trade foster a high probability that external crises will continue recurring. Heavy dependence on primary exports implies exposure to greater volatility (as well as slower long run growth), than can be expected when exports include a fair percentage of competitive industrial exports. Peru's exceptional dependence on mining exports is doubly unfortunate: they are particularly vulnerable to swings in world markets and, even when growing well, are singularly little help for employment. Beyond the question of erratic ups and downs, this structure of trade sets up a persistent block on sustained economic growth. Each period of domestic expansion leads to rising external deficits because it both raises demand for imports and pulls primary products away from exports into domestic markets instead (Tello 1990). In the absence of exceptional luck with external prices, this pattern means that any period of expansion will generate rising deficits on current account. What Peru needs—among its many needs—is a competitive industrial sector that can both provide a stimulus to growth of its own and help restrain external deficits during periods of expansion. Without it, sustained growth is almost impossible. How did economic liberalization in the 1990s change these factors, if it changed them at all?

The 1990s: Growth and Structural Change

Liberalization as implemented in Peru helped with some of the preceding problems but failed to help with others. The issues can be sorted out in terms of five interrelated dimensions: the capacity for more sustained economic growth, structures of production and trade, poverty and inequality, access of the majority to education of decent quality, and labor market conditions. The basic problems are too entrenched to be cleared up in one decade by any kind of economic strategy but a decade should have been long enough to permit discernable progress on some of them, if the strategy was appropriate to the problems. Was it?

For the 1990s as a whole, gross domestic product (GDP) per capita increased at an average rate of 2.2 percent a year, superior to the rate in any decade since the 1950s and well above the regional average (Table 1). But for Peru, as for the majority of the countries cited in Table 1, the last three years of the decade turned adverse. From a growth rate of 3.4 percent a year for 1990–97, Peruvian GDP per capita fell at a rate of 0.6 percent for 1997–2000. The region as a whole suffered a parallel, though more modest, change: from a growth rate of 2.2 percent for the first period to a low, though still positive, 0.4 percent for the second. In contrast, for reasons considered below, two countries managed to stand out with a different pattern: the growth rates for Costa Rica and for Mexico

Table 1   Gross national product and rates of growth for selected countries.

	GNP per Capita, 2000	Average Annual Rates of Growth, 1990s (in 1995 U.S. dollars; percent)		
	(in dollars adjusted for purchasing power)	1990–97	1997–2000	1990–2000
Argentina	$12,377	5.4%	−1.3%	3.2%
Bolivia	2,424	1.8	0.3	1.4
Brazil	7,625	1.6	0.5	1.3
Chile	9,417	6.6	1.3	5.0
Colombia	6,248	2.0	−2.1	0.8
Costa Rica	8,650	2.5	3.9	2.9
Ecuador	3,203	1.0	−3.5	−0.3
Mexico	9,023	1.0	3.7	1.8
Peru	4,799	3.4	−0.6	2.2
Uruguay	9,035	3.6	−0.6	2.3
Venezuela	5,794	1.1	−2.9	−0.2
Latin America and Caribbean region	7,273	2.2	0.4	1.6

SOURCE: World Bank 2002.

increased in the second period instead of falling, to the high rates of 3.9 and 3.7 percent, respectively. Differences in their versions of liberalization contributed to greater independence of performance.

The main immediate cause of the downturn after 1997 was a familiar external shock: the previously strong inflow of capital from world financial centers reversed to an outflow. As proponents of liberalization have emphasized, that reversal was not Peru's fault: it did not demonstrate any imbalance in the country's own macroeconomic management (Velarde and Rodríguez 2001). That interpretation is valid as far as it goes but it misses the more important issue: the new economic strategy accomplished little or nothing that would have reduced the economy's built-in vulnerability.

What could have been done to reduce the damage of such external shocks? One possible solution would have been to gain more room for sustained growth by promoting new exports. Liberalization of trade helped exports to some degree, by reducing costs of inputs for production and by increasing pressure on industrial producers to seek technological improvement. But these helpful factors were undercut by adverse management of the exchange rate. The real exchange rate, a key incentive for exporters, was allowed to fall by 30 percent between 1990 and 1991 (BCRP 2000, 184).[2] It was held in a narrow band from then until 1999, when it was raised by 9 percent. Holding the real price of foreign exchange down through the decade made imports artificially cheap and the profitability of exports artificially low. Together, these effects made external deficits higher than they need have been, increased dependence on external credit, and had the particularly unfortunate effect of holding down the growth of productive employment.

Currency appreciation is especially negative for long-run growth of competitive industrial exports. By reducing their profitability it discourages investment in new export possibilities. Primary exports lose some of their profitability too but strong comparative advantage may make their supply relatively inelastic in response to such changes: they may not respond well to the stimulus of devaluation but they hold up better in the face of appreciation. Trade liberalization may similarly have a more powerful stimulating effect on industrial than on primary exports, for two reasons. One is that the industrial sector depends much more heavily on imported inputs for production, and it gains more in terms of costs when restrictions on imports are eased. The other is that the relative profitability of exporting as compared to selling on the domestic market increases when protection of the domestic market for manufactured goods is reduced. The problem was that the stimulus of trade liberalization ran into the braking effect of currency appreciation—the new economic strategy was a mixture that included a self-defeating component.

Why did the Peruvian government allow the real price of foreign exchange to fall, when this was practically certain to handicap exports, as well as give imports an artificial advantage over domestic alternatives? The possible answers are almost endless but a central concern was the high priority given to stopping inflation. Keeping foreign exchange cheap helped hold down the price level. That policy would not have been feasible if foreign exchange had become too scarce to finance imports and to handle debt service. But it became easy to follow when the favorable turn of external financing conditions of the early 1990s provided exceptionally open access to credit. The capital inflow was so great that, in the absence of intervention by the central bank (by buying dollars on a large scale), foreign exchange would have become even cheaper than it actually did. That policy held the real exchange rate within a very narrow range from 1991 to 1999. The trouble was that it had already fallen too far. The possibility of movement toward long-term structural change was lost through preference for short-run stabilization.

In the event, total imports increased from 14 to 18 percent of GDP, while exports grew more slowly and remained at 16 percent of GDP (Table 2). That was a weaker performance on the export side, though better restrained on the import side, when Peru is compared with the Latin American region, where exports increased relative to GDP by 3 percentage points, and imports by 6.

Both Peru and the region made progress toward more competitive manufacturing sectors, as measured by the share of manufactures in total exports. For the region, that share rose steeply, from 34 to 49 percent. For Peru, both the level and the increase were much lower: from 18 to 20 percent. All were helped by the growth of demand from the United States until 2000, though Mexico and Costa Rica, with their strong positions in manufacturing exports, were helped a great deal more than Peru. The share of exports coming from the industrial sector in Mexico shot up from 43 to 83 percent, and that of Costa Rica from 27 to 66 percent. Peru could have participated more fully in that kind of change if its exchange rate, or any substitute set of incentives, had been used for that purpose.

While the direct cause of the interruption of growth after 1997 was the adverse change in external financial markets, the political turmoil at the end of the decade added seriously to the difficulty of economic recov-

Table 2   Imports, exports, and manufactures for selected countries

	Imports (percentage of GDP)		Exports (percentage of GDP)		Manufactures/ Total Exports (percentage of total commodity exports)	
	1990	2000	1990	2000	1990	2000
Argentina	5	11	10	11	29	32
Bolivia	24	25	23	18	5	29
Brazil	7	12	8	11	52	59
Chile	31	31	35	32	11	16
Colombia	15	20	21	22	25	34
Costa Rica	41	46	35	48	27	66
Ecuador	27	31	33	42	2	10
Mexico	20	33	19	31	43	83
Peru	14	18	16	16	18	20
Uruguay	18	21	24	19	39	42
Venezuela	20	17	39	29	10	9
Latin America and Caribbean Region	12	18	14	17	34	49

SOURCE: World Bank 2002.

ery. The political upheaval was a response to widening public perception of the government's manipulation of the political system and corruption of basic institutions, made glaringly evident by the revelation of incriminating videotapes recorded by the head of the National Intelligence Agency. Peruvians have a gift for the dramatic. For those who emphasize the effect of institutional quality on economic performance, the joint economic and political strains were readily understandable: effective performance in a liberalized economy requires respect for at least minimal dependability of laws and their implementation.

The 1990s: Poverty, Inequality, Education, and Employment

Explanation of degrees of poverty needs to take account of at least two different lines of causation. On the simpler level, sustained economic growth dependably reduces poverty (Easterly 2001, 1–15). On the more complex side, many other factors enter into determining why particular countries, including Peru, have persistently higher incidences of poverty than others relative to their levels of income.

The first line of explanation, emphasizing the effects of economic growth, gives a good fit to the pattern of change in the 1990s. On that view, poverty should have fallen in the period of high growth up to 1997 but stopped falling, or turned back up, when growth stopped at that point. That is exactly what happened, but it is not the whole story.

Table 3 contains two sets of estimates of poverty, by the private Instituto Cuánto and by the National Statistics Institute (INEI), based on different methods of surveying and analysis. The longer series by Instituto Cuánto indicates a decrease of 4.6 percentage points, or 8 percent, from the peak in 1991 to the lowest point in 1997. This was also a relatively good period for the region as a whole: the average incidence of poverty for Latin America as reported by CEPAL (Comisión Económica para América Latina y el Caribe, or Economic Commission for Latin America and the Caribbean) came down by 12 percent between 1990 and 1997 (CEPAL 2000, 269–70).

The trend turned the other way after 1997. According to the Cuánto measures, the incidence of poverty increased by 7 percent between then and the year 2000. By the INEI measures, the increase was 13 percent for those three years, and a dismal 17 percent between 1997 and 2001. The incidence of extreme poverty, which had been cut by an impressive 39 percent between 1991 and 1997, also turned back up from then to 2001 but much more moderately so than the incidence of total poverty.

The preceding measures of poverty refer to levels of income, which are only part of what matters. Poverty in the more comprehensive sense of living standards and ability to respond to new opportunities depends

Table 3 Estimates of incidence of poverty and extreme poverty in Peru (percentages of families below poverty lines)

| | Poverty | | Extreme poverty | |
	Instituto Cuánto	INEI	Instituto Cuánto	INEI
1985	41.6	—	18.4	—
1991	55.3	—	24.2	—
1994	53.4	—	19.0	—
1997	50.7	42.7	14.7	18.2
2000	54.1	48.4	14.8	15.0
2001	—	49.8	—	19.5

SOURCE: PNUD-PERU 2002, 18; Herrera 2002 (for INEI and the Institut de recherche pour le developpement), 82, 84.

NOTE: The INEI estimates given for 2001 are comparable to those from the same source for 1997 and 2000. INEI also gives a different set of estimates for 2001 that are based on new methods intended to provide a more complete picture. The new estimates are 54.8 percent for poverty and 24.4 percent for extreme poverty. These are presumably better measures of actual poverty but they are not comparable to the preceding figures for 1997 and 2000.

heavily on questions of public health, water supply, sanitary facilities, life expectancy, access to social services, and other crucial variables not measured by money incomes. Many specific improvements in these dimensions are reported and discussed in a World Bank (1999) study covering the years of strongest gains, from 1994 to 1997. Still, the needs remain great. One measure of their severity is given by the index of deprivation, or "human poverty," published by the United Nations Development Program (2001, 171–73). That index takes into account the probability at birth of dying before age forty (12 percent in Peru for 1995–2000, contrasted to a low of 5 percent in Uruguay), the adult illiteracy rate, the percentage of population not using improved water sources, and the percentage of children below age five who are underweight. Of the countries listed in Table 1, Costa Rica and Uruguay had, equally, the lowest level of deprivation. The index for Peru was 3.2 times as high as theirs. It was equal to that for Brazil and greater than those of all other countries except Bolivia and Ecuador.

Changes in education and literacy rates are too slow to have much discernable effect on poverty in a single decade, but their levels may account for exceptionally high (or low), incidence of poverty at given national incomes. A simple test is possible for 1970, a year for which CEPAL provided comparable measures of poverty in six Latin American countries. Higher GDP per capita was associated with lower incidence of poverty, though the correlation was weak. Lower degrees of illiteracy were also correlated with lower incidence of poverty, and this relationship was much stronger (Sheahan 2002, 38–39).

Public expenditures on education provide some evidence of effort for long-run improvement, though always subject to questions about their character and efficacy. Comparisons of public spending on education in ten countries for 1985–87 and for 1995–97, plus 1998–2000 data for eight of them, are shown in Table 4. For the ten countries, the median ratio of public expenditures on education to GDP increased from 3.4 percent in 1985–87 to 4.5 percent in 1995–97. In contrast, the ratio for Peru fell from 3.6 to 2.9 percent. Peru was the only one of the ten for which the ratio decreased. It partially recovered in the following few years, to 3.3 percent for 1998–2000, but that ratio remained below the median for the eight countries with comparable data.

Inequality in the distribution of income had been exceptionally high in 1960 but came down moderately through the 1970s and 1980s. Table 5 contains two pairs of estimates for Gini coefficients of inequality in Peru, one by CEPAL that should be comparable to the other seven coun-

Table 4   Public expenditures on education (percentage of GDP)

	1985–1987	1995–1997	1998–2000
Bolivia	2.1	4.9	5.5
Brazil	4.7	5.1	4.7
Chile	3.3	3.6	4.2
Colombia	2.6	4.1	—
Costa Rica	4.5	5.4	4.4
Ecuador	3.3	3.5	1.6
Mexico	3.5	4.9	4.4
Peru	3.6	2.9	3.3
Uruguay	3.2	3.3	2.8
Venezuela	5.0	5.2	—
Median	3.4	4.5	4.3

SOURCE: UNDP 2001, 170–72; 2003, 266–68.

Table 5   Estimated Gini coefficients of inequality in nationwide income distribution

	1990 or closest year	1999 or closest year
Brazil	.63	.64
Chile	.55	.56 (2000)
Colombia	.60 (1994)	.57
Costa Rica	.44	.47
Mexico	.54 (1989)	.54 (2000)
Peru (CEPAL)	.53 (1997)	.55
(Alternative estimates)	.44 (1991)	.46 (2000)
Uruguay	.49	.44
Venezuela	.47	.50

SOURCE: CEPAL 2002, 227–29 for all except alternative estimates for Peru. Alternative estimates from Pascó-Font and Saavedra 2001, 217. The alternatives cover a longer period for Peru but are not comparable to levels for the other countries.

NOTE: Argentina, Bolivia, and Ecuador are omitted because the CEPAL estimates for them apply to urban areas only.

tries cited and the other by leading Peruvian research economists. The CEPAL estimates place Peru practically at the median for the countries with nationwide estimates. The estimates by Pasco-Font and Saavedra cover a longer time period (starting in 1991 rather than 1997) and show a slight rise from .44 to .46 between those years. That fits the common picture of relative stability, with a tendency to small increases except for the pronounced decrease in Uruguay.

Inequality is the product of many forces, including social failures to provide anything like equal access to education and opportunities, differences in personal capacities, concentrated ownership of capital, and structures of production and trade (Sheahan and Iglesias 1998). For Peru, the long-term weakness of labor markets, especially for low-skill labor, has certainly been among the main factors that worsen inequality. This is in part a matter of open unemployment but more fundamentally of the growing share of workers caught in occupations of extremely low productivity.

Measures of open unemployment in urban areas vary in response to current levels of economic activity, though for metropolitan Lima in the 1990s they were consistently higher than averages for the region through good years and bad (CEPAL 2000, 96). Unemployment in Lima fell below 8 percent only once in the decade. The regional average, in contrast, was below 8 percent in eight years out of ten.

Employment in low-productivity activities, with earnings too low for the earner to escape poverty, is a much more pervasive problem than open unemployment. In rural areas, the basic reason is the insufficient availability of arable land relative to the agricultural labor force. In urban occupations, it is the lack of adequate employment opportunities in the formal sector. Low-productivity occupations are concentrated in the informal sector, though that sector also includes many activities that yield decent incomes, as well as workers who prefer independence from formal wage-paying employment. A study of the composition of the labor market in Lima, for the mid-1990s, suggests that approximately two-thirds of the workers in the informal sector were there because they did as well or better in that sector—given their education and other characteristics—than they would have if employed in the formal sector (Yamada 1996). The remaining third were not there by preference but because of the lack of sufficient opportunities for more productive employment in the formal sector.

A particularly telling marker of poor employment conditions between 1970 and 1990 was that the share of the labor force in Lima trying to survive by selling things in the street increased from 2.5 to 13.1 percent (Verdera 1994, 21). The first half of the 1990s was an improvement on this score: the proportion fell to 11.6 percent. Still, the share of the labor force in the informal sector kept right on rising even through the years of good economic growth. Between 1994 and 1997, the last three years of good growth, urban employment in the formal sector increased by 430,000 workers, but that was far from sufficient to keep up with the growth of the labor force: the informal sector increased by 585,000 (World Bank 1999, 32). In the more difficult period from 1997 to 2002, formal-sector employment fell in absolute numbers: the informal sector had to absorb both the full increase of the labor force and the workers who lost employment in the formal sector (Saavedra 2002, 3).

Real wages for hourly paid workers in the private sector took a drastic beating in the course of the 1980s, then started a modest recovery in the early 1990s. But from 1994 on they began to fall once more, even while economic growth continued. Between 1994 and 1997 real wages of hourly paid workers, in firms with ten or more workers, fell by 15 percent (BCRP 1998, 65).

Real wages of the low-skilled majority of the labor force cannot rise in any sustained way until the competitive strength of the economy makes it possible to maintain fairly high rates of growth, less subject to the erratic swings of external demand for primary products and less dependent on external capital. To approach the problem of external dependence by closing down access to imports, prior to the 1990s, was a fundamental mistake. That strategy reduced incentives to pursue technological progress, to improve quality and reduce costs, in order to compete in the world economy. It worked against the development of competitive strength by the modern sectors of the economy, and thus against any sustained improvement of employment conditions.

Liberalization of trade in the 1990s was a vital step toward long-run improvement but its potential was undercut by adverse management of the exchange rate. By restraining both the cost of imported manufactures and the earnings of exporters, it held the growth of production below the growth of demand. In turn, that held down the growth of productive employment. A careful attempt to measure the degree of damage suggests that industrial employment would have been about 12 percent higher than it actually was in 1994 if the increase in production up to that point had matched the increase in demand for industrial products (Saavedra 1997a). It is not that liberalization was overdone; it is rather that, in this crucial respect, the accompanying structure of incentives was poorly managed.

Degrees and Kinds of Economic Liberalization

Economic liberalization is in effect a commitment to withdraw from extensive state intervention in the operation of the economy. If followed strictly, that would constitute a rejection of the very idea of politically determined measures to promote changes in structures of production and trade. In practice, it has been implemented in significantly different ways among Latin American countries and has been changed considerably in some of them when its results proved to be unacceptable. From the viewpoint of the international development agencies, that is usually considered a defect: "structural reform" has not been complete. From the viewpoint of long-term prospects for development, it may instead be seen as a potential advantage in that the countries have retained some scope for promotional intervention. Whether that actually turns out to be a defect or an advantage in the particular case depends on the nature of the policies adopted.

As of the mid-1990s, Peru had implemented one of the highest degrees of liberalization in Latin America. Table 6 shows Inter-American Development Bank (IDB) indexes of reform in 1995, for the eleven countries cited in Tables 1 and 2. The indexes are based on averages for reform in five different dimensions: trade, finance, labor, privatization, and fiscal (IDB 1997, 31–96). The indexes could, in principle, go from zero up to unity for complete fulfillment of reformers' dreams. For 1995, they go from a low of .46 (Venezuela, understandably), to highs of .71 and .72 for Peru and Bolivia. Argentina is a close third, at .68.

In Table 6 these countries are divided into three groups: those most clearly neoliberal (group A); six others that liberalized considerably as compared to their pasts but fell short in their reforms, if judged in terms

Table 6   Degrees of liberalization as of 1995 for selected countries

	IDB index of structural reform
Group A: strongly neoliberal	
Bolivia	.72
Peru	.71
Argentina	.68
Group B: liberal compared to the past but more moderate than group A	
Chile	.63
Colombia	.59
Brazil	.58
Uruguay	.57
Mexico	.56
Costa Rica	.51
Group C: unstable changes during the 1990s	
Ecuador	.58
Venezuela	.46

SOURCE: For index of structural reform, IDB 1997, 9.

of the IDB index (group B); and two—Ecuador and Venezuela—that went through such erratic policy changes in the course of the 1990s that they do not fit readily in either of the more stable groups (group C). Group A had an average structural reform index of .70 in 1995; group B only .57. If "more liberalization is better" were a dependable rule, group A should be expected to perform better than group B. If "some liberalization is highly desirable but more is not necessarily better," group B might in some respects do as well or better than group A.

Econometric tests of the consequences of liberalization have given considerable evidence of its positive effects with respect to economic growth, productivity improvement, and possibly even income distribution (Fernández-Arias and Montiel 1997; IDB 1997, 31–96). For employment, on the contrary, the apparent consequences were negative.[3] The component of liberalization found to be most effectively favorable for growth was trade liberalization. A good deal of improvement in growth was attributed to separate (but closely associated) changes in stabilization policies.

Such econometric tests can be much more precise than simple comparisons between groups A and B in Table 6, but these particular tests may have lost some of their relevance because of changes in economic conditions subsequent to the period studied. They cover performance in the first half of the 1990s, a period in which it looked as if the most thoroughly liberalized countries were doing better and better. Peru and Argentina seemed to be the stars in that period, but then both fell into serious trouble shortly thereafter. The period observed in the econometric studies was a good one in terms of overt performance but not in terms of building capacity for sustained growth.

On the criterion of performance that comes most naturally to economists, the average rate of growth of GDP per capita for group A was 2.3 percent a year (from Table 1). By the coincidences of fate, the average for group B was almost exactly the same, at 2.4 percent. Differences in degrees of structural reform did not seem to matter much in this respect. Still, the two groups show an interesting pattern of differences in their reactions to the change between easy external financing from 1990 to 1997 and the more difficult conditions of 1997–2000. When external conditions were favorable, group A raised incomes notably faster than group B. When external financing contracted, and growth became more a matter of domestic economic management, group B fared much better. Lower liberalization was associated with somewhat greater stability, by better performance when external conditions worsened.

The superior performance of group B in the period 1997–2000 was the result, above all, of the striking improvements for Costa Rica and Mexico. They were the only two countries that raised their growth rates in this period (see Table 1). That achievement was closely related to their export performances. Both for increases in exports relative to GDP and for increases in the shares of manufacturing exports, they made the greatest gains through the 1990s of all the countries included in Tables 1 and 2. Only one other country came even close to their record of strengthening exports of manufactures. It happened to be a country in group A, namely, Bolivia. That was not the kind of change one would expect from such a low-income country. The explanation seems to be that Bolivia carried out a substantial real devaluation from 1988 to 1995. An econometric test of the consequences concluded that a devaluation of 10 percent in real terms leads to a rise of 13 percent in manufactured exports (Jenkins 1996).

The most significant difference between the neoliberal group and group B was in export performance, particularly the results of Mexico and Costa Rica in the latter group. For Mexico, that difference might be explicable mainly by its long-standing promotional intervention to foster industrial exports, prior to liberalization, supported by the effects of the North American Free Trade Agreement (NAFTA) in a period of strongly rising demand in the United States. For Costa Rica, a possible explanation is its continuance of promotional measures despite its partial liberalization, combined with activist exchange-rate policies to favor the profitability of exports. One of the reasons it has been regarded as an example of incomplete reform is that the government continued to promote new exports by tax incentives through Export Processing Zones, and to use activist promotion to bring in foreign investment in fields associated with high technological progress (IDB 2001b, 258). The biggest catch, Intel, proved to be a strong stimulus to the entry of new firms in fields associated with its activities. By continuing to use selective promotion, and using it effectively, Costa Rica did better than Peru in terms of growth as well as export development. Less structural reform, in this case, proved superior to more.

The observed differences between degrees of liberalization refer mainly to policies with respect to labor market regulations, privatization, fiscal reforms, and modest forms of promotion (as in Costa Rica for exports, and Chile for the use of capital controls in order to limit exchange-rate appreciation). That kind of promotion seems to have been successful for growth, though not especially helpful for distribution. Brazil, Costa Rica, and Uruguay all avoided the extreme antilabor policies of Chile in its authoritarian phase of liberalization. Uruguay's version of liberalization even allowed a democratic vote on proposed privatization, and acceptance of the popular decision against it. That did not prevent the country from achieving a growth rate above the regional average and the best record for reduction of inequality among the countries compared in Table 5. A modest score in terms of structural reform—below the median for the countries considered—proved to be consistent with more than usually appealing social consequences.

Clues for the Future

The mixed experiences of the 1990s included some important gains that deserve to be recognized and maintained. But they also they point to missed opportunities that could have been realized with a different—though not wholly contrary—economic strategy.

The central question about Peru considered in this chapter is how the new economic strategy of the 1990s affected the structural factors that underlie long-run performance. Three of the main factors emphasized are access to effective education, employment conditions, and possible transformation of the structures of production and trade toward a more competitive industrial sector. They are bound together in shaping the evolution of the economy, along with a host of other relevant factors, including institutional changes and the complex of political-economic influences that determine policy decisions. Fortunately, institutional changes are discussed in this volume by Carol Wise (Chapter 9) and more fully in her book on the Peruvian state (2003b). The decision-making process is an elusive matter that goes far beyond the scope of this chapter but it might be helpful to offer some tentative suggestions about why Peru kept so close to its relatively extreme version of structural reform all through the 1990s.

For the life chances of the majority of Peruvians, the most important single improvement needed is to raise the quality of public education: to reduce the enormous inequality of opportunities between the minority who have a chance for decent education and the majority who do not. The government of the 1990s, pushed and helped by the World Bank, seemed to be willing to promote serious reforms, but the simple indicator cited in Table 4 is not encouraging: of that of the ten countries compared for 1995–97, the ratio of public spending on education to GDP remained lowest in Peru. Of the eight countries with data available for 1998–2000,

Peru had the sixth-highest ratio, better than in the preceding period but still below the median.

Education and other social programs need tax revenue if they are to be carried out within reasonable fiscal restraint. The government of the 1990s made striking improvements in tax collection through the creation of Superintendencia Nacional de Administración Tributaria (National Superintendency of Revenue Administration [SUNAT]) early in the decade, repairing the damage of corrupted tax administration under the García government. That looked like an impressive case of true institutional reform. But then, as the manipulations of the Fujimori administration spread throughout the government, even that success was twisted into a weapon of blackmail and political pressure. No battle is ever over. For many reasons, a good test of future governments will be their ability to maintain an honest and effective tax agency.

Wider access to effective education can help people get out of poverty through increased productivity, reduced inequality of opportunity and earnings, and greater national capacity for technical progress. It comes close to being a necessary condition for a competitive industrial sector, able to provide more stable growth and in the process more opportunities for productive employment. Peru made modest progress in this direction in the 1990s: exports of manufactures increased from 18 to 20 percent of total exports. How small the change was may be seen by comparing to results for the region as a whole: the share of manufacturing exports jumped from 34 to 49 percent. That record owed a great deal to the unusual strength of external demand for imports of manufactures, though it surely also owed something to trade liberalization in Latin America. The pity is that Peru's participation in this period of opportunity was so limited.

Trade liberalization could have either undercut the industrial sector or on the contrary, stimulated domestic entrepreneurship. The threat from liberalization was that access to more competitive imports might have driven much of Peruvian industry out of business. The more positive possibility was that increased competitive pressure might have stimulated more active and effective entrepreneurship: that some firms, perhaps many, might have proved able to respond through increased efficiency and greater technological progress. In the event, trade liberalization was neither a disaster nor an adequate success. Many firms responded well, and output of the industrial sector increased, but its shares of the domestic market and of Latin American industrial markets both decreased. One helpful clue for the future is that Peruvian firms can respond positively to open markets. A second is that they need the support of favorable incentives to respond adequately. Throughout the 1990s the price of foreign exchange was kept so low that incentives to enter new export markets were weaker than they could and should have been.

William Easterly (2001) makes a powerful case for the importance of incentives: firms will take the kinds of actions that a country needs if the incentives are positive and will fail to do so if they are not. This is not the same idea as the familiar slogan "Get the prices right." That slogan usually presumes that markets will get the prices right if allowed to operate without intervention. That is a particularly dubious assumption for currency markets. They are dominated by capital flows that can make foreign exchange too cheap for successful competition by the industrial sector. That was a major problem for Peru in the 1990s. The government allowed a strong appreciation in real terms between 1990 and 1991, intended to help check inflation, and then kept the real exchange rate close to this new level until 1999. Fortunately, the central bank kept things from getting worse by massive purchases of dollars to moderate the impacts of the capital inflow. That intervention prevented further appreciation but did not go far enough to promote positive structural change. These are useful clues!

The weakness of employment conditions in the 1990s was mainly an inherited problem of an overwhelming imbalance between the numbers of low-skill workers and the openings available for productive employment. Up to 1997, the redirection of economic strategy proved to be consistent with distinctly faster growth of formal-sector employment than during the preceding two decades, though that growth was still not fast enough to reduce the initial imbalance. Even in the 1994–97 period of high economic growth, the number of workers who gained employment in the formal sector was less than half the number entering the urban labor force. Consistent with this context, real wages of hourly paid production workers fell even in this period of output growth. The problem of deficient opportunities for productive employment remained unanswered.

Why did the Fujimori government stay so rigidly within the lines of the economic strategy adopted at the beginning of the 1990s, when the results in terms of such crucial variables as employment and industrial exports remained weaker than they might have been, and even when growth stopped and poverty increased so markedly from 1997 on? What were the motives and what were the methods by which policies were kept on this narrow path? These questions go beyond the relative security of economic analysis, but it may be useful to suggest two themes that should be part of the picture, one on the domestic side and one concerned with external influences.

On the domestic side, the government's economic strategy had a good deal of public support, led by members of the business community but shared by many other Peruvians, in reaction to the disastrous results of the populist policies of the preceding government. The late 1980s were harrowing years for nearly all Peruvians, in terms of runaway inflation and economic breakdown as well as rising violence. The conservative economic program adopted in 1990–91 provided a response that proved successful in stopping at long last a process of accelerating inflation that everyone detested. Further, once the threat of Sendero Luminoso (Shining Path) was answered, in 1992, the same economic strategy encouraged a massive capital inflow that helped the economy resume economic growth at a rate that had not been seen for many years. When the capital inflow and the growth stopped after 1997, doubts and criticisms grew, but the government managed to keep selling the delusion that any retreat from its conservative principles would lead straight back to the costly populism of the 1980s. As many governments do, it kept pointing to a scarecrow in order to obscure the reality of alternatives to its own preferences. Beyond that common practice, it used bribes and threats to silence critics who were in a position to have wide influence, in an effort particularly to control the content of television news and commentary.[4]

This interpretation of how the basic economic strategy was maintained leaves open the question of why the government chose to cling to it even after it began to show increasing weaknesses. In part, that could be explained by the personal ideologies of some of the key members of and advisors to the government, notably that of the economist most closely identified with it, Carlos Boloña. But perhaps in larger measure it might be attributed to the powerful influence of the international financial community. The official institutions of finance and development did all they could to make sure that the government stayed close to the strategy of economic liberalization that was backed by monetary and fiscal restraint, and, in return, to make sure that financial flows to Peru would remain favorable as long as the country followed that course. The private international banks followed the same orientation for much of the decade, though they pulled out for their own reasons after 1997.

All this could be viewed as a story of considerable success in supporting policies that were in many respects desirable for the economy, even if
they fell short in such key respects as employment and promotion of a
more competitive industrial sector. But the external influences became
more subject to question in the last years of the decade, as the government intensified its political manipulation and began to subvert some of
its own institutional reforms. The World Bank and the IDB in particular
faced difficult questions of whether they should continue all-out approval
and support for a government headed in such damaging directions. In
both cases, they continued to issue favorable evaluations and to provide
financial support, despite serious internal questioning in the case of the
World Bank. After the fall of the Fujimori government the World Bank
sponsored an external evaluation of the policies it had followed in Peru
in the 1990s. That evaluation, summarized in an unpublished 2002 review of the "Country Assistance Strategy" for Peru, praised much that
was done in the first half of the decade but was severely critical of the
way in which the bank kept on giving full support in the last years of the
1990s to a government that was increasingly distorting economic and
social programs for partisan purposes and at the same time subverting
the country's political process. Yet another clue for the future is that the
chances of meaningful development could be improved if the international development agencies could bring themselves to spell out such
problems and withhold support in severe cases, even when the country
concerned is oriented to the general lines of structural reform that the
institutions favor.

A brief review of the Peruvian economy by the IDB in 2001 provided
an informative summary of developments up to that time, though with a
troublesome conclusion about desirable future direction. The prospects,
in this interpretation, will be favorable provided that new governments
remain committed to "build on the achievements of the nineties" (IDB
2001a). It is easy to see the rationale for such a conclusion if attention is
restricted to the achievements of trade liberalization, fiscal and monetary
restraint, and the institutional reforms of the early 1990s. But in crucial
respects it is not a helpful guide. It ignores the ways in which economic
policies became twisted to political ends. And it leaves critical economic
issues out of sight. Peru needs to promote structural change that is more
favorable to the growth of opportunities for productive employment, a
competitive industrial sector, and industrial exports. Both for these objectives and for human development it also needs to devote far more

serious attention and resources to public education. The changes made in the 1990s were helpful in important ways but they were not even remotely adequate to the needs of the country.

NOTES

1. The estimates of poverty reported by the Economic Commission for Latin America indicate that its incidence in Peru was higher than the regional average in 1970—at 50 percent versus the average of 40 percent—and remained higher in 1986 at 52 percent versus the average of 37 (ECLAC 1994, 158–59). In contrast to this picture of slightly worsening poverty in Peru, a more recent study places the incidence in 1970–71 at the much higher level of 64 percent, which suggests that the incidence of poverty decreased between that point and 1986 (Escobal, Saavedra, and Torero 1998, 7).

2. The real exchange rate as intended here refers to the ratio between external and domestic prices, when both are expressed in terms of domestic currency. In Peru's case during 1990–91, this ratio fell (external prices decreased relative to domestic), because domestic inflation remained at first much higher than external inflation, without sufficient devaluation of the currency to offset the difference. For a thorough analysis of the meaning and role of real exchange rates, see Edwards 1989.

3. Regressions for effects on employment are given in IDB 1997, 90 (appendix 2). After controlling for the effects of economic growth and real wages, "the evidence consistently tends to estimate that structural reforms have reduced the rate of employment growth."

4. The present administration in the United States has not needed to be quite so aggressive in concealing and distorting information presented on television, but the symbiotic relationship between the Fox news channel and the Republican White House presents some disturbing echoes of Fujimori's control over what the public is told.

NINE

Against the Odds:
The Paradoxes of Peru's Economic Recovery in the 1990s

CAROL WISE

The 1990 dark-horse presidential victory of the little-known, inexperienced politician Alberto Fujimori did not appear at the time to be a recipe
for Peru's sound economic recovery. The immediate context was the
country's first bout with hyperinflation and its international financial isolation that resulted from the repeated failure to stabilize the economy in
the aftermath of the 1982 debt shocks and a related debt default. The
traditional political parties had collapsed, civil strife was rampant, and
large segments of the hinterland were governed de facto by guerrilla
bands and drug traffickers (Webb 1991, 4). But despite these warlike
circumstances and the worst crisis the country had faced in more than a
century, Peru's economic performance in the 1990s easily outstripped
that of any of its neighbors in the Andean region (Vial and Sachs 2000).
Moreover, as can be seen in Tables 1 and 2, Peru held its own along with
the fastest-growing countries in the region during the 1990s, namely, Argentina and Chile, and it outperformed Argentina and Mexico in the
growth of income and real wages.

In retrospect, the loss of political and economic control by the country's entrenched elite paved the way for new actors and fresh approaches
to the country's enormous backlog of problems, some of which finally
began to pay off. As made clear by Fujimori's abrupt resignation in September 2000 and his subsequent self-exile to Japan, some of these new
actors and approaches proved to be corrupt. But herein lies the main

Table 1   Macroeconomic and external indicators in Argentina, Brazil, Chile, Mexico, and Peru, 1991–2000

	Argentina	Brazil	Chile	Mexico	Peru
GDPGRO	4.7	2.7	6.6	3.5	4.7
GNPPCGRO	5.0	1.3	6.7	1.3	4.3
INF	21.4	579.0	9.5	18.7	60.1
PRIVGDP	16.5	15.5	18.8	15.4	16.7
PUBIGDP	1.6	4.4	4.9	3.5	3.7
INVEST	18.1	19.9	23.7	18.9	20.4
RER	57.1	91.3	78.9	83.5	75.4
TRADEBAL	− 283	2,718.5	− 19.0	− 6,045.7	1,142.4
CURACCT	− 8,701.3	− 15,223.0	− 2,000.2	− 14,848.9	− 2,613.9
FDI	6,347.5	12,517.6	2079.7	8,793.1	1,533.3
PORT	6,952.2	13,752.1	565.0	9,312.5	140.1
DEBT	106,642.6	179,496.8	27,995.7	147,070.2	27,365.4

SOURCE: GDP, GNP, and debt from World Bank 2000, 2001c; GDP growth and debt from Economist Intelligence Unit Country Reports, March, April 2001; GNP per capita data from IDB (http://www.iadb.org), 2001. Data on investment from Bouton and Sumlinski 2000, http://www.ifc.org/economics/pubs/discuss.html. Inflation, exchange rates, and payments calculated from IMF 2001.

NOTE: Abbreviations in table are as follows:

GDPGRO	Growth of real GDP
GNPPCGRO	Growth of real per capita GNP
INF	December–December inflation
PRIVGDP	Private investment as percentage of GDP based on data through 1998
PUBIGDP	Public investment as percentage of GDP based on data through 1998
INVEST	Total domestic investment as percentage of GDP based on data through 1998
RER	Real exchange rate (1990 = 100), calculated using period average exchange rates, U.S. Wholesale Price Index and domestic Consumer Price Index
TRADEBAL	Trade balance (mil$) = merchandise exports − merchandise imports
CURACCT	Current account (mil$)
FDI	Foreign direct investment (mil$)
PORT	Foreign portfolio investment (mil$)
DEBT	Total external debt (mil$)

departure point for this chapter: my purpose is to sort out the remarkable confluence of factors, both positive and negative, that contributed to Peru's highly unexpected economic turnaround in the 1990s. My argument is largely an institutional one, as the flip side of Peru's 1988–90 hyperinflationary crisis was the emergence of a long-overdue consensus that major reforms could no longer be postponed. In turn, the growing demand for reform fostered strong incentives for institutional renovation, as the very survival of the first Fujimori administration hinged on the president's ability to deliver on those basic services and economic necessities that had been promised on the campaign trail.

This included, for example, the renovation of long-standing financial

Table 2   Macro versus micro performance in five countries, 1990–2000

		Argentina	Brazil	Chile	Mexico	Peru
GDP (growth)	1991–00	4.2	2.5	5.8	3.4	4.8
GDI (GDI/GDP)	1990–98	17.6	20.8	25.2	22.7	20.9
EXGDP (EXP/GDP)	1990–00	9.2	9.0	30.0	24.3	13.6
INF	2000	−1.7	8.0	2.6	13.9	4.8
RW	1990–00	0.0	0.5	3.7	0.8	0.9
EMP	1990–00	1.3	1.7	1.9	3.2	2.9
LPRO	1990–95	4.1	−0.1	3.3	−2.2	2.2
URUN	1990–00	11.9	5.6	7.3	3.7	8.5
EDGAP	1994	1.9[a]	4.7	1.5	3.1	2.6[a]
DIST: poorest 40%	1986	16.2	9.7	12.6	12.7[c]	14.1
DIST: poorest 40%	1990	14.9	9.6	13.4	11.7[b]	NA
DIST: poorest 40%	1994	13.9	11.8	13.3	10.8	14.1
DIST: poorest 40%	1998	NA	8.2	NA	NA	13.5
DIST: richest 10%	1986	34.5	44.3	39.6	34.3[c]	35.4
DIST: richest 10%	1990	34.8	41.7	39.2	39.0[b]	NA
DIST: richest 10%	1994	34.2	42.5	40.3	41.2	34.3
DIST: richest 10%	1998	35.8	44.3	39.1	42.8	35.4

SOURCE: GDP from ECLAC (http://www.eclac.org), 2001; GDI from World Bank 2001a; EXGDP calculated from IMF 2001, "National Accounts," September; INF from World Bank 2001c; RW, EMP, LPRO, URUN from ECLAC 2001; EDGAP from Behrman, Birdsall, and Szekly 1998. DIST: data for Chile and Brazil are based on data for urban areas, and data for Argentina are based on data for Buenos Aires, all from ECLAC 1997; data on national income distribution for Peru from World Bank 1993b, 1996, 2001a.

NOTE: Abbreviations in table are as follows:
GDP   Gross domestic product, average annual percentage growth
GDI   Gross domestic investment, average annual rate, as percentage of GDP
EXGDP   Ratio of exports of goods and services to GDP
INF   Percent change in consumer prices over previous year
RW   Real wages, average annual growth rate
         EMP Employment, average annual growth rate
LPRO   Labor productivity, average annual growth rate
URUN   Urban employment, average annual rate
EDGAP   Average years behind in school for ages 15–18
DIST   Percentage of national income accruing to groups

[a]1996
[b]1989
[c]1984

entities such as the Banco Central de Reserva del Perú (Central Reserve Bank of Peru [BCRP]) and the Ministry of Economy and Finance (MEF), that were essential for the successful completion of the macroeconomic stabilization effort. Another key aspect of institutional reform in the early 1990s was the reinvention or creation of new state entities geared toward achieving the longer-term goals of economic restructuring along market lines. The purpose of these longer-term institutional goals was, first, to modernize and sustain the state's revenue stream at levels that would allow for the proper provision of essential public goods and, second, to rationalize the new market-based development strategy through the design of institutions that sought to guarantee property rights and to promote a competitive business environment. In essence, Peru's economic turnaround is testimony to a pattern of "autonomous" institutional reform, which entailed the siphoning off of strategic pockets of the public sector and the management of these units as if they were private entities (Nuñes and Geddes 1987; Keefer 1995).

While candidate Fujimori had asserted the need for a gradual *dirigiste* reform program (S. Stokes 2001, 50–53), once he was elected it took just ten days for the newly inaugurated administration to realize that hyperinflation had rendered gradualism a foreclosed option. The complete collapse of state finances, combined with the halt of capital flows to Peru, meant there was zero financial room to maneuver. Other leaders elected at this time on similar gradualist platforms, such as Venezuela's Carlos Andrés Pérez and Argentina's Carlos Menem (Corrales 2002) moved immediately in launching market shock programs, and Fujimori followed suit. Hence, it came as no real surprise when Peru quickly adopted the blueprint package of stabilization and adjustment measures, as well as the sweeping structural reforms based on liberalization, privatization, and deregulation, that had come to be known as the Washington Consensus (Williamson 1990).

Less predictable were the cast of characters who coalesced around this market-oriented venture and the economic recovery that soon followed. For example, Fujimori's two main allies—domestic business and the Peruvian military—had not sustained a presence within the upper echelons of government since the country's return to civilian rule in 1980. Hindsight shows that the role of each in the leadership coalition lent credibility to the Fujimori administration at the very moment when public confidence in national leaders had sunk to an all-time low. However, as the 1990s wore on, and the president became intent on indefinitely prolonging his own incumbency, this tipped the balance of power uncomfortably on the side of the military. This disproportionate influence of the military, and along with it a lack of accountability and proper legislative oversight, did not bode well for the Fujimori team's ability to consolidate the policies that had been introduced as part of the initial shock program or to deepen this effort by launching another wave of necessary reforms.

In this chapter I analyze these tensions between economic recovery and impending political stalemate in the 1990s from three angles: the various paradoxes that underpinned the country's economic recovery, including the regime's own internal contradictions and the "outlier" status that this case came to occupy in the region; an assessment of Peru's economic restructuring in terms of the timing, sequencing, and content of market reforms; and the main legacies of the Fujimori era for the country's development trajectory.

On the last point, the analysis will show that impressive headway has been made in redressing those cumulative macroeconomic stabilization problems inherited from the 1980s; moreover, Peru's "first phase" of market reform based on liberalization, privatization, and deregulation has basically been completed. At the same time, few concrete gains have been made in the microeconomic realm, as distributional patterns and the competitive abilities of Peruvian workers and the predominantly small firms that employ them remain abysmal. This last set of challenges was passed on to the subsequent administration of Alejandro Toledo (2001–6), which is still struggling politically with the gridlock that has plagued economic progress since Fujimori's second term.

The Paradoxes of Economic Recovery

Against the Odds

Over the past decade a rich body of literature has evolved around one deceptively simple question: how is it that Latin America, a region that has sided historically with statist development strategies and varying degrees of authoritarianism, has sustained a combination of market reforms and civilian rule since the late 1980s? Answers to this question, as well as explanations for the highly variable outcomes that appear in Table 1, have centered on the ways in which market reforms have interacted with patterns of executive leadership, political-party structures, and the abilities of economic reformers to forge political coalitions that could credibly advance their new liberal initiatives (Haggard and Kaufman 1995; Mainwaring and Scully 1995; Corrales 2002; Wise 2003a). Briefly, while there may be some disagreement on the weight that should be assigned to these variables, there is a general consensus that reform efficacy stems from some combination of strong executive leadership, internal party renewal, and cohesive coalition building.

The Peruvian experience, of course, readily defies this view, not to mention an otherwise credible cluster of explanatory variables that have been used to defend it. Suffice it to say that the kinds of professional executive leadership, political-party renewal, and cohesive reform coalitions that roughly characterized such cases as Chile and Mexico in the 1990s have been sorely lacking in Peru. Rather, under Fujimori, a strong and overly autonomous executive leadership style failed to counter numerous other political asymmetries, including the internal unraveling of the country's traditional political-party system and the lack of a viable reform coalition. Yet, in contrast to Venezuela, where similar weaknesses provoked the abandonment of market reforms altogether, Peru was able to stay the course with market restructuring.

In the end, however, Peru's experience does not take away from those who have argued that the long-term success and sustainability of market reforms will require that they be firmly grounded in cohesive political-party systems and coherent state-society relations. If anything, this last point was confirmed by the need to call new elections after Fujimori's contrived reelection to a third term in May 2000, followed by the revelations of deep-seated corruption that finally brought Fujimori down in September 2000. It may have taken a decade, but the electorate's tolerance for authoritarianism finally diminished in the face of mounting frustration over unmet reform demands (Remmer 2003). A main question that I seek to address here is, How was Fujimori able to patch together a reform coalition and stretch a "short-term" political survival strategy out for so long? Further, in this interim, how is it that respectable economic returns were registered under these otherwise unfavorable circumstances?

The Least Likely of Reform Coalitions

As the dust began to settle on the mass of market measures that were implemented during Fujimori's first term, it became apparent that the business-military coalition that had catalyzed around the president's market reform program looked nothing like the elite party-controlled cliques that had ruled the country from 1980–90. How is it that an executive such as Fujimori, with no mentionable ties to the business community at the outset of his presidency, was able to forge a viable partnership with the Peruvian private sector when all prior attempts in the 1980s had patently failed? This unlikely alliance must be understood from the standpoint of Fujimori's own pragmatism, as he quickly grasped the need to bring the domestic private sector on board, as well as the institutional strengthening and internal reform that had occurred within the business community itself.

For the private sector's part, domestic business had come a very long way from the days when bank owners had chained themselves to their desks in protest against former president Alan Garcia Pérez's 1987 attempt to nationalize the country's financial institutions. This, in fact, was a critical turning point for Peruvian business, as a highly heterogeneous set of domestic interests finally began to unite as a peak association proper. Even before his inauguration in 1990, Fujimori began meeting with the representatives of the Confederación Nacional de Instituciones Empresariales Privadas (National Confederation of Private Business Institutions [CONFIEP]), the private sector's umbrella organization, and during his tenure as president he gave the closing speech at the annual conferences of CONFIEP and the Conferencia Anual de Ejecutivos (Annual Conference of Business Executives [CADE]) (Durand 1998, 270–72). This is not to say that the business community agreed with the entire package of market measures. However, the positive signals from higher growth and lower inflation, and the appointment of prominent business leaders to key ministerial posts through the course of the 1990s, helped forge a viable working coalition.

As for the military's strong presence in Fujimori's reform coalition, the armed forces' higher profile in national politics could perhaps be justified by the demands of quelling the long-running guerrilla insurgency led by Sendero Luminoso (Shining Path) and an explosion in drug trafficking in the 1980s. Prior to the 1990 presidential race the military had drawn up the "Green Book," its first sweeping plan of action since the installation of a populist military regime from 1968 to 1980 (Cameron 1997, 51). But in contrast to this earlier nationalist project, military leaders of the late 1980s called for the implementation of market reforms with solid backing from business, government, and the military as well as "a strong government that would last 20 years if necessary" (Crabtree 1998, 21–22). While Fujimori's last-minute ascendance in the 1990 presidential race took everyone, including the military, by surprise, the armed forces could not have found a better candidate to fulfill their newly articulated vision for Peru.

Antistatist Statism

As tempting as it may be to attribute Peru's turnaround in the 1990s to free markets and quasi-authoritarian rule, the discussion in this chapter points to a quiet process of state reconstruction and institutional reform that helped spur economic recovery in the 1990s. This explanation may seem paradoxical, given that Fujimori had become best known for his fierce independence and avowedly anti-institutional stance on all other matters. However, having inherited Latin America's most volatile political economy in 1990, the president had little choice but to delegate some bureaucratic authority and overhaul those state institutions that were crucial to economic recovery and hence to his own political survival.

The literature on bureaucratic delegation offers three insights with regard to the particularly strong reliance on autonomous agencies in Peru under the Fujimori administration (Przeworski 1999; Boylan 2000).[1] First, this was the first civilian administration since 1963 that did not command a majority vote in the Peruvian congress. This is the opposite scenario that awaited other civilian presidents who had inherited similarly daunting reform challenges, such as President Carlos Salinas in Mexico and President Carlos Menem in Argentina. The impulse of these other executives, relatively secure about their support bases and tenure in office, was to delay delegating authority to independent public entities such as central banks (Mexico) or regulatory boards (Argentina) for fear that such bureaucratic reforms would diminish their political control over the policymaking process. In contrast, Fujimori, with no guarantee of a "natural" legislative coalition to back him in Congress, pursued the autonomous-agency route up front as the only certain means for controlling his market reform agenda.

Accordingly, a second insight from the literature concerns the recognition that market reforms will flounder in the absence of a proper institutional base. As Philip Keefer (1995, 25) has observed, the potential benefit of this institutional autonomy is that "it insulates agencies from the influence of different government entities that attempt to use their oversight capacity to distort agency decisions in favor of narrow interests. The agency is relieved of the burden to balance every technical decision against the parochial concerns of a multitude of entities with oversight responsibilities." In a very real sense, then, the cultivation of a cluster of autonomous agencies to act as the standard-bearer for implementing and sustaining market reforms became part and parcel of the reforms themselves.

A third insight on bureaucratic insulation concerns policy efficacy. As voters in Peru had virtually abandoned party affiliation and instead cast their ballots according to the government's ability to visibly improve the delivery of essential public services (Graham and Kane 1998), the more efficient outputs from autonomous agencies became a main factor in enhancing Fujimori's electoral prospects. In short, they enabled the president to vastly improve the productivity and efficiency of fiscal spending while simultaneously attending to the needs of key constituencies. There was, however, a distinct downside to this new link between political survival and the development of autonomous public agencies in Peru.

For example, in other bureaucratic settings autonomous entities have more commonly been used as the surest way to render policy reforms irreversible (Boylan 2000, 5–7). As such, they tend to be governed by commissions composed of public and private representatives who serve staggered terms and are appointed by Congress (Keefer 1995). Not so in Peru, where autonomous agencies remain under the direct control of the president, who can hire and fire agency staff at will. Thus, while tremendous strides have been made in the way of efficiency, transparency, and service delivery, the future viability of this autonomous-agency approach will depend heavily on the extent to which it can be integrated into a broader legislative and managerial framework. Moreover, because this modernization process in the 1990s failed to fully penetrate the sectoral ministries, the state bureaucracy at large, or the legal-juridical apparatus, the degree of institutional reform achieved thus far constitutes a necessary, but not entirely sufficient, condition for more dynamic, equitable, and sustainable growth in Peru.

Market Reform, Phase One: Hyperpresidentialism and Congressional End Run

Similar to what was occurring with market reforms elsewhere in the region at this time, once the decision was made to finally buckle down to enacting a strict stabilization program, the policy package moved forward with little debate and just a handful of advisors. On the stabilization front, the first crucial step was to purge the country of hyperinflation, which was approached by way of a tight monetary policy, draconian spending cuts aimed at reducing public-sector deficits, and the unification of the multitiered exchange rate. Virtually overnight, government-controlled prices and subsidies were lifted on everything from gasoline to utilities, from sugar and rice to medicines. Between August 1990 and February 1991, emergency taxes were introduced, a new managed floating-exchange-rate system was established around a unified rate, domestic credit was tightened, and interest rate ceilings were basically lifted (C. E. Paredes 1991, 301).

During the first half of 1991, the economic team forged ahead with the implementation of deeper structural reforms and the renegotiation of the country's external debt. Tariffs on trade were reduced to a maximum of 25 percent; the capital account of the balance of payments was liberalized; numerous labor market regulations left over from the statist military regime (1968–80) were eliminated; land-tenure laws were amended to offer a broader scope for private initiative; the tax code was broadened and simplified; and the sale of some twenty-three state-owned enterprises (SOEs) had been announced (C. E. Paredes 1991, 313–15; Boloña 1996).

By 1990 there was a general consensus in the policy community that the adoption of structural reforms of this magnitude in the midst of the initial stabilization plan could detract from achieving the goals of that initial plan (Edwards 1990). Nevertheless, the economic team proceeded apace, apparently convinced that the benefits of launching the entire range of structural reforms simultaneously, along with mending Peru's relations with its external creditors, would outweigh the potential threat to the stabilization effort. Although this type of crash course in market reforms prompted macroeconomic blowups in any number of developing countries in the 1990s, and in line with the paradoxes discussed in the preceding section, Peru managed to beat these odds. Again, I would argue that it was renovation of economic institutions and Peru's autonomous-agency strategy that helped save the day.

After some initial success with the stabilization effort and the unilateral resumption of payments to service the country's external debt, the government initiated negotiations for settling the arrears it had run up with all the main multilateral lenders, including the World Bank, the Inter-American Development Bank (IDB), and the International Monetary Fund (IMF). This was a hurdle that had to be overcome before Peruvian policymakers could reschedule some $8 billion in debt with the consortium of Western country lenders known as the Paris Club, not to mention another $9.2 billion in commercial bank debt. However, the president's decision to take matters into his own hands in April 1992—closing the congress, suspending the constitution, and dismantling the judiciary—threw a quick wrench into any of the planned debt rescheduling. The Paris Club, in particular, insisted on a credible timetable for the restoration of democratic rule as a precondition for the rescheduling of Peru's debt.

Thus, the neoliberal strategy surged forward against a highly ambivalent political backdrop. The president garnered broad public support for the autogolpe, as he continued to hammer away at the moral corruption of the country's traditional legal and political institutions. But subsequent voting patterns suggested that the results of his political reform were not entirely embraced. For example, voters barely approved the new 1993 constitution and were especially wary of that document's expansion of presidential power (S. Stokes 1996b, 66; Gonzales de Olarte 1998, 44–45), including a new constitutional clause that allowed for the executive's immediate reelection to a consecutive term, and then further reelection after the lapse of one term. Alas, President Fujimori now became incumbent Fujimori, a turn of events that rendered solid economic performance and favorable public opinion ratings of the utmost importance for his political survival—regardless of how these were achieved.

Economic Recovery and the Launching of Structural Reforms

As can be seen in Table 3, the first convincing signs of economic recovery appeared in 1993, as growth rates and investment (both private and public) began to recuperate from the rock-bottom levels to which they had fallen during the García era. Moreover, for the first time in a decade, the annual inflation rate was below 50 percent. On the upside, because of the steep losses in personal income and the high levels of idle capacity that prevailed at the outset of the reform effort, there was considerable room for economic expansion. On the downside, the combination of rapid unilateral trade liberalization, tight monetary policy, and the continued appreciation of the exchange rate threw Peru's external accounts into disequilibrium.

While capital repatriation and a burst of privatization-related foreign direct investment (FDI) helped to finance the current-account deficit, the external gap increased nearly threefold from 1991 to 1995. Peruvian policymakers thus found themselves in straits similar to those of other market reformers in the region. Policymakers in Chile, and eventually Mexico and Brazil, had moved to rectify these problems, for example, by adopting a more flexible and competitive exchange-rate regime and by more aggressively promoting an export-led model of growth. In contrast, the Fujimori administration stood out for its insistence on a hands-off strategy, and it chose instead to assign the task of economic adjustment primarily to market forces.

Although this theme holds steady across the main components of the structural-reform program reviewed below, it does not detract from the integrity of this early stage of market restructuring in Peru. Rather, the

Table 3 Macroeconomic and external indicators in Peru, 1991–2000

Year	1991	1992	1993	1994	1995	1996	1997	1998	1999	2000
GDPGRO	7.0	−1.8	6.4	13.1	7.5	2.5	6.8	0.3	1.4	3.6
GNPPCGRO	19.1	−9.0	4.5	11.2	5.8	0.8	5.0	−3.3	NA	NA
INF	409.5	73.5	48.6	23.7	11.1	11.5	8.6	7.2	3.5	3.8
PRIVGDP	11.7	12.0	13.4	16.8	19.6	18.8	20.8	20.7	NA	NA
PUBIGDP	2.7	3.1	3.4	4.2	4.3	3.8	3.8	3.8	NA	NA
INVEST	14.5	15.2	16.8	21.0	23.9	22.6	24.6	24.5	NA	NA
RER	79.8	75.0	81.6	73.8	70.4	70.3	70.3	70.4	79.2	83.3
TRADEBAL	−188	−341	−605	−999	−2,166	−1,987	−1,723	−2,463	−617	−335
CURACCT	−1,500	−2,087	−2,287	−2,555	−4,117	−3,429	−3,056	−3,638	−1,822	−1,648
FDI	−7	150	687	3,108	2,048	3,242	2,697	1,881	1,969	558
PORT	NA	NA	201	492	159	181	156	−348	−372	−423
DEBT	20,716	20,338	23,573	26,528	30,852	29,328	30,523	32,397	29,100	30,300

SOURCE: GDP, GNP, and debt from World Bank 2000, except 1999 and 2000 GDP growth and debt, from Economist Intelligence Unit Country Reports (March, April 2001); GNP per capita data from IDB (http://www.iadb.org). Data on investment from Bouton and Sumlinski 2001, http://www.ifc.org/economics/pubs/discuss.htm. Inflation, exchange rates, and payments calculated from IMF 2001. Data for 1998 current account figures and Peruvian FDI and portfolio investment from IDB (www.iadb.org).

NOTE: Abbreviations in table are as follows:

GDPGRO   Growth of real GDP
GNPPCGRO   Growth of real per capita GNP
INF   December–December inflation
INVEST   Total domestic investment as percentage of GDP
PRIVGDP   Private investment as percentage of GDP
PUBIGDP   Public investment as percentage of GDP
RER   Real exchange rate (1990 = 100), calculated using period average exchange rate, U.S. Wholesale Price Index, and domestic Consumer Price Index.
TRADEBAL   Trade balance (mil$) = merchandise exports–merchandise imorts
CURACCT   Current account (mil$)
FDI   Foreign direct investment (mil$)
PORT   Foreign portfolio investment (mil$)
DEBT   Total external debt (mil$)

problem of policy inflexibility reared its head later, during Fujimori's second term, when challenges from the external sector demanded a more nuanced or hands-on approach to market reform, but policy responses moved in the opposite direction. In other words, although the institutional bases necessary to orchestrate a cohesive and effective economic policy response were finally being laid, an increasingly dominant president and his isolated inner circle mistakenly came to associate political survival with a strict adherence to the economic laissez-faire that had marked the initial phase of market reform under Fujimori's first term.

Trade Liberalization

In the wake of the shocking hyperinflation of the 1990s, Peru, having once set the pace for protectionist trade and investment norms within the Andean Community, now led the way as a champion of liberalization. The baseline for commercial-policy reform under Fujimori was a tariff structure that ranged from 10 to 110 percent; within this framework, 539 import items were banned outright. However, by March 1991, non-tariff barriers had been dismantled, and a dual tariff structure had been established under which 87 percent of tariff items were subject to a 15 percent tariff and the remainder to a 25 percent tariff (Boloña and Illescas 1997). In this sense Peru had quickly joined with other emerging market countries in the region, where unilateral trade liberalization had similarly been embraced both as a tool for promoting macroeconomic stabilization and as a means of forcing competitive changes at the microeconomic level. But unlike other reformers, who were more aggressive in coordinating macroeconomic policy with export promotion, Peruvian policymakers remained steadfastly committed to a laissez-faire economic policy.

Fiscal Shock

By the mid-1990s, Peru had recuperated from the outright fiscal collapse that had occurred a decade earlier. The rationalization of public finances was such that tax revenues had doubled, rising from their depths during the Garcia administration, when they had fallen to just 7 percent of GDP, to nearly 16 percent of GDP by the end of Fujimori's first term. At the same time, public expenditures were brought more realistically in line with tax revenues: the government deficit was less than 1 percent of GDP from 1990 to 1994, and public debt as a percentage of GDP—while still high by regional standards—had been reduced from nearly 50 percent in the mid-1980s to 32 percent in the mid-1990s. Three underlying factors contributed to Peru's fiscal overhaul, which was considered by some to be the most successful component of this first wave of structural reforms under Fujimori (Durand and Thorp 1998).

First, in the wake of hyperinflation, fiscal soundness was imperative, as policymakers and economic agents could no longer hide behind inflation in the setting of completely unrealistic revenue targets. Second, deep institutional changes underpinned the tax reform that was carried out between 1991 and 1994, including a complete revamping of the national tax agency (Superintendencia Nacional de Administración Tributaria, or National Superintendency of Revenue Administration [SUNAT]) and a strengthening of its capabilities in all areas of revenue collection (for example, streamlining of the tax structure, creation and updating of tax rolls, technical staff training, and computerization).[2] Third, the increase in tax revenues was bolstered by the more stable base for economic recovery and higher growth that had been established as a result of the implementation of the entire package of structural reforms reviewed in this section.

As impressive as these advances have been, few inroads were made in shifting the tax structure toward greater reliance on direct taxation or taxes on income and property. Apart from the fierce political resistance by powerful economic groups to these more progressive tax categories, fiscal reform along these lines was further hampered by the very small percentage of Peruvians who were actually in the habit of paying taxes (Durand and Thorp 1998, 221). Thus, while the tax structure had been simplified to just five categories (income tax, assets tax, excise duties, a housing and urban tax, and a value-added tax [VAT]), revenue collection came to depend disproportionately on indirect taxes and the tax on consumption (VAT) in particular. Peru is not unique in this respect, as the increased reliance on the more regressive VAT tax is a regionwide trend in the 1990s (ECLAC 1998, 67–71). But as the VAT came to account for 44 percent of all taxes collected by 1994, Peru's shift toward greater regressivity only exacerbated preexisting levels of inequality.

Privatization

The fiscal collapse of the late 1980s also rendered privatization inevitable at this point, as annual operating losses on the eve of the privatization drive were running at an astonishing $2.5 billion (Manzetti 1999, 248). In late 1991, with strong backing from the multilaterals, a new privatization law had been passed, and within a year the government's newly created privatization commission (Comisión de Promoción de la Inversión Privada, or Commission for Promotion of Private Investment [COPRI]) had begun to quickly unload state assets. In contrast to the foot-dragging and political charades that had surrounded previous efforts at privatization in Peru, COPRI staff moved forcefully in selling off some $9.1 billion in state assets by the end of 2000. During Fujimori's first term, for example, seventy-two privatizations had been completed, and the privatization program had generated commitments for another $11.3 billion in project investments (Araoz et al. 2001, 40). What explains this abrupt departure from past practices?

Certainly the liberalization of Peru's foreign investment regime and the overall economic recovery were important contributing factors, but it was the creation of COPRI and the long-overdue professionalization of the privatization strategy that accounts for these advances.[3] First, with the creation of COPRI, the legal guidelines for privatization were finally in place, the most important being an explicit set of instructions for assessing the value of individual firms and concrete procedures for divestiture. Second, the technical and financial expertise of COPRI's staff was such that the agency actively involved itself in the restructuring of companies to make them more attractive to potential buyers. Third, apart from better preparing state firms for sale and assisting in the preparation of proposals for financial backing, COPRI started its sell-off campaign with smaller firms, which are easier to unload; the strategy with the larger firms was to begin by offering stock options in a more piecemeal fashion. This latter approach represented a major difference from past efforts, which hinged on grand privatization schemes that simply stalled.

This is not to say that privatization's enemies had been completely neutralized, or that the strategy was free of problems. Along each step of the legislative way congressional foes sought to exclude key sectors such as mining and petroleum, which set the stage for a bruising fight over the privatization of the state oil company (Petróleos del Perú, or Petroleum of Peru [PETROPERU]) during the 1995 presidential campaign. This, in turn, helped to sour public opinion against the government's plan to sell off every last firm in its portfolio. Other problems, such as the challenge of raising sufficient funds to restructure the large number of SOEs that were in a semiliquid financial position, meant that potential buyers had to be guaranteed lucrative returns for some time to come. This made it all the more difficult to apply the kinds of antitrust criteria that typically prevail in the developed countries: in the absence of a sufficient competition policy to guide the process, the lack of transparency and solid financial information eased the way for new private owners to set above-market prices for public goods (for example, transportation, electricity, telephones) previously provided by the SOEs.[4]

Financial Reform

On the foreign front, financial reform meant completing the unfinished business of renegotiating Peru's outstanding debt and interest arrears with the multilaterals, the Paris Club, and the commercial banks. Because the statutes of the IMF and the World Bank stipulated that no new credit could be obtained from these institutions by a country that had fallen into arrears on previous loans, policymakers began repairing Peru's damaged borrower status by negotiating with the IMF through its Rights Accumulation Program (Boloña 1996, 216). It took Fujimori's entire first term to restore Peru's good standing with the multilaterals. This, plus the reinstallation of "democratic" political procedures by 1995, then paved the way for the renegotiation of Peru's Paris Club debt in 1996 and the rescheduling of some $10.6 billion in arrears and interest on the country's commercial debt under a Brady deal in 1997.

The remainder of the financial reforms involved an entire redefinition of the government's presence in this sector (C. E. Paredes 1991, 314). A new legal framework was written that simplified the rules of the domestic financial system and deregulated financial markets (for example, the lowering of reserve requirements, the liberalization of interest rates, and a reduction of the tax on debits). At the same time, the capital account of the balance of payments was liberalized, and this included the opening of the banking system to foreign interests and the freeing of foreign-exchange transactions. These measures, along with the launching of the privatization program and the Foreign Investment Promotion Act of 1991, contributed to the development of the Lima stock exchange.[5] Having long been hampered by low transparency and a burdensome regulatory backdrop, the combined effects of financial-sector reform helped to increase the capitalization of the Lima stock exchange from just $800 million in 1990 to $19.5 billion by 1997 (Manzetti 1999, 275).

Social Compensation

After a first year of false starts, the president sidestepped the relevant ministries that had long proved inadequate in rectifying the poverty rates that stand out in Table 2 and instead created the Fondo Nacional de Compensación y Desarrollo Social (National Fund for Development and Social Compensation [FONCODES]) in August 1991. Similar to short-term compensatory social programs that had been implemented simultaneously with sweeping market reforms in Bolivia, Chile, and Mexico, FONCODES relied on a combination of traditional social-welfare relief and on new demand-based criteria requiring that communities generate specific proposals for assistance (Graham 1994). The bulk of FONCODES funding was spent on economic infrastructure (road-maintenance projects, irrigation, deforestation) and social-infrastructure projects (health facilities, schools, basic housing).[6] As was the case with those safety net schemes mentioned above, FONCODES was never meant to resolve long-standing structural inequities in Peru.

Almost inadvertently, FONCODES enabled Fujimori to accomplish two main goals: bolstering his own political capital and offering high-profile but very temporary poverty relief to his most marginal constituents. Especially after the 1993 constitutional referendum, in which the president lost in all departments outside Lima, FONCODES became a main venue for channeling public resources to those regional districts where he had fared particularly poorly at the polls. This image of greater inclusion at the local level was reinforced by an overall increase in social expenditures within the line ministries, from 16 percent of government spending in 1990 to 40 percent in 1995 (Sheahan 1999, 125). This, in turn, helped deliver Fujimori's victory in all but one regional department (Loreto) in the 1995 presidential election. However, this opportunistic mix of politics and temporary social relief also distracted from the need to formulate a cohesive long-term strategy for poverty reduction and income distribution in Peru.[7] By 1994, 48 percent of the population was still living below the poverty line (Sheahan 1999, 108) and "for the average household, 1997 incomes were lower than those of 1975" (Webb 2000, 280).

Market Reform, Phase Two: Waiting in Limbo

By the end of Fujimori's first term the economic rules of the game had been radically transformed. In other words, a first generation of market reforms had basically been completed against a political-administrative backdrop that resonated with the management strategies adopted by other market reformers in the region during this time: "presidents and technocratic economic cabinets were able to design and implement changes in macroeconomic rules with relatively little interference from the rest of the political system or the public sector" (Naím 1994, 35). Having implemented a somewhat generic Washington Consensus program in the early 1990s, political leaders and policymakers in Latin America began to turn their attention to the consolidation of these reforms from the mid-1990s on. While all market reformers faced continuing challenges in the areas of macroeconomic management, income distribution, and the modernization of state organizations, the more specific content of "second phase" reforms varied according to a given country's political, social, and institutional legacies.

Although the tasks varied by country, second-phase reforms presented similar challenges in terms of the complexities and difficulties of following through on the initial "shock" program. First, because the gains from the kinds of policies that were now required (civil service reform, administration of justice, antitrust enforcement) were much more subtle than the obvious benefits of macroeconomic stabilization, while the pain (downsizing, loss of access to patronage, abiding by the new legal regimen) was more concentrated. Second, apart from the need to involve a much larger chunk of the central government in the reform process, the implementation of this next round of reform required debate and negotiation with those most affected. In other words, second-phase market reforms required a more inclusive and accountable style of politics. For Peru, it was the failure to shift to a more open and participatory mode of politics that constituted the most glaring reform gap in the second half of the 1990s.

As reelection in 1995 had afforded Fujimori a much longer time horizon on his tenure in office, the president's appetite for further reform was visibly curbed (Durand and Thorp 1998; Boylan 2000). As a result, privatization slowed considerably, exports were still lackluster and too dependent on raw materials (fishmeal, mining, and services related to the processing of primary goods), and social policy had yet to reach sufficiently beyond the executive's concern for political survival and hence his doling out of immediate adjustment relief. Moreover, because the prospect of a third term predictably provoked broad opposition (national opinion polls showed that nearly 70 percent of Peruvians felt that it was time for the president to move on), this prompted Fujimori and his congressional allies to exert their will through direct intervention in the country's legal and judicial apparatus. The relationship between Peru's democratic transition and Fujimori's designs on a prolonged incumbency, which were increasingly at odds, became even more conflictual; as a result, second-phase reforms were relegated to the back burner, and unfortunately remain so to this day.

Fujimori's Economic Legacy: Flirting with Mediocrity

Admittedly, the Peruvian economy went far in the 1990s under a purist market approach backed by sound institutional reform, and it did so despite an increasingly dysfunctional political backdrop. By definition, the sheer magnitude of market measures that had been introduced during Fujimori's first term implied a fundamental shift in the balance of public and private influence over the economy. Public activity, in particular, had been restructured by way of the reconstruction and renovation of the country's main economic institutions and through the creation or overhaul of numerous autonomous state agencies involved in revenue collection, regulatory oversight, and the delivery of essential public services. Again, the underlying argument here is that, while laying the necessary groundwork for an impressive economic turnaround in the 1990s, the confinement of institutional reform to the state's internal organizations was a necessary but not sufficient condition for triggering a full-fledged economic takeoff.

At a minimum, such an economic advance would require a deeper commitment from those private actors who, in turn, were still demanding additional reform in numerous areas (among them tax incidence, financial deregulation, judicial oversight, and property rights). Moreover, as the Chilean case had shown in the 1990s (Sheahan 1999; Wise 1999), higher sustainable growth would mean a much more aggressive approach toward improving income inequality and the strengthening of institutional ties between the state and those societal groups that represented the ultimate stakeholders in the reform process. Yet rather than broaden the development coalition and deepen reforms along these lines, the Fujimori cohort instead moved in the opposite direction.

For example, the main institutional locus for launching executive initiatives became the previously defunct Ministry of the Presidency, which came to capture around 23 percent of the central-government budget by 1995 (Graham and Kane 1998, 85). At heart, the Ministry of the Presidency became Fujimori's slush fund for reining in stray constituents and evolved into the very symbol of Peru's semiauthoritarian regime. A deeper problem was that these everyday concerns for political survival distracted the ruling coalition from articulating a cohesive development strategy for the longer term. Tellingly, both Fujimori terms passed without the generation of an integrated development plan that reflected the government's policy goals, or even its commitment to tackle glaring reform gaps in such areas as income distribution, the restructuring and modernization of small and medium-sized firms, and export promotion.[8]

This failure to better harness the country's considerable technocratic talent to a development strategy surely had to do with the peculiar circumstances that led to the vetting of executive access by the likes of National Security Advisor Vladimiro Montesinos (Bowen and Holligan 2003). The situation was also worlds away from those of the other countries in Tables 1 and 2, where executives had purposefully armed themselves with large high-profile technical teams that themselves came to signal reform credibility. However, although the Fujimori legacy clearly fell short of an economic takeoff, the reform inroads that were made on multiple fronts since 1990 mean that the country is still better positioned to break through those growth, trade, and investment barriers that define Chile's success in Tables 1 and 2. But this will entail the shift to a more competitive strategy, which now seems as much a matter of decision makers' vision and fortitude as of the particular policies and expertise that are brought to bear on such a project.

In the post-Fujimori era, domestic-policy debates have centered on these very questions, and a rich base of local social science research has emerged to inform public discourse concerning the future of the Peruvian political economy.[9] According to these diagnoses, a competitive strategy would entail a more dynamic role for public policy in two main areas: first, the adoption of an explicit export-led development strategy and, second, the depoliticization of social policy in favor of more targeted human capital investments. Below I review the unfinished business of the Fujimori era within each of these categories, as well as the policy challenges that lie ahead.

A Trade-Led Development Strategy

By definition, the sweeping liberalization that occurred in the 1990s implied a commitment to an export-led strategy along Chilean or Mexican lines. This option for Peru is especially compelling in light of the country's proven success in promoting both traditional and nontraditional exports with higher value-added content during a brief period in the late 1970s (Sheahan 1999). And although economists are known to disagree more so than not, one point of consensus is the crucial role that such higher value-added exports can play in spurring growth, productivity, jobs, and income gains (Edwards 1995; Londoño and Székely 1997). Peru's failure to follow this path and instead stick with a hands-off management strategy based on traditional exports and comparative advantage can be attributed, first and foremost, to the ideological blinders worn by some within Fujimori's economic team, regardless of the failure of markets alone to infuse more dynamism into the micro economy.[10] Moreover, an overly insulated leadership coalition further deterred debate about the proper role for public policy in facilitating innovation and microeconomic adjustment.

It thus makes sense that in a recent ECLAC study published by Barbara Stallings and Wilson Peres (2000), Peru emerges as an aggressive reformer, but a laggard one with regard to the dynamism of trade in relation to other market reformers, the efficiency of investment, and the impact of both on employment and equity. Under the impulse of market reforms, Peru's sectoral contribution to value-added followed a regional trend: a decline in manufacturing, a growth spurt in services, and a dominant pattern of output in agriculture and mining that is more or less a continuation of prereform trends. Similar to those of its neighbors, the Peruvian economy saw an increase in patterns of heterogeneity within these four main sectors during the 1990s. The underside of market transformation for Peru and others, it seems, has been the worsening plight of those smaller producers and less-skilled workers who have yet to reap the benefits of or integrate into international markets for investment and trade.

Where Peru stands out, according to Stallings and Peres (2000, 160–70), is in its disproportionate decline in investment in potentially dynamic manufacturing or semimanufacturing sectors (foodstuffs, metal products, pharmaceuticals, chemicals, pulp and paper), and the exceptional growth of nonagricultural low-skill rural employment in the 1990s. Meanwhile, in the urban setting, the bulk of employment creation came from those micro enterprises and small firms operating in the largely informal service sector, while big capital-intensive firms continued to dominate in their contribution to GDP but not employment. Outside telecommunications, banking, and mining, Peru also trailed in attracting investments that would have promoted the greater application of technology to the country's productive structures. This is not to take away from the productivity and wage gains that appear in Table 2, but the fact is that the dualist tendencies that have long plagued the Peruvian economy are still present.

Another point of consensus is that these shortcomings in the way of innovation and dynamism are amenable to public policy. For example, Brazil, Chile, and Mexico have countered these trends by promoting higher value-added exports in both the traditional (mining, agriculture) and the nontraditional sectors of the economy. More specifically, such approaches have included incentives to promote business clusters and strengthen production chains for companies that have been weakened by trade liberalization, and the offering of a range of tax and credit incentives to foster outward-oriented production (Stallings and Peres 2000; Pastor and Wise 2003). These efforts differ from the heavy-handed industrial policies of the past in that they are designed with an eye toward fostering horizontal cross-sectoral links and toward supporting firms in the market through training, support services, and access to know-how (Chudnovsky 1997). Whereas such interventions were unthinkable in Peru in 1990, the magnitude of reform is now such that they are advisable for infusing greater dynamism into domestic markets.

The Human Capital Frontier—Back to the Basics

Despite the fact that "income either stagnated or fell slightly between 1985 and 1997" (Webb 2000, 217) in the average Peruvian household, distributional demands were basically papered over right up until the very end of Fujimori's tenure. It was the president's tight control over social expenditures in ways that provided short-term relief to the poor, but did little to tackle the underlying causes of inequality, that perhaps most reflected the authoritarian bottlenecks that had built up around the office of the executive. This is so, even though the 1990s saw the proliferation of an impressive body of data and research on both the sources of inequality and the most direct ways to address it.[11] Peru, of course, is hardly alone with regard to its chronic patterns of inequality.

Across the region, the tenacity of regressive distributional patterns flies in the face of neoliberal thinking, which holds that market reforms will expand the national pie and enable a wider segment of the population to gain access to this newly found wealth (Baer and Maloney 1997). Recent research on Latin America's distributional shortcomings in the aftermath of market reforms offers two main explanations for this counterintuitive outcome. First, income inequality has lingered in the region because of the high levels of asset concentration—both productive and human capital assets—that are still present in these economies (Birdsall and Londoño 1997). And second, the failure of liberalization and privatization to penetrate these entrenched dualistic structures is no longer seen as an adjustment lag, but rather as an endogenous feature of market reforms that must be addressed through more aggressive public policies (Sheahan 1997). In other words, the region's track record suggests that, over time, microeconomic adjustment will not occur solely at the hand of market forces.

Although the struggle for greater upward social mobility is region-wide, Peru's social policy was especially hampered by Fujimori's heavy reliance on social-capital expenditures to keep his incumbency alive through the 1990s. This, in essence, slowed the momentum for reform within frontline social ministries such as education and health and distracted policymakers from launching the more targeted human capital investments that will be essential for sustaining poverty reduction in Peru. Thus, education reform faltered very early on (C. Parodi 2000), and health care saw some isolated pockets of success but nothing near the overhaul that current trends call for (Ewig 2000a). This failure to clear up the overlap and redundancy between public-sector institutions, or to make use of that professional talent that existed within the public sector to advance this larger set of social-policy goals, constitutes one of the main lost opportunities under Fujimori.

Conclusion

Up until 1990, the tendency in Peru had been for each successive administration to hand over an even bigger bundle of political and economic problems than it had inherited upon taking office. The crisis of the late 1980s finally put an end to these delay tactics, as the combination of state collapse, hyperinflation, and civil war made it virtually impossible for politicians and policymakers to avoid implementing a long-overdue set of reforms. In hindsight, a maverick independent politician such as Fujimori may have seemed the least likely candidate of all to succeed in restructuring the economy along market lines. Yet the magnitude and longevity of the crisis of the 1980s, combined with Fujimori's own fortitude, created a unique set of opportunities for the initiation of sweeping political economic change.

There is simply no disputing that the country that emerged from the decade of the 1990s is considerably different from the one that entered it. This is so both in regional terms and when Peru is assessed according to the macroeconomic and institutional variables discussed in this chapter. For example, when Peru is compared with the rest of Latin America, the data in this chapter confirm that the country's main reference point for measuring economic performance is no longer an Andean bloc still struggling to implement market reforms. Rather, the notable headway that Peru has made in resolving its dire macroeconomic difficulties renders its track record more comparable with those of such emerging market countries as Argentina, Chile, and Mexico. With regard to institutional reform, the modernization of key entities such as the central bank and a handful of ministries (Economy and Finance, Energy and Mines, Industry and Commerce), as well as the renovation or creation of a range of highly professional and efficient autonomous agencies, further distinguishes Peru from its less developed neighbors in the Andean Community (Vial and Sachs 2000, 10–11).

Clearly, however, there is much more to political economic success than the inroads just mentioned. While I have argued throughout this chapter that Peru's cup may be more than half full on the reform front, progress in eradicating poverty and bridging the distributional gap failed to keep pace with the country's impressive growth and investment performance in the 1990s. Peru is certainly not alone on this count, but regressive distributional trends were exacerbated by the politicization of social spending and by the bias toward short-term adjustment relief at the expense of initiatives that more aggressively target human capital development over the longer term.

These shortcomings in social policy are symptomatic of a larger problem; the failure to articulate an integrated trade-led development strategy geared toward the promotion of higher value-added exports, the expansion of local labor markets, and the strengthening of domestic firms. As Brazil, Chile, and Mexico have all ventured down this path, Peru's reticence stemmed not from the lack of technical expertise, but rather from the concentration of economic policymaking in an elite executive-level clique that prevented the kinds of policy debate and ideological flexibility that gave rise to more competitive development strategies in these other countries.

Although the Fujimori coalition was patently successful in launching the first phase of market reforms in Peru, this same coalition emerged as the main bottleneck in the pursuit of second-phase market reforms. This was a result of Fujimori's rejection of the kinds of interest intermediation and inclusive politics that underpinned the implementation of second-phase reforms—not to mention the transition to democracy—in other emerging market countries in the region. At the very moment when Fujimori's leadership coalition became unstable, it collapsed amid a swirl of scandals involving bribery, blackmail, and the trafficking of various illicit goods. The moral of this story appears to be that neopopulism, or the doling out of state largesse in ways that endear a leader to the masses without undermining market reforms, can take a politician such as Fujimori far; but in the end, the country's disorganized mass of poor could not save him from his own political excesses.

While the tasks of fine-tuning Peru's market model in a more dynamic and distributive direction have been left to the Toledo administration, the question now is not which policy course to follow, but whether Fujimori's successors will have the wherewithal and tenacity to tackle the numerous reform gaps analyzed here, and to more fully institutionalize the reforms now in place. What is at stake is the difference between giving in to a political stalemate that could condemn the country indefinitely to mediocre growth, social instability, and regressive income returns versus forging ahead with a broad-based reform coalition that can craft a pragmatic set of political and economic policies able to render open markets and liberal politics more compatible in Peru.

NOTES

1. Peru's autonomous agencies can be grouped into four categories: those that deal with financial regulation (SBS), those that handle tax administration (SUNAT), other miscellaneous regulatory agencies (INDECOPI; OSINERG), and new agencies that relate directly to the goals of sustaining market reforms (COPRI, FONCODES). All these entities, which staff sparsely and pay salaries two to six times higher than those paid in the central government ministries, quickly came to symbolize highly professional service delivery in the 1990s. For further detail, see Wise 2003b, 199–205.

2. For more detail on the bureaucratic and administrative aspects of fiscal reform that has taken place in the region over the past decade, see ECLAC 1998.

3. These insights are based on my interviews conducted in Lima with two former COPRI directors, Carlos Montoya (May 25, 1992) and Manuel Llosa (July 18, 1995), and with COPRI official Carolina Castillo (December 17, 1998).

4. In March 1993 the National Institute for the Defense of Competition and Protection of Intellectual Property (INDECOPI) was created. INDECOPI functions as an umbrella agency that oversees intellectual property protection, consumer rights, the elimination of barriers to entry, and antitrust matters. Given the magnitude of these tasks, it was decided at the outset that INDECOPI would establish ex-post rather than ex-ante controls on economic activity (Beatriz Boza, INDECOPI director, interview by the author, Lima, December 8, 1998). In the after-

math of privatization, many have questioned the efficacy of this ex-post approach.

5. Under the new FDI regime, foreigners were allowed to invest in Peru and to repatriate profits and capital equipment as they saw fit. Although additional legislation was passed that protected all investors, domestic and foreign, from sudden changes in existing laws and that established procedures for the resolution of disputes over investment (Manzetti 1999, 251), in the post-Fujimori era it came to light that these new laws were poorly honored. In fact, numerous foreign-investment disputes that erupted in the 1990s have yet to be resolved (Vladimir Radovic, director of the Inter-American Development Bank mission in Peru, interview by the author, Lima, December 16, 2003).

6. This information is derived from various issues of the agency's published monthly report titled FONCODES: *Nota mensual.*

7. For example, Fujimori focused on visible projects, such as school buildings, rather then on core institutions, such as the education system itself, with obviously weak results.

8. As a matter of planning by default, the national budget served as a guideline of sorts, as did the periodic sectoral plans generated by the line ministries (Reynaldo Bringas, former director of the national budget at the Ministry of Economy and Finance, interview by the author, Lima, December 10, 1998).

9. See, for example, Gonzáles de Olarte 1998; Abusada et al. 2000; Boza 2000; C. Parodi 2000; Portocarrero 2000; Webb 2000.

10. In late 1998, when Peru was in the throes of adjusting to the Asian shocks and interest rates had skyrocketed, I asked a top policy official at the Ministry of Industry in an off-the-record in-person interview about the kinds of adjustment support available for smaller companies with burgeoning debt burdens. The response: "None . . . the private sector just doesn't get it, this is a generation that still clamors for protectionism . . . we are fully committed to relying on comparative advantage."

11. This statement holds for the policy community at large (see, for example, Birdsall and Londoño 1997; Londoño and Székely 1997; Sheahan 1997; Stallings and Peres 2000) and for the impressive array of social sector research that has been produced locally in Peru by think tanks and the academic community (see n. 9, this chapter).

TEN

The Often Surprising Outcomes of Asymmetry in International Affairs: United States–Peru Relations in the 1990s

DAVID SCOTT PALMER

The Regional and International Context

During the decade of the 1990s, United State–Latin American relations responded to four principal priorities, according to official statements: democracy and human rights, economic growth through economic liberalization and integration, reduction of poverty and discrimination, and environmentally sustainable development (U.S. Department of State 1996). However, there are other high-priority U.S. policy issues as well that have had a significant impact on U.S. relations in the region in recent years, such as drugs and immigration. While specifically subsumed within the officially stated priorities, they are important enough in their own right for inter-American relations to merit separate consideration.

The end of the Cold War provoked a sea change in the international system. As a result, for the first time in fifty years, opportunities were presented for the United States to respond to Western Hemisphere issues on their own terms rather than through the filter of national security. The U.S. government initially used the foreign-policy space that opened up in the international system in a variety of ways to make significant adjustments in relations with other countries in the Western Hemisphere. From the Enterprise for the Americas Initiative (trade) to the Andean Initiative (drugs), from the Santiago Resolution (OAS [Organization of American States] 1080) (democracy) to the Brady Plan (debt), from the El Salvador

Peace Accords (multilateral conflict resolution) to the North American Free Trade Agreement (NAFTA) (trade and investment), the late 1980s and early 1990s were replete with new departures in U.S. relations with Latin America. In numerous ways, pragmatism and partnership replaced the security-driven unilateralism that had characterized many U.S. policy initiatives toward the region since the 1950s. The high-water mark of this new policy as it related to Latin America came with the ratification by the U.S. Congress of the NAFTA in November 1993.

As the 1990s advanced, however, multiple domestic constraints in the United States increasingly limited U.S. foreign-policy makers' ability to continue to take advantage of the opportunities provided by the changes in the international system in relations with Latin America. These included massive federal-government deficits, cutbacks in fiscal resources for the Department of State, interagency rivalries, a variety of domestic economic and political concerns that took precedence over foreign policy, and major tensions between the executive and legislative branches after 1995—culminating in Congress's unsuccessful effort in 1998 to impeach the president. In addition, a number of major international crises in other parts of the world—including Bosnia, Burundi, Russia, South Asia, and the Middle East—tended to deflect the U.S. foreign-policy community's attention away from Latin America.

Such considerations significantly affected United States–Latin American relations in spite of the long-standing reality of dramatic asymmetry between the so-called Colossus of the North and the individual countries of the region (as reflected, for example, in a U.S. economy more than eleven times larger than all the Latin American economies combined). This meant that U.S. policy, however important its perceived role to Latin American actors over the course of the 1990s, was often not in a very good position to ensure outcomes favoring stated objectives. In other words, the hegemonic presumption and the concomitant assumption of dominance in bilateral as well as multilateral relations were often not borne out in practice.

Beginning in the months after NAFTA's ratification, U.S. policy initiatives toward the region were often characterized by improvisation; drift; subordination to domestic politics; and lost, even squandered opportunities (Palmer 2004). Several examples serve to illustrate the shift.

1. The Clinton administration, with an eye on the 1994 midterm elections, chose not to seek an extension of fast-track authority, so it

lapsed. It was regained only eight years later, by the George Walker Bush administration, but with new limiting conditions.

2. Haiti policy was plagued by the specter of Somalia, bureaucratic infighting, and multiple political pressures, which enabled the repressive military regime of Raoul Cedras to take advantage of the confusion for its own nefarious purposes.

3. Decertification of Colombia in 1996 and 1997 failed to reduce drug production and trafficking levels. It also weakened the legitimacy of the Colombian government and emboldened guerrillas and paramilitaries alike to expand their activities, thereby introducing a new cycle of destructive political violence in that beleaguered country.

4. The United States did play an important, if largely behind-the-scenes, role over several years in helping to achieve the Guatemala Peace Accords in December 1995.[1] However, their finalization and implementation depended primarily on a serious and continuing multilateral commitment by the United Nations and its peacekeeping mission, not on U.S. policy.

5. NAFTA and Brady debt reduction and restructuring agreements aside, the economic growth that boosted the region between 1993 and 1998 came about largely through independent initiatives of Latin American governments and the international private sector rather than through direct U.S. government actions.

6. Environmental initiatives after the 1992 Rio Summit debacle were few and far between in spite of the rhetorical commitment to sustainable development by the Clinton administration.

7. The Summit of the Americas in Miami in 1994 and, to a lesser degree, the Santiago Summit of 1998 served to symbolize the limits of U.S. policy. While these were long on head-of-state camaraderie and rhetoric, there was little U.S. government follow through.

8. The counterdrug foreign-policy arena was the only one to see increased U.S. resources for the region over the decade. However, not only were there embarrassing examples of official praise for Latin American officials subsequently found to be involved in the drug trade themselves, but both production and trafficking levels actually increased, as did drug-consumption levels in the United States.

In most policy arenas over the course of the 1990s, Latin American governments pursued their own agendas, with or without U.S. support. In short, asymmetry did not translate into hegemonic influence. U.S. policy toward the region was far from being the dominating product of an all-powerful juggernaut, as so often portrayed.

Asymmetry in United States–Peruvian Relations: The Historical Context

United States–Peru relations over the past forty years or so offer multiple examples of outcomes that did not favor the dominant partner in the relationship in spite of its asymmetrical nature (as can be illustrated by a U.S. economy approximately 175 times greater than its Peruvian counterpart). They began with the successful coup in 1962 by Peru's armed forces in spite of initial strenuous objections by the administration of John F. Kennedy (St. John 1999, 188). They continued with the elected Peruvian government's decision in 1967 to go against U.S. government arms control policy in the hemisphere and the United States' two-decade-long monopoly of military assistance to Latin America after the United States vetoed Peru's request to purchase the U.S.-made F5A jet fighter plane. The Peruvian government then turned to the French and purchased the Mirage (St. John 1999, 190–91).

The relationship between the United States and the military government of General Juan Velasco Alvarado (1968–75) was particularly strained. Against U.S. government wishes, the Peruvian regime nationalized important U.S. private investments—including the International Petroleum Company (IPC), of Standard Oil; Cerro de Pasco Mining, of Phelps-Dodge; and the Marcona Mining Company. Peruvian authorities also seized U.S. tuna boats, expelled the U.S. military mission, terminated Peru's twelve-year relationship with the Peace Corps, normalized relations with Cuba, and began a massive reequipping of the army and air force with a $1.2 billion arms and training agreement with the Soviet Union. Although the U.S. government opposed all these initiatives, with the modest exception of under-the-table compensation for IPC, it was unable to reverse them (McClintock and Vallas 2003, 25–29).

While the United States enthusiastically supported the return to democracy in Peru between 1977 and 1980, relations were often conflictive with the elected governments of Fernando Belaúnde Terry and Alan García Pérez. During the Belaúnde government, there were prolonged disagreements over landing rights and trade, leading Peru's president to cancel a state visit to the United States in 1982. President García railed frequently in official speeches against the United States, insisted on limiting foreign-debt repayments to 10 percent of foreign exchange revenues over strong U.S. objections, and then stopped paying altogether. Were it not for cooperation on drug production and trafficking, bilateral relations with the García administration could well have broken down altogether (St. John 1999, 199–206).

Such bilateral tensions and conflicts between the United States and Peru from 1962 to 1990 frequently produced results that enabled the smaller, less favored country in the relationship to accomplish national and international objectives over U.S. opposition. Many times these outcomes did not favor U.S. interests. They also required that U.S. policymakers devote much attention to a relationship that is normally considered to be only a second or third priority in U.S. foreign affairs. The case of Peru, in short, illustrated the principle over several decades that a clearly asymmetrical relationship such as that with the United States does not necessarily mean that the larger and stronger party is consistently able to impose its will on the smaller.

Peru and the United States Since 1990

The surprise election of Alberto Fujimori as president of Peru in 1990 produced a new set of challenges for United States–Peru relations. In many respects, the conflictive patterns of prior decades continued. During the early weeks of the Fujimori regime, Peru unexpectedly declined an offer of significant military support within the Andean Initiative, the regional counterdrug program of George Herbert Walker Bush's administration. President Fujimori argued that such assistance did not meet Peru's needs. He pushed instead for greater economic assistance to promote alternative development in coca-growing areas, and eventually prevailed (St. John 1999, 213).

After months of slow, laborious marshaling of support within executive and legislative offices of the U.S. government, in September 1991 the U.S. Congress approved a significant counterdrug economic and military assistance program for Peru. Six months later, however, President Fujimori unilaterally scuttled the aid with his April 5, 1992, autogolpe. The timing of the pronouncement, with the U.S. State Department's Assistant Secretary for Inter-American Affairs Bernard Aronson in Lima at that very moment awaiting his appointment for the following day with President Fujimori, represented a direct affront to the United States. Among other effects, the significant new U.S. assistance earmarked for Peru under the $1.2 billion Andean Initiative was suspended and eventually reallocated to Peru's neighbors (McClintock and Vallas 2003, 136–39).

However, Peru's autogolpe also provided an opportunity for the OAS to invoke Resolution 1080, the historic instrument forged by OAS member states in Santiago, Chile in June 1991, by which they agreed to call a special meeting to decide collectively what measures to take to respond to threats to democracy within a country. The meeting was called and held in the Bahamas in May. Here the United States tried to put together an agreement to take specific multilateral measures against Peru. However, President Fujimori sidetracked U.S. goals at the meeting by appearing personally and promising to reestablish democracy within a year, while deft diplomatic footwork by Peru's OAS ambassador Luis Marchand avoided censure or sanction.[2]

Limited but crucial counterterrorism aid in 1992, as Peru's beleaguered government fought to overcome the mounting threat of the Sendro Luminoso (Shining Path) guerrilla organization, and the continuation of counterdrug programs responded more to larger U.S. policy objectives in the region than to support for the Fujimori government itself. True, significant new assistance was forthcoming after democratic procedures were reestablished in late 1993, but overall bilateral relations often remained tense and even problematic. As Ambassador David Passage, director of the Office of Andean Affairs of the Department of State at that time, noted, "Our bilateral relations with Peru . . . are in various senses the most complex and subtle of any in the Hemisphere."[3]

Policies During the Clinton Administration

Tension with Normalization

During the early months of the William Jefferson Clinton administrations (1993–2001), the executive branch continued to press the Fujimori government to restore democratic procedures promptly and to improve its dismal human rights record. The National Security Council (NSC) representative for Latin America, Richard Feinberg, was able to influence the Department of the Treasury as well as the International Financial Institutions (IFIs) to postpone the economic support that Peru was seeking to help reinsert the country into the international economy until democracy was fully restored.[4] Successive annual State Department human rights reports highlighted the serious abuses that both the government and the Shining Path guerrillas were continuing to commit and, along with the work of Americas Watch and the Washington Office on Latin America (WOLA), had a significant impact. Even in the midst of such pressure, however, the Peruvian government rejected a critical report on the judicial state of exception, with summary trials of alleged subversives by "faceless judges" (Goldman et al. 1993), and continued with this system for almost four more years.

The new constitution of 1993 reestablished electoral procedures and a legislative body. However, it also included various adjustments that substantially increased the power of the executive in relationship to the legislative and judicial branches. Even though democratic forms were reinstated, President Fujimori both took advantage of these new powers and carried out extraconstitutional initiatives, particularly after his reelection in 1995, to slowly increase his personal political control and to manipulate the political system to his advantage. He also benefited from gaining a legislative majority in both the 1992 constitutional convention elections and the 1995 national elections. These gave him the support in Congress he needed to ensure implementation of his ambitious agenda (LASA 1995).

Some U.S. agencies, such as Treasury, Commerce, and the White House Office on Drug Control Policy, were anxious to support Peru in its efforts to implement significant economic liberalization reforms and to stem drug production and trafficking.[5] They tended to overlook the growing deficiencies in the restored democratic process over the continuing objections of the NSC representative. Over the course of 1994, IFI loans to Peru resumed and bilateral economic assistance through the United States Agency for International Development (USAID) increased significantly, to more than $100 million annually. Peru became the largest recipient of USAID support in the region through 1996.[6] Economic reinsertion proceeded, culminating in agreements with the Paris Club in July 1996 and in the Brady Plan in March 1997, which together reduced Peru's foreign-debt obligations by some $9.4 billion, more than a third of the total owed to foreign creditors. Over the four years between 1994 and 1998, private foreign capital inflows totaled about $8 billion.[7] While U.S. investment increased significantly in the 1990s, from about $600 million to $1.8 billion, the U.S. share of total foreign investment declined from 55 percent in 1980 to 20 percent in 1998 (McClintock and Vallas 2003, 99–100).

Even as President Fujimori and his economic ministers were succeed-

ing in restoring economic growth through economic reinsertion and access to significant private and IFI capital investment, however,
relationships with the U.S. ambassadors of the period remained problematic. For more than four years through the mid- to late 1990s, President
Fujimori regularly snubbed Ambassadors Alvin Adams and Dennis Jett
as he pushed forward with his increasingly authoritarian approach to
ensure executive domination of the political process and the media in
order to continue in power.

The counterdrug program, given its high priority for U.S. policymakers, was one bilateral policy arena that would be most likely to proceed
without major problems, in spite of Peru's political contretemps. Even
here, however, although U.S. drug assistance continued, the policy met
with multiple difficulties because of differences between agencies over
how best to proceed.

When Peru began to force down or destroy presumed drug-carrying
planes in 1994, the United States suspended for almost a year the sharing
of information on these flights that it had gathered from its radar installations because of concerns over military engagement of civilian aircraft.
Another suspension occurred with the outbreak of hostilities between
Peru and Ecuador in January 1995. Periodic problems occurred over coordination of U.S. and Peruvian military drug-interdiction flights, as the
shooting down of a plane carrying American missionaries in 2001 attests.
As a consequence, such flights were suspended immediately in order to
assess the reasons for this tragic error and to institute new safeguards
against a future occurrence. The suspension has remained in effect even
though evidence mounted that drug flights were increasing. Although
there was a dramatic reduction in the area that was planted for coca
production between 1997 and 2001 (from 68,800 to 34,200 hectares),
much of that decline can be attributed to the spread of a fungus and to
aggressive initiatives by the Peruvian government itself.[8]

In the area of defense, the United States played a significant behind-
the-scenes role in providing technical support for Peruvian officials in
the Grupo Especial de Inteligencia (Special Intelligence Group [GEIN]),
established in the waning months of the García administration in 1990
to track leaders of Shining Path and Peru's other guerrilla movement, the
Movimiento Revolucionario Tupac Amaru (Tupac Amaru Revolutionary
Movement [MRTA]). Such assistance was instrumental in the capture of
Shining Path leader Abimael Guzmán Reynoso in September 1992. The
United States also provided important assistance that contributed to the
resolution in April 1997 of the hostage crisis at the Japanese ambassa-

dor's residence that was initiated by the MRTA (McClintock and Vallas 2003, 71–76).

The role of the United States, as one of the four guarantors of the Rio Protocol of 1942, which ended the 1941 war between Peru and Ecuador and set national boundaries, assumed new importance in the aftermath of renewed hostilities between the parties from January to March 1995. The multilateral civil and military response served to defuse the crisis and gradually worked toward establishing levels of confidence and trust between the parties that helped to set the stage for a final resolution in October 1998 of the hemisphere's longest running border dispute (Palmer 2001).

However, definitive resolution of this historic conflict would not have been possible, whatever the significance of the U.S. presence, without the courageous personal initiatives of Presidents Jamil Mahuad of Ecuador and Peru's Fujimori. Furthermore, the United States was unable to prevent the significant new expenditures for arms that Peru carried out as it tried to recover from the embarrassment of failing to oust Ecuador's military from the positions it had occupied within Peruvian territory during the conflict.[9]

On balance, even though United States–Peru relations were gradually normalized over the course of the 1990s, there continued to be challenges and difficulties in their day-to-day conduct. While Peru's ambassador to the United States, Ricardo Luna, succeeded over time in smoothing relations with public, multilateral, and private entities in Washington, his U.S. counterparts in Lima found it difficult to interact at all with President Fujimori. The Peruvian government succeeded in benefiting from normalization to pursue its own domestic- and international-policy objectives without allowing itself in various instances to be forced to accept U.S. conditions.

Limits of Support for Democracy

Given the strong U.S. commitment since the late 1980s to supporting and deepening democracy in Latin America and the U.S. government's vehement opposition to Peru's 1992 autogolpe, quite puzzling was the Fujimori government's ability to take several steps that progressively undermined democratic procedure and practice in Peru after 1995 without U.S. retaliatory measures (Palmer 2000).

One such initiative was the June 1995 general amnesty for military and police human rights abuses in the counterinsurgency campaign, this amnesty serving to cement armed and police forces support. Another was a blatantly unconstitutional vote in 1996 by Peru's Congress, where Fujimori supporters were in the majority, reaffirming an "authentic interpretation" that indeed he could run for a third term. This was followed by the removal in May 1997 of three members of the Constitutional Tribunal who had asserted publicly that President Fujimori was indeed not eligible to run again in the 2000 elections. Adding insult to injury in 1998 was the thwarting of a popular referendum permitted under the constitution on the third-term issue, even though organizers had gathered more than the constitutionally mandated 1.2 million signatures.

During the same period, the government rescinded the Peruvian citizenship of Baruch Ivcher, majority owner of a television channel that had broadcast unflattering information on the administration, especially on key presidential advisor Vladimiro Montesinos. The action forced Ivcher to relinquish control of the station to the Winter family, minority shareholders who were Fujimori supporters. In another government initiative, intelligence service employees suspected of leaks were brutally attacked—one was killed, the other permanently disabled.

Over the course of Fujimori's second term, government supporters progressively replaced members of the election commission and oversight boards, and provisional judges packed the judiciary, forced by their nonpermanent status to do the government's bidding. As the 2000 election campaign began, clear evidence that the government's party had forged up to one million signatures was thrown out by the courts (Palmer 2000, 61–62).

There are several reasons that help explain the failure of the United States to force President Fujimori and his advisors to adhere to democratic practice. These include Peru's new openness to foreign investment, the efforts to resolve the conflict with Ecuador, and the counterdrug campaign. During most of the 1995–2000 period, top U.S. officials, especially Ambassadors Adams and Jett, were shut off from contact with the upper echelons of the Peruvian government. Although Ambassador Jett in particular voiced his concerns over the erosion of Peru's democracy in various public forums, these views were overshadowed by the active involvement in Peru of General Barry McCaffrey, the White House drug czar. His regular trips to Peru during his four-year tenure between 1996 and 2000, with unfettered access to top officials, including Montesinos and Fujimori, made it appear that the U.S. government was not overly concerned with the Peruvian government's assaults on democracy as long as there was close cooperation on the counterdrug front. Although Montesinos used his meetings with McCaffrey to suggest a much closer relationship than actually existed, and McCaffrey responded publicly by disavowing that tie, Montesinos's power remained intact. It appears that the U.S. government was unwilling to jettison its relationship with Montesinos, both because of his reputation as a "fixer" and because of his continuing ability to provide the Central Intelligence Agency (CIA) with what agency officials considered to be valuable intelligence (McClintock and Vallas 2003, 86–87).

After Ambassador John Hamilton arrived in Peru in late 1998, his efforts to reestablish official contact with top Peruvian officials bore fruit. However, the price paid, it appears, was a further muting of the message on the need to observe democratic practices. While Hamilton felt that he could have an impact behind the scenes and that he was indeed getting the prodemocracy message across,[10] the way events played out indicate that he was mistaken in his assessment.

It was not until January 2000, just three months before the elections were to be held, that the United States and its representatives began to speak out officially, consistently, and in a coordinated manner against the gross manipulation of democratic process that was unfolding. Certainly the coordinated effort between U.S. officials, the OAS, and the United Nations to protest the electoral manipulation in the April 2000 vote—their effort inducing almost simultaneous statements by Secretary of State Madeleine Albright, Secretary-General César Gaviria of the OAS, and OAS electoral observer mission chief Eduardo Stein—had an impact. However, it was insufficient to keep Fujimori from being elected unopposed in the second-round of voting after second place finisher Alejandro Toledo withdrew in protest.

Nevertheless, soon after Fujimori's inauguration for a third term, the Peruvian government began to implode in the face of continuing popular protests, videotaped revelations of congressional-support buying by Montesinos, and public revelations of arms trafficking to Colombia's guerrilla movement, the Revolutionary Armed Forces of Colombia (FARC). Even as the United States officially jettisoned Montesinos for this gross betrayal of his long relationship with U.S. authorities, Ambassador Hamilton did everything in his power to keep Fujimori in charge. This included his help to facilitate Montesinos's exile to Panama and personal visits to Fujimori to persuade him to stay in office. Even as the crisis deepened amid growing popular indignation and protest, the U.S. goal was to preserve order with Fujimori at the helm during the transition to new elections rather than to commit its influence to working with the democratic opposition to bring democracy back to Peru. Once again, and at this critical juncture, in the face of growing national indignation in Peru at the continuing affronts to democracy by Fujimori and Montesinos, U.S. damage-limitation policy was thwarted.

Alternative Explanations

There are two competing explanations for the inability of the United States to accomplish its objectives. One is that the United States was willing to go along with the travesty of democratic process in Peru in order to ensure cooperation in intelligence gathering, counterdrug efforts, and continued economic liberalization. The other is that President Fujimori and Vladimiro Montesinos successfully pursued their policies even when the United States opposed them, even manipulating their larger partner at times for their own purposes.

There appear to be valid elements in each explanation. U.S. policy certainly tolerated and provided substantial economic support for the Fujimori government after mid-1995, when the multiple steps to restrict Peruvian democratic practice and process began. This is the result of a combination of domestic factors and competing foreign-policy objectives that came to have significant effects on United States–Latin American relations during these years.

First, Republicans regained control of both houses of Congress in the 1994 elections and introduced, beginning in 1995, a pernicious partisan political dynamic that spilled over into foreign affairs. Second, top leadership in the State Department had little interest in or commitment to Latin American matters, in a context, moreover, of significant and increasing budget constraints. Third, drug czar McCaffrey came to fill the Latin America policy vacuum with strong and decisive initiatives in counterdrug policy and enjoyed the support of the Republican Congress. Fourth, Peru's ambassador to the United States, Ricardo Luna (1993–2000), skillfully presented his country's positions in Washington and contributed in important ways to overcoming resistance there to what was happening to Peruvian democracy (Palmer 1998, 31–32). Fifth, the dramatic hostage crisis of 1996–97, when the MRTA took over the Japanese ambassador's residence, galvanized U.S. and world attention and generated new support for the Fujimori government. Sixth, the Peru-Ecuador conflict in 1995 and U.S. efforts as a guarantor through 1998 focused attention on working with the Peruvian government to find a solution rather than on raising questions about its domestic policies. Finally, U.S. interagency rivalries, particularly those between the Department of Defense, the Drug Enforcement Administration, the White House Office on Drug Control Policy, the CIA, and the State Department, often generated conflicting foreign-policy signals and enabled presumed beneficiaries to play one off against another.

The overall effect on United States–Peru relations of these various factors was to maintain an official U.S. policy of support for the Fujimori regime with a particular and growing emphasis on counterdrug relationships. The predominance of this aspect of policy during a critical period led to a willingness to work closely with key figures, especially Montesinos, and to play down their less savory actions.

This changed only between April and August 2000 as the CIA became convinced that Montesinos and several Peruvian generals were behind illegal arms shipments to the FARC in Colombia. When Montesinos broke the news in Peru in August that Peruvian intelligence had uncovered an arms-smuggling ring, his efforts to manipulate the media in his favor backfired, and the United States formally broke with its erstwhile ally (McClintock and Vallas 2003, 87–88).

However, it was also the case that the Peruvian government successfully worked around U.S. officials in various ways to accomplish its objective of remaining in power. For instance, Ambassador Jett repeatedly called attention to the deteriorating political situation, but he was ignored and sidelined by Peruvian authorities. General McCaffrey was embarrassed to find himself used in a doctored video disseminated on national television to suggest his (and therefore U.S. government) support for Montesinos. Ambassador Hamilton, the first U.S. representative in almost a decade to be able to meet regularly with top Peruvian officials, including President Fujimori, found that he was unable to move the government back toward a democratic opening. Finally, at the meeting in Washington, D.C., that preceded the June 2000 OAS gathering of foreign ministers in Windsor, Ontario, the United States sought once again and failed to secure invocation of Resolution 1080 after the tainted April and May elections. In part, this was a result of Peru's ability to outmaneuver the United States by securing Mexico's and Brazil's support for not taking action. This, in effect, left the Fujimori government in place for yet another term, however tainted.

The dramatic collapse of the Fujimori regime just weeks later, between September and November 2000, was largely the result of growing internal pressures brought to bear by tens of thousands of courageous Peruvians. For all intents and purposes, U.S. diplomacy was left on the sidelines during this critical juncture.

Conclusion: The Limits of Asymmetry

On balance, the Peruvian case illustrates the capacity of a smaller and weaker country to pursue its objectives in spite of efforts by a larger and more powerful actor to materially influence outcomes. Part of the explanation for this result most certainly rests on a variety of domestic forces and factors that tended to divide and weaken U.S. policy toward Peru. Equally significant, however, is the ability of the weaker party to manipulate the bilateral dynamic to its own advantage. United States–Peru relations in the 1990s illustrate in multiple ways the degree to which a dramatically asymmetrical relationship can be used to advantage by the smaller and weaker party, however inimical the ultimate outcome for that country.

NOTES

1. Richard Nuccio, special advisor, U.S. State Department, 1995–97, interview by the author, Pell Center, University of Salve Regina, Newport R.I., October 30, 2001.

2. Luis Marchand Stein, ambassador of Peru to the Organization of American States (OAS), 1990–92, interview by the author, Santiago, Chile, June 30, 1992.

3. David Passage, ambassador and director of the Office of Andean Affairs, U.S. State Department, interview by the author, by telephone from Washington, D.C., June 4, 1997.

4. Ricardo Luna, ambassador of Peru to the United States, interview by the author, Americas Society, New York City, June 3, 1997.

5. Luna, interview.

6. Embassy of Peru, "Preguntas en el Ambito Político," Embassy of Peru, Washington, D.C., February 1997, 5, typescript; Embassy of Peru, "Memoria de la Embajada del Perú en los Estados Unidos de América," Washington, D.C., annual typescript, 1994–1997.

7. "Peru/Brady Deal." *Latin American Weekly Report,* March 11, 1997, 125.

8. Al Matano, deputy chief, Americas and Caribbean Division, Office of Program Management, Bureau for International Narcotics and Law Enforcement Affairs (INL) at the Department of State, interview by the author, Washington,

D.C., June 12, 1997; Ernest R. Rojas Peru desk officer, U.S. Agency for International Development (USAID), presentation to the author of the hard copy of a PowerPoint presentation, "Peru: 2001 Coca Estimates," March 14, 2002.

    9. See n. 2, this chapter; see also Palmer 2001.

    10. John Hamilton, U.S. ambassador to Peru, interview by the author, January 20, 2000.

ELEVEN

Electoral Authoritarian Versus Partially Democratic Regimes: The Case of the Fujimori Government and the 2000 Elections

CYNTHIA MCCLINTOCK

In a series of articles titled "Elections Without Democracy?" published in the *Journal of Democracy* in April 2002 (Diamond 2002; Schedler 2002; Levitsky and Way 2002), leading scholars advanced a new regime classification: "electoral authoritarianism." Schedler (2002, 47) explained that, "While democracy is 'a system in which parties lose elections,' electoral authoritarianism is a system in which opposition parties lose elections."[1] Elaborated Levitsky and Way (2002, 52): "[Although] formal democratic institutions are widely viewed as the principal means of obtaining and exercising political authority," incumbents "violate these rules so often and to such an extent . . . that the regime fails to meet conventional minimum standards for democracy."

As Carrión suggests in the introduction and conclusion to the present volume, most scholars now agree that the government of Alberto Fujimori in Peru was an "electoral authoritarian" regime. However, for many years, U.S. experts at the key institutions Freedom House and Polity had classified the Fujimori government as partially democratic or "democratic with an adjective."[2] Despite the autogolpe, the apparently

The author would like to thank Julio Carrión, Charles Kenney, and Gregory Schmidt for their helpful comments and their insights about Peru's 1995 congressional elections over the course of many years.

free and fair presidential election in 1995 had persuaded the U.S. government and most U.S. analysts to restore the label of partial democracy to the Fujimori government. As the 2000 elections approached, international organizations and the U.S. government maintained a low bar for classification of the regime as partially democratic—despite the increasing concentration of presidential power, the obstructionist policies against Peru's mayors, and the mounting evidence of corruption that have been shown by other authors in this volume. And finally, although international observers did not give a passing grade to Peru's 2000 elections, international organizations and the U.S. government did.

Indeed, the line between "electoral authoritarianism" and "partial democracy" is blurry. The purpose of this chapter is to help draw the line. The discussion here supports the authors in the April 2002 *Journal of Democracy* issue and Carrión in their arguments that, in our regime classifications, analysts should carefully assess not only electoral processes but also incumbents' record of respect or disrespect for democracy and the rule of law. As Diamond (2002, 22) declares, "Regime classification must, in part, assess the previous election, but it must also assess the intentions and capabilities of ambiguously democratic ruling elites, something that is very hard to do." Using Peru's 2000 presidential election as a case study, in this chapter I point out that evaluating electoral processes can be difficult. In the case of Peru's 2000 elections, I show that, not taking into account Alberto Fujimori's record of disrespect for democracy and the rule of law, and unable to secure key evidence for judgment of the 2000 election, international observers almost gave the election a passing grade.

How might we assess the intentions and capabilities of elites? Examining the Fujimori government, I propose various indicators: (1) a record of assault against the constitutional order (such as a coup or coup attempt); (2) a record of constitutionally dubious attempts to extend presidential term limits; (3) a record of credible charges of manipulation of the playing field, of the vote count in previous elections, or both; and (4) a substantial majority of citizens (and a larger percentage than during previous democratic eras) judging the regime authoritarian in opinion polls. These indicators are quite different from those proposed by Diamond (2002); drawing on the African experience, Diamond (29) proposes an assessment based on seat and vote percentages and years of incumbency.

A fifth indicator would be relevant for many cases: a state's or ruling party's use of political violence to punish, terrorize, or demoralize the opposition (28). In the case of the Fujimori government, outright repression was limited. However, it did occur. The most notorious cases were those of two army intelligence agents, Mariella Barreto and Leonor La Rosa Bustamante; in retaliation for their apparent leaking of information about a government death squad, in 1997 former colleagues killed Barreto and, it was widely believed, badly beat La Rosa Bustamante. Commented an opposition legislator: "Fear became more palpable after Barreto. People think, 'if they [the National Intelligence Service] do this to one of their own, what might they do to us?'"[3] Also, after the regime's demise, evidence emerged that it was responsible for an attack against opposition journalist Fabián Salazar and possibly complicit in the death of the opposition leader Gustavo Mohme.

In the first section of this chapter I assess the Fujimori government's record, describing the four indicators of authoritarian intentions and capabilities stated above. In the second section I examine Peru's 2000 election, showing that these intentions and capabilities were not considered by key international actors as they sought to evaluate the election. Without the capacity to consider the government's intentions and capabilities, and also without clear thresholds for freedom and fairness, it was especially difficult for election monitors to fail the elections on the basis of its tilted playing field—despite the steepness of the tilt. Although, ultimately, international election observers judged Peru's 2000 elections "far from free and fair," this conclusion was a cliff-hanger; also, despite observers' criticism, the international community recognized Fujimori as Peru's new president.

I also highlight the special challenges raised by an electoral authoritarian regime for the political opposition. Especially—as in the case of Fujimori's Peru—when a regime is incorrectly classified as partially democratic rather than electoral authoritarian, analysts tend to perceive the shortcomings of the political opposition as the key reason for its losses at the polls. This tendency, however, is to blame the victim. As Schedler (2002, 42) points out, electoral authoritarians "find ways to engineer the failure of opposition parties." During Peru's 2000 elections, the evidence of current manipulation and abuse by the regime remained limited, and as a result—despite the government's past record—it was very difficult for the political opposition to make its case that the election did not meet democratic standards.

Classification of the Fujimori Government
Prior to the 2000 Elections

While elections are pivotal to regime classification, one previous electoral process is often weighted too heavily in U.S.-based experts' classifications. For example, President Fujimori won Peru's 1995 presidential election freely and fairly. Accordingly, although he had previously been responsible for various authoritarian measures and took additional ones between 1996 and 1999, neither Freedom House's nor Polity's scores for Peru became more negative.[4]

By contrast, I believe that, by December 1999 at the latest (when Fujimori formally launched his third consecutive presidential campaign), his record should have led U.S. analysts to withdraw Peru from the "partially democratic" classification and place it within the "electoral authoritarian" camp. As described in this section, prior to December 1999, the Fujimori government's record on three of the four indicators cited above were negative: the government was responsible for a coup against the constitutional order in April 1992, it had been credibly charged with the manipulation of elections between 1992 and 1995, and it was judged authoritarian by an increasing majority of citizens. In 1996, the regime embarked on its attempt to override the constitutional ban on a third consecutive term. Within Peru, the Fujimori government's past record plus this attempt were sufficient for the vast majority of analysts to adopt the "electoral authoritarian" classification.[5]

I also indicate the difficult challenges posed to Peru's political opposition by the electoral-authoritarian government. Although various strategies were pursued by the opposition to delegitimate or oust Fujimori—a countercoup attempt in 1992, a boycott of the 1992 legislative elections, a referendum on Fujimori's right to a third consecutive term in 1998, and frequent denunciation's of the government's human rights violations—none of these proved particularly successful.

President Fujimori, the Autogolpe, and Its Aftermath

On April 5, 1992, President Fujimori ruptured Peru's electoral democracy and adopted a series of repressive measures. The regime arrested the presidents of both houses of Congress as well as several other legislators. Troops occupied the offices of most of Peru's main newspapers, newsmagazines, and television and radio stations, and at least twenty-three journalists and twelve political leaders were detained.[6]

Eleven of the twelve political leaders were members of Alianza Popular Revolucionaria Americana (American Popular Revolutionary Alliance [APRA]), Peru's longest-standing political party. At the time of the autogolpe, APRA's leader, former president Alan García Pérez, had just been cleared by Peru's Supreme Court of charges of illicit enrichment and appeared likely to galvanize opposition to the government. A determined but ultimately unsuccessful attempt was made to capture García; in the security forces' effort to locate him, his secretary was detained and her husband badly beaten.[7] Subsequently, the Fujimori government brought more suits against García, and he did not return to Peru until after the regime's downfall.

Although the autogolpe was supported by most Peruvians, it was repudiated not only by the vast majority of the country's intellectuals and political leaders but also by the international community. On April 6, the secretary general of the Organization of American States (OAS) invoked Resolution 1080, declaring that Peru's democratic process had been interrupted and convening an emergency meeting of the OAS Permanent Council; the council condemned the autogolpe and called an ad hoc meeting of Latin America's ministers of foreign affairs for April 13. The U.S. government immediately suspended most of its aid to Peru as well as its participation in a "Support Group" of industrialized nations that was to facilitate Peru's return to the good graces of the international financial community.

Negotiations between the Fujimori government and the international community were intense. Both sides compromised. For its part, the Fujimori government retreated from its blatantly repressive course: most political detainees were released and media outlets reopened. On the other side, the international community decided not to seek the immediate departure of Fujimori.

Not surprisingly, this compromise dismayed the Peruvian opposition. On April 21, Peru's first vice president, Máximo San Román, was declared legal president by the country's dissolved congress. On May 15, a rally on behalf of San Román was supported by Peru's traditional parties—APRA, Acción Popular, the Partido Popular Cristiano (Popular Christian Party [PPC]), and Izquierda Unida (United Left [IU]).[8] Although the replacement of Fujimori by his vice president was logical—and indeed was the political outcome in somewhat similar crises in

Guatemala in 1993 and Ecuador in 2000—there is no indication that this possibility was seriously considered by the international community. San Román, who had become Fujimori's vice presidential candidate as a representative of Peru's small and medium-sized businesses, did not have a significant political base within Peru and was a virtual unknown outside it.

On May 18, at a meeting of Latin America's foreign ministers in the Bahamas, the Fujimori government conceded to the international community's demand for the election of a congress that would both draft a new constitution and assume conventional legislative functions. These Congreso Constituyente Democrático (Democratic Constituent Congress [CCD]) elections were held on November 22, 1992. Although the government's machinations for these elections were numerous—electoral authorities, procedures, and schedules were altered to the government's benefit—and although in part for these reasons the election was boycotted by most of Peru's major traditional parties, the elections were given the international community's stamp of approval (McClintock 1993, 118–19; Acevedo and Grossman 1996, 141).

Just prior to the elections for the CCD, officers from a sector of Peru's military plotted what was called a "countercoup." Led by retired general Jaime Salinas Sedó, these officers resented the flagrant politicization of military appointments and dismissals by Fujimori's national security advisor, Vladimiro Montesinos, and sought a return to constitutional government—before the CCD elections that, they feared, would relegitimize the Fujimori government. However, on November 13, Fujimori learned of Salinas's plotting and arrested him and a dozen-odd other high-ranking military officers. Although Salinas's credentials and reputation were good, a military resolution to Peru's political crisis was not favored by the international community.

After the autogolpe, the Fujimori government decreed draconian counterinsurgency laws. Suspects were denied most legal-defense rights and were tried before hooded judges or even in military courts; between 95 and 97 percent of suspects were declared guilty, and thousands of people were unjustly detained (Youngers 2003, 255–56). In July 1992, nine students and a professor "disappeared" from La Cantuta University in Lima, and it was rumored that a government-sponsored death squad, subsequently called the Grupo Colina (Colina Group), was responsible. In May 1993, the third-highest-ranking officer in Peru's army, General Rodolfo Robles, presented information linking Montesinos and the commander-in-chief of Peru's armed forces to the Grupo Colina—and simultaneously sought refuge in Argentina.

In October 1993, a referendum was held for the approval of the new constitution that had been drafted by the CCD. The new constitution was approved only narrowly (52 to 48 percent in favor, in the official result). Numerous flaws in the referendum process were identified by critics (LASA 1995, 7–10). As in the 1992 CCD election, the Fujimori government tightly controlled decisions about scheduling and format. In highland areas where the military continued to wield maximum authority under state-of-emergency provisions, it was charged that ballots and tallies were manipulated. A long six weeks elapsed between the referendum and the announcement of the official result, and one member of Peru's electoral commission denounced the result as fraudulent. However, the opposition was pleasantly surprised by the closeness of the referendum, and it did not rigorously criticize the various anomalies. The referendum was pronounced fair by the OAS's Observer Group, and the OAS's positive assessment was followed by that of the U.S. Department of State.

The 1995 Elections

Between 1992 and 1995, the Fujimori government enjoyed major counterinsurgency and economic successes. Fujimori was at the apex of his popularity, and he won a landslide victory in the 1995 presidential elections (Schmidt 2000). Although the government resorted to dirty tricks in the presidential campaign, it is extremely likely that Fujimori would have won without them. It is not at all clear, however, that Fujimori's 1995 electoral vehicle, Cambio 90/Nueva Mayoría (Change 90/New Majority), won the majority-party status in Congress that it was officially awarded. Peru's domestic election-observer group, named Transparencia, requested a formal investigation of the congressional results, but this request was not heeded.

In the April 9 presidential race, Fujimori's tally was an impressive 64 percent of the valid vote in a field of fourteen candidates. The runner-up, with 22 percent of the valid vote, was Javier Pérez de Cuéllar, a distinguished former secretary-general of the United Nations—but an ineffective campaigner. Peru's opposition parties had sought Pérez de Cuéllar's candidacy in the hope that he would unify them (which did not happen) and in the hope that his prestige would enhance international respect for the opposition (which did not happen either). At numerous intervals, Pérez de Cuéllar criticized the government's dirty tricks. His criticisms were widely considered sour grapes—until 1998, when a former intelligence agent, Luisa Zanatta, disclosed the scope and sophistication of a clandestine telephone-tapping operation, used against hundreds of Peruvian leaders (Youngers 2003, 313–14).

Most problematical, however, was the seriously flawed vote count in the congressional race. In the official tally, Cambio 90/Nueva Mayoría was awarded 51 percent of the vote, versus 49 percent for twenty opposition parties (Tuesta Soldevilla 2001, 456). However, 40 percent of all congressional ballots were voided—more than quadruple the percentage in the 1995 presidential race and more than triple the percentages in the previous 1990 and 1985 legislative races (Tuesta Soldevilla 2001, 44, 456, 505–6, 531–32). About 50 percent more ballots were declared invalid as were cast for Cambio 90/Nueva Mayoría. On its face, this outcome would have appeared to require a formal investigation by impartial officials and possibly a repeat vote.

However, the Fujimori government strongly defended the congressional count. Election officials argued that the invalid vote was caused by errors in the casting and tabulating of the "preferential vote" (the voters' indication of up to two preferred candidates from a political party's list of candidates). Election officials explained that citizens had cast their preferential votes incorrectly; that voting-table officials had added preferential votes incorrectly; and that incorrect voting-tally sheets had been rejected by election officials' computers. It was indeed the first time that Peru had used computers for electoral tabulation, and a larger percentage of null ballots than in the past would indeed be expected.[9]

At first, Peru's opposition was inclined to accept the result because it appeared to be confirmed by the quick count made by Transparencia, which, founded in July 1994, was at the time a fledgling domestic election-monitoring organization. Transparencia's quick count was virtually identical to the official result. Over time, however, criticisms mounted. Could pollsters—most of whom had predicted that Cambio 90/Nueva Mayoría would win only one-third of the legislative vote—really have been so wrong?[10] The preferential vote had been in use in Peru since 1985; why had such an unprecedented percentage of voters and voting-table officials suddenly erred? The government said that voting-table officials were poorly trained; but their task was simple addition, three officials (chosen in part for their educational qualifications) worked together, and at this time most Peruvians had attended secondary school.[11] Also, why was the rate of nullification 45 percent in sophisticated Lima but 20 percent in remote Ucayali and Ancash? (Tuesta Soldevilla 2001, 339).

These criticisms were fueled by ongoing revelations of wrongdoing with *actas* (voting-table tally sheets, totaling roughly seventy thousand in 1995).[12] Just before the election, 3,024 *actas* were revealed to have been stolen from the elections office in Huánuco; on April 21, it was charged that 206 fraudulent *actas* had altered the preferential vote in Juliaca; and on April 26, it was discovered that 37,000 *actas* were missing from the storage facility of the national elections office in Lima. To contain the escalating controversy, in early May election officials invited opposition leaders to their main Lima office, where for ninety hours the original copy of each *acta* was compared to the scanned version in official computers. It was not clear, however, exactly how opposition leaders were invited and how they could make complex comparisons for three days straight.[13]

The critics were joined by Transparencia. On April 30, Transparencia declared that the presidential and legislative races had to be distinguished from each other and cited "possible frauds" in the legislative results.[14] In its September report, Transparencia backed away from its own quick count and asked that its concerns be "calmly investigated."[15] At least one 1995 Transparencia staff person has said that, indeed, Transparencia—which, it will be recalled, was less than a year old at the time—did not actually conduct a quick count for the congressional race.[16]

The criticisms were not echoed by the international community, however. The head of the OAS observation mission, Santiago Murray, championed the elections.[17] Secretary-General César Gaviria declared that problems had been "small" and "had not compromised the final result."[18] Neither the OAS nor the U.S. Department of State expressed concern about the whopping invalid vote in the congressional race.[19]

Ultimately, not only most opposition leaders but also Eduardo Stein (head of the 2000 OAS Electoral Observation Mission [Misión de Observación Electoral]) came to believe that the congressional results had been manipulated.[20] However, there was no "smoking gun." Concludes Fernando Tuesta Soldevilla, Peru's foremost elections scholar and 2001–4 head of Peru's elections office: "With respect to the 1995 congressional race, there was a murder. We haven't yet found the knife, but there was still a murder."[21]

The Government's Pursuit of a Third Consecutive Term

Assuming that the presidential term limits in a country's constitution are representative of its political traditions and are supported by the public, a sitting president's effort to extend these limits for his own benefit is one indicator of authoritarian intentions. What came to be called Fujimori's "reelection project," a third consecutive term in a country that had traditionally not allowed two consecutive terms, began in 1996. As Conaghan (2001, 4) wrote, the reelection project "became the political equivalent of a cluster bomb, as it spewed out its destructive effects across institutions."

In August 1996, Fujimori's congressional majority passed a law permitting Fujimori to run for a third consecutive term: the "Law of Authentic Interpretation of the Constitution." This law was ridiculed by most constitutional experts. They pointed out that Fujimori had been Peru's president between 1993 and 1995 under the new constitution, and they derided the government's mathematics: 1[term] plus 1 [term] plus 1 [term] equals 2.[22]

Still, despite various concerted efforts on several fronts, groups opposed to this law were unable to prevail. First, Peru's National Election Board ruled that a 1996 law imposing a new hurdle to Peru's referendum process—subjecting referenda to prior congressional approval—could not be applied retroactively to the Law of Authentic Interpretation. The Fujimori government's response was to change the provisions for election to the board. In 1998, when several members were newly elected and at least one other was bribed, the board reversed its position, endorsing the requirement for congressional approval (Conaghan 2001, 7; the bribe was videotaped).

Also, Lima's Bar Association disputed the constitutionality of the Law of Authentic Interpretation, taking its case to Peru's Constitutional Tribunal (which was charged with the interpretation of Peru's constitution). In January 1997, three of the seven judges on the tribunal announced their ruling that the law was "inapplicable" to President Fujimori; the president of the tribunal abstained. Although the legal upshot of these rulings was unclear, the government was not pleased. Its congressional majority voted to remove the three judges from office and the Constitutional Tribunal ceased to function.

The opposition coalition the Democratic Forum vigorously sought a referendum on the law. Opinion polls consistently indicated that Peruvians were opposed to a third consecutive Fujimori candidacy (Conaghan

2001, 4; see also Chapter 6, this volume). The Democratic Forum collected the 1.25 million signatures that were necessary for a referendum on the issue. However, because of the rulings mentioned above, the referendum was conditional not only on the 1.25 million signatures but also on the votes of 48 of the 120 members of Congress. In August 1998, the referendum initiative fell three votes short of the necessary forty-eight—after the government had bribed or intimidated several legislators to be absent (Youngers 2000a, 53).

Among the Fujimori government's machinations in pursuit of a third consecutive term, its increasing control over Peru's media was especially important. In particular, in 1997, after the Channel 2 television station broadcast the government's human rights violations and also Montesinos's vast income, the government revoked the citizenship of Baruch Ivcher, the Israeli-born majority stockholder of the station. Ivcher went into exile.

Peruvians' Classification of the Regime Type of the Fujimori Government

To date, in their regime classifications, U.S.-based experts rarely consider the judgments of the country's citizens, as expressed in opinion polls. Clearly, opinion polls are problematical for various reasons. First, in many nations such as Peru, there are numerous polls, and the reliability and validity of their results may vary. Indeed, some poll results compared below in this section are from different companies. Second, with respect to polling items about *democracy* and *authoritarianism*, these terms are not defined, and respondents may have definitions at odds with those of U.S.-based experts. Still, I believe that, when considered as one indicator among several and when the results of the most prestigious polls are consistent, opinion poll data are valuable.

Between 1990 and 1998, the percentage of Peruvians who did not believe that their country was democratic increased markedly. Whereas in 1990, in Lima, 59 percent of people believed that Peru was "only a little democratic" or "not at all democratic," in 1998 the figure was 80 percent; there was a similar increase in the percentage who believed that people were afraid to express their opinions publicly.[23] The increase was especially noteworthy given that Peru's Shining Path (Sendero Luminoso) guerrilla movement had been decimated and that, concomitantly, political violence had sharply declined. Also, in various polls, more than 70 percent of respondents deemed the Fujimori government not merely "authoritarian" but downright "dictatorial."[24]

Relevant also is the jump in the percentage of Peruvians who considered the country's elections fraudulent. Whereas 32 percent of Limeños in 1990 judged Peru's elections generally fraudulent, the figure in 1998 was 64 percent.[25] In smaller, informal surveys by Mónica Villalobos in Huancayo and Trujillo in February 2000, 35 percent deemed Peru's 1985 and 1990 elections fraudulent, but 57 percent expected fraudulent elections in 2000.[26]

Peru's 2000 Elections

As we have seen, despite the mounting evidence of the Fujimori government's authoritarianism, Polity, Freedom House, and the U.S. government continued to classify the regime as partially democratic. As the 2000 elections loomed, it was clear to the Fujimori government, the opposition, and the international community that the elections were pivotal to subsequent regime classification. However, assessment of an election is more difficult than analysts traditionally acknowledge (Diamond 2002, 22). First, most observers are experts in elections, not in the politics of particular countries. They tend to hope that electoral processes will be free and fair and consider their role to be, at least in part, the encouragement of a free and fair process.[27] Also, as independent as most observers try to be, they are aware that their mission is both at the invitation of the host government and supported financially by other governments, all of which are likely to feel entitled to contact with the observers.

Observers' checklists for freedom and fairness are numerous, and thresholds are difficult to establish. For example, a Polity criterion for judging fairness is "If the incumbent uses his/her official powers to . . . unduly influence the electoral process to benefit themselves or their party."[28] Of course, what is the measurement of "unduly"? Another criterion is " '[I]rregularities,' while present, did not significantly affect the outcome of the vote." What is the measurement of "significantly"?[29] Observers tend to make these decisions as if they were jurors in a trial, listening to the claims made by government and opposition and considering the evidence advanced by the two sides. Just as in a U.S. trial, where the defendant's prior record is not presented, the government's and opposition's prior records are not taken into account (Middlebrook 1998).

This approach is problematic for the opposition in an electoral-authoritarian regime. The opposition's goal is to show that it does not have a fair chance to defeat the government in the elections. But, especially without recourse to the historical record, how can the opposition make its case? In actuality, the election is not a trial in which, after the fact, responsibility for a crime is assessed and evidence has been carefully pursued. Rather, it is an event in real time. The monitors usually decide if a crime has been committed within a day or two of the election; at that point they often go home. As in the Peruvian case, evidence of the crime—which of course the government is trying to hide—may surface only months or years after the monitors have left. In part for these reasons, in Latin America since the late 1980s, international observers have rarely repudiated elections. Indeed, they have repudiated only the 1994 elections in the Dominican Republic and the 2000 legislative elections in Haiti. In both cases, the repudiation was based on clear evidence of vote fraud.

Also, despite scholars' emphasis on the importance of "political freedoms to speak, publish, assemble, and organize" to the definition of democracy (Huntington 1991, 7), international election observers have not established clear thresholds for these freedoms and to date have not repudiated any elections in Latin America on these grounds. Given the lack of clear thresholds, how might observers decide that an electoral playing field is "too" tilted—that the opposition does not have the necessary freedom to campaign and get out its message?

Here is the rub for a political opposition: logically, if opposition parties are competing on the playing field, they are saying that it is not too tilted to void their chance to win. Only if the opposition boycotts the election does it clearly state that the playing field is too tilted. The political opposition's charge might not be endorsed by observers; but if the opposition does not make this charge, it is almost impossible for observers to do so. Not surprisingly, if the opposition argues that the playing field was too tilted only after the election, its argument is likely to be dismissed as sour grapes. For the political opposition, the question whether or not—and at what precise moment—it should boycott an election may be very difficult.[30] In an electoral-authoritarian regime, by definition the opposition is already struggling—as Juan Linz (2000, 170) describes, not so much persecuted but frustrated and, often, co-opted.

What are the advantages of a decision to boycott? First, as indicated above, a boycott is the signal that the opposition does not believe that the government will allow an opposition victory. With this signal, the opposition has a chance to deny the regime legitimacy.[31] Participation in rigged elections may also cost the political opposition its moral authority; it is considered willing "to bargain away [its] integrity for a few meaningless parliamentary seats."[32] Worse yet, the incumbent government may choose to recognize only the electoral victories of the opposition candidates it can manipulate (Johnson 1984, 145).

However, there are advantages to participation. First, while by definition an electoral-authoritarian regime is conspiring not to lose the election, there is usually at least a slight possibility that, despite its best effort, it will not prevail. During the course of an electoral campaign, scandals erupt, presidential planes crash, and international actors' positions evolve. Second, although a boycott is an effort to signal that the electoral process is fraudulent, this effort might fail; the electoral authoritarian regime will then endure, but the opposition will have a smaller political presence. Third, even a rigged election provides some opportunity for political debate.

In this section I delineate three distinct stages of the 2000 elections: the electoral campaign through February 29, 2000; the period from February 29 through mid-April 2000; and from mid-April through Fujimori's inauguration on July 28. My research on these political actors was conducted by document analysis, interviews, and participation in scores of relevant meetings during 1999–2000 (see the sources in McClintock and Vallas 2003, 207).

The First Stage: Mid-1999 Through February 29, 2000

During the first stage, it appeared that Fujimori and Perú 2000 would defeat the political opposition easily, without significant manipulation of the vote count. Although it was clear that Peru's electoral playing field was tilted in the government's favor, the margin of victory seemed likely to be large and international observers likely to decide that the outcome had not been "significantly" affected by this tilt. During this period, the opposition front-runners were Alberto Andrade (Lima's mayor and the candidate of Somos Perú) and Luis Castañeda Lossio (former head of the social security institute and the candidate of Solidaridad Nacional). They faced a steeply tilted playing field—indeed, a virtual cliff. It was obvious at the time that, except on cable, Peru's television news was blatantly biased; it was also obvious that progovernment tabloids that engaged in mocking and slandering opposition candidates were proliferating (Conaghan 2005). However, the government claimed that these media were only expressing their opinions, and at the time there was no evidence to the contrary. It was only after the government's demise that evidence of its bribing of media magnates became available. (For example, Montesinos paid the owner of Peru's most watched television station $1.5 million a month, for a total of about $9 million; he paid tabloid publishers about $5,000 for a front page with headlines that he himself chose).[33]

Peru's playing field was skewed in other ways as well.[34] Opposition candidates were harassed and their campaigns obstructed. The government greatly increased its expenditures for public works and for food programs and sought votes in exchange for these expenditures. In an apparent effort to signal the military's stance toward the elections, enormous Perú 2000 inscriptions were made on military property. The Fujimori government was aware that, given the skewed playing field, the opposition might decide to boycott and might also win the international community's approval of this decision. One of the government's shrewdest initiatives enticing candidates' participation was a dramatic salary increase for congresspersons: 1999–2000 annual salaries were approximately $120,000, an extremely handsome sum for many candidates. Also, the government manipulated the media and opinion polls both to entice opposition participation and to obstruct opposition unity around a boycott. A "high-level source" described Montesinos's "magic wand" for the electoral process: "[The magic wand] is the seesaw—the defamation campaigns and the surveys, to always keep at least one of the candidates with the illusion that his popularity is rising and, accordingly, it is not in his interest to collaborate with the others. This is how it had been first with Andrade, then with Castañeda [Lossio], and now with [Alejandro] Toledo; next, after destroying Toledo, the illusion [of victory] would be manipulated for [Federico] Salas."[35]

During this period, Andrade and Castañeda did not seem to understand the significance to the international community of a decision to participate in the 2000 elections.[36] In Lima and in Washington, their political allies denounced the tilted electoral playing field but then said that they would fight—and even forecast that they would win.[37] The contradiction between repudiation of the elections as illegitimate and participation in them was not addressed.[38] Commented *The Economist*, for example: "[T]he opposition has legitimized the election by taking part."[39]

For its part, the international community was mounting a serious election-monitoring effort. In 1999–2000, the United States Agency for International Development provided approximately $1 million for the most prominent domestic observer group, Transparencia, and roughly another

$1 million for a joint National Democratic Institute (NDI)/Carter Center effort.[40] The first NDI/Carter Center preelectoral delegation visited Peru in November–December 1999, and the second during February 7–11, 2000. The resulting first report found "serious flaws" in the electoral process, but also emphasized that these flaws could be addressed and that the electoral process could meet international standards.[41] The February report was more critical, but also stated that "significant improvements in the electoral process are still possible."[42]

Threatened by the NDI/Carter Center's criticisms, the Fujimori government vigorously sought the establishment of an OAS election-monitoring delegation. On the basis of its previous experience with OAS monitors, the Fujimori government was confident that the OAS delegation would be more positive, balancing the more critical position of NDI/Carter Center (Conaghan 2005).

Meanwhile, the tone at the U.S. Department of State was very cautious. Their statements were not only without criticism of the Fujimori government's past political abuses but without reference to them; it was as if the nine-year-old government had a clean democratic record. The U.S. Department of State *Report on Human Rights Practices for Peru* for 1999 said nothing more than, "Questions remain about the openness and fairness of the electoral process."[43] On December 28, 1999, the day after Fujimori formally declared his presidential candidacy, the U.S. Department of State declared that the U.S. government was "neutral on whatever government is elected in Peru," but "not neutral about the process."[44] In Lima, U.S. ambassador John Hamilton was even less inclined to criticize Peru's electoral process.[45]

In mid-February 2000, the funds became available for the OAS Electoral Observation Mission. The U.S. Department of State provided $560,000; Canada allocated $81,000 and Japan $200,000.[46] The head of the delegation, former Guatemalan foreign minister Eduardo Stein, was a Fujimori acquaintance.[47]

The Second Stage: February 29, 2000 Through Mid-April 2000

During this stage, the presidential race became much closer. As it appeared that the government might have to manipulate the vote count in order to win, evidence emerged that it was indeed willing and able to coordinate fraud. The possibility that there would be a rigged election and that it would be repudiated by the international community became significant. This stage began on February 29, when Peru's most serious newspaper, *El Comercio*, published a five-page report on the falsification of 1.2 million signatures for the inscription of Perú 2000 as a competing party in the 2000 elections.[48] The scandal of a "signatures forgery factory" (as it was called) was serious; witnesses described complicity in the forgery by election officials at the Oficina Nacional de Procesos Electorales (National Office of Electoral Processes [ONPE]) (Conaghan 2005). Of course, if election officials were complicit in the falsification of signatures, it is logical that they would also be complicit in the falsification of vote counts.

Amid this scandal, the U.S. government became much more critical of the Fujimori government. On March 9, Department of State spokesperson James P. Rubin called for a rapid investigation of the signatures scandal and for a leveling of the electoral playing field.[49] On March 29, the U.S. Congress passed, and on April 5 President Clinton signed, Resolution 43, which called for "modifications" in U.S.-Peruvian relations if the elections were not free and fair. Still, in the U.S. government's view, Peru's elections could yet be saved. On March 12, Ambassador Hamilton said that the NDI/Carter Center recommendations had not been satisfactorily implemented, but that that there was still time for the monitors' recommendations to be implemented and that he "did not even want to think about the possibility" that the electoral outcome would be repudiated by the international community.[50] On March 28, the White House called for the implementation of the monitors' recommendations "to ensure a fully democratic process."[51]

In March, a third opposition candidate, Alejandro Toledo, began to rise in the polls. He was a much more engaging speaker than the previous front-runners, and his emphasis on job creation resonated strongly. Toledo's résumé was impressive: as a teenage *cholo* (person of indigenous descent who speaks Spanish and wears Western dress) from Peru's provinces, he had secured a fellowship for study in the United States and had eventually earned a doctorate from Stanford University and worked for the World Bank. Having lived for many years in the United States, he was knowledgeable about the country and its norms. Although the Fujimori government originally expected to slander Toledo as it had his predecessors, character assassination was now more difficult for the government. First, vilification campaigns were less credible among better-educated Peruvians. And second, the government was trying to appear responsive to election observers' concerns.

The first round was held on April 9. After balloting ended, exit polls and then Transparencia's quick count indicated that Fujimori had not won the "50 percent plus one vote" necessary for a first-round victory. Transparencia's quick count put Fujimori at 48.73 percent and Toledo at 41.04 percent. OAS officials indicated that their quick count was similar. However, ONPE officials put Fujimori's tally at more than 49 percent and insisted that the tally could rise above the 50-percent-plus-one-vote threshold. Vote-counting slowed. For three days, incomplete tallies hovering around 50 percent were released. Analysts inferred that the delay reflected divisions in the government between "hard-liners" who wanted an end to the electoral process at any cost and the "soft-liners" who hoped to mollify international actors.

Not surprisingly, Toledo was angry. On election night, wearing an Inca-style red headband, he rallied his supporters in Lima, charging fraud. (At the end of the demonstration, there was some property damage, the perception grew that Toledo was a rabble-rouser). Also not surprisingly, international actors were dismayed. Stein warned that "something sinister is happening in Peru" (Conaghan 2001, 13–14). U.S. officials, including Secretary of State Madeleine Albright and drug czar Barry McCaffrey, called the Fujimori government to urge a second round.

Finally, on the evening of April 12, Peru's election authorities announced that Fujimori's tally was below 50 percent. The runoff was on.

The Third Stage: Mid-April Through July 2000

During this period, the stakes were of course the highest. For many weeks, it appeared that Fujimori would win an accurate vote count in a second round on May 28. However, in mid-May, Peru's election officials suddenly announced that they were introducing new computer software for the runoff. At this point, all bets on the eventual outcome were off.

For the runoff, Peruvians were taking a second look at Toledo. Some became uneasy about his character, in part because of negative portrayals in the government-controlled media. Unflattering images of Toledo's leadership of the election-night protest—suggesting that he was drunk—were broadcast ad nauseam on television. It was charged (and in fact was true) that Toledo had been separated for years from his wife and had fathered an out-of-wedlock child.

Just as Peruvians were taking a second look at Toledo, so were U.S. officials (McClintock and Vallas 2003, chap. 7). They too were concerned about Toledo's behavior the night of the first round, perceiving him as erratic and emotional. They became less confident that Toledo would maintain the collaboration on security issues, free-market reform, and narcotics control that had been established by the Fujimori government.

Accordingly, Fujimori appeared to be on his way to a third consecutive term that would be deemed legitimate by the U.S. Department of State. Public-opinion polls suggested that Fujimori was likely to win, albeit not by a large margin.[52] U.S. officials were praising electoral improvements and arguing that a free and fair election was possible.[53] For their part, observers remained very critical, but did not reject the possibility that reforms would yet raise the elections over the bar.[54] Then, suddenly, in mid-May, Peru's electoral authorities announced that they were introducing a new computer program for the runoff. On May 18, a dismayed Stein announced that his team could not verify the new program in the mere ten days before the May 28 runoff and asked for a postponement.

Crucial decisions followed. For their part, citing Article 111 of the 1993 constitution, which required that the runoff be held within thirty days of the declaration of the official results of the first round, Peru's electoral authorities declined the OAS mission's request. Toledo announced that he would boycott the runoff unless the date were postponed to June 18, his campaign given equal time on all television channels, and new poll-watchers selected.[55] The U.S. Department of State commented, "We regret both the unilateral decision of the opposition candidate to withdraw from the May 28 electoral contest and the hasty ruling by the National Board of Elections."[56]

Toledo's decision to boycott was widely criticized.[57] In the government-controlled media, he was denigrated as a "whiner" and "crybaby" who was not playing by the rules for the scheduling of the election.[58] However, as we have discussed, the boycott was the only way by which he could signal his judgment that the playing field was "too" tilted. If he had not boycotted and the government had allowed the review of the computer software, it was likely that he would have lost—amid a count that might even have been accurate. In this event, Toledo's complaints about the playing field would probably have been dismissed as sour grapes, and observers' criticisms of the elections would have been relatively muted.

The following week, the various parties negotiated intensely. The OAS mission, U.S. officials, and Latin American leaders urged postponement. The OAS mission threatened to withdraw if the government did not delay the runoff. Although by this time Stein had lost all confidence in the

Fujimori government (he feared for his life and was taking numerous security precautions),[59] he was also under U.S. pressure to seek a compromise. Said a "senior U.S. official," "The situation is hot, and we're trying to cool it down. We're trying to find an exit route so that both Fujimori and Toledo can save face and democracy can somehow be salvaged here. But foremost, it's vital for the region that we defuse this situation and allow free and fair elections to take place in Peru."[60]

Apparently, the OAS mission and the Fujimori government came close to a compromise agreement of a delay of only ten days. Finally, however, on May 25, Peru's electoral authorities categorically rejected the international community's appeals. Said a U.S. Department of State official: "The U.S. government deeply regrets this outcome. Even a relatively brief delay would have put the OAS in a position to speak to the integrity of the results."[61]

The Fujimori government's refusal to postpone the vote was surprising. Its claim of concern about the constitution's Article 111 was hardly credible. Why did it not accede to the international community's request, as it had at the end of the first round? There are no definitive answers. Probably, despite the opinion polls showing a likely Fujimori victory, the government did not feel confident and wanted to be able to rig the count if necessary. It should be kept in mind that among the many actors bribed by Montesinos were pollsters.

Possibly, the government feared that if the campaign were extended, new reversals would occur. In particular, on May 24, an opposition journalist, Fabián Salazar, was brutally attacked and his office burglarized. Salazar said that he had obtained a videotape showing Montesinos meeting with ONPE officials about the rigging of the election and that the intruders had seized the videotape and tortured him in pursuit of the identity of the person who had leaked the videotape.[62] Fortunately for the Fujimori government, amid the turbulent electoral process, both domestic and international coverage of the attack on Salazar was limited and for the most part echoed the official view that Salazar's account was wildly exaggerated. Subsequently, Salazar's word was proved good; since the demise of the Fujimori government, videotapes showing Montesinos meeting with ONPE officials have emerged (Conaghan 2005).

Other factors may have been at work as well. In the course of lengthy conversations with Ambassador Hamilton and Secretary-General César Gaviria of the OAS, Fujimori may have decided that, whatever the observers concluded, international reprisals would be limited.[63] Also, as Conaghan describes in Chapter 5 in this volume, the "display of arbitrary power" was a key strategy in the maintenance of the regime; capitulation to monitors could be interpreted as weakness and, over time, could lead to the government's downfall.

The May 28 exercise proceeded as scheduled, but it was not monitored by the OAS or any other group. Toledo called on his supporters to spoil their ballots or abstain. The official result was 51 percent of the vote for Perú 2000, 31 percent null or blank, and 18 percent for Perú Posible (which remained on the ballot). For NDI/Carter Center, Peru's 2000 elections had "failed dramatically to meet minimum international standards."[64] Said Stein: "The Peruvian electoral process is far from one that could be considered free and fair."[65]

Still, Alberto Fujimori claimed a third consecutive term, and his claim was not denied by the international community. The U.S. Department of State neither called for new elections nor suspended aid (McClintock and Vallas 2003, 151–53). For its part, at its June General Assembly meeting, the OAS decided to send a high-level mission to Peru, charged with "strengthening democracy" in the country; however, the mission's mandate was not a review of the 2000 elections but the proposal of future reforms (Cooper and Legler 2001, 128).

Conclusion

In this chapter I have argued that the Fujimori government should have been judged authoritarian prior to the fraudulent elections of 2000. The executive's 1992 responsibility for the rupture of the previous constitutional order was a serious authoritarian act. The government's 1996 indication that it would seek a constitutionally prohibited third consecutive term, and its subsequent egregious manipulation of many rules and institutions to make this possible, was a second major authoritarian act. If these two acts were insufficient to persuade analysts of the government's authoritarian intentions and capabilities, to them may be added the pattern of controversial elections and the considerable increase in the percentages—well surpassing 50 percent—of Peruvians who judged the government as authoritarian and elections as fraudulent.

Even in the wake of the failed 2000 elections, Peru was not classified as an electoral-authoritarian regime by the OAS General Assembly or the U.S. government. Also, international observers' repudiation of the 2000 elections had been far from a foregone conclusion. If the Fujimori government had not suddenly introduced new computer software and had not rejected the OAS mission's request for a postponement of the election so that it could review the software, a passing grade would have been likely.

How might the possibility of a correct judgment of the 2000 elections been increased? First, elections should not be assessed in a historical vacuum. When an incumbent president is competing, his or her record on democracy and the rule of law should be considered so that the credibility of both government and opposition arguments can be evaluated. Amid the real time in which an election takes place, often without evidence to validate or invalidate charges, it is necessary to include assessments of intentions and capabilities based on the historical record.

Second, it is necessary to establish standards for the electoral playing field. Without clear thresholds, observers are reluctant to repudiate elections on the basis of the playing field. Although observers regularly criticized Peru's tilted playing field, they also said—even mere weeks before the elections—that the field could yet be leveled and given a passing grade by monitors. Without clear thresholds, if opposition parties continue to play on a tilted field, observers are virtually obliged to monitor the competition. The difficult burden of the boycott decision is placed on the opposition parties.

NOTES

1. Schedler's statement is a play on the definition of democracy by Adam Przeworski (1991, 10).

2. For a discussion of the phrase "democratic with an adjective," see D. Collier and Levitsky 1997. On the classification of Peru as partially democratic or "democratic with an adjective," note Peru's scores by global democracy measures. From 1990 through 2000, Peru was ranked "partially free" by Freedom House; its lowest combined political rights–civil liberties score, 11, occurred after the 1992 autogolpe; between January 1995 and January 2000, the combined score was 9 (5 for political rights and 4 for civil liberties) every year except in January 1997, when the combined score was better, at 7 (4 for political rights and 3 for civil liberties). In Freedom House's rankings, 1 represents the most free and 7 the least free; nations whose combined political rights–civil liberties score is 11 are sometimes ranked "partly free" and sometimes "not free;" nations whose combined score is 12 or below are ranked "not free." Polity's score for Peru in 1992 was -3 (a classification as autocratic), but Polity's score during 1993–99 was +1, just reaching into the ranks of democracies. Polity's scores range from +10 to -10; 0 is the threshold between democratic and autocratic. Available at http://www.freedomhouse.org and http://www.bsos.umd.edu/cidcm/inscr/polity. U.S. scholars' "democratic with an adjective" labels for the Fujimori government

include "delegative democracy" (O'Donnell 1994); "degenerated delegative democracy" (Cameron and Mauceri 1997, 241); "semidemocratic" (Levitsky 1999, 78); "top-down democracy" (Palmer 1996, 74); and "autocratic democracy" (Mauceri 1997a). A post-1995 "restoration of democracy in a formal sense" is cited by S. Stokes (1996b, 70).

3. Legislator Anel Townsend, cited in Burt 2002, 28. State complicity is suspected in various other cases as well.

4. See n. 3, this chapter.

5. Most adopted the label even earlier. See Rospigliosi 1994; Cotler 1994, 222–24; Pease García 1999, 80–83; Degregori 2000, 62–77; Lynch 2000.

6. U.S. Ambassador Anthony Quainton, Memorandum from U.S. Embassy in Lima, no. 05167, April 7, 1992, 2 (made available through the Freedom of Information Act).

7. Ibid., 1–3.

8. *Resumen Semanal* 15, no. 670, May 15–21, 1992, 1.

9. Oscar Medrano, "Réquiem por un Cómputo Parlamentario," *Caretas*, April 20, 1995, 10–17; Schmidt 2000, 116.

10. Conaghan 1995b, 9; *Latin American Weekly Report* 11, March 23, 1995, 124.

11. Calculation from data in World Bank 1993a.

12. For further discussion, see Conaghan 2005; Schmidt 2000.

13. *Resumen Semanal* 17, no. 818, May 3–9, 1; "Cierre con Bulla," *Caretas*, May 11, 1995, 19.

14. *Resumen Semanal* 17, no. 818, May 3–9, 1.

15. Transparencia 1995, 75–78. Transparencia cautioned: "Our observation was limited to the presidential vote and the congressional vote for the political organizations, and for technical reasons, did not include the preferential vote." So, was it possible that, for every single one of the twenty political parties, the difference between Transparencia's quick count and the official tally was less than one percentage point?

16. Transparencia staffperson in communication with Julio Carrión, August 24, 2004; the substance of the communication was e-mailed to the author. See also the points raised in n. 15, this chapter.

17. See, for example, "El Perú tiene una democracia consolidada y no necesita verificación electoral," *Expreso*, April 11, 1995, A3.

18. "Secretario general de OEA presentó informe sobre comicios en el Perú," *El Comercio*, June 2, 1995, A4.

19. Unit for the Promotion of Democracy 1997, 28–29; U.S. Department of State 1995.

20. Eduardo Stein, "La memoria del observador," *El Comercio*, June 16, 2001, 1. Stein noted that officials involved in the 1995 count had admitted to him that the congressional vote had been altered. Interview by the author, Washington, D.C., January 10, 2002.

21. Fernando Tuesta Soldevilla, interview by the author, Lima, July 26, 2002.

22. See, for example, the publications of the Instituto de Defensa Legal, in particular its e-mail updates, during the electoral period.

23. Unfortunately, the polls were by different agencies; the 1990 poll was by

Datum, while the 1998 poll was by Apoyo. In the later 1990s, Datum changed its scale for the item, and results were not comparable. However, poll results were generally consistent; for example, in a 1999 poll by the University of Lima, 64 percent said that "the government does not respect freedom of the press;" see Universidad de Lima—Grupo de Opinión Pública, *Coyuntura sociopolítica mayo 1999: Opinión ciudadana en Lima y El Callao,* courtesy of Universidad de Lima. For information on the precise question and samples, see McClintock 1999, 94.

24. See, for example, a survey by the Empresa Peruana de Investigación de Mercado cited in *La República,* September 6, 1998, 3; and a survey by the University of Lima reported on Peru's weekly television news program *Panorama* on June 15, 1997.

25. Again, unfortunately the surveys were by different companies (Datum in 1990 and Apoyo in 1998), but the trend was not disputed; see, for example, Schmidt 2000, 127. A 1996 Apoyo poll showed that only 40 percent considering the elections fraudulent, suggesting that the jump occurred after 1996. See McClintock 1999 for more information about the items and surveys. In 1995, 17 percent believed the presidential elections results to be fraudulent. That figured jumped to 47 percent in the wake of the 2000 elections, as Carrión reports in Chapter 6 in this volume.

26. Nonrandom surveys of 35 respondents in each of the two cities. Respondents in Huancayo were considerably more skeptical of the 2000 electoral process than those in Trujillo. Mónica Villalobos, who has worked for various polling companies, was contracted for this research by the author.

27. See, for example, the National Democratic Institute and Carter Center (NDI/Carter Center) reports cited below, available at http://www.ndi.org and at http://www.cartercenter.org.

28. Available at http://www.bsos.umd.edu/cidcm/inscr/polity.

29. Ibid.

30. In Latin America, the decision split the major opposition party in Nicaragua in 1963, Paraguay in 1963, and the Dominican Republic in both 1970 and 1974; see Walter 1993, 144–75; Miranda 1990, 76–100; Hartlyn 1998, 110–15.

31. For example, to try to deny legitimacy to the FSLN (Frente Sandinista de Liberación Nacional [Sandinista National Liberation Front]) government in Nicaragua, Reagan administration hard-liners encouraged opposition parties to boycott the 1984 elections. See Carothers 1991, 88–89, among other accounts.

32. A comment about Paraguay's opposition by Lewis (1980, 185).

33. Scott Wilson, "Camera Has Turned on Peru's TV Stations," *Washington Post,* December 18, 2001, A23.

34. See "Statement of the NDI/Carter Center February 2000 Pre-Election Delegation to Peru," Lima, February 11, 2000, 5–6, http://www.ndi.org and http://www.cartercenter.org.

35. "Very high level sources," quoted in *Ideele Alerta* 6, March 7, 2000, 1.

36. For example, the very first question posed by principal deputy assistant secretary of state for inter-American affairs Jack Leonard to Peruvian opposition leaders in a June 2, 1999, meeting in Washington, D.C. was, "Are you participating in the elections?" The very first sentence of the first preelection report by the NDI/Carter Center highlighted that the opposition was participating; see "State-

ment of the NDI/Carter Center December 1999 Pre-Election Delegation to Peru," Lima, December 3, 1999, http://www.ndi.org/perurep1.htm.

37. Congresswoman Lourdes Flores Nano in a meeting with Jack Leonard, cited in n. 36, and vice presidential candidate for Somos Perú, Beatriz Merino, at an invitation-only workshop, "A Dialogue Among Peruvian Opposition Leaders and International Policymakers," co-sponsored by the George Washington University and the Washington Office on Latin America, Washington, D.C., January 28, 2000. The workshop followed a January 27, 2000, all-day conference by the same co-sponsors.

38. The contradiction is emphasized by Eduardo Stein (*El Pregonero*, March 9, 2000, 21).

39. "The Andean Autocrats Dig In for the Long Haul," *Economist*, February 5, 2000, 27.

40. On the amount for Transparencia, see Levitt 2001. The amount for NDI/Carter Center was an estimate from Patrick Merloe, senior associate and director of Programs on Election Processes at NDI, telephone interview by the author, July 10, 2002.

41. "Statement of the NDI/Carter Center December 1999 Pre-Election Delegation to Peru," Lima, December 3, 1999, 2.

42. "Statement of the NDI/Carter Center February 2000 Pre-Election Delegation to Peru," Lima, February 11, 2000, 2, http://www.ndi.org and http://www.cartercenter.org.

43. Available at http://www.state.gov/www/global/human_rights/999_hrp_report/peru, 2.

44. U.S. Department of State, "Decision of Peru's President Fujimori to Seek Third Term," statement released on December 28, 1999, http://secretary.state.gov/www/briefings/statements/1999.

45. See, for example, his comments in *La República*, February 15, 2000, 2.

46. Figures courtesy of Elizabeth Spehar, Unit for the Promotion of Democracy, OAS, July 1, 2002.

47. *El Comercio*, March 23, 2000, A4.

48. As Perú 2000 was a new party in Peru, it was required to supply a list of 4 percent of Peru's total number of registered voters (with signatures and the number of the voter's identification card) who were adherents of the party.

49. Joanna Drzewieniecki, *Peru Unofficial*, no. 27, March 13, 2000, 2. *Peru Unofficial* is a newsletter sponsored by Peru Peace Network (http://www.perupeace.net).

50. "Recomendaciones del Centro Carter no han sido atendidas," *La República*, March 12, 2000.

51. "Statement by the Press Secretary," the White House, Washington, D.C., March 28, 2000, http://www.whitehouse.gov/library/PressReleases.

52. "Poll Track: Voter Preference in the Second Round of the Presidential Election," Peru Election 2000 Web site (http://www.qsilver.queensu.ca/csd/peru2000), accessed May 23, 2000.

53. Clifford Krauss, "International Observers Say They Fear Fujimori May Steal Peru's Election Runoff," *New York Times*, May 15, 2000, A8.

54. See "Statement of the National Democratic Institute for International Af-

fairs/Carter Center May 2000 Pre-election Delegation to Peru," May 5, 2000, http://www.ndi.org.

55. Clifford Krauss, "Insurgent in Peru Calls for Election Boycott," *New York Times,* May 20, 2000, A5.

56. Krauss, "Insurgent in Peru," A5; Anthony Faiola, "Fujimori's Rival Threatens to Quit Peruvian Election," *Washington Post,* May 19, 2000, A23.

57. In an Apoyo poll, 59 percent of the respondents disagreed with Toledo's boycott. See "Toledo Pulls Out of Peruvian Run-Off and Courts Reprisals by Urging Abstention," *Latin American Weekly Report,* May 23, 2000, 229.

58. "Fujimori Stands Firm on 28 May as Election Day; Toledo Calls for Mass Protest," *News Briefs: May 2000,* Peru Election 2000 Web site (http://www.q silver.queensu.ca/csd/peru2000), accessed May 23, 2000.

59. "La memoria del observador," interview with Eduardo Stein, *El Comercio,* June 16, 2001, A4.

60. "One source close to the talks"—presumably a U.S. official—quoted by Anthony Faiola ("OAS Issues New Fraud Warning in Peru Runoff," *Washington Post,* May 23, 2000, A23).

61. Quotation is of "a senior U.S. Embassy official," cited by Anthony Faiola ("Peru Refuses to Postpone Vote," *Washington Post,* May 26, 2000, A25).

62. "Crimen electoral," *Caretas,* May 26, 2000, 11–13.

63. There is no evidence to this effect. However, these leaders did hold several long conversations, and it would be assumed that the intensity of reprisals would be among the topics. See Clifford Krauss, "Angry Election Monitor Leaves Peru 2 Days Before Runoff Vote," *New York Times,* May 27, 2000, A5; Anthony Faiola, "Election Monitors Extend Deadline in Peru," *Washington Post,* May 24, 2000, A27; "OAS Envoy Leaves Peru, Criticizes Vote," *Washington Post,* May 27, 2000, A18.

64. "Statement of the National Democratic Institute (NDI)/Carter Center Post-Election Delegation to Peru," issued in Lima on July 14, 2000, http://www.ndi.org.

65. Krauss, "Angry Election Monitor," A5.

TWELVE

Endogenous Regime Breakdown:
The Vladivideo and the Fall of Peru's Fujimori

MAXWELL A. CAMERON

Dramatis Personae

Bello, Elesván. Commander general of the armed forces. Loyal to Vladimiro Montesinos.

Boloña, Carlos. Cabinet minister under Fujimori. Held economy portfolio twice.

Bustamante, Alberto. Cabinet minister under Fujimori. Served as prime minister and minister of justice.

Camell del Solar, Eduardo. Director of newspaper *Expreso*. Caught on videotape with Montesinos.

Castillo Castillo, Víctor Raúl. President of the Supreme Court. Served on Council of Judicial Coordination. Captured on video meeting with Montesinos.

I am grateful to Julio Carrión, Charlie Kenny, Pablo Policzer, and two anonymous reviewers for comments and to Catherine Hirbour for research assistance. The Social Sciences and Humanities Research Council of Canada provided a grant to conduct research in Peru that enabled this chapter to be written. During the period between January 2 and January 14, 2002, interviews were conducted with five members of Congress, six congressional staffers, a retired member of the intelligence service, and a senior government official. All interviews were conducted on a not-for-attribution basis. No member of Congress from the Fujimori camp agreed to be interviewed. Specific interviews are indicated by numbers. The author is exclusively responsible for the analysis.

Crousillat, José Francisco. Director of América Televisión (Channel 4). Caught on video with Alberto Kouri and Montesinos.

Cuculiza, Luisa María. Cabinet minister under Fujimori. Caught on videotape with Montesinos.

Delgado Parker, Manuel. President of RPP (radio broadcasting company), influenced by Montesinos.

Dufour Martinez, Oscar. Director of Interandina de Publicidad, owner of the newsmagazine *Oiga*.

Fujimori, Alberto. President of Peru, 1990–2000.

García Pérez, Alan. President of Peru, 1985–90.

Hildebrandt, César. Journalist. Persecuted by government.

Ibárcena, Antonio. Commander of navy. Loyal to Montesinos.

Ivcher, Baruch. Majority owner of Frecuencia Latina (Channel 2). Stripped of Peruvian citizenship after exposing criminal activity by the intelligence service.

Joy Way, Víctor. Member of Congress and leader of Perú 2000. Involved in arms deals with Montesinos.

Kouri, Alberto. Member of Congress, elected in 2000. Caught on videotape accepting a bribe from Montesinos to defect from Perú Posible.

Montes de Oca, Alipio. President of National Election Board. Controlled by Montesinos.

Montesinos, Vladimiro. De facto head of National Intelligence Service, 1990–2000.

Muñoz Arce, Rómulo. Member of National Election Board. Controlled by Montesinos.

Nélida Colán, Blanca. State attorney responsible for public ministry. Controlled by Montesinos.

Olivera, Fernando "Popi." Leader of Frente Independiente Moralizador (Independent Moralizing Front [FIM]).

Paniagua, Valentín. Transitional president of Peru, 2000–2001.

Pinchi Pinchi, Matilde. Montesinos's secretary and confidante.

Robles, Rodolfo. Military whistle-blower. Accused the high command of human rights abuses.

Rodríguez Medrano, Alejandro. Provisional judge on the Supreme Court. Considered a key figure in Montesinos's influence over the judiciary.

Salas, Federico. Presidential candidate in 2000, became prime minister under Fujimori. Accepted money from Montesinos.

Schutz, Ernesto. President of Panamericana Televisión, influenced by Montesinos.

Toledo, Alejandro. President of Peru, 2001–
Vargas Llosa, Mario. Writer and presidential candidate in 1990.
Vera Abad, Julio. Majority owner of Andina de Televisión (Channel 9).
  Influenced by Montesinos.
Villanueva Ruesta, José. Served as minister of Interior and commander
  general of the armed forces. Loyal to Montesinos.

> If it were done when 'tis done, then 'twere well
> It were done quickly. If th' assassination
> Could trammel up the consequence, and catch,
> With his surcease, success; that but this blow
> Might be the be-all and the end-all—here
> But here, upon this bank and shoal of time,
> We'd jump the life to come. But in these cases
> We still have judgment here; that we but teach
> Bloody instructions, which, being taught, return
> To plague th' inventor; this even-handed justice
> Commends th' ingredients of our poisoned chalice
> —*Macbeth*, Act 1, Scene 7

The rise and fall of President Alberto Fujimori is a story of the concentration of political power in the hands of a tiny clique around the president and his informal security advisor, Vladimiro Montesinos, and how their power evaporated into thin air when the alliance between them fell apart. It is about the construction of an electoral-authoritarian political regime in which the core relationships and practices that sustained political power were based not upon formal and established institutions, norms, and practices, but upon a set of informal mechanisms involving coercion, deception, blackmail, and bribery—all veiled behind a masquerade of legality that was used to insulate the regime from public scrutiny, guarantee impunity for the key power-brokers, and persecute regime opponents.[1]

There is an intimate link between how Fujimori acquired power and how he lost it; the collapse of the Fujimori regime was primarily the product of forces endogenous to the regime itself, forces that can be traced to its very origin. Even before he swore the presidential oath, on July 28, 1990, Fujimori had forged a relationship with Montesinos that would ultimately prove to be his undoing; the key event in his fall was the release of a videotape that provided a rare glimpse into the sort of bribery and blackmail that had glued together the governing clique from its inception. The release of this video, colloquially known as the Vladivideo, stripped away the regime's assiduously cultivated veneer of legality; it made allegations of corruption and blackmail by the political opposition irrefutable in the court of public opinion; it effectively dissolved the congress as a functioning institution; it further damaged the already severely questioned electoral legitimacy of the president; it placed everyone complicit with Montesinos—a vast network of judges, lawyers, journalists, businesspeople, and the president himself—on notice that they were similarly vulnerable to exposure; and, most crucially, it undermined the alliance between Fujimori and Montesinos.[2] The fact that Fujimori announced his decision to call new elections following the release of the videotape underscores the indissoluble bond that tied him to Montesinos. Montesinos became a liability, yet Fujimori was unable to govern without him; caught between the proverbial sword and the wall, the president was compelled to resign.

Fujimori's resignation was the key—and by no means inevitable—event in the collapse of the regime. In a functioning electoral democracy, presidents leave office because they choose not to run, because they cannot get reelected, or because they are impeached or otherwise removed by constitutional means. None of these options was available in Peru's competitive-authoritarian system.[3] Fujimori's occupancy of the palace was the only real guarantee that Montesinos and his cronies would be able to continue to enrich themselves and accumulate influence while avoiding prosecution or exile. Montesinos needed Fujimori in power to retain control over his vast network of influence. Fujimori needed Montesinos, in part because they were bound together by ties of complicity in illegal activity. As long as Fujimori and Montesinos controlled Congress and the judiciary (including the Public Ministry and the Constitutional Tribunal), impeachment was out of the question. Just as important, Fujimori could not run for or resign from office without breaking with Montesinos—an outcome neither could possibly relish.

Dislodging the president through electoral competition had proved impossible. The main obstacle was Fujimori's remarkable popularity, in spite of a decade in office. It was precisely his popularity that made it possible for an authoritarian regime to be built around competitive elections. Fujimori had an uncanny ability to read the public mood and the public resources necessary to mold opinion, including control over much of the media—the tax-collection agency was especially helpful in this respect—and programs of assistance to the poor that were run out of the Ministry of the Presidency. More important, Montesinos, driven to desperation in an effort to ensure Fujimori's bid for a third term in office, captured control over the electoral institutions (the Jurado Nacional de Elecciones, or National Election Board [JNE], and the Organización Nacional de Procesos Electorales, or National Organization of Electoral Processes [ONPE]) that were responsible for registering parties and collecting and counting the votes. Add the ineffectiveness of the opposition, and the conclusion is almost inevitable: the end of the Fujimori regime would occur not as a consequence of electoral competition based on respected rules and according to the constitutional calendar, but as a result of the inevitable internal tensions within the regime given the massive concentration of executive power.[4] Speculation about the regime's denouement often involved scenarios that included a coup, assassination, accident, capture, exile, or some other unscripted event.

A well-established literature on the breakdown of authoritarian regimes stresses the interaction between internal tensions and external forces. This literature finds that fissures within the ruling bloc—typically between hard-liners and soft-liners—are often a necessary condition for transitions to occur.[5] For the better part of a decade the key power brokers in the regime demonstrated remarkable discipline and cohesion. The Vladivideo led to the first public schism between Fujimori and Montesinos. The role of the political opposition is well understood and easily documented, yet a complete and accurate appreciation requires an understanding of the regime's vulnerability. The efforts of the opposition were necessary but not sufficient to topple of the regime; a fully fledged regime crisis required the internal dynamics prompted by the release of the Vladivideo. The most significant achievement of the opposition—at least those who were neither intimidated nor corrupted—was to withstand the onslaught of bribes and dirty tricks by the government long enough to reap the benefits of an imploding regime.

A Faustian Bargain

The relationship between Fujimori and Montesinos can be dated to the presidential election campaign in 1990. On April 8, 1990, Fujimori placed second in the first round of voting, trailing Mario Vargas Llosa by a narrow margin. The result was a shock to Peru's political establishment, but an opportunity for Montesinos. Fujimori presented himself as a practical man of modest means and claimed that he had sold a house, a tractor, and a couple of vehicles to finance his campaign. This was an exaggeration. Fujimori declared campaign expenses of less than two hundred thousand dollars.[6] However, investigations by FIM leader Fernando "Popi" Olivera revealed that Fujimori (in partnership with his wife) owned a large number of properties (which were publicly recorded in the National Public Registry Office) and had significantly underreported the value of many of these properties. Fujimori was discovered to have more than twenty properties in Lima and to have sold twelve between 1977 and 1989, according to journalist Cesar Hildebrandt.[7] The total value of the properties was estimated between $600,000 and $1 million.[8]

Further investigation revealed that Fujimori had received a twelve-hectare plot of land, called Pampa Bonita, from the government under the Agrarian Reform law—a law implemented for the benefit of peasants. The seriousness of Fujimori's history of tax evasion was a matter for debate. According to a prominent politician, "The charges were trivial. If you threw Fujimori in jail for them, you would have to do the same for half of Peru."[9] The public seemed to understand. In one poll, only 4 percent of people surveyed were troubled by the allegations enough to question whether Fujimori was fit for office.[10] In a country where a majority of the work force was in the informal sector (and hence routinely evaded taxes), the allegations were hardly a major political liability. Nevertheless, Fujimori feared that even minor tax-fraud problems provided his adversaries with the opportunity to derail his campaign by legal means.[11]

Fujimori was introduced to Montesinos, who offered to help him with his legal problems.[12] Montesinos had been cashiered from the army in the 1970s for selling military secrets to the U.S. Central Intelligence Agency (CIA), and he subsequently developed a network of connections within the judiciary as a lawyer for drug traffickers and military officers charged with human rights crimes in the 1980s. Montesinos was not the sort of lawyer who won cases by arguing the merits; he was the kind who would walk out of a judge's office leaving behind a briefcase of cash. He also knew the value of a well-timed threat. Suspiciously, a car bomb was placed in front of Fernando Olivera's house, presumably to warn him to stop investigating Fujimori's real estate dealings. Olivera also received warning phone calls at work and in Congress.[13] In retrospect, these acts have the earmarks of a Montesinos operation.

Fujimori responded to the allegations of tax fraud using stratagems of subterfuge and evasion that would be perfected throughout his tenure in office. He refused to appear before a judge to demonstrate his innocence;

he responded selectively to certain allegations while obfuscating more serious ones; and he complained of being the victim of a "dirty war" of verbal mudslinging, and then underhandedly hurled similar allegations back at his adversaries. He insisted that all the allegations against him were not isolated events, but part of an orchestrated campaign.[14] This rhetorical style would become Fujimori's trademark. Once in office, he would repeatedly deny any wrongdoing within his government until it became impossible to do so, and thereafter, once such wrongdoing had been proved beyond any shadow of a doubt, the cases would be called "isolated events" and efforts to expose them would be "campaigns" by the opposition to discredit his government. Finally, he slyly commented, "I have not fallen from an avocado tree" ("No soy un caído del palto," meaning, roughly, "I was not born yesterday"). This became the campaign's most celebrated phrase and earned Fujimori the grudging admiration that in Peru is accorded to the *vivo,* one who gets the better of someone else—especially when the other person is more powerful.[15]

Legal defense was not all Fujimori needed. He had virtually no team; nor had he prepared a program for governing in the event of a second-round victory. Potential advisors were assembled in a popular but discrete Chinese restaurant in Lima, and among the invitees was an intelligence officer associated with Montesinos, Rafael Merino. Merino presented an analysis of the fight against terrorism that appealed to Fujimori, who professed to know little about terrorism. The analysis, originally written for the Ministry of Defense and archived after the assassination of the minister, suggested that too much effort had been expended attacking the social base of the Shining Path (Sendero Luminoso), and not enough energy spent on going after the leadership. Later, Montesinos presented this 40-page document to the candidate. The analysis criticized the expenditure of resources devoted to attacking the base of the movement and called for a strategy that would go after the organization's senior leadership.[16] Although the strategy was not Montesinos's, he took credit for it and thereby won the admiration of the president-to-be.

Montesinos also presented Fujimori with a secret government program devised by a cabal within the armed forces plotting a military coup. The document, known as the Plan Verde (Green Plan), outlines the need for a "guided democracy" coupled with a "market economy."[17] The existence of a plot to overthrow the winner of the second round increased Fujimori's anxiety and his inclination to rely on Montesinos for advice on how to manage the armed forces and thwart an eventual coup. Signaling the importance that Fujimori placed on securing control over the armed forces, he moved into military installations (the Círculo Militar) in downtown Lima, where he remained virtually sequestered during the period leading up to the presidential inauguration on July 28, 1990.

From the inauguration onward, Montesinos became Fujimori's de facto head of intelligence and his primary advisor on security issues. He used his control over the Servicio de Inteligencia Nacional (National Intelligence Service [SIN]) to run black operations using operatives who came to be known as Grupo Colina (Colina Group). The single worst crime committed by the group was the massacre of Barrios Altos, where gunmen murdered fifteen people. Thereafter, any threat to Fujimori's tenure in office would also necessarily imply the threat of prison time, for the all signs pointed to Montesinos's involvement and Montesinos and Fujimori were by then inseparable.[18] The mutual complicity of Fujimori and Montesinos, and the desire to cover their tracks, is believed by some to be a key motivating factor behind Fujimori's decision in April 1992 to close Congress, suspend the constitution, and rule by decree.[19]

In one sense, impunity was written in the genetic code of the political system developed by Fujimori from 1990 onward. The precariousness of the rule of law is a constant in Peruvian politics, but the process of regime decay under Fujimori can only be understood in terms of the need for ever more drastic measures to cover up previous crimes. From seemingly benign beginnings, Fujimori compromised himself through actions with Montesinos that would implicate him in a series of progressively more serious legal difficulties. These, in turn, would require further steps to control and curtail mechanisms of accountability, in a dynamic process that would ultimately lead to the co-optation of all major state institutions. In the end, however, like those of Macbeth, Montesinos's "bloody instructions" would indeed "return to plague the inventor"—and the "poisoned chalice" would take the form of a scandalous videotape.

Bribes, Lies, and Videotapes

The fall of Fujimori was precipitated by a video leaked to the opposition by Montesinos's personal secretary and confidante, Matilde Pinchi Pinchi. The video showed opposition legislator Alberto ("Beto") Kouri accepting a bribe of fifteen thousand dollars in cash from Montesinos to cross over to the government benches. Pinchi gave this video to an intermediary, Germán Barrera. Posing as an emissary for a group of disgruntled naval officers, Barrera contacted various members of the opposition.[20] Initial contacts with Perú Posible, the leading challenger to Fujimori in the 2000 elections, were fruitless. Preoccupied with the March of the Four Suyos, and put off by the demand for $1 million in return for the videos, Toledo's advisor Carlos Bruce did not respond to the offer to purchase the videos.

Although initially skeptical, representatives of FIM were, nevertheless, more receptive. FIM member Luis Iberico asked to see the video to confirm its authenticity, and a meeting was arranged in a private home in an affluent district of Lima. Barrera played a tape showing Montesinos bribing Kouri. He also showed Iberico a contract that television executives José Francisco Crousillat, vice president of América Televisión (Channel 4), and Mendel and Samuel Winter, owners of Frecuencia Latina (Channel 2), had signed pledging loyalty to Montesinos. The Winter brothers were minority shareholders who had seized control of Channel 2 in 1997 after its owner, Baruch Ivcher, was stripped of his Peruvian citizenship by the Ministry of the Interior. Ivcher was exiled because he refused to squelch *Contrapunto,* an aggressive investigative news program that exposed Montesinos's links with drug traffickers, his accumulating fortune, and intrigue within the SIN. Iberico had worked as a journalist for *Contrapunto* before it was terminated. Now he would have his revenge.

Iberico offered to buy the videos, suggesting that a half million dollars might be more feasible, and then attempted to contact Ivcher for the money. Before Ivcher could be contacted in Israel, however, Olivera secured the money from another local source. While Olivera and the private donor drove around Lima in search of a bank with a sufficient sum of cash on hand, Iberico negotiated with Barrera and they agreed on a sum of one hundred thousand dollars per video, to be paid pro rata. In the end, one video was sufficient to topple the regime.[21]

While the reasons for Pinchi's betrayal of Montesinos are unclear, and may have involved a combination of public and private motives, the choice of the video revealed either acumen or luck. The Kouri brothers posed as "independent" politicians but they had financial dealings with Víctor Joy Way, a corrupt Fujimori cabinet minister involved in government procurement contracts with China and arms deals. They were courted by Montesinos—who may have been using Beto to reach his more powerful brother, Alex Kouri, the mayor of Callao. Moreover, Beto was a prime example of the *tránsfuga* (turncoat) phenomenon that had been denounced by the opposition.

Fernando Olivera paid one hundred thousand dollars for the video, which he immediately took to the FIM headquarters in a Lima hotel, where he called an impromptu press conference. He demanded the dismissal of Montesinos, the resignation of the president, an interim government, and new elections. A little more than forty-eight hours later, over the opposition of his cabinet, Fujimori convened new elections, in which he would not run; fired Montesinos; and promised to dismantle the SIN.[22]

The Logic of Blackmail: Why the Vladivideo Brought Down the Regime

In-depth interviews with political leaders from across the political spectrum confirmed widespread agreement that the release of the Vladivideo was the decisive event in the fall of Fujimori.[23] Two interviewees independently used the same metaphor, that the video was the "detonator" of regime change.[24] "Were it not for the Vladivideo," said another, "we would still be under the Fujimori regime."[25] A fourth was still more emphatic: "The video brought Fujimori down."[26] While no one argued that the Vladivideo was exclusively responsible, few doubted its decisive impact.

Yet while legislators were convinced that the Vladivideo had a powerful impact, explanations for why varied widely. According to one leader, the video demonstrated the "power of images." It turned "mere gossip into something real." Or rather, surreal: there was something postmodern about actually seeing bribery performed on videotape. Moreover, the case of Alberto Kouri was immediately assumed to be "emblematic" of a deeper and more pervasive problem of corruption.[27] A number of leaders suggested that the video might not have had the same impact had it not been for the climate of crisis in the country that had been produced by the growing opposition to Fujimori following the 2000 elections and the deteriorating economic situation. A leader of Alianza Popular Revolucionaria Americana (American Popular Revolutionary Alliance [APRA]) suggested that, although the video was the key event in toppling the government, "the principle actor was the people."[28] A member of Congress from the Partido Popular Cristiano (Popular Christian Party [PPC]) said that the video enabled the people to "understand the opposition."[29] Still another pointed out that the video was released in the middle of a dialogue between the government and the opposition under the auspices of the Organization of American States (OAS) and in the aftermath of the March of the Four Suyos. However, he also noted that "with the results of the march, there was a backward movement; I think they fell into an ambush. But there was a mobilization throughout the country, not just in Lima."[30]

The Vladivideo may have bolstered the opposition and undercut support for Fujimori, but it is not clear that the collapse of the regime was caused by Fujimori's declining popularity, much less the rising strength of the opposition. Moreover, these views may overstate the impact of the video on public disapproval of the regime and understate its effect on the interior of the regime. They rest on counterfactual reasoning, of the sort expressed in the statement "Had Fujimori not resigned, there would have been a revolt."[31] The point is, however, Fujimori *did* resign and his resignation was, in the words of opposition daily newspaper *La República*, "the beginning of the end for Fujimorismo."[32] It is the resignation we must explain.

The most compelling reason offered for the impact of the video was that it occasioned the president's resignation by breaking up his relationship with Montesinos. Said one lawmaker: "The video made Fujimori decide to get rid of Montesinos, something that Sofía [Fujimori's daughter and, after his turbulent divorce, his surrogate first lady] had wanted for some time and had been pressing her father to do. But [Montesinos's] control over the armed forces was such that he could not do so. So the video achieved the breakup of this relation. It exposed Montesinos; the man who managed everything, had let a bomb get away. Everyone connected with him was placed on guard."[33]

Montesinos's reaction to the airing of the Vladivideo in a press conference on September 14, 2000, was, "I am destroyed."[34] To understand why, we must analyze why the videos were taped in the first place. Montesinos was not interested in blackmailing those who appeared on the videos; it is obvious that such a threat would not be credible because it would damage Montesinos as much as his co-conspirators as *long as Montesinos was in power*.[35] The key to understanding the videos, then, is to consider how they would be used to avoid losing power since the threat to make them public could only be credible in a scenario in which Montesinos's power, was threatened. Deterrence was the logic underpinning this policy, and according to its logic, the weapon is useful as long as it does not have to be used.[36] Such a deterrent could only be of value against someone more powerful than Montesinos—someone like Fujimori (or a hypothetical rival or successor) who could dismiss him.

Evidence for this interpretation comes from the fight between Fujimori and Montesinos after the tape was released. Fujimori watched the video with his prime minister, Federico Salas, and his minister of justice, Alberto Bustamante. "Screw Montesinos" was Bustamante's angry response.[37] Salas encouraged Fujimori to fire Montesinos, and after a long pause, Fujimori gave the order: "Indicate the decision of the government that he present his immediate resignation." Salas spoke by phone with Montesinos, who reminded him that he was only a "little president of the council of ministers," that no government was going to fall over a fifteen-thousand-dollar bribe, and that "if the king falls, all the pages will fall." This last point was a clear allusion by Montesinos to his blackmail power over all the key operators within the political system. Despite the tough words, Montesinos knew he was weak, and this is indicated by the fact that he began to phone the embassies of various nations in search of a place of exile.[38]

In the language of deterrence, the release of the Vladivideo was like the accidental launch of a nuclear missile. A weapon of last resort, created solely for its deterrent value, had been used. The effect on Fujimori and the entire political establishment was explosive. Every member of Congress, judge, military officer, lawyer, business leader, media owner, and journalist who had visited Montesinos in his offices in the SIN and had received bribes or threats immediately knew that there was a chance that he or she too had been taped and was vulnerable to exposure. Nobody knew how many videos there were, and Olivera kept them guessing with an astute ruse: "This is only a sample," he said of the video with Alberto Kouri. "All will be known."[39] What was clear was that Montesinos had been wounded and his departure from power might create the conditions for the release of hundreds more videos. Among those with the most to lose was the president himself, for he had lived during substantial periods in the "Little Pentagon" out of which Montesinos ran his operations and where he kept his video archives.

With the release of the Vladivideo, Fujimori began to lose control over Congress. Government lawmakers were momentarily stupefied. Lacking initiative of their own, they waited for instructions while the president pondered his fate. According to Manuel Dammert, the role of Congress under Fujimori was not to legislate and hold the government accountable through parliamentary inquiry and oversight, but to provide disciplined support to the executive and enable the government to spend and rule in an autocratic and discretionary manner, often disregarding constitutional norms (Dammert Ego Aguirre, 2001, 57). Since this role was not a formal feature of the constitution, it required a legislative majority under extraparliamentary control. Control over Congress was also the key to Montesinos's strategy of sustaining power for the five-year term 2000–2005. In the Vladivideo, Montesinos is recorded saying to Kouri: "Image is everything. We're thinking about the international image of the country. How do we win it? We win it with a strong Congress, a solid majority, a thinking majority. We already have a majority, but I don't want this simple majority, I want to have a majority of seventy or seventy-five members of Congress."[40] At the time, the government had a majority of 64 votes out of 120, up from 52 members elected on the government ticket.

One opposition member of Congress described the virtual collapse of parliament on the day after the video was made public:

> There was an ordinary meeting of Congress of the Commission of Justice. It was presided over by [Luis] Delgado Aparicio. The meeting filled up with people because everyone wanted to talk about the affair, and the Fujimoristas accepted all the requests of the members of Congress, something unusual. We asked for an investigative commission and they agreed. I arrived late and like everyone else I went to the meeting and was sitting with others from [my party]. I received a call from [my party leader]. He said, "What are you doing there?" and I said, "I don't know." He said: "Break up the meeting, there is no Congress." So, I asked to speak, and I rose and said, "I do not recognize the authority of this commission and of this parliament," and with that the meeting came to an end. That is how we finished with the congress.[41]

Although the congress remained open, opposition members refused to return to normal activities until the *tránsfuga* phenomenon was clarified; serious political deliberations were shifted to the "dialogue tables" under the auspices of the OAS (Cooper and Legler, 2001).

Loss of control over Congress was merely the beginning. In his comment "If the king falls, all the pages will fall," Montesinos had hinted at much deeper damage. With the release of subsequent videos, we now know just how deeply he had penetrated all the branches of government. In the judiciary he controlled the Supreme Court, using Alejandro Rodríguez Medrano, a provisional judge, and Víctor Raúl Castillo Castillo, the president. He had Alipio Montes de Oca on his payroll and used him to control the Executive Commission of the Judiciary. Special attention was devoted to controlling the courts responsible for drug trafficking. The Constitutional Tribunal had been neutralized with the destitution of its only independent members in 1997, and the remaining magistrates were subservient to Montesinos. Similarly, in the Public Ministry, Montesinos controlled the Fiscalía de la Nación, the office of the nation's top investigative lawyer, a nominally independent post occupied by Blanca Nélida Colán, as well as the key investigative judges. This made a farce of his offer to turn his fate over to the Fiscalía de la Nación. He controlled the National Election Board through people like Rómulo Muñoz Arce.[42]

Without Montesinos, Fujimori would lose control over the armed forces. Montesinos had spent a decade staffing the senior posts with loyalists, including General Elesván Bello, General Jose Villanueva Ruesta, and Admiral Antonio Ibárcena. He controlled the key regional commanders and hundreds of officers. Outside the state institutions, Montesinos corrupted and controlled much of the media. In addition to Crousillat, he influenced media magnates Eduardo Calmell del Solar, Ernesto Schutz, Manuel Delgado Parker, and Julio Vera Abad. His influence in the cabinet extended to Víctor Joy Way, Carlos Boloña, and Luisa María Cuculiza. The threat to bring down "all the pages" was not idle.

Even if Fujimori had the stomach to govern without a parliament he could control, with the network of control over the judiciary and the Public Ministry in disrepair, and with a military stacked with Montesinos loyalists, he faced the fact that Montesinos had blackmail power over him too. This blackmail power dates back to the circumstances of their initial association; subsequently, Montesinos even insinuated himself into Fujimori's private life, spying on his wife and reporting on her daily activities.[43]

Montesinos was the architect of Fujimori's long, illegal, third election campaign, which began in 1996 with the introduction of the "Law of Authentic Interpretation of the Constitution." To sustain this law it was necessary to eviscerate the referendum law to prevent the opposition from submitting the issue of a second reelection to the public and then the removal of the magistrates on the Constitutional Tribunal who upheld a legal challenge to the constitutionality of the law. The stacking of the National Election Board, the fraudulent collection of more than a million false signatures to register Fujimori's electoral vehicle Perú 2000, and the use of the armed forces to finance the reelection campaign were part of the same effort to clear the path for Fujimori's reelection. Fujimori may not have wanted to run for reelection. He repeatedly expressed his misgivings, pointing out that his family members were pressing him not to run. Moreover, there was evidence of growing tensions with Montesinos and the armed forces. Fujimori was unhappy about the detention of re-tired general Rodolfo Robles; further, he seemed to support the restora-tion of Peruvian citizenship to Baruch Ivcher, and he was irritated by the Perú 2000 signatures scandal. Yet enormous political capital was ex-pended to clear the way for his reelection. The incongruity lends credence to the view that Montesinos brought great pressure to bear on Fujimori to run for a third term and that, in the end, Fujimori decided that no other candidate could guarantee the preservation of the political regime they had created.

So close was the association between Fujimori and Montesinos that they came to be known as "Siamese twins." The analogy is inexact (Dr. Jekyll and Mr. Hyde might be closer), for they are very different. Alberto Fujimori has been described as a man of energy and decisiveness. As pres-ident, he was calculating, hardworking, and dedicated. His original elec-toral slogan was "Honesty, technology and work," and these were touted as personal attributes. He liked to carry a laptop computer with him wherever he went, and he routinely worked into the early-morning hours. His detractors emphasized a paranoid style and extraordinary am-bition, to which one might add the can-do mentality of an engineer. Fuji-mori liked to fix problems, and results mattered more than means. He repeatedly acknowledged his autocratic style of rule, but could see this as no basis for objection as long as he obtained desirable results. Human rights abuses during his government did not appear to disturb him, be-cause he could point to a trend of diminishing violations as a result of a successful counterinsurgency strategy.

Fujimori's vulnerability was typical of the "man of action": the ten-dency to act, often with astonishing boldness, based on a desire for re-sults without measuring the effect of the means used, a tendency that manifests itself in the repeated failure to understand the importance of legality and accountability.[44] Fujimori was fond of saying, "My deeds are my words," a phrase that captures the impatience with dialogue and deliberation that often accompanies a preference for bold action. Driven by ambition and paranoia, and limited by an inability to appreciate the need for restraints on executive power, Fujimori was vulnerable to Mon-tesinos's wiles.

Whereas Fujimori was at least partially motivated by patriotism, Montesinos was driven by a naked greed for power. According to a for-mer intelligence officer, he is "amoral, and has no principles. He func-tions according to his interests and objectives. It does not matter to him whether he steals a little or a lot; whether he blackmails a few people or lots of people. He can be enchanting when he wants to and [when he] has something to gain. When angered, he is a mortal enemy; when he cries or laughs it is calculated."[45]

For many reasons it was impossible for Fujimori to dissociate himself from Montesinos without surrendering his own claim on power. Thus, the Vladivideo, by destroying Montesinos, also destroyed Fujimori and the entire informal network of power they had created. Fujimori hung on to power for long enough to bribe Montesinos into exile with a $15 million gift, and then led a dramatic manhunt against him when he made an unwelcome return—a manhunt that also served as a pretext for an illegal search of one of Montesinos's houses (which, by some accounts, was really a search for incriminating videos before they would fall into the hands of the judiciary). In November he loaded the presidential jet with baggage, the contents of which remain the subject of speculation, and used an official visit to Asia as a pretext to flee to Japan.[46]

Rival Views: The Regime Was Already Moribund

It is my contention that the Vladivideo created a rupture between Fujimori and Montesinos; Fujimori chose to resign because he knew he could not remove Montesinos without upsetting the entire political system. The Vladivideo is important primarily because of its impact on the interior of the regime, rather than its impact on public opinion and the political opposition. However, another interpretation is possible, and while it is not entirely incompatible with mine, the difference lies in the weight assigned to endogenous and exogenous forces. In the alternative view, the Vladivideo toppled a regime that was already moribund.

One version of this argument stresses that the regime had been debilitated by the 2000 election before the Vladivideo was released. As an electoral official in the post-Fujimori government put it: "The key event in Fujimori's fall was the elections in 2000. . . . After that, nobody expected him to complete his mandate."[47] In this view, the collapse of the regime followed a loss of legitimacy when the Fujimori government was unable to pass the litmus test of winning a free and fair election.[48] There are a number of problems with this view. In the first place, assessments of legitimacy tend to be subjective and can be hard to define and measure. Second, as Julio Carrión shows in Chapter 6 in this volume, Fujimori enjoyed a popularity rating of above 45 percent even after the 2000 elections—even though nearly half the public questioned the legitimacy of the electoral process. Third, the 2000 election weakened Fujimori but it is not obvious that his subsequent fall was inevitable. Lack of legitimacy does not always undermine regime stability; many illegitimate regimes have lasted for years. By adroit leadership, Mexico's Carlos Salinas de Gortari served out his six-year term, or *sexenio,* and governed vigorously despite the fraudulent elections that brought him into office in 1988. Finally, Fujimori's lack of legitimacy did not necessarily translate into support for Alejandro Toledo. Fujimori had survived tough political tests before, and rarely did the opposition best him. Toledo's deficiencies could be summed up in the word *character.* Notorious for boozing and womanizing, he was also an intellectual lightweight whose personal insecurity interfered with his judgment and capacity for decision making. Even harsh critics of Fujimori found Toledo an implausible aspirant to the presidential palace.

Another version of the argument that the regime was already moribund stresses the rising influence of the SIN and Montesinos to the detriment of Fujimori and his own supporters within and outside the regime, especially the business and international communities. In an intriguing analysis, Francisco Durand (2003) argues that there were three "institutional mafias" within the regime (Conaghan aptly calls them "greed rings" in Chapter 5 in this volume). One mafia revolved around Montesinos and the SIN; another encircled Fujimori and his entourage of Japanese-Peruvian allies; and a third linked the regime to business through a network in the Ministry of Economy and Finance (MEF) under Jorge Camet. As the mafias around Fujimori and Camet saw their influence eclipsed by Montesinos and the SIN, doubts arose about the viability of a third term in office—especially in the eyes of the larger business community and in the United States State Department.

A revealing anecdote exposes the tensions between the mafias within the regime. According to Durand, at one point between the first and second rounds of the 2000 election, Montesinos considered deposing Fujimori. He had succeeded in appointing Carlos Boloña as the minister of economy and finance after Camet stepped down. When Fujimori appeared to flounder in the first round, Montesinos toyed with the idea of making Boloña a puppet president. Boloña, who later acknowledged that conversations along these lines had occurred, had emerged as a key figure articulating the mafias around the SIN and the MEF. Although the plan never materialized, the fact that such behind-the-scenes machinations occurred underscores the divisions between the key mafias within the regime and the near-absolute power to which Montesinos aspired. "At the outset of the third term, the equilibrium between the kleptocratic mafias had been broken," says Durand (2003, 446). Without power to balance Montesinos, Fujimori would reign but not govern.

The merit of Durand's analysis is that it links internal tensions with erosion of external regime support. The notion that the regime depended on an intermafia equilibrium, however, requires qualification. The three mafias—if, indeed, that is the best term, for only the SIN used violence to achieve its ends—were never on an equal footing.[49] The SIN under Montesinos was the decisive pillar of the regime, not only during the election of 2000, but throughout the Fujimori period. Jorge Camet never had the power of Montesinos. His influence ranked, perhaps, with that of Nicolas de Bari Hermoza Ríos. He was a player at the cabinet level, but not an indispensable one. Moreover, while it is true that Montesinos, Fujimori, and Camet all occupied the apex of respective groups or networks within the regime, the power of Fujimori never depended on the loyalty and influence of his kin and collaborators so much as his own personal capacity to win votes. That was his main asset, and the primary reason why Montesinos needed him. No other figure in the regime ever matched Fujimori's popularity, and talk of a successor—whether Jaime Yoshiyama, Joy Way, Martha Chávez, or Carlos Boloña—invariably came to naught. The laughable notion of Boloña as marionette for Montesinos may be dismissed as little more than a measure of the former's opportunism and the latter's delusions of grandeur. As long as Fujimori and Montesinos had the power to expose each other's crimes and a mutual interest in what the other had to offer politically, the regime persisted. Only when this relationship was broken did it collapse, and that is the sense in which the Vladivideo was critical.

There is a third version of the moribund-regime explanation. In a meticulous and thoughtful account of the collapse of the Fujimori regime, Conaghan (2001, 29) argues that the Vladivideo "brought scandal to a new level in Peru," but she credits the opposition with laying the groundwork for the transition. "The footage confirmed all the arguments that the opposition had long been making about the criminal and illegitimate nature of the regime and the elections. For the first time, a scandal was internalized by the regime, as *oficialistas* were forced to wrestle with an uncomfortable truth. The undeniable nature of the evidence and a consensus that something had to be 'done'—even shared by *oficialistas*—turned the matter into a subjective crisis that Fujimori had to deal with." She goes on to say that "dealing with the Montesinos issue in a way that would be satisfactory to veteran opponents and the international community meant that Fujimori would have to drive a stake into the *head* of what made the strange regime work. Removing Montesinos from official duties in name only would not be enough. Domestic opponents, all too acquainted with the regime's chicanery, would not be taken in by cosmetic changes."

As Conaghan implies, quite apart from the demands of the opposition, Fujimori could not fire Montesinos, nor could he sustain his own power when his key ally had been destroyed. "Once Fujimori distanced himself from Montesinos," notes Conaghan, "his own vacuity and tenuous hold over power were fully revealed." Not only because he relied upon the "expertise of his 'co-president,'" but also because, as Conaghan notes, "given Montesinos' vast control over the upper ranks of the armed forces and the intelligence agency," the only way Fujimori could "fire Montesinos was to fire himself as well" (29, 23).

While Montesinos maintained internal cohesion through coercion, bribery, and blackmail, Fujimori provided the facade of electoral popularity. Fujimori must have felt that he had upheld his end of the bargain, and at considerable cost. Reluctantly, he agreed to run for a third term. The results of the first round were a bitter pill for the president, judging by his state of virtual stupor at a press conference following the election-night results. He failed to win an outright first-round victory and was forced into a second round. It is widely believed that the final tally was manipulated to give Fujimori a greater advantage over Toledo,[50] but the results were not dramatically different from what opinion polls had predicted (most placed Fujimori as the front-runner).[51] When Toledo withdrew from the second round, Fujimori was placed in the embarrassing position of running unopposed.

It is worth reiterating that Fujimori remained Peru's most popular leader throughout the 2000 election campaign; that the poll results and the election outcome of the first round were roughly consistent; and that while Fujimori could not win an outright first-round victory, he might well have won in a second round held under competitive conditions.[52] Indeed, one of Fujimori's biggest advantages was the weakness of the opposition. During the 1990s, most of Peru's opposition parties splintered into a series of loose coalitions around individual politicians who pursued short-term electoral strategies that offered little challenge to the functioning of the regime.[53] They insisted that the 2000 elections were going to be fraudulent, but failed to agree to boycott them or run behind a unified candidate. Unable to dislodge the president at the urns, they professed surprise that the government had not allowed free and fair elections. Finally, they vowed to prevent the inauguration with a mass mobilization that might in fact have unintentionally reinforced the regime. The March of the Four Suyos on July 28, 2000, demonstrated the depth of opposition to the government, but also reinforced regime cohesion (which was beginning to fray under the pressure of the electoral competition) by offering a pretext for the government to use violence—deadly fires and street battles started by the SIN—to discredit the protesters and blame the mayhem on the leaders of the march.[54]

Could Fujimori have weathered the storm of international disapproval and domestic resistance stemming from the 2000 elections without the release of the Vladivideo? We do not know whether the political opposition could have parlayed the post-2000 election crisis into a mass mobilization to repudiate the regime. Such a confrontation was avoided by Fujimori's resignation and the internal implosion that followed. The main achievement of the opposition—and of Alejandro Toledo in particular—was to withstand pressures from the regime long enough to be able to replace Fujimori when he fell. The decision to resign was decisive, and Fujimori knew it; he, better than anyone, understood the extent to which the regime rested on a set of coercive and illegal mechanisms that had been exposed and thus neutralized.[55] The track record of the political opposition over the previous decade was not auspicious, but the vulnerability of the regime to internal tensions was more than apparent.

Conclusions

Well before the collapse of the Fujimori regime it was evident that President Fujimori was caught in a web of illegality in which he was under the constant threat of scandal. Trapped between Montesinos's blackmail and the risk of public exposure, he prolapsed into ever more brazen abuses of power. The key feature of the regime was an executive power unaccountable to the legislative and judicial branches, and thus able to shield itself from public scrutiny. As I have argued elsewhere, before its collapse, the main threat to the regime was publicity (Cameron 1998, 126).

The Vladivideo graphically exposed the complicity of the executive in illegal and illegitimate activity and publicly demonstrated how blackmail had trapped the president and a widening network of public officials. Undoubtedly, it had an impact on the public that supported the president, including those who disliked Montesinos. However, I suspect that

the more important effect was on the interior of the regime. The vulnerability of Montesinos's network of informal coercion and control was that
it had to remain hidden in order to be effective. This does not mean that
nobody knew how the system operated. Since at least 1996 it had been
clear to anyone who read the independent daily newspapers that Montesinos was collecting protection money from drug traffickers, accumulating
spectacular illicit earnings, bullying the media, and using terrorist tactics—including torture and assassination—against adversaries within the
armed forces as well as opponents in society. In fact, what the Vladivideo
exposed was minor in comparison with the human rights crimes that
could be traced to the SIN and its shadowy chief. Nor is it accurate to
say that the video confirmed what the opposition suspected but could not
prove. Only the most naive supporters of Fujimori could have doubted
that the *tránsfuga* phenomenon was real; the opposition never enter-
tained serious doubt. What the release of the Vladivideo did was weaken
Montesinos's blackmail power over Fujimori by making public evidence
that had no strategic value unless withheld. The blackmailer loses power
when the compromising material in his or her possession is made public.
Once Montesinos lost power, Fujimori could cling to it no longer.

The Fujimori regime had two faces: a popular and effective president,
on the one hand, and a corrupt government within the government, on
the other. Put slightly differently, the political system, especially post-
1992, was built on a combustible mix of formally democratic institutions—above all, elections—and the erosion of the separation of powers.
Elections without the separation of powers might be an apt characterization of "delegative democracy."[56] However, once the checks and balances
inherent in a presidential democracy are eroded past a certain point, one
is more apt to speak of "electoral authoritarianism." The line between
delegative democracy and electoral authoritarianism is drawn when the
minimal conditions necessary to guarantee that elections are free and fair
are no longer present (see Chapter 6).

The rationale for the constitutional separation of powers is to guarantee the rights and freedoms of citizenship necessary to sustain democracy
over the long haul. Failure to appreciate this lesson entails a major risk:
that we may ignore the fact that a substantial number of Peruvians supported an autocratic president not in spite of his repeated violations of
fundamental rights and freedoms but because such violations were believed to be necessary to create a stronger, more "authentic" democracy.
This sentiment, rooted in the catastrophic experience with democracy in
the 1980s, is what generated both the popularity of Fujimori and the

public's tolerance for Montesinos, and this sentiment did not disappear with the collapse of the regime.

A defining feature of electoral, as opposed to military, authoritarianism is the ability of the leadership to win elections, albeit under unfair conditions. The retention of significant levels of popular support for President Fujimori marks the primary distinction between the Peruvian transition from electoral authoritarianism in 2000–2001 and earlier transitions from authoritarian rule, including Peru's 1978–80 transition. The transition from electoral authoritarianism involved an effort to dismantle the informal network of bribes, threats, and blackmail that neutralized the agencies within the state apparatus that might have held the president to the terms of his own constitution.

There are also important differences between the recent and earlier patterns of regime change or transition in terms of the evolving international context. The popularity of electoral authoritarianism resides precisely in the benefits of preserving the appurtenances of electoral democracy in an international environment that is hostile to military rule but yet unable to effectively chastise *elected* leaders who behave undemocratically. Although the international community was stumped by the 1992 autogolpe, many leaders grew increasingly alarmed by the erosion of democracy in the 1990s (especially in Guatemala, Haiti, Paraguay, and Venezuela). Alarm translated into action in the Peruvian transition in 2000, which became the first major regime change in Latin America in which the OAS played a significant and largely constructive role. It is unlikely that the OAS-sponsored dialogue tables would have been able to play the historic role of facilitating the transition from the collapsing Fujimori regime to the interim government of Valentín Paniagua had it not been for the release of the Vladivideo. Nevertheless, once the process of decomposition of the regime began in earnest, the international community offered the best available vehicle for redemocratization.

In one key respect, the literature on transitions from authoritarian rule remains relevant to the dynamics of electoral-authoritarian-regime breakdown. The transitions literature identified the strategic dynamics between factions within authoritarian regimes and regime opponents.[57] Transitions can be thought of as games between hard-liners and soft-liners within the regime and radicals and moderates in the opposition. Typically, some form of alliance between soft-liners and moderates guides a negotiated transition. The process is an uncertain one, in which the possibility of reversals and the imposition of even harsher measures is always present. In Peru, Montesinos and Fujimori (the hard-liners) remained in undisputed control of the coercive agencies of the state until the resignation of Fujimori. Soft-liners never had any real power within the regime and never lasted long. The opposition had no choice but to challenge the regime, coupling maximalist rhetoric with minimal chances of defeating the regime on its own terms. As would be predicted by the transitions literature, the decisive event that made it possible to initiate a transition was the division in the ruling clique and breakdown from within.

Contemplating his endgame after the release of the Vladivideo, Fujimori must have envisioned his own growing isolation, the defection of key allies, and mounting external opposition—a lonely end, like Macbeth's. Yet while Macbeth faced his final battle with a world-weary existential resignation, Fujimori's flight from Peru to his ancestral Japan—where he would launch a campaign in cyberspace to rehabilitate his image, defend his record, and plot his return—was a denouement more pathetic than tragic for a president who sought to play a hero's part.

NOTES

1. On informal institutions, see O'Donnell 1999a; Helmke and Levitsky 2004; Chapter 5 in this volume.

2. Although I refer to the Vladivideo in the singular, the first video was only one in a massive archive of videotapes that would expose graft and corruption throughout the regime. See Chapter 5.

3. I concur with the characterization of Peru as an electoral-authoritarian regime (see Chapters 6 and 11, this volume). Over the course of the decade 1990–2000, Peru degenerated from a delegative democracy into electoral authoritarianism. Elections alone do not suffice as a criterion to demarcate the line between democratic and authoritarian regimes. See also McClintock 1999.

4. Philip Mauceri also emphasizes the concentration of executive power and the evisceration of checks and balances as a defining characteristic of the Fujimori regime in Chapter 2 in this volume.

5. See O'Donnell and Schmitter 1986. A lucid game-theoretic analysis of transition dynamics is found in Przeworski 1991. See also O'Donnell 1999a.

6. Fujimori offered this breakdown of campaign expenses: television advertisements, $120,000; radio spots, $20,000; plane rental, $10,000; and printing of posters, $40,000, for a total of $190,000. The lack of expenditure on newspaper advertisements is noteworthy. See "Candidatos investigados," *Caretas*, May 21, 1990, 13.

7. "Revelan Fujimori tiene mas de 20 propiedades y vendio 12," *Expreso*, May 23, 1990, 3.

8. "Los bienes de Fujimori," *Caretas,* April 23, 1990, 10–15.

9. Member of Congress, interview no. 3, Lima, January 8, 2002.

10. Poll results were reported in "El Perú en juego," *Caretas,* May 28, 1990, 10–17. Only 4 percent of Peruvians were troubled by Fujimori's tax evasion, according to a Datum poll (16). Another poll, by the firm Imasen, suggested that the public was split roughly in thirds on the question of whether Fujimori had actually committed tax evasion, with 30 percent saying yes, 40 percent saying no, and another 30 percent saying they did not know. "Cambio 90 pierde credibilidad," *Expreso,* May 13, 1990, 2.

11. For speculation about whether Fujimori was born in Japan and the authenticity of his Peruvian citizenship papers, see Jochamowitz 1993.

12. On Fujimori's early contacts with Montesinos, see Bowen 2000, 51–70.

13. "Olivera descarta que atentado sea subversivo: 'Quieren silenciarme por denunciar a Fujimori," *Expreso,* June 1, 1990, 2.

14. "Olivera desafía al candidato de cambio," *Expreso,* May 23, 1990, 3; "Fujimori dice solo tiene 4 propiedades: Denuncia campaña de difamación," *Expreso,* May 24, 1990, 5. In a May 23, 1990 letter to the press, Fujimori stated that he only owned four properties; the rest had been sold and were occupied by others. He argued that the allegations made in the media were not isolated or unconnected events, but part of a campaign of defamation directed at himself and Cambio 90. He reiterated that he sold a house, a tractor, and two vehicles to finance his modest campaign, and he asked where his adversaries got all the money for their campaigns.

15. Literally meaning "alive," *vivo* refers to anyone who is sharp, clever, sly, crafty, or unscrupulous (see *Collins Spanish-English Dictionary,* 5th ed. [HarperCollins, 1997]). The opposite of the *vivo* is the *zonzo,* one who is silly or stupid. "Los vivos viven de los zonzos," goes a popular saying, which could be translated as "The sly live off the stupid." True to the logic of the prisoner's dilemma, it is often argued that in a world of *vivos,* one must be *vivo* to succeed. Or, in President García's also celebrated phrase, "In Peru one must not be ingenuous."

16. Member (retired) of intelligence services, interview no. 5, January 9, 2002.

17. The Plan Verde and the rise of Montesinos is discussed in greater depth in Cameron 1997, 50–54. It is fair to say that there is much conjecture in efforts to reconstruct the use of the Plan Verde by Montesinos.

18. For example, Santiago Fujimori's vehicle was used in the Barrios Altos massacre. See Rospigliosi 2000, 31.

19. "Montesinos used Barrios Altos and Japanese nationality to squeeze Fujimori" (member of Congress, interview no. 3). In other words, Fujimori's tenure was insecure because of wrongdoing that ranges from inconsequential (fraudulent real estate dealings), to atrocious (human rights crimes). The autogolpe was one way of ensuring the sort of political control that would immunize the regime and its incumbents against investigation and prison. Although many observers remain skeptical that Fujimori was born in Peru, and thus doubt his legal entitlement to hold the office of president, others believe that this argument is at best legalistic and at worst racist. See n. 9, this chapter.

20. Member of Congress, interview no. 7, Lima, January 14, 2002. The inter-

viewee had direct knowledge of the events described in this section and the story is consistent with other reports.

21. Barrera subsequently claimed he was swindled.

22. "El día siguiente," *La República*, September 18, 2000. See "Mensaje al país del Sr. Presidente de La República, Ing. Alberto Fujimori." September 16, 2000. See Bowen and Holligan 2003.

23. A survey cited by Cynthia McClintock (2001) also reinforces this. Other analysts have emphasized the importance of the videotape. "One videotape became the symbol of the power of the truth, helping to knock over a crooked regime that had been built on a labyrinth of lies" writes Ernesto García Calderón (2001, 58).

24. These exact words were used in two interviews: member of Congress, interview no. 4, Lima, January 9, 2002, and member (retired) of intelligence services, interview no. 5.

25. Member of Congress, interview no. 7.

26. Member of Congress, interview no. 3.

27. Member of Congress, interview no. 3.

28. Member of Congress, interview no. 4.

29. Member of Congress, interview no. 3.

30. Member of Congress, interview no. 7.

31. Member of Congress, interview no. 3.

32. "Se abre la transición con muchas esperanzas y no pocas incertidumbres," *La República*, September 17, 2000.

33. Member of Congress, interview no. 7.

34. Member (retired) of intelligence services, interview no. 5. This is an eyewitness account, but for obvious reasons cannot be verified by other sources. The same source went on to suggest that Montesinos's decline began before the release of the Vladivideo. His Central Intelligence Agency patronage came under scrutiny following the discovery of his involvement in the sale of arms to the Revolutionary Armed Forces of Colombia (FARC), and his sloppy attempt to cover up the connection with the FARC only worsened the problem and further isolated the Peruvian government. The video was the first major crisis for Montesinos following the loss of his international protection. But the release of the Vladivideo was his undoing.

35. The claim that the videos were taped to blackmail those filmed does not withstand a moment's reflection. See Angel Páez, "Esa sería una de las razones que precipitó la caida del gobierno: Hay más videos que comprometen a tránsfugas y al mismo Fujimori," *La República*, September 17, 2000.

36. Deterrence can be a form of nuclear blackmail. See Schelling 1960, 119.

37. This episode is described in Wiener 2001, 495–500.

38. Member (retired) of intelligence services, interview no. 5. Again, this is difficult to confirm and comes from a single source.

39. "Peruanos piden la cabeza de asesor de Fujimori," Reuters, September 15, 2000. In retrospect, we know that Olivera only bought one video, but he could have purchased five more.

40. "Tránsfugas al borde de un ataque de nervios," Imediaperu.com, September 15, 2000.

41. Member of Congress, interview no. 7. For a similar account, see "Delgado Aparicio levantó abruptamente sesión de la comisión de Justicia," *El Comercio,* September 15, 2000.

42. For documentation of the penetration of the judiciary and Public Ministry by the Fujimori-Montesinos mafia, see Comisión investigadora de la influencia irregular ejercida durante el gobierno de Alberto Fujimori (1990–2000) sobre el Poder Judicial, Ministerio Público y otros poderes e instituciones del estado vinculado a la administración de justicia, presidido por Fausto Alvarado Dodero, *Informe Preliminar,* December 2002.

43. Member (retired) of intelligence services, interview no. 5.

44. This impression is partially based on the author's observation of Fujimori during a two-hour meeting with representatives of nongovernmental organizations in Ottawa, Canada, October 28, 1998.

45. Member (retired) of intelligence services, interview no. 5.

46. Whereas substantial sums of money have been traced to bank accounts of Montesinos, the evidence against Fujimori is weaker. Nevertheless, Anel Townsend's investigative commission has found evidence of corruption among various members of the Fujimori clan. Comisión Investigadora sobre los dineros de Vladimiro Montesinos y su evidente relación con Alberto Fujimori, presidida por Ana Elena Townsend Diez Canseco, *Dictamen Preliminar,* January 2002.

47. Interview no. 9, Lima, January 8, 2002. In a similar vein, see Conaghan 2001.

48. There is a polemical—even partisan—dimension to this debate. Supporters of Alejandro Toledo chafed at the idea of Fernando Olivera and the FIM taking credit for the fall of Fujimori. Partisanship aside, the source of the collapse of the regime remains an important part of the assessment of Fujimori's legacy.

49. The SIN and Montesinos used coercion, while the other did not. I am grateful to Phil Mauceri for this observation.

50. Post-Fujimori government official, interview no. 9.

51. Julio Carrión, in his chapter in this volume, provides survey data that indicates that as late as August 2000 Fujimori enjoyed an approval rating of 46 percent, roughly comparable to the results of the first round of voting. His popularity did decline over his second term, but remained fairly robust until the end.

52. A senior official of the Organization of American States who was closely involved in the election observation mission in Peru confided that he believed that Fujimori could have won the 2000 election without fraud and was puzzled by the meddling of Montesinos in the election process (conversation with the author, Vancouver, Canada, November 15, 2002). I would argue that it was in the interests of Montesinos to have a hand in helping Fujimori win the 2000 election, for this would bolster his power within the regime relative to the president.

53. See Levitsky and Cameron 2003; Chapter 4, this volume.

54. This is the "ambush" mentioned above (see n. 28).

55. Conaghan (2001, 23) has a different interpretation: "[I]t is probably fair to conclude that Fujimori did not fully appreciate how strange and ultimately uncontrollable the consequences of his announcement would be."

56. See O'Donnell 1994; for a discussion, see Diamond 1999, 34–42.

57. See Przeworski 1991; O'Donnell 1999a.

Conclusion:
The Rise and Fall of Electoral Authoritarianism in Peru

JULIO F. CARRIÓN

The 1960s were years of guarded hope for Latin America, particularly in Peru. The decade was characterized by a general disposition toward mild social reform meant to tackle long-standing issues of social injustice—if only to diminish the likelihood of "another Cuba." With occasional help from the United States (in the form of the Alliance for Progress), reform-oriented parties attempted to implement change within the confines of existing political arrangements in various Latin American countries. Policies were proposed to enact mild land reform, reduce extreme income inequalities, address urban overcrowding, and foster industrial growth. Unfortunately, at least in the Peruvian case, these policies were either blocked or significantly watered down by conservative forces that used their considerable clout in Congress to stall reform. In Peru, the unresolved issues and the promise of social reform encouraged the organized mobilization of the urban and rural working classes, who demanded greater participation in national decision making. The increasing social mobilization, the rapid growth of forces favoring radical change, and the emergence of guerrilla groups all signaled to the Peruvian military that fundamental political transformations would be required to stop these developments. The regime installed after the 1968 coup in Peru was only part of the widespread wave of military governments that swept Latin America during the 1960s and 1970s. Some of these military regimes exerted a mild rule, such as in Peru, while others were extremely repressive, but all saw as their mission the political exclusion (and in some cases the physical elimination) of political forces that they considered inimical to the well-being of their nations. Echoing some early skepticism about the region's cultural readiness for democracy (W. Stokes 1952), the prevalence of militarism led some to question whether Western democracy could ever take root in Latin American soil (Wiarda 1973).

As Latin America gradually returned to civilian rule in the 1980s, a sense of cautious hope resurfaced. After years of military dictatorship, Latin Americans were looking forward to a new era of democratic coexistence. Although with some delay in Central America, during these years significant gains were made in terms of political inclusion. All political forces willing to participate, even those that were previously considered "dangerous," were now allowed to organize and run in elections. Countries such as Peru that had denied the vote to people who were illiterate now expanded their franchises to include them. In Peru, as in other nations of the region, voting-age requirements were lowered. In other respects, however, the experience of civilian rule during the 1980s was generally disappointing. For Peru, the "lost decade" was characterized not only by severe economic crisis and increased political violence but also by overbearing executives. Nevertheless, unlike military regimes, these "delegative democracies" (O'Donnell 1994) did not seek to exclude opponents from the political game.

Regrettably, in the 1990s a new kind of political regime began to crystallize in such places as Peru and Venezuela. President Alberto Fujimori of Peru went beyond the boundaries of a delegative democracy when in April 1992 he decided to shut down Congress, dismiss the Supreme Court, and rule by decree. He then used elections as a legitimizing mechanism in his efforts to remain in office. Fujimori's frequent violations of democratic procedures were aimed at more than simply passing a preferred set of policy proposals in Congress; they were attempts to perpetuate him in office. Although Fujimori was reelected in relatively competitive elections in 1995, these elections—as was shown in the Introduction—were flawed in many respects and sanctioned an essentially authoritarian regime. Chávez seems to have embarked on a similar path in Venezuela.

Unfortunately, governments like those of Fujimori and Chávez are not exceptional in contemporary times. Many of the so-called third-wave democracies have evolved into regimes that are neither dictatorial in the traditional sense nor truly democratic (Carothers 2002; Diamond 1999; Ottaway 2003). Under these regimes, limited but real political competition exists; one dominant player seeks to remain in power using question-able means but without completely abandoning the forms of electoral democracy. Schedler (2002), among others, uses the term "electoral au-thoritarianism" (EA) to describe these governments, although "competi-tive authoritarianism" (Levitsky and Way 2002), "pseudo-democracy" (Diamond 1999), or "semi-authoritarianism" (Ottaway 2003) could be employed similarly.

In the following pages, the emergence and demise of EA in Peru is placed in a historical and theoretical perspective. I briefly discuss the way in which scholarship has dealt with issues of political accommodation and authoritarianism in the region, followed by a brief review of the emergent literature on EA. Drawing on the book's contributions, the re-maining part of the chapter is dedicated to examining the factors that made the emergence of EA in Peru possible and the factors that led to its downfall. I finish by summarizing the most important legacies of this controversial regime for Peruvian democracy.

Early Elite Accommodation, Military Authoritarianism, and the Transition to Democracy

Before Latin America became engulfed in the wave of military govern-ments initiated by the 1964 Brazilian coup, there was a growing realiza-tion among scholars that the roots of political instability were to be found in the region's rigid social and economic structures (Kling 1956). In addition, it was acknowledged that actors seeking political accommo-dation failed to recognize an ultimate source of political authority, which made the democratic resolution of political crises extremely difficult (Needler 1963). Elections, coups d'état, national strikes, mass rallies, and military force were all available avenues to gaining power. The challenge was in explaining the paradoxical situation of frequent political instabil-ity and yet the persistence of traditional socioeconomic structures. The accepted explanation at the time was that politics in the region were mainly characterized by violent confrontation between various power contenders who were seeking access to power and government spoils rather than actual social or political change (W. Stokes 1952).

In a context in which no single source of legitimate authority was unanimously accepted, access to political power depended upon the as-piring power contenders' ability to deploy some power capability while assuring the other contenders that the latter's established position would not be threatened (Anderson 1967). Ruling elites could thus find accommodation and admit new actors in a piecemeal fashion without having to completely change the oligarchic nature of the state. However, the equilibrium that this game provided was unstable, since it required artful elite statecraft as well as a demobilized civil society.

By the mid-1960s this limited political inclusion began to be challenged as the urban poor, recent rural migrants, and industrial workers demanded greater political power (Graciarena 1967). The continuation of elite rule could be ensured only if it was significantly expanded to include these new urban sectors, although in a subordinated position.[1] The problem was that this expansion was largely dependent on the state's ability to buy out newcomers through an increase in expenditures (36–37). Since the expansion of the political system could not be done without affecting the prospects for economic accumulation, the effort generated much elite resistance.

Cardoso (1972, 18) rightly laments that just when some Latin American societies had matured to the point of making possible the enlargement of their restricted democracies, military regimes took over. Sparked by the 1964 coup in Brazil, the region quickly became overwhelmed by military governments that would ultimately alter the foundations of its political system. The early scholarly preoccupation with the politics of elite accommodation began to recede as the region underwent the dramatic transformation caused by military authoritarianism. Some of these regimes were highly repressive and others less so, but all attempted to alter the traditional bases of domination in their respective countries. Scholarship rapidly shifted to the analysis of this "new authoritarianism" (D. Collier 1979).

The extensive presence of military regimes generated a healthy body of literature whose authors sought to examine the roots of authoritarianism in the region. Some attempted to find these roots in cultural variables, noting the region's Catholic and Iberian tradition (Wiarda 1973). Others preferred to explore structural variables linking authoritarianism with the specific characteristics of Latin American capitalism. For instance, O'Donnell ([1973] 1979) linked these regimes to national capitalism's needs facing the exhaustion of the "easy phase" of horizontal industrialization. Others examined the role that corporatism, clientelism, and the mobilization of the working and middle classes played in the genesis and functioning of these regimes (D. Collier 1979; Schmitter 1974; Malloy 1977; Nun 1967).

Some military governments, in an effort to undermine popular support for traditional political parties, both encouraged a controlled mass mobilization and introduced social and economic reforms. Regimes such as those of Alfredo Ovando and Juan José Torres in Bolivia, Omar Torrijos in Panama, and Juan Velasco Alvarado in Peru fill this description. The military regime in Peru (1968–80), especially during its first phase, led by Velasco Alvarado (1968–75), was probably the most far-reaching in terms of economic and social transformations (Lowenthal 1975; McClintock and Lowenthal 1983). The regime, self-defined as the Revolutionary Government of the Armed Forces, sought the mobilization and integration of the lower classes into the political process, albeit in a rigidly controlled and corporatist fashion (Cotler 1980; Dietz 1980; Malloy 1974).

While most influential analyses of democratic breakdown privileged explanations rooted in systemic responses to societal contradictions, Linz (1978) approached it in a different manner. Instead of structural variables, Linz favored "more strictly political variables that tend to be neglected in many other approaches to the problem of stable democracy" (5). His model was quite parsimonious and rested on the interaction between political legitimacy and elites' behavior. He argued that unsolvable problems, usually generated by the regime's own ineptitude, produce a loss of efficacy that ultimately leads to a loss of legitimacy and "to a generalized atmosphere of tension, a widespread feeling that something has to be done" (75). In this context, "disloyal oppositions offer themselves as a solution" (50).

As the third wave of democratization began to take shape, Linz's emphasis on political variables and actors' behaviors in understanding regime change was sustained in a new set of important studies (Baloyra 1987; Di Palma 1990; Huntington 1991; Karl and Schmitter 1991; O'Donnell, Schmitter, and Whitehead 1986). The shift away from the sociostructural variables that had characterized most analyses of military rule to a more strategic, even game-theoretic, approach can be clearly seen in the influential project directed by O'Donnell, Schmitter, and Whitehead (1986), especially in its concluding volume (O'Donnell and Schmitter 1986). Many contributors to this project analyzed the transition as the outcome of complex, strategic interactions between soft-liners, hard-liners, moderates, and maximalists. Przeworski (1986), for instance, focuses his discussion around the coalition size necessary to generate regime change in a clearly game-theoretic fashion, while O'Donnell and Schmitter (1986, 48) examine the role of elite dispositions and calculations during the outset of liberalization.[2]

The understandable early optimism caused by the region's transition from authoritarian rule quickly faded as the realities of existing civilian governments set in. Many of the newly established civilian regimes showed such serious democratic deficits that some observers doubted whether democracy in Latin America was at all consolidating. Rustow's (1970) prescient contention that the factors that make transition to democracy possible are not identical to those that make democracy endure was proved correct. New studies have offered competing views on the conditions affecting democratic consolidation in Latin American and elsewhere. Some believe that institutions are crucial (Linz 1994); others stress cultural norms (McDonough, Barnes, and Lopez Pinto 1998; Plasser, Ulram, and Waldrauch 1998), and some emphasize civil society and working-class activism (Avritzer 2002; R. B. Collier 1999). However, when one looks at the condition of existing third-wave democracies, the inescapable conclusion is that whatever the reason—institutional, cultural, or otherwise—these regimes are more likely to be stuck in a "gray zone" between authoritarianism and democracy (Carothers 2002) than to be engaged in a process of democratization. Increasingly the term *electoral authoritarianism* is being used to describe many of these gray-zone regimes.

Defining Electoral Authoritarianism (EA)

Many of the book's contributors use the term *electoral authoritarianism* (EA) to characterize the Fujimori regime. What is EA and how prevalent is it? Schedler (2002, 36) defines these regimes as those "that hold elections and tolerate some pluralism and interparty competition, but at the same time violate minimal democratic norms so severely and systematically that it makes no sense to classify them as democracies, however qualified." He estimates, as of 2001, that as many as 58 out of 151 regimes could be classified as such (he classifies 25 additional regimes as having a system of "closed authoritarianism"). There is a clear difference between traditional or "closed" authoritarianism and its electoral variant. In the former, opposition parties are not allowed to compete for office, or if they are, they have no real chance of winning. In the latter, opposition parties do exist and they do have more than a token chance at winning elections but the electoral field is so tilted that an opposition victory requires an inordinate amount of effort and mobilization.

Clearly, democracy requires elections, "but not just any kind of elections" (Schedler 2002, 37). Recent experience tells us that the presence of competitive elections does not automatically ensure the democratic character of the regime (Karl 1986; Diamond 1999). Many electoral-based regimes systematically violate civil liberties (Diamond 1999; Mainwaring 1992); keep extensive "reserved domains" outside democratic control (Valenzuela 1992; O'Donnell 1996); fail to provide a sufficiently open, free, and fair arena for political competition (Diamond 2002); or systematically exclude from the arena some religious, ethnic, or other national minorities (Mainwaring 1992). It is not sufficient that voters' preferences are counted honestly at election time; these preferences must also be allowed to form freely before the actual election day. The free formation of these preferences entails a set of procedures and institutions designed to guarantee a basically level field between governments and their oppositions (Schedler 2002, 40–41). Although these regimes provide what Levitsky and Way (2002) call "arenas of democratic contestation," they still actively seek to control or restrict them.

For many years Mexico provided probably the best example of EA in Latin America (Centeno 1998), but the Mexican regime was based on the hegemonic control of the Partido Revolucionario Institucional (Institutional Revolutionary Party [PRI]) and thus resembled more traditional one-party rule. The Fujimori regime comes closer to the more competitive, personality-based variant of EA that Diamond, Schedler, and Levitski and Way discuss. After his April 1992 coup, Fujimori sought to obliterate any opposition to his three main policies goals, namely, defeat domestic insurgency, implement market reforms, and secure reelection. In the process he engaged in a pattern of governance that can only be characterized as authoritarian, as Mauceri, Conaghan , McClintock, and Cameron argue in this volume (Chapters 2, 5, 11, and 12). Tilting the electoral playing field to his advantage was certainly an aspect of the regime. Another authoritarian aspect was its use of its congressional majority and control of the judiciary in order to pass legislation that greatly undermined civil liberties and changed traditional rules of the game. Fujimori's overall record after the 1992 coup makes his regime's designation as authoritarian almost inescapable.

After years of scholarly focus on the politics of transition and the examination of the democratic deficiencies of new civilian regimes, the political realities of Latin America and other third-wave democracies have stimulated a renewed interest in personalistic politics and authoritarianism. Concepts such as "delegative democracy," "neopopulism," and now "electoral authoritarianism" have been developed to explain the region's political dynamics. In a sense, we are coming full circle, re-creating the early academic shift from the analysis of elite accommodation to the study of personalistic and authoritarian politics. However, the authoritarianism that we face today is significantly different from the authoritarianism the region encountered in the 1970s. The region no longer has a "legitimacy vacuum" in the sense that Needler (1963) gave to this term. There is now a clear consensus that the ultimate source of authority emanates from the people in the form of elections. For this reason, this newer form of authoritarianism needs electoral validation in order to establish itself in the eyes of domestic and international players. The problem is that the bar used by international organizations and foreign governments to classify elections as "free and fair" is, as McClintock shows in Chapter 11, generally too low, focusing mostly on the honesty of the count and paying little attention either to the process itself or to the government's overall record.

The introduction of the notion of EA requires us to address its similarities to and differences from the well-established notions of delegative democracy and neopopulism. The following section provides such discussion.

Delegative Democracy, Neopopulism, and Electoral Authoritarianism: A Conceptual Map

Shattering the early optimism of the "transition to democracy" literature, O'Donnell (1994) questioned whether some Latin American democracies were headed toward democratic consolidation. Noting a disturbing pattern of excessive executive predominance, lack of "horizontal accountability" (checks and balances), and sporadic governmental effectiveness, O'Donnell described delegative democracy (DD) as a "new species" of democracy (55), one that was "more democratic, but less liberal, than representative democracy" (60). According to him (1994, 59), presidents in DDs, claiming to be the true representatives of the nation, rule as they see fit and are constrained only by the existing power relations and a limited term of office.

DD presidents exhibit anti-institutional bias (for, as O'Donnell contends, institutions are perceived as "encumbrances" to presidential power), and they usually resort to legislative decrees as their preferred method to enact policy. But DDs *are* democratic regimes, since they are the product of clean elections and meet Dahl's criteria for the definition of polyarchy (O'Donnell 1994, 56). Moreover, despite the clear anti-institutional bias, institutions do retain the ability to occasionally check presidential power. To this set of characteristics, we may add that DDs do not systematically engage in the exclusion of political competition. DD presidents may seek to change constitutional rules to be able to run for reelection, but "vertical accountability" (voters' ability to hold elected officials accountable at election time) remains fully in effect.

In the mid-1990s, Roberts (1995) and Weyland (1996) coined the term *neopopulist* to describe many of the governments that O'Donnell had previously characterized as DDs: Fujimori's in Peru, Carlos Menem's in Argentina, Fernando Collor de Mello's in Brazil. But these scholars were addressing a different research puzzle, namely, the adoption of neoliberal market reforms by leaders who evoked the old populism with their personalistic governments and their broad-based support. The challenge was to explain the "unexpected affinity," as Weyland put it, between this new breed of populism and neoliberalism. The solution has been to reconceptualize the very notion of populism, stripping from it some of its early characteristics (Knight 1998; Weyland 2001). Nevertheless, the use of the word *neopopulist* to describe leaders who can also be characterized as DD presidents requires us to identify the conceptual overlaps of and differences between neopopulism and DD. Is *neopopulism* just another term for delegative democracy? If not, what is the conceptual contribution of neopopulism?

In a suggestive article, Weyland (2001, 12) redefines populism as a political strategy in which "an individual leader seeks or exercises government power based on support from large numbers of followers." Populist leaders rely on unorganized masses in order to come to power and then rule with weak or nonexistent organizational intermediation with these masses. Weyland goes further by identifying subtypes of populism based on their degree of organizational intermediation. The classical populism of the 1930s to 1960s, he argues, displays some minimal traces of organization; populist leaders appeal to the masses as a collective entity. Neopopulist leaders of the 1980s and 1990s, by contrast, display no organizational intermediation with the masses and appeal to them not as a collective entity but as "a disperse set of private individuals" (15).[3]

This redefinition allows us to set clear boundaries between populism (and its modern subtype neopopulism) and DD. It can be argued that DD depicts a type of political *regime,* whereas neopopulism describes a political *strategy.* DD is a subtype of democratic regime in which elected leaders use their popular support to surmount the constitutional checks and balances that limit their power. Neopopulism, however, is a political strategy used by leaders in weak party systems to win and exercise power. Although there are substantial overlaps between these concepts (they both stress personalistic rule and broad-based support), they speak to different dynamics. While the concept of DD calls our attention to over-bearing executives and institutional fragilities, neopopulism speaks to the nature of the relationship between elected leaders and their supporters.

Given the extraordinary powers that presidents enjoy and the weaknesses that institutions exhibit under DDs, what makes DD regimes different from EA regimes? The answer lies in two crucial variables: one, whether the regime is willing to accept meaningful political competition by providing free and fair elections and, two, the regime's overall record in respecting democratic procedures. Admittedly, these criteria still leave room for disagreement, since *meaningful political competition* and *overall record of respect for democracy* are phrases open to wide interpretation. But the point to be made is that the mere presence of relatively free suffrage does not guarantee the democratic character of the regime. As Przeworski et al. (2000, 18) rightfully note, "[T]he mere fact that elections have been held does not suffice to qualify the regime as democratic. Only if the losers are allowed to compete, win, and assume office is a regime democratic." According to them (Przeworski et al. 2000, 16), democratic regimes honor the three dimensions of contestation: ex-ante uncertainty, ex-post irreversibility, and repeatability. I would argue that DDs fulfill Przeworski and associates' definition of effective contestation, whereas EA regimes do not. Moreover, while civil and political rights are occasionally violated in DDs, they are not systematically or extensively infringed upon. EA regimes, by contrast, violate democratic criteria so systematically that they create "an uneven playing field between government and opposition" (Levitsky and Way 2002, 53). In sum, while "vertical accountability" remains in full effect under DDs, it is severely curtailed under EA regimes.

Certainly, relying on the fairness and openness of elections to distinguish between electoral democracy and EA (Schedler 2002) is a sensible choice, but in classifying regimes it is also necessary to examine the regime's overall record. Is the overall pattern of governance consistent with democratic procedures, even of the delegative variety? Or does the regime engage in a pattern of governance that shows utter disregard for democratic procedures, unfairly undermines the opposition, and aims at retaining power? Here the conceptual benefits of using EA to distinguish between neopopulist leaders become apparent. While the label *neopopulist* could be employed to describe both Alan García Pérez and Alberto

Fujimori, it is clear that they presided over substantially different governments. Despite his many democratic faults and his abrasive style, García honored the competitive nature of the political game. Fujimori, however, showed a behavioral pattern that violated this competition.

There is a fine line between DD and EA, one that is important to establish. For instance, courts are under pressure in DD regimes but they can occasionally block executive acts. Such behavior is extremely rare under EA regimes, since courts are under tighter controls. Similarly, the media often operates freely under DD regimes, whereas it is usually coerced and even under control in EA regimes. Likewise, even though presidents usually exert a great deal of control over parties and legislatures in DD regimes, the opposition (and even the ruling party) can sometimes pose congressional obstacles to presidential power. Such obstacles are far less likely under EA regimes. Finally, DD presidents tend to end their terms in ordinary ways or in complete passivity, whereas transitions in EA regimes are more dramatic. O'Donnell (1994, 67) mentions that DD presidents frequently go from omnipotence to impotence as policy failures accumulate. When that happens, the president's overarching goal "is just to hang on until the end of his term" (idem). This dynamic is less likely under EA. Once entrenched, EA leaders do not abandon power easily. Transfer of power in the wake of EA is rarely routine, as President Leonid Kuchma's dramatic failure to get his prime minister, Viktor Yanukovich, elected as president of Ukraine shows. In some cases, EA leaders depart after they fail to win plebiscites in order to legitimize their authoritarianism (as in the case of Albania's Sali Berisha in 1994). In other instances, they resign (as did Fujimori in Peru and Ter Petrosian in Armenia), or decay into more traditional forms of authoritarianism (as in the cases of Robert Mugabe in Zimbabwe and Ilham Aliyev in Azerbaijan).

Is neopopulism compatible with electoral authoritarianism? Since EA refers to the nature of the regime (severe curtailment of political competition without abandoning the forms of democracy) and neopopulism describes a strategy to win and exercise power, the answer is clearly affirmative. In fact, neopopulism is compatible with both DD and EA regimes. Neopopulist leaders, as Barr and Dietz argue in Chapter 3, seek to obliterate "independent hubs of public support" to stifle the opposition. If, by a number of circumstances they face little obstacles in this effort, the regime may tip over to electoral authoritarianism, as was the case for Fujimori in Peru. However, if the neopopulist leader faces effective opposition, then the regime will remain a DD without decaying into EA (as was the case for Menem in Argentina and Collor in Brazil).

The Rise of Electoral Authoritarianism in Peru

Delegative democracies seem to live on the edge of EA, for they already exhibit some features that are detrimental to democratic health: overbearing executives, weak checks and balances, and plesbicitarian political cultures (O'Donnell 1994). For this reason, a dramatic change in the political environment of these democracies could tip them over to EA. In Peru, the deepening crisis of the late 1980s and early 1990s (fueled by economic recession and political violence) and the significant weakening of civil society and intermediary organizations marked a dramatic change in the political environment. Fujimori, whose initial election was in great part a result of these changing conditions, took advantage of Peru's strong presidential tradition, of people's yearning for order, and of his growing public approval in order to embark on an authoritarian project. In addition, he took advantage of a permissive international community, which saw him as the lesser of the many evils Peru was facing at the time.

A Crisis Situation

Scholars (O'Donnell 1994; Roberts 1995) have noted that situations of extreme crisis in Latin America are usually associated with the emergence of personalistic leadership. At least two different reasons have been advanced for this association. Weyland (2000, 2002), relying on prospect theory, argues that extreme crisis situations place people in the "domain of losses," making them more likely to support risky, untried alternatives. Linz (1978), however, associates crisis situations with a loss of power and a power vacuum. He maintains that a crisis condition usually arises in the presence of an unsolvable problem to which outsider forces offer themselves as a solution.

Whatever the mechanism at work linking crisis situations with authoritarian rule, it is undisputed that Peru was undergoing—to use Pocock's expression—a "Machiavellian moment" in the late 1980s and early 1990s, the moment "in which the republic was seen as confronting its own temporal finitude" (Pocock 1975, viii). Hyperinflation, economic recession, declining wages, growing unemployment, and brutal political violence were ravaging this Andean nation. As Weyland rightly notes in Chapter 1 in this volume, crises discredit the established political class and pave the way for outsiders; they also weaken intermediary organizations, opening up opportunities for personalistic leadership and inducing citizens to support risky political alternatives. The widespread feeling that the nation was on the verge of collapse may have led people to grant Fujimori the benefit of the doubt when he claimed that he needed unfettered powers to deal with the crisis.

Fujimori's early success in dealing with the crisis situation cemented his political appeal. He stabilized the economy and reduced inflation. He reinserted Peru into the international financial community. He reconstituted and modernized state agencies. He defeated an entrenched domestic insurgency. He implemented small developmental programs in many urban and rural communities. An effective handling of crisis situations will certainly cement the popularity of any elected official, and such was the case with Fujimori. Unfortunately for Peruvian democracy, his policy successes also led people to overlook his authoritarian traits. Although his landslide reelection in 1995 came in the wake of an essentially flawed electoral process, nobody could dispute that he was very popular that year.

If a crisis situation enhances the likelihood of authoritarianism, its resolution (as Weyland argues here) removes its rationale. After 1995, with the defeat of both domestic insurgency and hyperinflation but with a decline in the country's economic situation, Fujimori began to face increased scrutiny from the public. As his popularity dropped, he relied more and more on the shady operations of his chief security advisor, Vladimiro Montesinos. As I show in Chapter 6, Fujimori's obsession with a third term alienated many upper- and middle-class voters, dissolving the electoral coalition that had reelected him in 1995. Although he eventually secured reelection in 2000, that event polarized the country; many perceived it as not only unfair but even outright fraudulent. The revelations that the regime operated a vast corruption network triggered a deep crisis—for the reasons that Cameron discusses in Chapter 12—that would eventually lead to its downfall.

A Weakening Civil Society and a Vanishing Party System

In the late 1970s, Peru's civil society had participated remarkably in the transition process to democracy. As in many other Latin American countries, this societal activism subsided somewhat after the transition. In the particular case of Peru, this decline was particularly severe and lasting because of two developments mentioned by Mauceri in Chapter 2. First, the situation of declining wages, high inflation, and growing unemployment in the 1980s depleted the resource base of many civil society organizations. Second, rising political violence from both guerrilla groups and security forces weakened the ability of some organizations to mobilize. As a consequence, society's ability to resist authoritarianism was dramatically reduced by the late 1980s and early 1990s. In addition to this weakening of civil society, the party system also underwent a severe crisis. As both Roberts (Chapter 4) and Mauceri document, Peru's party system—which was never too solid to begin with—suffered a surprising blow at the beginning of the 1990s (see also Kenney 2004).

Established and well-functioning parties, unlike political outsiders, have an incentive to keep the democratic game going, for it enhances their chances of having access to power at a later time. Even if they engage in less than fully democratic governance while in power, established parties honor the competitive nature of the political game, and in so doing augment the prospects of democratic survivability. Outsiders, by contrast, especially if they are of the "populist" variety (as Roberts labels them in Chapter 4) lack both the partisan ties and political experience. As a result, outsiders are more likely to develop what Roberts calls a "profit while one can" mentality, which usually leads them to seek an ever expanding tenure in office—thus diminishing the competitive nature of the political game. The weakening of party systems has an additional negative consequence: it weakens institutional barriers against authoritarianism. The opposition to Fujimori lacked strength because its parties were weak, fragmented, and unpopular.

A clear example of how a debilitated party system helped Fujimori proceed with his authoritarian project was evident in the parties' behavior during the crucial November 1992 legislative election. This election was to produce a new congress to replace the one dismissed by Fujimori; this new legislature would have the additional task of drafting a new constitution. The manipulations leading to this election were such (see Introduction) that most traditional parties refused to participate, arguing (correctly, as it would turn out) that the election would only legitimize an authoritarian regime. However, this principled action did not have a lasting impact, as some of the parties faced internal dissension and divisions on this issue, while newly created organizations decided to participate. In fact, two powerful electoral alliances (Frente Democrático, or Democratic Front [FREDEMO], and Izquierda Unida, or United Left [IU]) dissolved and some of their component organizations did participate in the contest. Despite its obvious flaws, the election was given a seal of approval by the Organization of American States (OAS), thus sanctioning Fujimori's legitimacy as president and producing a flawed legislature that would ultimately draft the constitution that allowed Fujimori to run for reelection in 1995. Stronger parties perhaps would have been able to derail the electoral legitimacy of the 1992 coup.

An additional example of how a weak party system undermined institutional resistance against Fujimori can be found in the conflicting relations between Fujimori and Lima's majors. Throughout his regime, Fujimori consistently tried to undermine and erase the powers of Lima's elected mayors (Ricardo Belmont and Alberto Andrade) in order to eliminate them as potential political competitors (see Chapter 3). In this effort Fujimori was largely successful, in part because both Belmont and Andrade were independent figures—further confirming the declining nature of the party system in Peru—and thus lacked the support of strong national parties and their respective congressional representations.

Strong Presidentialism

In most of Latin America and especially in Peru, overbearing executives frequently overshadow legislatures and exert a degree of power that goes beyond those granted in the constitution. This strong presidentialism provides the opportunity for authoritarian abuse. As has been long acknowledged, in many occasions presidential predominance is such that "is apt to conceal dictatorships under the veneer of constitutional forms" (Lambert 1967, 324). Mauceri shows in Chapter 2 that Fujimori raised presidential prerogatives to such a new level that his government could no longer be described as democratic, however qualified. Yet he argues that the practices Fujimori abused were not unknown in Peru. Indeed, studies of the presidencies of Fernando Belaúnde Terry and Alan García Pérez describe their frequent misuse of executive power: bypassing Congress out of major policymaking initiatives as well as demanding and obtaining the power to legislate by decree (Abugattas 1987; Carrión 1998; Conaghan, Malloy, and Abugattas 1990; Mauceri 1997b; McClintock 1994).

For a full description of the ways in which Fujimori took presidential prerogatives to new heights, I refer the reader to Chapter 2. Suffice it to say that the new constitution enacted under Fujimori's supervision further undermined check and balances by giving the president even greater involvement in legislative and judicial matters. A "superpresidency," similar to what Fish (2001, 69) finds in some postcommunist regimes, was thus created. Superpresidentialism already poses significant challenges for democratic survivability, but its deleterious effects are compounded further when it operates with a weak or declining party system and an outsider has been elected to the presidency. Under these circumstances, the emergence of EA seems likely.

Societal Support

One would like to describe the emergence of EA in Peru as a ruthless imposition on Peruvian society, but nothing would be further from the truth. Fujimori commanded significant popular support, which enabled him to build an electoral-based authoritarian regime without resorting to openly repressive rule. This broad-based support was driven by many factors. First, many Peruvian citizens have a documented predisposition toward what is perceived as strong and beneficent leadership (J. Parodi 1993; Murakami 2000). Second, this support was a function of Fujimori's unquestionable policy successes (see Chapters 1, 6, 8, and 9, this volume). Third, Fujimori was able to target key societal groups such as women (see Chapter 7) and the poor in order to maximize this support. Fourth, Fujimori was able to clamp the opposition through his shrewd use of fear and intimidation (Burt 2004, 264–65). Finally, the support was driven by the perception that Fujimori was a "can-do president" (especially when compared with the largely ineffective administrations that preceded him). Although his approval ratings fell significantly after 1995, nobody can deny that he retained considerable public support even when he ran for a third term in the highly controversial 2000 election.

At the peak of his popularity, Fujimori attracted support from all social classes, yet it is undisputable that at critical junctures his support came disproportionately from the poor. He was initially elected in 1990 because he was able to draw extraordinary support from the poorest sectors of Peru's society (Degregori and Grompone 1991), and when he ran in the controversial 2000 elections the poor were again his main base of support. To court this vote, Fujimori used food-relief programs and community-development projects that were timed to the electoral calendar (Schady 2000). Indeed, levels of state spending in food programs were unprecedented in Peru. In 1999, the number of beneficiaries of diverse food programs was close to 11 million, almost 40 percent of Peru's total population. Toward the end of the regime, about 60 percent of Lima's households in extreme poverty participated in two or three food programs (Carrión 2001).

But societal support for this electoral-based authoritarian project was not realized only in opinion polls and electoral returns. In his plans to "reengineer" Peru, Fujimori enjoyed the active support of *poderes fác-*

ticos (de facto powers): prominent members of the business community, transnational technocrats, media executives, and high-ranking military officials all colluded with the regime (Cotler and Grompone 2000; Degregori 2000; Durand 2003; Pease García 2003). In fact, as Conaghan shows in Chapter 5, this collaboration could only be described in some cases as complicity, since so many of them became integral parts of what she describes as "greed rings," the informal institutions that sustained the regime.

Despite all the spending and corruption, Fujimori could not prevent the increasing societal mobilization against his attempts to secure reelection in 2000 (Conaghan 2001). Whether this mobilization was *the* crucial factor in the eventual collapse of the regime remains a source of contention (in Chapter 12, Cameron prefers to stress the regime's internal contradictions), but it was undoubtedly a contributing factor. Declining societal approval may not have finished the regime, but it certainly made the continuation of "politics as usual" much more difficult.

A Permissive International Community

The emergence of EA in Peru was in part the result of the timid attitude adopted by the international community, particularly the United States (see McClintock and Vallas 2003). When Fujimori suspended Peru's democracy in April 1992, the OAS reacted with ambivalence. The OAS secretary-general made use of Resolution 1080 to call an emergency meeting of foreign-relations ministers. At the meeting a statement was issued "deeply deploring" the disruption of the democratic process in Peru and Uruguay's foreign relations minister was appointed as the OAS representative to negotiate with Fujimori. Participants at the OAS meeting failed, however, to pass any real sanction against Fujimori (Bowen 2000, 109–12). Moreover, as Palmer shows in Chapter 10, the United States was reluctant to break with Fujimori and eventually came to accept the status quo. A few weeks after the autogolpe, the United States recognized Fujimori as Peru's legitimate president; Bernard Aronson, under-secretary of state for the Americas, declared to a congressional committee: "[N]either we nor the OAS are seeking a return to the status quo ante. Peru is a country in deep crisis which needs a deep reform" (quoted in Bowen 2000, 108–9).

For all practical purposes, both the OAS and the United States were content to leave Fujimori—he who had broken Peru's democratic continuity in the first place—with the task of bringing Peru back to democracy. Yet Fujimori had no serious intention of democratizing Peru. Unfortunately, neither the United States nor the OAS paid attention to the significant alterations of the electoral rules that Fujimori enacted in order to secure his party's position in the upcoming legislative election. As McClintock notes in Chapter 11, the OAS gave its stamp of approval to the 1992 election despite these irregularities.

Between 1992 and 1999, the OAS was largely absent from Peruvian politics, even though there was increasing evidence of Fujimori's systematic violations of accepted democratic practices in order to secure the continuation of his regime. Fujimori's overwhelming reelection in 1995 brought him a renewed legitimacy that allowed him to escape from the probing eyes of the international community. When he started manipulating his own constitution as well as Peru's institutions in order to secure an illegal reelection bid in 2000, neither the OAS nor the United States administration publicly criticized the regime. As Palmer describes in chapter 10, it was not until January 2000 that the U.S. administration began to speak out "officially, consistently, and in a coordinated manner" against Fujimori's manipulations.

Even as the OAS electoral mission declared the 2000 election virtually illegitimate, the oas General Assembly declined to take a forceful stance against Fujimori. The assembly held at Windsor, Canada, in June 2001 failed to follow the logical step of declaring the Fujimori government illegitimate (despite Canadian and American efforts to do so). Instead, it appointed a high-level mission to "strengthen democracy" in Peru. Thus, the OAS mounted only a very timid response to an election that it labeled as falling short of international standards of fairness.

The Limits of Electoral Authoritarianism

Fujimori's sudden resignation and the swift unraveling of his regime made apparent the serious obstacles that he faced in consolidating his authoritarian experiment. There were a number of underlying factors that debilitated the regime, and these should be analytically distinguished from the precipitating factor that led to its eventual downfall.

One could begin the analysis of the severe difficulties that the EA regime faced in consolidating its rule by pointing out, almost tongue in cheek, that no regime in Peru—democratic or otherwise—seems to be able to last for long (McClintock 1999). But EA regimes—especially of the presidential variety, and most of them are—face particularly difficult obstacles for their consolidation since their leaders have finite periods and therefore must face the electorate at regular intervals, forcing them to deal with the problem of succession when rulers are no longer eligible to run for reelection (Ottaway 2003, 157).

The problem of succession is particularly acute because, as Ottaway notes, in very few cases can a strong EA personality transfer the post to another. In addition, electoral contests open a route for the opposition to rally against the regime, thus increasing the likelihood of regime termination (as the recent case of Ukraine illustrates). In the Peruvian case, one could argue that such a moment was reached in 2000, when the regime's efforts to reelect Fujimori for a third term generated deep fissures in his electoral coalition (see Chapter 6). The problem of succession is aggravated because the personalistic nature of EA makes it more difficult to transfer the electoral appeal of the regime's leader to the its appointed successor. In Peru, Fujimori's inability to transfer his electoral appeal was repeatedly demonstrated through the regime's candidates' failure to win the important Lima mayoralty.

A possible solution to the problem of succession is to create a party to replace the strong personality when he or she is no longer eligible to run, thus ensuring the regime's continuation. This avenue, however, is rarely taken because the creation of such a party sets limits to the authoritarian leader's power. The lack of institutionalization makes the regime highly dependent on the leader's sustained popularity and his or her ability to "deliver the goods," as Weyland argues in Chapter 1.

In the absence of a party apparatus and an ideology from which to elicit loyalty, the Fujimori regime relied on both corruption networks and the security apparatus to keep it together. The extreme reliance on Montesinos and his intelligence operation generated internal tensions that ultimately undermined the regime's popularity and thus its legitimacy (Crabtree 2000; Durand 2003). Similarly, the regime's corruption was widespread and served not only to personally benefit the regime's key members but to also finance the regime's reelection effort, as Conaghan argues in Chapter 5.[4] Corruption in a personalistic regime such as Fujimori's is a double-edged sword. While it may "grease the wheels" of government and buy political allegiance, it creates a predatory state that encourages rent-seeking behavior (Evans 1989), thus affecting economic growth and further undermining the regime's electoral appeal. As both Sheahan and Wise illustrate in Chapters 8 and 9, respectively, the regime's corruption and its political needs end up affecting economic growth. In addition, corruption exposes the regime to severe danger because EA regimes, as Cameron contends in Chapter 12, need to keep a veneer of legality. The disclosure that key members of the regime are implicated in widespread corruption can thus lead to what Cameron aptly labels "endogenous breakdown": a collapse caused by internal tensions.

In sum, the regime faced severe obstacles to its consolidation, the most important being its inability to solve the problem of succession. It was forced to keep Fujimori as its public face in the 2000 electoral race, yet in order to counteract his sagging popular support it had to rely increasingly on corruption and open manipulations as a way to improve its electoral chances. In addition, a revitalized civil society and an increasingly hostile international community severely undermined the regime's strength. The precipitating factor that led to its demise was the public exposure of its widespread corruption, which completely removed any of its pretenses of legality.

The Fujimori Legacy

In this concluding section I highlight what I consider to be the most lasting legacies of the Fujimori regime: market reforms, a further debilitated civil society and party system, political corruption, and—as a reaction to the regime—an emerging regional commitment to competitive politics.

Market Reforms

Fujimori adopted one of the most systematic programs of market reform in Latin America. Both Sheahan (Chapter 8) and Wise (Chapter 9) show persuasively that this program was largely successful in macroeconomic terms. Fujimori's economic policy was particularly effective at ending inflation, a problem that had plagued Peru for many years. Moreover, as Wise argues, the regime was quite successful in creating or "reinventing" state agencies in order to foster economic performance. By redefining traditional state-market relations and ending the inefficiencies associated with the old import-substituting-Industrialization model, Fujimori modernized Peru's economy. This is a positive legacy. Fujimori's economic policy, however, as again both Sheahan and Wise point out, was less than stellar in dealing with Peru's pressing social and economic needs (especially income and job growth). Fujimori's political goals prevented the adoption of measures that could have created the necessary conditions for economic takeoff.

For instance, Sheahan demonstrates that Peru remained vulnerable to external shocks because Fujimori allowed the country's currency to appreciate, which negatively affected exports. The reason for this policy, Sheahan notes, was the high priority given—for political reasons—to keeping low inflation. Similarly, reelection considerations prevented Fujimori from following his impressive first-term economic achievements with much needed "second phase" reforms (reforms of the civil service and the administration of justice reforms, antitrust enforcement, and so on). As Wise contends here, these reforms could not be tackled because they required "a more inclusive and accountable style of politics" than Fujimori could ever deliver.

The reorganization of the economy along market lines has also reconfigured Peru's class structure (Portes and Hoffman 2003), through a decrease in the size of blue-collar workers and the middle class and an increase of the informal sector. As a result, a shift in the political clout of these classes and their peak associations has occurred. The clear winner has been the capitalist class, whose "structural power . . . increased dramatically" (Durand 2002, 11). This "business empowerment," as Durand calls it, is an important consequence of market reforms and thus a legacy of the Fujimori regime.

A Further Debilitated Civil Society and Party System

As has been said before, Peru's civil society and party system were already deteriorating in the early 1990s. Many factors contributed to this decline: the severe economic crisis, which created unemployment; increasing political violence that made social or communal activism risky, and the parties' mediocre governmental performance, which sunk their electoral fortunes. In its quest to obliterate opposition parties and to reduce resistance to its policies, the Fujimori regime further undermined civil society, local governments, and the party system. In Chapters 2, 3, and 4, Mauceri, Barr and Dietz, and Roberts, respectively, discuss the numerous ways in which this was accomplished. They are briefly mentioned below.

First, in an effort to keep a tight control over provincial governments, Fujimori reversed a policy of state decentralization that had been timidly begun in the late 1980s. After the 1992 autogolpe, regional governments became an extension of the executive. Second, to prevent the emergence of political competitors, Fujimori pursued a policy of confrontation against municipal governments, especially Lima's, depriving them of their traditional sources of revenues and thus limiting their functions. Neighborhood food programs that were either autonomous or funded by municipal governments were transferred to the powerful Ministry of the Presidency. Lima's municipal government was financially choked. Third, to reduce the effectiveness of the opposition, the regime severely curtailed the bargaining power of labor unions by introducing new restrictive labor laws and by easing restrictions on the ability of employers to dismiss workers. Finally, civil society organizations were greatly affected by the atmosphere of fear and intimidation that permeated Peru's poorest communities as a result of the regime's efforts to repress domestic terrorism (Burt 2004). The regime may not have engaged in generalized repression, but its human rights record was deplorable and widely criticized by independent observers, which included the U.S. State Department.

As the regime pushed for a third term, Peru saw a renovated spirit of societal activism. New organizations sprang up to denounce, ridicule, and mobilize against the reelection machinations. The highest point of this process was the extremely successful Marcha de los Cuatro Suyos (March of the Four Suyos). This activism, however, has receded. In a similar vein, Peru's existing parties, with the possible exception of Alianza Popular Revolucionaria Americana (American Popular Revolutionary Alliance [APRA]), are in flux and after the transition have not been able to consolidate. Of the four top vote-getter parties in the 2000 presidential elections, only one finished among the top four in the 2001 presidential elections. This single organization, President Alejandro Toledo's Perú Posible, is currently facing serious organizational problems, and it is highly unlikely that it will be among the top presidential contenders in 2006.

It is now clear that the inchoate party system that existed in the 1980s, organized around the traditional left-right cleavage, collapsed in the wake of the 1992 autogolpe (Levitsky and Cameron 2003). But some parties that were part of this incipient system (especially the APRA party) were able to come back in post-Fujimori Peru. Given this return, it makes sense to speak of a "partial rebirth" of the party system in Peru (Kenney 2003). However, this "rebirth" should not be overstated. The multiplicity of new personality-based parties and the fluid and fragmented electoral politics that it encourages poses a significant challenge for the working of democracy in Peru (Levitsky and Cameron 2003). In fact, the demise of ideological discourse that characterizes Peruvian politics today

(Carrión 2001) opens the way to the emergence of media-based candidates eager to replicate Fujimori's electoral fortune. On the positive side, the lack of ideology that characterizes these new organizations may help governability by making postelectoral coalitions easier to achieve.

Political Corruption

A degree of political corruption exists almost everywhere, and it is certainly embedded in many Latin American political systems. In Peru, the administrations that preceded the Fujimori regime did not escape allegations of corruption. In fact, President García faced a congressional accusation that eventually ended only because the statute of limitations had expired. The Fujimori regime, however, made corruption a pillar of its functioning. Given the existing evidence, one must agree with Conaghan's assertion in Chapter 5 that the regime "was not just a government, it was also a vast criminal conspiracy." As she also points out, the elaborate system of corruption and clientelism provided an informal institutionalization to the declining institutionalization of formal intermediary organizations in Peru. As both Conaghan and Cameron (Chapter 12) argue, the spiraling corruption deepened the regime's authoritarian inclinations by forcing it to resort to increasingly drastic measures to cover up its previous crimes. The consequences of this generalized corruption have been far-reaching and have already negatively affected Toledo's government.

Indeed, uncovering, prosecuting, and convicting the vast corruption networks were unavoidable tasks for both the caretaker Valentín Paniagua presidency and the currently elected Toledo administration. If for no other reason, this task has not been easy, because the very institution that is supposed to investigate all these crimes, the judicial branch, is not only painfully inadequate but was also actually involved in the corruption network. As a consequence, the population perceives very little progress in the fight against corruption, something that greatly undermines the legitimacy of democracy. At the same time, prosecuting these crimes certainly distracts the Toledo administration from paying full attention to other more pressing—and politically rewarding—concerns such as unemployment.

This legacy of corruption runs even deeper than simply creating extra work for democratic administrations. The disclosure that such a significant number of high-ranking state officials, military officers, media executives, and elected representatives were involved in the regime's corruption network has undoubtedly lowered the public's already low regard for the political class, making governance even more difficult. In this context, revelations of even minor corruption could have earth-shaking consequences, for they only increase the public's deep skepticism of the political class. President Toledo's already low popularity rating has been further depressed by revelations that some members of his family as well as his personal lawyer and former intelligence chief were involved in corruption schemes. Some called for his resignation as a result of these accusations. This is a clear example of how governments are now fragile and vulnerable to new accusations of wrongdoing. In the long term, the public's reduced tolerance for and heightened awareness of corruption could have positive consequences for democracy by signaling to politicians and state officials that even minor corruption will not be tolerated. In the short term, however, the deep mistrust of institutions and their leaders is making governance more difficult.

Perhaps the most lasting consequence of this controversial regime is that in seeking to return order and governability to Peru in order to deal with a serious crisis, it effectively destroyed the democratic institutions and public trust that are so necessary to achieving long-term governability in this Andean nation.

A Renewed Regional Commitment to Democracy

To conclude on a more positive note, an important legacy of the Fujimori regime has been a redefining of the dangers that Latin American democracies face today. The 2000 electoral process in Peru made evident that the main collective legal instrument to protect democracy in the region, Resolution 1080, had become obsolete and inoperative in a context in which military coups were rare. The rise of electoral authoritarianism in Peru demanded a new regional response. It is no accident that the new democratic government in Peru took the initiative in developing a new legal instrument to defend democratic governance. After a series of drafts and negotiations, the historic OAS Inter-American Democratic Charter was approved at a meeting of the region's foreign ministers held in Lima on September 11, 2001.

The new Inter-American Democratic Charter goes beyond Resolution 1080 by asserting in its Article 2 that "the effective exercise of representative democracy is the basis for the rule of law and of the constitutional regimes of the member states." Moreover, in Article 19 the charter recognizes that democracy can be placed at risk not only by the "unconstitutional interruption of the democratic order" (that is, old-fashioned military coups) but also by the "unconstitutional alteration of the constitutional regime that seriously impairs the democratic order in a member state." Despite the awkwardness of the wording, it is clear that the inclusion of this clause that alerts against "alteration of the constitutional regime" is aimed at situations like the ones created by Fujimori in 1992 and 2000.

Accepting that threats to democracy can come from within elected governments is a significant regional accomplishment. Hopefully, in the coming years this acceptance will prevent the kind of timid responses that the international community adopted vis-à-vis the unsavory practices of the Fujimori regime.

NOTES

1. In some countries an alternative route for the political integration of the lower classes had been tried before in the form of populism.

2. To be sure, not all scholars devoted to the analysis of transitions shared this strategic, actor-based approach. See, for instance, Malloy 1987.

3. Redefining populism as a political strategy has the advantage of making the concept more general and therefore increases its applicability. However, the redefinition strips from it all references to the class alliances that were part of standard definitions of populism. For a critique of this conceptual strategy see Lynch 1999a; Quijano 1998.

4. For additional analysis of the regime's corruption, see Dammert Ego Aguirre 2001; Pease García 2003; Durand 2003.

BIBLIOGRAPHY

Abugattas, Luis A. 1987. "Populism and After: The Peruvian Experience." In *Authoritarians and Democrats: Regime Transition in Latin America,* edited by James M. Malloy and Mitchell A. Seligson. Pittsburgh: University of Pittsburgh Press.

Abusada, Roberto, Fritz Du Bois, Eduardo Morón, and José Valderrama. 2000. "La reforma incompleta." In *La reforma incompleta.* Vol. 1, edited by Roberto Abusada et al. Lima: Universidad del Pacífico and Instituto Peruano de Economía.

Acevedo, Domingo, and Claudio Grossman. 1996. "The Organization of American States and the Protection of Democracy." In *Beyond Sovereignty,* edited by Tom Farer. Baltimore: Johns Hopkins University Press.

Aldrich, John H. 1995. *Why Parties? The Origin and Transformation of Political Parties in America.* Chicago: University of Chicago Press.

Alvarado Pérez, Betty M. 1994. *Relaciones fiscales: Entre el gobierno central y los gobiernos locales.* Lima: Fundación Friedrich Ebert.

Americas Watch. 1992. *Peru Under Fire: Human Rights Since the Return of Democracy.* New Haven: Yale University Press.

Anderson, Charles W. 1967. *Politics and Economic Change in Latin America: The Governing of Restless Nations.* Princeton, N.J.: D. Van Nostrand.

Apoyo. 1990–2000. *Informe de Opinión.* Lima: Apoyo.

Araoz, Mercedes, José Luiz Bonifaz, Carlos Casas, and Fernando González Vigil. 2001. *Factores limitantes de la inversion extranjera en el Perú.* Lima: Universidad del Pacífico.

Arce, Moisés. 2003. "Political Violence and Presidential Approval in Peru." *Journal of Politics* 65:572–83.

Asociación de Comunicadores Sociales Calandria. 2000. *Buscando la equidad en el Congreso: Encuesta sobre participación política de la mujer.* Lima: Calandria.

Avritzer, Leonardo. 2002. *Democracy and the Public Space in Latin America.* Princeton: Princeton University Press.

Baer, Werner, and William Maloney. 1997. "Neoliberalism and Income Distribution in Latin America." *World Development* 25:311–27.

Balbi, Carmen. 1996. "El Fujimorismo." *Pretextos* 9:187–223.

Balbi, Carmen, and David Scott Palmer. 2001. "Political Earthquake." *LASA Forum* 31 (Winter): 7–11.

Baloyra, Enrique, ed. 1987. *Comparing New Democracies: Transition and Consolidation in Mediterranean Europe and the Southern Cone.* Boulder, Colo.: Westview Press.

Barr, Robert R. 2002. "Between Success and Survival: Devolution and Concentration in Latin America." Ph.D. diss., University of Texas, Austin.

————. 2003. "The Persistence of Neopopulism in Peru?" *Third World Quarterly* 24 (December): 1161–78.

Banco Central de Reserva del Perú. 1998. *Nota Semanal* 32 (August). Lima: BCRP.

————. 2000. *Memoria 1999*. Lima: BCRP.

————. 2002. *Memoria 2001*. Lima: BCRP.

BCRP: *See* Banco Central de Reserva del Perú.

Behrman, Jere, Nancy Birdsall, and Miguel Szekly. 1998. "Workshop on Social Mobility," Brookings Institution, Washington, D.C., June 4-5.

Birdsall, Nancy, and Juan Luis Londoño. 1997. "Asset Inequality Does Matter: Lessons from Latin America." *American Economic Review* 87 (May): 32–38.

Blondet, Cecilia. 1995. "El movimiento de mujeres en el Perú 1960–1990." In *Perú 1964–1994: Economía, sociedad y política*, edited by Julio Cotler. Lima: Instituto de Estudios Peruanos.

————. 1998. "La emergencia de las mujeres en el poder ¿Hay cambios?" Working paper no. 92, Instituto de Estudios Peruanos, Lima.

————. 1999. "Percepción ciudadana sobre la participación de la mujer: El poder político en la mira de las mujeres." Working paper no. 98, Instituto de Estudios Peruanos, Lima.

Blondet, Cecilia, and Carmen Montero. 1994. "La situación de la mujer en el Perú 1980–1994." Working paper no. 68, Instituto de Estudios Peruanos, Lima.

Boggio, María, Fernando Romero, and Juan Ansión. 1991. *El pueblo es así . . . y también asá*. Lima: Instituto Democracia y Socialismo.

Boloña, Carlos. 1996. "The Viability of Alberto Fujimori's Economic Strategy." In *The Peruvian Economy and Structural Adjustment*, edited by Efraín Gonzáles. Miami: North-South Center Press.

Boloña, Carlos, and Javier Illescas. 1997. *Políticas arancelarias en el Perú, 1980–1997*. Lima: Instituto de Economía de Libre Mercado and Universidad San Ignacio de Loyola.

Bouton, Lawrence, and Mariusz A. Sumlinski. 2000. "Trends in Private Investment in Developing Countries: Statistics for 1970–1998." International Finance Corporation Discussion Paper 41, Washington, D.C.

Bowen, Sally. 2000. *The Fujimori File: Peru and Its President, 1990–2000*. Lima: Peru Monitor.

Bowen, Sally, and Jane Holligan. 2003. *The Imperfect Spy: The Many Lives of Vladimiro Montesinos*. Lima: Peisa.

Boylan, Delia. 2000. "Bureaucratic Design in Comparative Perspective." Paper presented at the Twenty-third Congress of the Latin American Studies Association, Miami, March.

Boza, Beatriz, ed. 2000. *The Role of the State in Competition and Intellectual Property Policy in Latin America*. Lima: INDECOPI-PROMPERU, Universidad del Pacífico.

Burgos, Hernando. 2000. "La inagotable caja China de Fujimori." *Quehacer* 126 (September–October): 18–21.

Burki, Shahid Javed, and Guillermo E. Perry, eds. 1999. *Beyond the Washington Consensus: Institutions Matter*. Washington: World Bank.

Burt, Jo-Marie. 2002. "'*Quien Habla es Terrorista*': Fear and Loathing in Fujimori's Peru." Paper presented at the conference "The Fujimori Legacy and Its Impact on Public Policy," Dante B. Fascell North-South Center and the University of Delaware, March 14.

———. 2004. "State Making Against Democracy: The Case of Fujimori's Peru." In *Politics in the Andes: Identity, Conflict, Reform*, edited by Jo-Marie Burt and Philip Mauceri. Pittsburgh: University of Pittsburgh Press.

Cambio 90. 1990. *Lineamientos del Plan de Gobierno 1990*. Lima: n.p.

Cameron, Maxwell A. 1997. "Political and Economic Origins of Regime Change in Peru: The *Eighteenth Brumaire* of Alberto Fujimori." In *The Peruvian Labyrinth*, edited by Maxwell Cameron and Philip Mauceri. University Park: Pennsylvania State University Press.

———. 1998. "Self-Coups: Peru, Guatemala, Russia." *Journal of Democracy* 9, no. 1:125–39.

Cameron, Maxwell A., and Philip Maurceri, eds. 1997. *The Peruvian Labyrinth: Polity, Society, Economy*. University Park: Pennsylvania State University Press.

Camp, Roderic. 1999. *Politics in Mexico: The Decline of Authoritarianism*. 3d ed. New York: Oxford University Press.

Canel, Eduardo. 1992. "Democratization and the Decline of Urban Social Movements in Uruguay: A Political-Institutional Account." In *The Making of Social Movements in Latin America: Identity, Strategy, and Democracy*, edited by Arturo Escobar and Sonia E. Alvarez. Boulder, Colo.: Westview Press.

Cardoso, Fernando Henrique. 1972. *Estado y sociedad en América Latina*. Buenos Aires: Ediciones Nueva Visión.

Carey, John M. 2003. "Transparency Versus Collective Action: Fujimori's Legacy and the Peruvian Congress. *Comparative Political Studies* 36, no. 9: 983–1006.

Carothers, Thomas. 1991. *In the Name of Democracy: U.S. Policy Toward Latin America in the Reagan Years*. Berkeley and Los Angeles: University of California Press.

———. 2002. "The End of the Transition Paradigm." *Journal of Democracy* 13, no. 1:5–21.

Carrión, Julio, F. 1998. "Partisan Decline and Presidential Popularity: The Politics and Economics of Representation in Peru." In *Deepening Democracy in Latin America*, edited by Kurt von Mettenheim and James Malloy. Pittsburgh: University of Pittsburgh Press.

———. 1999. "La popularidad de Fujimori en tiempos ordinarios, 1993–1997." In *El juego político: Fujimori, la oposición y las reglas*, edited by Fernando Tuesta Soldevilla. Lima: Friedrich Ebert Stiftung.

———. 2000. "La campaña electoral y la opinión pública en el Perú actual." Paper presented at the Twenty-second Latin American Studies Association Congress, Miami, March 16–18.

———. 2001. "Las elecciones Peruanas de 2001: Desmantelando la herencia autoritaria." *Reflección Política* 3, no. 6:107–18.

Centeno, Miguel Angel. 1994. *Democracy Within Reason: Technocratic Revolution in Mexico*. University Park: Pennsylvania State University Press.

——. 1998. "The Failure of Presidential Authoritarianism." In *Politics, Society, and Democracy: Latin America,* edited by Scott Mainwaring and Arturo Valenzuela. Boulder, Colo.: Westview Press.

CEPAL: *See* Comisión Económica para América Latina.

Comisión Económica para América Latina. 2000. *Panorama social de América Latina, 1999–2000.* Santiago: Comisión Económica para América Latina.

——. 2002. *Panorama social de América Latina, 2001–2002.* Santiago: Comisión Económica para América Latina.

Chirinos Soto, Enrique. 1995. *Constitución de 1993: Analisis y comentario.* 2d ed. Lima: Nerman.

Chudnovsky, Daniel. 1997. "Beyond Macroeconomic Stability in Latin America." In *The New Globalism and Developing Countries,* ed. by John H. Dunning and Khalil A. Hamdani. New York: United Nations University Press.

Collier, David, ed. 1979. *The New Authoritarianism in Latin America.* Princeton: Princeton University Press.

Collier, David, and Steve Levitsky. 1997. "Democracy with Adjectives: Conceptual Innovation in Comparative Research." *World Politics* 49 (April): 430–51.

Collier, Ruth Berins. 1999. *Paths Toward Democracy: The Working Class and Elites in Western Europe and South America.* Cambridge, U.K.: Cambridge University Press.

Collier, Ruth Berins, and David Collier. 1991. *Shaping the Political Arena: Critical Junctures, the Labor Movement, and Regime Dynamics in Latin America.* Princeton: Princeton University Press.

Comisión de la Verdad y Reconciliación. 2003. *Informe final.* http://www.cverdad.org.pe/ifinal.

Conaghan, Catherine M. 1995a. "Polls, Political Discourse, and the Public Sphere: The Spin on Peru's Fuji-golpe." In *Latin America in Comparative Perspective: New Approaches to Methods and Analysis,* edited by Peter H. Smith. Boulder, Colo.: Westview Press.

——. 1995b. "Troubled Accounting, Troubling Questions: Looking Back at Peru's Election." *lasa* Forum 26 (Summer): 9–12.

——. 2001. *Making and Unmaking Authoritarian Peru: Re-election, Resistance, and Regime Transition.* North-South Agenda Paper 47. Miami: University of Miami North-South Center.

——. 2002. "Cashing In on Authoritarianism: Media Collusion in Fujimori's Peru." *Harvard International Journal of Press/Politics* 7 (Winter): 115–25.

——. 2005. *Fujimori's Peru: Deception in the Public Sphere.* Pittsburgh: University of Pittsburgh Press.

Conaghan, Catherine M., James Malloy, and Luis Abugattas. 1990. "Business and the 'Boys': The Politics of Neoliberalism in the Central Andes." *Latin American Research Review* 25, no. 2:3–30.

Congreso del Perú. 2004. *En la sala de la corrupción: Videos y audios de Vladimiro Montesinos (1998–2000).* 6 vols. Lima: Fondo Editorial del Congreso.

Cooper, Andrew, and Thomas Legler. 2001. "The OAS in Peru." *Journal of Democracy* 12, no. 4:123–36.

Coordinadora Nacional de Derechos Humanos. 2003. *Dossier Fujimori*. Lima: La Coordinadora Nacional de Derechos Humanos. Available at http://www. cnddhh.org.pe.

Corrales, Javier. 2002. *Presidents without Parties: The Politics of Economic Reform in Argentina and Venezuela in the 1990s*. University Park: Pennsylvania State University Press.

Cotler, Julio. 1978. *Clases, estado y nación en el Perú*. Lima: Instituto de Estudios Peruanos.

———. 1980. *Democracia e integración nacional*. Lima: Instituto de Estudios Peruanos.

———. 1994. "Crisis política, *Outsiders* y autoritarismo plebiscitario: El Fujimorismo." In *Política y sociedad en el Perú: Cambios y continuidades*. Lima: Instituto de Estudios Peruanos.

———. 1995. "Political Parties and the Problems of Democratic Consolidation in Peru." In *Building Democratic Institutions: Party Systems in Latin America*, edited by Scott Mainwaring and Timothy R. Scully. Stanford: Stanford University Press.

Cotler, Julio, and Romeo Grompone. 2000. *El Fujimorismo: Ascenso y caída de un régimen autoritario*. Lima: Instituto de Estudios Peruanos.

Crabtree, John. 1998. "Neopopulism and the Fujimori Phenomenon." In *Fujimori's Peru: The Political Economy*, edited by John Crabtree and Jim Thomas. London: Institute of Latin American Studies, University of London.

———. 2000. "Populisms Old and New: The Peruvian Case." *Bulletin of Latin American Research* 19, no. 2:163–76.

Daeschner, Jeff. 1993. *The War of the End of Democracy: Mario Vargas Llosa Versus Alberto Fujimori*. Lima: Peru Reporting.

Dalton, Russell J., and Martin P. Wattenberg. 2000. "Unthinkable Democracy: Political Change in Advanced Industrial Democracies." In *Parties Without Partisans: Political Change in Advanced Industrial Democracies*, edited by Russell J. Dalton and Martin P. Wattenberg. Oxford: Oxford University Press.

Dammert Ego Aguirre, Manuel. 2001. *Fujimori-Montesinos: El estado mafioso*. Lima: Ediciones El Virrey.

Dancourt, Oscar, Waldo Mendoza, and Leopoldo Vilcapoma. 1997. "Fluctuaciones económicas y shocks externos, Perú 1950–1996." Working paper no. 135, Pontificia Universidad Católica del Perú, Departamento de Economía.

de la Cadena, Marisol. 1999. *Indigenous Mestizos: The Politics of Race and Culture in Cuzco, Peru, 1919–1991*. Durham: Duke University Press.

Dealy, Glen. 1982. "Prologemena on the Spanish American Political Tradition." In *Politics and Social Change in Latin America: The Distinct Tradition*. 2d ed. Edited by Howard Wiarda. Amherst: University of Massachussetts Press.

Degregori, Carlos Iván. 1990. *Ayacucho 1969–1979: El nacimiento de Sendero Luminoso*. Lima: Instituto de Estudios Peruanos.

———. 2000. *La Década de la Antipolítica: Auge y huida de Alberto Fujimori y Vladimiro Montesinos*. Lima: Instituto de Estudios Peruanos.

Degregori, Carlos Iván, José Coronel, and Ponciano del Pino. 1998. "Government, Citizenship and Democracy: A Regional Perspective." In *Fujimori's Peru: The Political Economy*, edited by John Crabtree and Jim Thomas. London: Institute of Latin American Studies, University of London.

Degregori, Carlos Iván, and Romeo Grompone. 1991. *Demonios y Redentores: Una Tragedia en Dos Vueltas*. Lima: Instituto de Estudios Peruanos.

della Porta, Donatella, and Alberto Vannucci. 1999. *Corrupt Exchanges: Actors, Resources, and Mechanisms of Political Corruption*. New York: Aldine De Gruyter.

Di Palma, Giuseppe. 1990. *To Craft Democracies: An Essay on Democratic Transitions*. Berkeley and Los Angeles: University of California Press.

Diamond, Larry. 1999. *Developing Democracy: Toward Consolidation*. Baltimore: Johns Hopkins University Press.

———. 2002. "Thinking About Hybrid Regimes." *Journal of Democracy* 13, no. 2:21–35.

Dietz, Henry. 1980. *Poverty and Problem-Solving Under Military Rule*. Austin: University of Texas Press.

———. 1998. *Urban Poverty, Political Participation, and the State: Lima, 1970–1990*. Pittsburgh: University of Pittsburgh Press.

Dietz, Henry, and Martín Tanaka. 2002. "The Mayor of Lima and the President of Peru: Centralized Authority Versus the Struggle for Autonomy." In *Capital City Politics in Latin America*, edited by David Myers and Henry Dietz. Boulder, Colo.: Lynne Rienner.

Durand, Francisco. 1997. "The Growth and Limitations of the Peruvian Right." In *The Peruvian Labyrinth: Polity, Society, Economy*, edited by Maxwell A. Cameron and Philip Mauceri. University Park: Pennsylvania State University Press.

———. 1998. "Collective Action and the Empowerment of Peruvian Business." In *Organized Business, Economic Change, and Democracy in Latin America*, edited by Francisco Durand and Eduardo Silva. Miami: North-South Center Press.

———. 2002. "Business and the Crisis of Peruvian Democracy." *Business and Politics* 4, no. 3:319–41.

———. 2003. *Riqueza económica y pobreza política: Reflexiones sobre las elites del poder en un país inestable*. Lima: Pontificia Universidad Católica del Perú, Fondo Editorial.

Durand, Francisco, and Rosemary Thorp. 1998. "Tax Reform: The SUNAT Experience." In *Fujimori's Peru: The Political Economy*, edited by John Crabtree and Jim Thomas. London: University of London, Institute of Latin American Studies.

Easterly, William. 2001. *The Elusive Quest for Growth: Economists' Adventures and Misadventures in the Tropics*. Cambridge: M.I.T. Press.

ECLAC: *See* Economic Commission for Latin America and the Caribbean.

Economic Commission for Latin America and the Caribbean. 1994. *Social Panorama of Latin America*. Santiago: Economic Commission for Latin America and the Caribbean.

———. 1997. *The Equity Gap: Latin America, the Caribbean, and the Social*

Summit. Santiago: Economic Commission for Latin America and the Caribbean.

————. 1998. *The Fiscal Covenant.* Santiago: Economic Commission for Latin America and the Caribbean.

Edwards, Sebastian. 1989. *Real Exchange Rates, Devaluation, and Adjustment: Exchange Rate Policy In Developing Countries.* Cambridge, Mass.: MIT Press.

————. 1990. "The Sequencing of Economic Reform." *World Economy* 13, no. 1:1–13.

————. 1995. *Crisis and Reform in Latin America: From Despair to Hope.* New York: Oxford University Press for the World Bank.

Ellner, Steve. 2003. "The Contrasting Variants of the Populism of Hugo Chávez and Alberto Fujimori." *Journal of Latin American Studies* 35:139–62.

Epstein, Leon D. 1980. *Political Parties in Western Democracies.* New Brunswick, N.J.: Transaction Books.

Escobal, Javier, Jaime Saavedra, and Máximo Torero. 1998. "Los activos de los pobres en el Perú." Working paper no. 26, GRADE, Lima.

Evans, Peter. 1989. "Predatory, Development, and Other Apparatuses: A Conceptual Political Economy Perspective on the Third World State." *Sociological Forum* 4, no. 4:561–87.

Ewig, Christina. 2000a. "Democracia diferida: Un análisis del proceso de reformas en el sector salud." In *Políticas sociales en el Perú: Nuevos aportes,* edited by Felipe Portocarrero Suárez. Lima: Universidad del Pacífico.

————. 2000b. "Engineering Development: The Reform of Family Planning in Peru Under Fujimori." Paper presented at the Twenty-first International Congress of the Latin American Studies Association, March 16–18, Miami.

Felch, Jason. 2004. "Letter from Lima: Have Peru's Press Heroes Gone Too Far?" *Columbia Journalism Review* 43, 2 (July–August): 43–47.

Fernández-Arias, Eduardo, and Peter Montiel. 1997. "Reform and Growth in Latin America: All Pain and No Gain?" Working paper no. 351, IDB-OCE, Washington, D.C.

Fernández Segado, Francisco. 1994. "El nuevo ordenamiento constitucional del Perú: Aproximación a la constitución de 1993." In *La Constitución de 1993: Análisis y comentarios I,* edited by Comisión Andina de Juristas. Lima: Comisión Andina de Juristas.

Fish, Steven M. 2001. "The Dynamics of Democratic Erosion." In *Postcommunism and the Theory of Democracy,* edited by Richard Anderson, M. Steven Fish, Stephen E. Hanson, and Philip G. Roeder. Princeton: University of Princeton Press.

Fisher, Louis. 1987. *Politics of Shared Power.* 2d ed. Washington D.C.: Congressional Quarterly.

Foley, Michael, and Bob Edwards. 1996. "The Paradox of Civil Society" *Journal of Democracy* 7, no. 3:38–52.

Fowks, Jacqueline. 2000. *Suma y resta de la realidad: Medios de comunicación y elecciones generales 2000 en el Perú.* Lima: Friedrich Ebert Stiftung.

Fujimori, Alberto. 1991. "Mensaje al país del Presidente Fujimori el 8 de agosto de 1990." *Encuentro* (Lima) 58 (May): 96–97.

————. 1992. *Hacia la reconstrucción nacional: Mensaje a la nación y memoria anual, 2do año de gobierno.* Lima: Secretaría General de la Presidencia.

————. 1994. *4to año de gobierno: Mensaje a la Nación y Memoria Anual.* Lima: Presidencia de la República.

————. 1998. "Speaking Out: President Alberto Fujimori." *Countdown 2005: The Newsletter of the Microcredit Summit Campaign* 2, nos. 2–3. http://www.microcreditsummit.org/newsletter/newsletter5.htm.

Gamarra, Rodolfo. 1995. *Terrorismo: Tratamiento jurídico.* Lima: Instituto de Defensa Legal.

García Calderón, Ernesto. 2001. "Peru's Decade of Living Dangerously." *Journal of Democracy* 12, no. 2:46–58.

Geddes, Barbara. 1994. *Politicians' Dilemma: Building State Capacity in Latin America.* Berkeley and Los Angeles: University of California Press.

Goldman, Robert, León Carlos Arslanian, Ferdinando Imposimato, and José Rafucci. 1993. *International Jurists Commission Report on the Administration of Justice in Peru.* Washington, D.C.: Washington College of Law, American University.

Gonzales de Olarte, Efraín. 1998. *El neoliberalismo a la peruana.* Lima: Instituto de Defensa Legal.

Gonzales de Olarte, Efraín, and Lilian Samamé. 1993. *El pendulo peruano: Política económica, gobernabilidad, y subdesarrollo, 1963–1990.* Lima: Instituto de Estudios Peruanos.

Graciarena, Jorge. 1967. *Poder y clases sociales en el desarrollo de América Latina.* Buenos Aires: Paidós.

Graham, Carol. 1994. *Safety Nets, Politics, and the Poor: Transitions to Market Economies.* Washington, D.C.: Brookings Institution.

Graham, Carol, and Cheikh Kane. 1998. "Opportunistic Government or Sustaining Reform? Electoral Trends and Public-Expenditure Patterns in Peru, 1990–1995." *Latin American Research Review* 33, no. 1:67–104.

Grompone, Romeo. 1998. *Fujimori, neopopulismo y comunicación política.* Working paper no. 93, Instituto de Estudios Peruanos, Lima.

————. 2000. "Al día siguiente: El Fujimorismo como proyecto inconcluso de transformación política y social." In *El Fujimorismo: Ascenso y caída de un régimen autoritario,* edited by Julio Cotler and Romeo Grompone. Lima: Instituto de Estudios Peruanos.

Guillermoprieto, Alma. 1990. "Letter from Lima." *New Yorker,* 29 October, 116–29.

Haggard, Stephan, and Robert Kaufman. 1995. *The Political Economy of Democratic Transitions.* Princeton: Princeton University Press.

Hartlyn, Jonathan. 1998. *The Struggle for Democratic Politics in the Dominican Republic.* Chapel Hill: University of North Carolina.

Helmke, Gretchen, and Steven Levitsky. 2004. "Informal Institutions and Comparative Politics: A Research Agenda." *Perspectives on Politics* 2, no. 4:725–40.

Herrera, Javier. 2002. *La pobreza en el Perú.* Lima: Instituto Nacional de Estadística e Informática and Institut de Recherche pour le Développment.

Htun, Mala N. 1998. "Women's Political Participation, Representation, and

Leadership in Latin America." Women's Leadership Conference of the Americas Issue Brief, Inter-American Dialogue/International Center for Research on Women, Washington, D.C.

Htun, Mala N., and Mark P. Jones. 2002. "Engendering the Right to Participate in Decision-Making: Electoral Quotas and Women's Leadership in Latin America." In *Gender and the Politics of Rights and Democracy in Latin America,* edited by Nikki Craske and Maxine Molyneux. Houndmills, U.K.: Palgrave.

Huntington, Samuel. 1991. *The Third Wave: Democratization in the Late Twentieth Century.* Norman: University of Oklahoma Press.

IDB: *See* Inter-American Development Bank.

Iguíñiz, Javier. 1998. "The Economic Strategy of the Fujimori Government." In *Fujimori's Peru: The Political Economy,* edited by John Crabtree and Jim Thomas. London: University of London, Institute of Latin American Studies.

Iguíñiz, Javier, and I. Muñoz. 1992. *Política económica de industrialización del Perú, 1980–1990.* Lima: Cuadernos Desco.

IMF. *See* International Monetary Fund.

INEI. See Instituto de Estadística e Informática.

Instituto Cuánto. 1990. *Perú en números: Annuario estadístico, 1990.* Lima: Instituto Cuánto.

Instituto de Estadística e Informática. 2001a. *Perú: Compendio Estadístico 2001.* Lima, Instituto de Estadística e Informática.

———. 2001b. *¿Qué Sabemos Sobre el Desempleo en el Perú?* Lima: Instituto de Estadística e Informática.

Inter-American Development Bank. 1997. *Economic and Social Progress in Latin America.* Washington, D.C.: Inter-American Development Bank.

———. 2001a. *Economic Situation and Prospects.* Country Report on Peru. Washington, D.C.: Inter-American Development Bank.

———. 2001b. *Economic and Social Progress in Latin America.* Washington, D.C.: Inter-American Development Bank.

International Monetary Fund. 2001. *International Financial Statistics.* CD-ROM. Washington, D.C.: International Monetary Fund.

Jenkins, Rhys. 1996. "Trade Liberalization and Export Performance in Bolivia." *Development and Change* 27, no. 4:693–716.

JNE. *See* Jurado Nacional de Elecciones.

Jochamowitz, Luis. 1993. *Ciudadano Fujimori.* Lima: Peisa.

Johnson, Kenneth. 1984. *Mexican Democracy: A Critical View.* New York: Praeger.

Jurado Nacional de Elecciones. 1997. *Elecciones municipales: Resultados de las elecciones municipales generales de 1995. Resultados de las elecciones municipales parciales de 1996.* Lima: Jurado Nacional de Elecciones (JNE), Fundación Internacional para Sistemas Electorales (IFES), and Agencia para el Desarrollo Internacional (USAID).

———. 1999. *Elecciones municipales 1998 y complementarias 1999. Resultados generales.* Lima.

Karl, Terry Lynn. 1986. "Imposing Consent? Electoralism vs. Democratization in El Salvador." In *Elections and Democratization in Latin America*, edited by Paul Drake and Eduardo Silva. San Diego: University of California.

Karl, Terry Lynn, and Philippe C. Schmitter. 1991. "Modes of Transition in Latin America, Southern and Eastern Europe." *International Social Science Journal* 128 (May): 269–84.

Kay, Bruce. 1996. "'Fujipopulism' and the Liberal State in Peru, 1990–1995." *Journal of Interamerican Studies and World Affairs* 38, no. 4: 55–98.

Keefer, Philip. 1995. "Reforming the State: The Sustainability and Replicability of Peruvian Reforms in Its Public Administration." World Bank, Washington, D.C. Mimeo.

Kelly, Jana Morgan. 2003. "Counting on the Past or Investing in the Future? Economic and Political Accountability in Fujimori's Peru." *Journal of Politics* 65, no. 3:864–80.

Kenney, Charles. 1996. "Por qué el Autogolpe? Fujimori y el Congreso, 1990–1992." In *Los enigmas del poder: Fujimori 1990–1996*, edited by Fernando Tuesta Soldevilla. Lima: Fundación Friedrich Ebert.

———. 2003. "The Death and Rebirth of a Party System, Peru, 1978–2001." *Comparative Political Studies* 36, no. 10: 1210–39.

———. 2004. *Fujimori's Coup and the Breakdown of Democracy in Latin America*. Notre Dame: University of Notre Dame Press.

Kitschelt, Herbert. 1994. *The Transformation of European Social Democracy*. Cambridge, U.K.: Cambridge University Press.

Klarén, Peter. 2000. *Peru: Society and Nationhood in the Andes*. New York: Oxford University Press.

Kling, Merle. 1956. "Toward a Theory of Power and Political Instability in Latin America." *Western Political Quarterly* 9, no. 1:21–35.

Knight, Alan. 1996. "Corruption in Twentieth Century Mexico." In *Political Corruption in Europe and Latin America*, edited by Walter Little and Eduardo Posada-Carbó. London: Macmillan.

———. 1998. "Populism and Neopopulism in Latin America, Especially Mexico." *Journal of Latin American Studies* 30 (March): 223–48.

Kogan, Liuba. 1999. "¿Llegamos tarde a la fiesta?" *Quehacer* 21 (November–December): 96–99.

Lambert, Jacques. 1967. *Latin America: Social Structures and Political Institutions*. Berkeley and Los Angeles: University of California Press.

Latin American Studies Association. 1995. "The 1995 Electoral Process in Peru: A Delegation Report of the Latin American Studies Association." Latin American Studies Association and the North-South Center, Pittsburgh and Miami, March.

LASA. *See* Latin American Studies Association.

Levitt, Barry Steven. 2001. "Beyond Fraud: The 2000 (and 2001) Elections in Peru." Paper presented at the twenty-third meeting of the Latin American Studies Association, Washington, D.C., September 6–8, n.p.

Levitsky, Steven. 1999. "Fujimori and Post-party Politics in Peru." *Journal of Democracy* 10, no. 3:78–92.

———. 2000. "The "Normalization" of Argentine Politics." *Journal of Democracy* 11, no. 2:56–69.

Levitsky, Steven, and Maxwell A. Cameron. 2003. "Democracy Without Parties? Political Parties and Regime Change in Fujimori's Peru." *Latin American Politics and Society* 45, no. 3:1–33.

Levitsky, Steven, and Lucan A. Way. 2002. "The Rise of Competitive Authoritarianism." *Journal of Democracy* 13, no. 2:51–65.

Lewis, Paul H. 1980. *Paraguay Under Stroessner.* Chapel Hill: University of North Carolina Press.

Linz, Juan J. 1978. *The Breakdown of Democratic Regimes: Crisis, Breakdown, and Reequilibration.* Baltimore: Johns Hopkins University Press.

———. 1994. "Presidential or Parliamentary Democracy: Does It Make a Difference?" In *The Failure of Presidential Democracy: Comparative Perspectives,* edited by Juan J. Linz and Arturo Valenzuela. Baltimore: Johns Hopkins University Press.

———. 2000. *Totalitarian and Authoritarian Regimes.* Boulder, Colo.: Lynne Rienner.

Linz, Juan J., and Alfred Stepan. 1996. *Problems of Democratic Transition and Consolidation: Southern Europe, South America, and Post Communist Europe.* Baltimore: Johns Hopkins University Press.

Loayza Galván, Francisco.1998. *El rostro oscuro del poder.* Lima: San Borja Ediciones.

Londoño, Juan Luis, and Miguel Székely. 1997. "Distributional Surprises After a Decade of Reforms: Latin America in the Nineties." Paper presented at the annual meeting of the Inter-American Development Bank, Barcelona, March.

Loveman, Brian. 1993. *The Constitution of Tyranny: Regimes of Exceptions in Spanish America.* Pittsburgh: University of Pittsburgh Press.

Lowenthal, Abraham F., ed. 1975. *The Peruvian Experiment: Continuity and Change Under Military Rule.* Princeton: Princeton University Press.

Lynch, Nicolás. 1999a. "Neopopulismo: Un concepto vacío." *Socialismo y Participación* 86 (December): 63–81.

———. 1999b. *Una tragedia sin héroes: La derrota de los partidos y el orígen de los independientes en Peru, 1980–1992.* Lima: Fondo Editorial Universidad Nacional Mayor de San Marcos.

———. 2000. "Posibilidades de reconstrucción de un sistema de partidos en el Perú." Paper prepared for presentation at the Latin American Studies Association meeting, Miami, March 16–18.

McClintock, Cynthia. 1993. "Peru's Fujimori: A Caudillo Derails Democracy." *Current History* 92 (March): 112.

———. 1994. "Presidents, Messiahs, and Constitutional Breakdowns in Peru." In *The Failure of Presidential Democracy: Comparative Perspectives,* edited by Juan Linz and Arturo Valenzuela. Baltimore: Johns Hopkins University Press.

———. 1996. "La voluntad política presidencial y la ruptura constitucional de 1992 en el Peru." In *Los enigmas del poder: Fujimori 1990–1996,* edited by Fernando Tuesta Soldevilla. Lima: Fundación Friedrich Ebert.

———. 1998. *Revolutionary Movements in Latin America: El Salvador's* FMNL and Peru's Shining Path. Washington, D.C.: United States Institute of Peace Press.

————. 1999. "¿Es autoritario el gobierno de Fujimori?" In *El juego político: Fujimori, la oposición y las reglas,* edited by Fernando Tuesta Soldevilla. Lima: Friedrich Ebert Stiftung.

————. 2001. "Room for Improvement." *Journal of Democracy* 12, no. 4:137–40.

McClintock, Cynthia, and Abraham F. Lowenthal, eds. 1983. *The Peruvian Experiment Reconsidered.* Princeton: Princeton University Press.

McClintock, Cynthia, and Fabian Vallas. 2003. *The United States and Peru in the 1990s: A Handshake for a Peruvian Caudillo.* New York: Routledge Press.

McDonough, Peter, Samuel Barnes, and Antonio Lopez Pinto. 1998. *The Cultural Dynamics of Democratization in Spain.* Ithaca: Cornell University Press.

McGuire, James. 1997. *Peronism Without Perón.* Stanford: Stanford University Press.

Mainwaring, Scott. 1992. "Transitions to Democracy and Democratic Consolidation: Theoretical and Comparative Issues." In *Issues in Democratic Consolidation: The New South American Democracies in Comparative Perspective,* edited by Scott Mainwaring, Guillermo O'Donnell, and J. Samuel Valenzuela. Notre Dame: University of Notre Dame Press.

Mainwaring, Scott, and Timothy Scully. 1995. "Party Systems in Latin America." In *Building Democratic Institutions: Party Systems in Latin America,* edited by Scott Mainwaring and Timothy Scully. Stanford: Stanford University Press.

Mainwaring, Scott, and Matthew Shugart, eds. 1997. *Presidentialism and Democracy in Latin America.* Cambridge, U.K.: Cambridge University Press.

Mainwaring, Scott, and Matthew Soberg Shugart. 1997. Introduction to *Presidentialism and Democracy in Latin America,* edited by Scott Mainwaring and Matthew S. Shugart. Cambridge, U.K.: Cambridge University Press.

Malloy, James M. 1974. "Authoritarianism, Corporatism, and Mobilization in Peru." In *The New Corporatism: Social-Political Structures in the Iberian World,* edited by Frederick B. Pike and Thomas Stritch. Notre Dame: University of Notre Dame Press.

————, ed. 1977. *Authoritarianism and Corporatism in Latin America.* Pittsburgh: University of Pittsburgh Press.

————. 1987. "The Politics of Transition in Latin America." In *Authoritarians and Democrats: Regime Transition in Latin America,* edited by James M. Malloy and Mitchell A. Seligson. Pittsburgh: University of Pittsburgh Press.

Mancini, Paulo, and David L. Swanson. 1996. "Politics, Media, and Modern Democracy: Introduction." In *Politics, Media, and Modern Democracy: An International Study of Innovations in Electoral Campaigning and Their Consequences,* edited by David L. Swanson and Paulo Mancini. Westport, Conn.: Praeger.

Manrique, Nelson. 1988. *Yawar Mayu: Sociedades terratenientes serranas, 1879–1910.* Lima: Desco.

Manzetti, Luigi. 1999. *Privatization South American Style.* New York: Oxford University Press.

——. 2000. "Market Reforms Without Transparency." In *Combating Political Corruption in Latin America,* edited by Joseph S. Tulchin and Ralph H. Espach. Washington, D.C.: Woodrow Wilson Center Press.

Marcus-Delgado, Jane, and Martín Tanaka. 2001. *Lecciones del final del Fujimorismo.* Lima: Instituto de Estudios Peruanos.

Mauceri, Philip. 1995. "State Reform, Coalitions, and the Neoliberal *Autogolpe* in Peru." *Latin American Research Review* 30, no. 1:7–37.

——. 1996. *State Under Siege: Development and Policy Making In Peru.* Boulder, Colo.: Westview Press.

——. 1997a. "Return of the Caudillo." *Third World Quarterly* 18, no. 5:899–911.

——. 1997b. "The Transition to 'Democracy' and the Failures of Institution Building." In *The Peruvian Labyrinth: Polity, Society, Economy,* edited by Maxwell A. Cameron and Philip Maurceri. University Park: Pennsylvania State University Press.

Middlebrook, Kevin, ed. 1998. *Electoral Observation and Democratic Transitions in Latin America.* La Jolla: Center for U.S.-Mexican Studies, University of California at San Diego.

Ministerio de Relaciones Exteriores del Perú. 1999. *Boletín,* May.

Miranda, Carlos. 1990. *The Stroessner Era: Authoritarian Rule in Paraguay.* Boulder, Colo.: Westview Press.

Mouzelis, Nicos. 1985. "On the Concept of Populism: Populist and Clientelist Modes of Incorporation in Semiperipheral Polities." *Politics and Society* 14 (September): 329–48.

Murakami, Yusuke. 2000. *La democracia según C y D: Un estudio de la conciencia y el comportamiento político de los sectores populares de Lima.* Lima: Instituto de Estudios Peruanos–The Japan Center for Area Studies.

Naím, Moisés. 1994. "Latin America: The Second Stage of Reform." *Journal of Democracy* 5, no. 4:32–48.

Needler, Martin. 1963. *Latin American Politics in Perspective.* Princeton, N.J.: D. Van Nostrand.

Nun, José. 1967. "The Middle Class Military Coup." In *The Politics of Conformity in Latin America,* edited by Claudio Véliz. Oxford: Oxford University Press.

Nuñes, Edson de Oliveira, and Barbara Geddes. 1987. "Dilemmas of State-Led Modernization in Brazil." In *State and Society in Brazil: Continuity and Change,* edited by John D. Wirth, Edson de Oliveira Nuñes, and Thomas E. Bogenschild. Boulder, Colo.: Westview Press.

Nye, Joseph. 1967. "Corruption and Political Development: A Cost-Benefit Analysis." *American Political Science Review* 6 (June): 417–27.

Obando, Enrique. 1996. "Fujimori and the Military: A Marriage of Convenience." *nacla*: Report on the Americas, 30, no. 1:31–36.

O'Donnell, Guillermo. [1973] 1979. *Modernization and Bureaucratic-Authoritarianism. Studies in South American Politics.* Berkeley: Institute of International Studies, University of California.

——. 1994. "Delegative Democracy." *Journal of Democracy* 5, no. 1:55–69.

——. 1996. "Illusions About Consolidation." *Journal of Democracy* 7, no. 4:34–51

————. 1999a. *Counterpoints: Selected Essays on Authoritarianism and Democratization.* Notre Dame: University of Notre Dame Press.

————. 1999b. "Notes for the Study of Processes of Political Democratization in the Wake of the Bureaucratic-Authoritarian State." In *Counterpoints: Selected Essays on Authoritarianism and Democratization.* Notre Dame: University of Notre Dame Press.

O'Donnell, Guillermo, and Philippe C. Schmitter. 1986. *Transitions from Authoritarian Rule: Tentative Conclusions About Uncertain Democracies.* Baltimore: Johns Hopkins Press.

O'Donnell, Guillermo, Philippe C. Schmitter, and Laurence Whitehead, eds. 1986. *Transitions from Authoritarian Rule: Comparative Perspectives.* Baltimore: Johns Hopkins University Press.

Oficina Nacional de Procesos Electorales. 2002. http://www.onpe.gob.pe/.

O'Neill, Kathleen Marie. 1999. "Decentralization in the Andes: Power to the People or Party Politics?" Ph.D. diss., Harvard University.

ONPE: *See* Oficina Nacional de Procesos Electorales.

Ortiz de Zevallos, Gabriel, and Pierina Pollarolo, eds. 2000. *Gobiernos locales.* Lima: Instituto Apoyo.

Ottaway, Marina. 2003. *Democracy Challenged: The Rise of Semi-authoritarianism.* Washington, D.C.: Carnegie Endowment for International Peace.

Oxhorn, Philip. 1994. "Where Did All the Protestors Go? Popular Mobilization and the Transition to Democracy in Chile." *Latin American Perspectives* 21 (Summer): 49–68.

Palmer, David Scott. 1992. "United States–Peru Relations in the 1990s: Asymmetry and Its Consequences." In *Latin America and Caribbean Contemporary Record,* no 9, 1989–90, edited by Eduardo Gamarra and James Malloy. New York: Holmes and Meier.

————. 1994. *The Shining Path of Peru.* 2d ed. New York: St. Martin's Press.

————. 1996. "Fujipopulism and Peru's Progress." *Current History* 95 (January–December): 70.

————. 1998. "Llegando al "Sí" en la disputa Perú-Ecuador." *La República* (Lima), June 7, 16–17.

————. 2000. "Democracy and Its Discontents in Fujimori's Peru." *Current History* 99, no. 634:60–65.

————. 2001. "Overcoming the Weight of History: 'Getting to Yes' in the Peru-Ecuador Border Dispute." *Diplomacy and Statecraft* 12, no. 2:29–46.

————. 2004. "Opportunities Lost or Opportunities Squandered? United States–Latin American Relations During the Clinton Years." Paper presented at the Twenty-fifth International Congress of the Latin American Studies Association, Las Vegas, October 7–9.

Paniagua, Valentín. 1995. "Acusación constitucional, antejuicio o juicio político?" In *Comisión Andina de Juristas, Constitución de 1993: Analisis y comentarios II.* Lima: CAJ.

Paredes, Carlos E. 1991. "Epilogue: In the Aftermath of Hyperinflation." In *Peru's Path to Recovery: A Plan for Economic Stabilization and Growth,* edited by Carlos E. Paredes and Jeffrey D. Sachs. Washington, D.C.: Brookings Institution.

Paredes, Martín. 2000. "Hijos de La medianoche." *Quehacer* 127 (November–December): 65–69.

Parodi, Carlos. 2000. *Peru, 1960–2000: Políticas económicas y sociales en entornos cambiantes.* Lima: Universidad del Pacífico.

Parodi, Jorge. 1993. "Los pobladores, la ciudad y la política: Un estudio de actitudes." In *Los pobres, la ciudad, y la política,* edited by Jorge Parodi. Lima: Centro de Estudios de Democracia y Sociedad.

Pastor, Manuel, and Carol Wise. 2003. "A Long View on Mexico's Political Economy: What's Changed? What Are the Challenges?" In *Mexican Politics and Society in Transition,* edited by Andrew Selee and Joseph Tulchin. Boulder, Colo.: Lynne Rienner Press.

Pease García, Henry. 1999. *Electores, partidos y representantes: Sistema electoral, sistema de partidos y sistema de gobierno en el Perú.* Lima: Departamento de Ciencias Sociales de la Pontificia Universidad Católica del Perú.

———. 2003. *La autocracia Fujimorista: Del estado intervencionista al estado mafioso.* Lima: Fondo Editorial de la Pontificia Universidad Católica del Perú-Fondo de Cultura Económica.

Planas, Pedro. 1999. *El Fujimorato: Estudio politico constitucional.* Lima: n.p.

———. 2000. *La democracia volátil: Movimientos, partidos, lideres políticos y conductas electorales en el Perú contemporáneo.* Lima: Friedrich Ebert Stiftung.

Plasser, Fritz, Peter Ulram, and Harald Waldrauch, eds. 1998. *Democratic Consolidation in East-Central Europe.* New York: St. Martin's Press.

PNUD-Peru: *See* Programa de las Naciones Unidas para el Desarrollo–Oficina del Perú.

Pocock, J. G. A. 1975. *The Machiavellian Moment: Florentine Political Thought and the Atlantic Republican Tradition.* Princeton: University of Princeton Press.

Poole, Keith, and Steven Daniels. 1985. "Ideology, Party, and Voting in the US Congress, 1959–1983." *American Political Science Review* 79 (June): 373–99.

Portes, Alejandro, and Kelly Hoffman. 2003. "Latin American Class Structures: Their Composition and Change During the Neoliberal Era." *Latin American Research Review* 38, no. 1:41–82.

Portocarrero, Felipe, ed. 2000. *Políticas sociales en el Perú: Nuevos aportes.* Lima: Red para el Desarrollo de las Ciencias Sociales en el Perú.

Programa de las Naciones Unidas para el Desarrollo–Oficina del Perú. 2002. *Informe sobre el desarrollo humano, Perú 2002: Aprovechando las potencialidades.* Lima: Programa de las Naciones Unidas para el Desarrollo.

Przeworski, Adam. 1986. "Some Problems in the Study of the Transition to Democracy." In *Transitions from Authoritarian Rule: Comparative Perspectives,* edited by Guillermo O'Donnell, Philippe C. Schmitter, and Laurence Whitehead. Baltimore: Johns Hopkins University Press.

———. 1991. *Democracy and the Market: Political and Economic Reforms in Eastern Europe and Latin America.* Cambridge, U.K.: Cambridge University Press.

———. 1999. "On the Design of the State: A Principle Agent Perspective." In

Reforming the State: Managerial Public Administration in Latin America, edited by Luiz Carlos Bresser Pereira and Peter Spink. Boulder, Colo.: Lynne Rienner.

Przeworski, Adam, Michael Alvarez, José Antonio Cheibub, and Fernando Limongi. 2000. *Democracy and Development: Political Institutions and Well-Being in the World, 1950–1990.* Cambridge, U.K.: Cambridge University Press.

Quijano, Aníbal. 1998. "Populismo y Fujimorismo." In *El fantasma del populismo: Aproximación a un tema (siempre) actual,* edited by Felipe Burbano de Lara. Caracas: Editorial Nueva Sociedad.

Ranis, Gustav, and Frances Stewart. 2001. "Growth and Human Development: Comparative Latin American Experience." Center Discussion Paper no. 826, Yale University, Economic Growth Center.

Remmer, Karen. 2003. "Elections and Economics in Contemporary Latin America." In *Post-stabilization Politics in Latin America: Competition, Transition, Collapse,* edited by Carol Wise and Riordan Roett. Washington, D.C.: Brookings Institution.

Reynolds, Andrew. 1999. "Women in the Legislatures and Executives of the World: Knocking at the Highest Glass Ceiling." *World Politics* 51, no. 4:547–72.

Roberts, Kenneth M. 1995. "Neoliberalism and the Transformation of Populism in Latin America: The Peruvian Case." *World Politics* 48 (October): 82–116.

———. 1998. *Deepening Democracy? The Modern Left and Social Movements in Chile and Peru.* Stanford: Stanford University Press.

———. 2003. "Populist Mobilization and Political Organization in Latin America: Historical and Contemporary Variations." Paper presented at the twenty-fourth annual meeting of the Latin American Studies Association, Dallas, March 27–29.

Roberts, Kenneth M., and Moisés Arce. 1998. "Neoliberalism and Lower-Class Voting Behavior in Peru." *Comparative Political Studies* 31, no. 2:217–46.

Rospigliosi, Fernando. 1992. "Las elecciones peruanas de 1990." In *Una tarea inconclusa,* edited by Instituto Interamericano de Derechos Humanos. San José, Costa Rica: Instituto Interamericano de Derechos Humanos.

———. 1994. "Democracy's Bleak Prospects." In *Peru in Crisis: Dictatorship or Democracy?* edited by Joseph S. Tulchin and Gary Bland. Boulder, Colo.: Lynne Rienner.

———. 2000. *Montesinos y las fuerzas armadas.* Lima: Instituto de Estudios Peruanos.

Rustow, Dankwart A. 1970. "Transitions to Democracy: Toward a Dynamic Model." *Comparative Politics* 2, no. 3:337–63.

Saavedra, Jaime. 1997a. "Liberalización comercial e industria manufacturera en el Perú." Lima: Consorcio de Investigación Económica, Investigaciones Breves, 2.

———. 1997b. "Quienes ganan y quienes pierdan con una reforma estructural: Cambios en la dispersión de ingresos según educación, experiencia y genero en el Perú urbano." Working paper no. 24, GRADE, Lima.

———. 2002. "Empleo en el Perú: Situación actual y perspectivas." Report presented to the GRADE-IDB seminar "Los Mercados Laborales en el Perú y en el Area Andina," Lima, July.

Sabatini, Chris. 2001. "The Emergence and Growth of Single Issue ('Quality of Politics') Parties in Latin America." Paper presented at the annual meeting of the American Political Science Association, San Francisco, August.

Salcedo, José María. 1995. *Terremoto: ¿Por qué ganó Fujimori?* Lima: Editorial Brasa.

Sartori, Giovanni. 1976. *Parties and Party Systems: A Framework for Analysis.* Cambridge, U.K.: Cambridge University Press.

Schady, Norbert R. 2000. "The Political Economy of Expenditures by the Peruvian Social Fund (FONCODES), 1991–95." *American Political Science Review* 94, no. 2:289–304.

Schedler, Andreas. 2002. "The Menu of Manipulation." *Journal of Democracy* 13, no. 2:36–50.

Schelling, Thomas. 1960. *The Strategy of Conflict.* London: Oxford University Press.

Schmidt, Gregory D. 1998. "Presidential Usurpation or Congressional Preference?" In *Executive Decree Authority,* edited by John Carey and Matthew Shugart. Cambridge, U.K.: Cambridge University Press.

———. 1999. "Crónica de una reelección." In *El juego político: Fujimori, la oposición y las reglas,* edited by Fernando Tuesta Soldevilla. Lima: Friedrich Ebert Stiftung.

———. 2000. "Delegative Democracy in Peru? Fujimori's 1995 Landslide and the Prospects for 2000." *Journal of Interamerican and World Affairs* 42, no. 1:99–132.

———. 2002. "Dale Uno a la Mujer: Preference Voting and Gender Quotas in Peru." Paper prepared for the annual meeting of the American Political Science Association, Boston, August 30.

———. 2003. "Ineffective but Successful: The Paradox of Gender Quotas in Lima's Municipal Elections." Paper prepared for the annual meeting of the American Political Science Association, Philadelphia, August 28.

Schmidt, Gregory D., and Saunders, Kyle L. 2004. "Effective Quotas, Relative Party Magnitude, and the Success of Female Candidates: Peruvian Municipal Elections in Comparative Perspective." *Comparative Political Studies* 37 (August): 704–34.

Schmitter, Philippe C. 1974. "Still the Century of Corporatism." In *The New Corporatism: Social-Political Structures in the Iberian World,* edited by Frederick B. Pike and Thomas Stritch. Notre Dame: University of Notre Dame Press.

Scott, James C. 1976. *The Moral Economy of the Peasant: Rebellion and Subsistence in Southeast Asia.* New Haven: Yale University Press.

Sheahan, John. 1997. *Patterns of Development in Latin America: Poverty, Repression, and Economic Strategy.* Princeton: Princeton University Press.

———. 1999. *Searching for a Better Society: The Peruvian Economy from 1950.* University Park: Pennsylvania State University Press.

———. 2002. "Alternative Models of Capitalism in Latin America." In *Models of Capitalism: Lessons for Latin America,* edited by Evelyne Huber. University Park: Pennsylvania University State Press.

Sheahan, John, and Enrique Iglesias. 1998. "Kinds and Causes of Inequality in Latin America." In *Beyond Trade-offs: Market Reforms and Equitable Growth in Latin America,* edited by Nancy Birdsall, Carol Graham, and Richard Sabot. Washington, D.C.: Brookings Institution and Inter-American Development Bank.

St. John, Ronald Bruce. 1999. *La política exterior del Perú.* Lima: Asociación de Funcionarios del Servicio Diplomático del Perú.

Stallings, Barbara, and Wilson Peres. 2000. *Growth, Employment, and Equity: The Impact of Economic Reforms in Latin America and the Caribbean.* Santiago: Economic Commission for Latin America and the Caribbean.

Stern, Steve, ed. 1998. *Shining and Other Paths: War and Society in Peru, 1980–1995.* Durham: Duke University Press.

Stokes, Susan. 1996a. "Economic Reform and Public Opinion in Peru, 1990–1995." *Comparative Political Studies.* 29, no. 5:544–65.

———. 1996b. "Peru: The Rupture of Democratic Rule." In *Constructing Democratic Governance,* edited by Jorge Domínguez and Abraham Lowenthal. Baltimore: Johns Hopkins University Press.

———. 2001. *Mandates and Democracy: Neoliberalism by Surprise in Latin America.* New York: Cambridge University Press.

Stokes, William S. 1952. "Violence as a Power Factor in Latin American Politics." *Western Political Quarterly* 5, no. 3:445–68.

Tanaka, Martín. 1998. *Los espejismos de la democracia: El colapso de un sistema de partidos en el Perú, 1980–1995, en perspectiva comparada.* Lima: Instituto de Estudios Peruanos.

———. 1999. "Los partidos políticos en el Perú, 1992–1999: Estatalidad, sobrevivencia y política mediática." Working paper no. 108. Lima: Instituto de Estudios Peruanos.

———. 2003. "The Political Constraints on Market Reform in Peru." In *Poststabilization Politics in Latin America: Competition, Transition, Collapse,* edited by Carol Wise and Riordan Roett. Washington, D.C.: Brookings Institution Press.

Teichman, Judith. 2001. *The Politics of Freeing Markets in Latin America: Chile, Argentina, and Mexico.* Chapel Hill: University of North Carolina Press.

Tello, Mario. 1990. *Exportaciones y crecimiento económico en el Perú, 1950–1987.* Lima: Fundación Frederich Ebert.

Toche, Eduardo. 1998. "La emergencia permanente." *Quehacer* 113 (May–June): 30–34.

Tovar, Teresa. 1985. *Velasquismo y Movimiento Popular.* Lima: Desco.

Transparencia. 1995. "Informe del conteo rapido y la observación electoral de las elecciones generales de 1995." Lima: Transparencia.

———. 2000. *Datos electorales,* no. 93. Lima. Available at http://www.transparencia.org.pe/elecciones2000/datos/datos29.pdf.

Tuesta Soldevilla, Fernando. 1994. *Perú político en cifras: Elite política y elecciones,* 2d ed. Lima: Fundación Friedrich Ebert.

———, ed. 1996a. *Los enigmas del poder: Fujimori 1990–1996.* Lima: Fundación Friedrich Ebert.

————. 1996b. *Simposio sobre reforma electoral*. Lima: IFES.

————. 2001. *Perú político en cifras, 1821–2001*.3d ed. Lima: Friedrich Ebert Stiftung.

UNDP: *See* United Nations Development Program.

Unit for the Promotion of Democracy. 1997. "Executive Summary: Electoral Observation, Peru, 1995." Organization of American States, Washington, D.C.

United Nations Development Program. 2001. *Human Development Report*. New York: Oxford University Press.

————. 2003. *Human Development Report*. New York: Oxford University Press.

U.S. Department of State. 1995. *Country Report on Human Rights Practices [Peru]*. Washington, D.C.: U.S. Department of State.

U.S. Department of State, Summit Coordinating Office. 1996. "Summit of the Americas: Implementation of the Summit Plan of Action," Report prepared for the U.S. Department of State, Washington, D.C., March 29.

Valenzuela, Samuel J. 1992. "Democratic Consolidation in Post-transitional Settings: Notion, Process, and Facilitating Conditions." In *Issues in Democratic Consolidation: The New South American Democracies in Comparative Perspective*, edited by Scott Mainwaring, Guillermo O'Donnell, and J. Samuel Valenzuela. Notre Dame: University of Notre Dame Press.

Vargas Llosa, Mario, and Alberto Fujimori. 1990. *El debate*. Lima: Centro de Investigación. Universidad del Pacífico.

Velarde, Julio, and Martha Rodríguez. 2001. "Efectos de la crisis financiera internacional en la economía peruana 1997–1998." Working paper no. 36, Universidad del Pacífico y Consorcio de Investigación Económica y Social, Lima.

Verdera, Francisco. 1994. "El mercado de trabajo en Lima metropolitana: Estructura y evolución, 1970–1990." Working paper no. 59, Instituto de Estudios Peruanos, Lima.

Vial, Joaquín, and Jeffrey Sachs. 2000. "Andean Competitiveness at a Glance." Paper prepared for the annual conference "Trade and Investment in the Americas," Washington, D.C., September 8.

Villanueva Flores, Rocío. 1998. "¿Están justificadas las cuotas de mujeres en las listas electorales?" In *Poder político con perfume de mujer: Las cuotas en el Perú*, edited by Ana María Yañez and Lisbeth Guillén. Lima: Movimiento Manuela Ramos and Instituto de Estudios Peruanos.

Walter, Knut. 1993. *The Regime of Anastasio Somoza, 1936–1956*. Chapel Hill: University of North Carolina.

Webb, Richard. 1991. Prologue to *Peru's Path to Recovery: A Plan for Economic Stabilization and Growth*, edited by Carlos E. Paredes and Jeffrey D. Sachs. Washington, D.C.: Brookings Institution.

————. 2000. "Pilot Survey on Household Perceptions of Mobility: Peru, 1998." In *New Markets, New Opportunities*, edited by Nancy Birdsall and Carol Graham. Washington, D.C.: Brookings Institution.

Webb, Richard, and Graciela Fernández Baca. 1999. *Perú en números*. Lima: Cuánto.

———. 2000. *Perú en números*. Lima: Cuánto.

———. 2002. *Perú en números*. Lima: Cuánto.

Weber, Max. 1976. *Wirtschaft und Gesellschaft*. 5th ed. Tübingen, Germany: J. C. B. Mohr.

Werlich, David. 1978. *Peru: A Short History*. Carbondale: Southern Illinois University Press.

Weyland, Kurt. 1996. "Neopopulism and Neoliberalism in Latin America: Unexpected Affinities." *Studies in International Comparative Development* 31, no. 3 :3–31.

———. 1998a. "The Politics of Corruption in Latin America." *Journal of Democracy* 9, no. 2:108–21.

———. 1998b. "Swallowing the Bitter Pill." *Comparative Political Studies* 31, no. 5: 539–68.

———. 2000. "A Paradox of Success? Determinants of Political Support for President Fujimori." *International Studies Quarterly* 44, no. 3:481–502.

———. 2001. "Clarifying a Contested Concept: Populism in the Study of Latin American Politics." *Comparative Politics* 34, no. 1:1–22.

———. 2002. *The Politics of Market Reform in Fragile Democracies*. Princeton: Princeton University Press.

———. 2003. "Neopopulism and Neoliberalism in Latin America: How Much Affinity?" *Third World Quarterly* 24, no. 6:1095–115.

Wiarda, Howard J. 1973. "Toward a Framework for the Study of Political Change in the Iberic-Latin Tradition: The Corporative Model." *World Politics* 25, no. 2:206–35.

Wiener, Raúl R. 2001. *Bandido Fujimori: El reelectionista, 2da edición*. Lima: n.p.

Williamson, John, ed. 1990. *Latin American Adjustment: How Much Has Happened?* Washington, D.C.: Institute for International Economics.

Wise, Carol. 1999. "Latin America Trade Strategy at Century's End." *Business and Politics* 2:117-153.

———. 2003a. "Latin American Politics in the Era of Market Reform." Introduction to *Post-stabilization Politics in Latin America: Competition, Transition, Collapse*, edited by Carol Wise and Riordan Roett. Washington, D.C.: Brookings Institution.

———. 2003b. *Reinventing the State: Economic Strategy and Economic Change in Peru*. Ann Arbor: University of Michigan Press.

WLCA. See Women's Leadership Conference of the Americas.

Women's Leadership Conference of the Americas. 2001. *Women and Power in the Americas: A Report Card*. Washington, D.C.: Inter-American Dialogue and International Center for Research on Women.

World Bank. 1993a. *Social Indicators of Development, 1993*. Baltimore: Johns Hopkins University Press.

———. 1993b. *World Development Report*. New York: World Bank and Oxford University Press.

———. 1996. *World Development Report*. New York: World Bank and Oxford University Press.

———. 1999. *Poverty and Social Developments in Peru, 1994–97*. Washington, D.C.: World Bank.

———. 2000. *World Tables of Economic and Social Indicators.* CD-ROM. Washington, D.C.: World Bank.

———. 2001a. *World Development Indicators.* CD-ROM. Washington, D.C.: World Bank.

———. 2001b. *World Development Report, 2002: Building Institutions for Markets.* Washington, D.C.: World Bank.

———. 2001c. *World Tables of Economic and Social Indicators.* CD-ROM. Washington, D.C.: World Bank.

———. 2002. *World Development Indicators, 2002.* CD-ROM. Washington, D.C.: World Bank.

Yamada, Gustavo. 1996. "Urban Informal Employment and Self-Employment in Developing Countries: Theory and Evidence." *Economic Development and Cultural Change* 44, no. 2:289–314.

Yáñez, Ana María, and Lisbeth Guillén, eds. 1998. *Poder político con perfume de mujer: Las cuotas en el Perú.* Lima: Movimiento Manuela Ramos and Instituto de Estudios Peruanos.

Yáñez, Ana María and Guillén, Lisbeth. 2001. "Sección especial: Elecciones 2001." *El Cuarto Femenino,* no. 10 (April): 16-23.

Youngers, Coletta. 2000a. "Deconstructing Democracy: Peru Under President Alberto Fujimori." Washington D.C.: Washington Office on Latin America.

———. 2000b. "Fujimori's Relentless Pursuit of Re-election." *nacla* Report on the Americas 33, no. 4:6–10.

———. 2003. *Violencia política y sociedad civil en el Perú: Historia de la Coordinadora Nacional de Derechos Humanos.* Lima: Instituto de Estudios Peruanos.

APPENDIX: PERU, 1990–2000: A BASIC CHRONOLOGY

1990

April 8	General elections are held. No candidate wins a majority of the vote and therefore a runoff election becomes necessary between the two top vote getters, the world-famous novelist Mario Vargas Llosa and the relatively unknown Alberto Fujimori.
June 10	Alberto Fujimori wins the runoff election with 62 percent of the vote.
July 28	Alberto Fujimori is sworn in as president.
August 8	Juan Carlos Hurtado Miller, minister of economy and finance as well as the president of the Council of Ministers, announces a dramatic plan for economic restructuring. The inflation rate will reach 7,650 percent by the end of the year, but falls dramatically in subsequent years.

1991

February 15	Carlos Boloña is appointed minister of economy and finance.
August 14	The Fondo Nacional de Compensación y Desarrollo Social (Compensation and Social Development Fund [FONCODES]) is created. This fund would later play a significant role in Fujimori's efforts to buy political support among the poor.
October 2	Congress votes to indict former president Alan García Pérez on corruption charges.
November 3	An army death squad known as Grupo Colina (Colina Group) kills fifteen people in the Barrios Altos neighborhood in Lima.

1992

April 5	Fujimori announces the dissolution of Congress, the Supreme Court, and the Tribunal of Constitutional Guarantees and suspends the 1979 constitution.
July 18	Grupo Colina strikes again. This time the victims are nine students and one faculty member from the Universidad Nacional de Educación, Enrique Guzmán y Valle, most commonly known as La Cantuta university.
July 21	By decree (Decreto Ley No. 25635), the Fujimori regime creates the Sistema de Inteligencia Nacional (National Intelligence System [SIN]). According to this decree, the SIN's budget and its supporting documents are classified as "secret." Fujimori's

right-hand man, Vladimiro Montesinos, although formally an "advisor," becomes the real head of the newly created SIN.

September 12   Abimael Guzmán Reynoso, leader of the Shining Path (Sendero Luminoso), is captured. In subsequent days, the police will also capture other prominent leaders of this guerrilla group.

November 13   General Jaime Salinas Sedó leads a failed coup attempt to depose Fujimori and arguably return the country to the 1979 constitution.

November 22   Elections for the Congreso Constituyente Democrático (Constitutional Democratic Congress [CCD]) are held. The pro-Fujimori alliance wins forty-four out of eighty seats in the new congress.

1993

January 29   Ricardo Belmont, an independent candidate, wins reelection as Lima's mayor with 45 percent of the vote. With the exception of Tacna's, no candidate of Fujimori's electoral vehicle Cambio 90 is successful in winning a single provincial mayoralty.

October 31   The referendum to ratify a new constitution is held. Amid accusations of vote irregularities and fraud, the yes vote wins with only 52 percent of the vote.

December 30   Fujimori enacts Legislative Decree No. 776. The decree strips municipalities of their authority to collect certain taxes. Mayors complain that municipal revenues will be reduced by 79 percent.

1994

February 28   The state-owned phone and telecommunications company (ENTEL/CPT) is sold to Telefónica of Spain for approximately US$1.4 billion.

1995

January 9   Border clashes between Peruvian and Ecuadorian troops in Cenepa River are reported. The conflict will escalate in subsequent days to include air clashes. A cease-fire accord is signed on February 17 in Brazil.

April 9   President Fujimori secures reelection with 64 percent of the vote.

June 14   Congress approves a blanket amnesty law (Ley de Amnistía General no. 26479) for military personnel accused of human rights violations. The amnesty also includes those who were involved in the November 13, 1992, coup attempt against Fujimori.

November 12   Alberto Andrade, founder of the recently created independent movement Somos Lima, is elected mayor of Lima with 52 percent of the vote.

1996

April 18 Law 26592 is enacted. According to the new legislation—which modifies a 1994 law—referendum initiatives require the approval of at least forty-eight members of the unicameral congress. No such proviso existed in the original law. The new requirement seeks to defeat a citizen initiative that calls for a referendum to rule on Fujimori's ability to run for reelection in 2000.

August 23 Congress passes the so-called Ley de Interpretación Auténtica de la Constitución (Law of Authentic Interpretation of the Constitution). This law declares Fujimori's second term to be his first, thus enabling him to run for reelection in 2000.

December 17 An MRTA (Movimiento Revolucionario Tupac Amaru) command seizes the Japanese embassy, taking more than five hundred hostages.

1997

January 3 Three members of the Constitutional Tribunal (TC) rules that the Law of Authentic Interpretation is inapplicable to President Fujimori.

April 2 Operation Chavín de Huantar—releasing hostages from the Japanese embassy—is completed successfully.

May 29 Congress impeaches and removes the three members of the TC who had ruled that the Law of Authentic Interpretation was not applicable to President Fujimori. As a result of this removal, the president of the TC resigns. The TC becomes inoperative for all practical purposes.

August 13 The government rescinds the nationality of Baruch Ivcher, owner of Canal 2–Frecuencia Latina, which had made explosive revelations regarding human rights violations. Ivcher becomes ineligible to own a media outlet. The Winter brothers, minority stockholders but supporters of the regime, gain control of the channel.

1998

January 16 The Supreme Court rules in favor of Congresswoman Martha Chávez's complaint against the TC's ruling declaring that the Law of Authentic Interpretation was inapplicable to Fujimori. This Supreme Court ruling opens the way for Fujimori's second reelection.

October 13 Alberto Andrade is reelected mayor of Lima, with 59 percent of the vote. He becomes the main opposition leader. He will go on to run for the presidency in 2000.

1999

July 8 Peru withdraws from the Inter-American Human Rights Court. The argument provided by the regime was that it could not accept the court's ruling demanding another trial for four Chilean citizens accused of treason. Opposition leaders claim that the regime's real intention is to preempt a legal challenge to the constitutionality of Fujimori's second reelection.

2000

February 28	The newspaper *El Comercio* reports that Fujimori's new electoral vehicle for the 2000 elections, Perú 2000, has been registered with more than 1 million fraudulent signatures.
April 9	General elections are held. Fujimori fails to win 50 percent of the vote and is thus forced to face Alejandro Toledo, the opposition's leader, in a runoff election.
May 22	Toledo announces his decision not to run in the scheduled runoff because of the severe flaws of the process.
July 28	Fujimori is sworn in for his third five-year term. Toledo leads the huge Marcha de los Cuatro Suyos rally.
September 14	A video is leaked showing elected opposition congressman Alberto Kouri being bribed by Montesinos to switch parties. A political storm ensues.
September 16	Fujimori announces the dissolution of the SIN and calls for new elections to be held in 2001. He declares his intention to not run in these elections.
September 23	Fujimori orders a US$15 million "severance payment" for Montesinos. Soon thereafter, Montesinos goes into exile in Panama.
October 23	In a surprising move, Montesinos returns to Peru. Six days later, he leaves Peru again. He will be finally captured in Caracas, Venezuela, on June 24, 2001.
November 13	Congress censures Martha Hildebrandt, the pro-Fujimori president of Congress.
November 20	Fujimori faxes his resignation from Tokyo, Japan.
November 21	Congress declares the presidency "vacant" because of Fujimori's "moral incapacity."

LIST OF CONTRIBUTORS

Robert Barr is an Assistant Professor of Political Science at the University of Mary Washington. He received his Ph.D. in political science from the University of Texas at Austin. Professor Barr has published numerous articles on populism and the politics of decentralization in Latin America. His current research concerns the sources and implications of contemporary political dissent.

Maxwell A. Cameron is Professor of Political Science at the University of British Columbia, Canada. He holds a Ph.D. from the University of California at Berkeley and specializes in comparative politics (Latin American) and international political economy. He authored *Democracy and Authoritarianism in Peru* and coedited *The Making of Nafta: How the Deal Was Done,* as well as many other books on similar subjects. Professor Cameron has published articles on democracy, trade liberalization, debt bargaining, and development. He is currently writing a book on democracies lacking checks and balances as manifested in Peru, Guatemala, Venezuela, and Russia.

Julio F. Carrión is an Associate Professor of Political Science and International Relations at the University of Delaware. He holds a Ph.D. from the University of Pittsburgh. Professor Carrión's work focuses on the analysis of public opinion in Latin America. His research has been published in edited books as well as in *Comparative Political Studies* and other journals. He is currently working on a book project dealing with issues of public opinion and governability in the Central Andes.

Catherine M. Conaghan is Professor of Political Studies at Queen's University, Canada. She received her Ph.D. from Yale University and specializes in Andean politics. Her books include *Restructuring Domination: Industrialists and the State in Ecuador* and *Unsettling Statecraft: Democracy and Neoliberalism in the Central Andes.* Her most recent book, *Fujimori's Peru: Deception in the Public Sphere,* provides an extensive account of the Fujimori presidency.

Henry Dietz is Professor of Government at the University of Texas at Austin. Professor Dietz's holds a Ph.D. from Stanford University, and his major areas of interest include Latin American politics, third-world urban politics, poverty and politics, comparative methodology, and survey research. He is the author or coauthor of many books, including *Urban Poverty, Political Participation, and the State: Lima, Peru, 1970–1990.* He is currently conducting research on the impact of socioeconomic inequality on democratic consolidation in Latin America.

Philip Mauceri is Professor in the Department of Political Science at the University of Northern Iowa. He holds a Ph.D. from Columbia University, and his research interests include constitutional reform, presidential politics, ethnic conflict, and state-elite relations in the Andean region. Among his publications are *Militares, insurgencia y democratizacion en el Peru, 1980–88* and *State Under Siege: Policy Making and Development in Peru.* He is also the coauthor of *Politics in the Andes: Identity, Conflict, and Reform,* among other books.

Cynthia McClintock is Professor of Political Science and International Affairs at George Washington University. A foremost authority on Peruvian politics, Professor McClintock has authored and edited many books, including *Revolutionary Movements in Latin America: El Salvador's* FMLN *and Peru's Shining Path.* Professor McClintock was president of the Latin American Studies Association in 1994 and 1995. She was also a member of the American Political Science Association Council from 1998 to 2000.

David Scott Palmer is Professor of Political Science and International Relations at Boston University. He received his Ph.D. from Cornell University and specializes in the analysis of U.S.–Latin America relations. He served at the Foreign Service Institute of the U.S. State Department as Chair for Latin American and Caribbean Studies and as a Dean of the School of Area Studies. Professor Palmer has published many scholarly articles on Latin America and Peru. His many books include *The Shining Path of Peru.*

Kenneth M. Roberts is Professor of Government at Cornell University. He holds a Ph.D. from Stanford University and researches comparative politics with a focus on Latin America. He is the author of *Deepening Democracy? The Modern Left and Social Movements in Chile and Peru* and has published widely in the *American Political Science Review, Comparative Politics, Comparative Political Studies, World Politics,* and *International Security.*

Gregory D. Schmidt is Professor of Political Science at Northern Illinois University. Since receiving his Ph.D. from Cornell University in 1984, Professor Schmidt has published extensively on Peruvian politics and institutions. He has contributed chapters to various books and has published *Donors and Decentralization in Developing Countries* along with numerous articles in *Comparative Politics, Comparative Political Studies, Studies in Comparative International Development,* and the *Journal of Inter-american Studies and World Affairs.*

John Sheahan is Professor Emeritus of Economics at Williams College. He holds a Ph.D. in economics from Harvard University. He was an economic analyst with the Marshall Plan, Paris, from 1951 to 1954, a teacher at Williams College from 1954 to 1994, and a visiting professor at El Colegio de México from 1969 to 1970. His main research interests include international trade and development, with a concentration on Latin American development issues. He is the author of many books, including *Searching for a Better Society: The Peruvian Economy from 1950.*

Kurt Weyland is Professor of Political Science at the University of Texas at Austin. He received his Ph.D. from Stanford University. He was a Fellow at the Woodrow Wilson Center in 1999 and 2000 and a Visiting Fellow at the Kellogg Institute for International Studies, University of Notre Dame. His publications include *The Politics of Market Reform in Fragile Democracies: Argentina, Brazil, Peru, and Venezuela* as well as articles dealing with social policy, neoliberal reform, and populism in Latin America.

Carol Wise is an Associate Professor of Political Science at University of Southern California. Having received her Ph.D. from Columbia University, Professor Wise researches political economy issues as they relate to the development process in Latin America. She has written on trade integration, exchange rate politics, and the political economy of state reform in the region. Most of her research efforts within Latin America focus on Argentina, Mexico, and Peru. She is the author of *Reinventing the State: Economic Strategy and Institutional Change in Peru,* among numerous publications.

INDEX

Acción Popular (AP), 67, 84, 101 n. 9; *auto-golpe* and, 246; defectors from, 87; Fujimori regime and, 94; Vargas Llosa candidacy and, 88
accountability, culture of, 43, 59, 83, 92
Adams, Alvin, 234, 236
Aken foundation, 108
Albania, 304
Albright, Madeleine, 237, 259
Alianza Popular Revolucionaria Americana (APRA), 20, 35, 77, 79 n. 2; *autogolpe* and, 246; demise of party system and, 84; Fujimori legacy and, 315; García election victory (2001) and, 99, 100; history of, 84; Lima's mayoral elections and, 67; market reforms and, 130; restoration of democracy and, 91; as "strong" party, 43; "Vladivideo" and, 277; women in, 152, 161
Aliyev, Ilham, 304
Aljovín, Cayetana, 159
Aljovín, Miguel, 116
Alliance for Progress, 294
Alvarado, Fausto, 104
American Popular Revolutionary Alliance. *See* Alianza Popular Revolucionaria Americana (APRA)
Americas Watch, 233
AMPE (national association of Peruvian mayors), 71
Andean Community, 201, 213, 224
Andean Initiative, 227, 232
Andrade Carmona, Alberto, 33, 61–62, 85, 90, 161, 308; as "defector," 87; as opposition front-runner, 255; as threat to Fujimori's power base, 68, 73–76; as victim of electoral fraud, 256
Andrés Pérez, Carlos, 14, 64, 204
antejuicio, 48
Antiterrorism Law, 134
Apenkai foundation, 108
Arana, Ana María, 155

Argentina, 14, 17, 31, 201; constitutional reform in, 32; economic growth in, 186, 224; gender-equity legislation in, 166, 167; Gross Domestic Product (GDP), 203; macroeconomic indicators in, 202; neoliberalism in, 192, 193; political parties, 32; populism in, 16; subnational government in, 78–79
Armenia, 304
Aronson, Bernard, 231, 310
Aritomi, Víctor, 108
Asia-Pacific Economic Cooperation (APEC), 155
authoritarianism, 2–5, 12, 45–46, 60, 165, 206; antistatist statism, 207–9; elections under, 10–11; legitimizing of, 304; Peru's history of, 44; progressive policies and, 9; public opinion and, 148; statist development strategies and, 205; women's social progress and, 171, 172. *See also* electoral authoritarianism (EA)
autogolpe (autocoup), 2, 18, 24, 36; aftermath of, 245–48; congressional resistance and, 94; criminal conspiracy and, 103; female cabinet members and, 153; foreign aid to Peru and, 79 n. 4; Fujimori's popularity and, 127, 129; international community and, 109, 146; judiciary and, 48; justification for, 113; political parties and, 315; *ropa donada* (donated clothes) scandal and, 156; U.S.–Peruvian relations and, 231, 246
Azerbaijan, 304

Banco Central de Reserva del Perú (BCRP), 203
Banco de la Micro-Empresa (MIBANCO), 158, 159
Banco Wiese, 110
Bank of the Nation, 70, 71
banks, 9, 110, 179; economic structural change and, 185; "greed rings" and, 106–7; nationalization of, 44, 53, 57,

banks (*continued*)
  87–88. *See also* Inter-American Development Bank (IDB); World Bank
Barr, Robert, 8, 304
Barrantes, Alfonso, 67, 87, 100–101 n. 5
Barrera, Germán, 275–76
Barreto, Mariella, 162, 244
Barrios Altos, massacre of, 275, 291 n. 19
Beijing conference (U.N. World Conference on Women), 158, 166, 176 n. 52
Belarus, military aircraft from, 105
Belaúnde Terry, Fernando, 44, 46, 67; Acción Popular party and, 84, 101 n. 9; approval ratings, 128; executive power and, 308; legislative authority and, 48; local autonomy and, 51; mayors of Lima and, 66; political parties and, 53; U.S.– Peruvian relations and, 230
Bello, Gen. Elesván, 268, 281
Belmont Casinelli, Ricardo, 61–62, 67, 308; as "populist outsider," 88, 89; as threat to Fujimori's power base, 68–73
Berisha, Sali, 304
Bertini, Enrique, 110
Bolivia, 188, 192, 194, 217, 298
Boloña, Carlos, 21, 22, 56, 120; appointment of, 135; economic strategy and, 198; Montesinos and, 281, 284, 285; "Vladivideo" and, 268
Boza, Beatriz, 159, 162, 174 n. 22
Bozzo, Laura, 164
Brady Plan, 227, 229, 233
Brazil, 14, 16, 188, 194; economic growth in, 186, 189; Gross Domestic Product (GDP), 203; macroeconomic indicators in, 202; market reforms in, 211; military rule in, 296, 297; value-added exports, 222, 224
Bresani, Augusto, 109–10
bribery, 31, 34, 103, 111, 270, 286; of media owners, 58; videotaped, 11–12, 277
Briones Dávila, Gen. Juan, 105, 115
Bucaram, Abdalá, 14
bureaucracy, 209
Bush, George H. W., administration of, 231
Bush, George W., administration of, 229
business community, 10, 56, 130, 198
Bustamante, Alberto, 268, 279
Bustamante, José Luis, 80 n. 6

Cabanillas, Mercedes, 152, 161
Cable Canal de Noticias, 110

caciques (strongmen), 51
Caja Militar, 105
Calmell del Solar, Eduardo, 110, 268, 281
Cambio 90 (C90), 50, 53, 74; after fall of Fujimori, 89; corruption and, 111, 114–15; Fujimori's relations with, 93–94; majority in Congress and, 248; Nueva Mayoría in congressional bloc with, 32, 94, 97, 131, 249; women in, 153, 169
Cameron, Maxwell, 11–12, 306, 313
Camet, Jorge, 106, 115, 284, 285
Canada, 257
Canale, Lilliana, 155
Cantuta case, 135, 149 n. 11, 175 n. 45, 247
capitalism, 297, 314
Cárdenas, Lázaro, 16
Cardoso, Fernando Henrique, 297
Caretas (newsmagazine), 3, 117
Carey, John M., 94, 101 n. 14
Carrera, Elsa, 158
Carrión, Julio F., 68, 242, 243, 283, 293 n. 51
Carter Center, 257, 258, 262
Castañeda Lossio, Luis, 33, 67, 75, 90; as "defector," 87; as opposition front-runner, 255; as victim of electoral fraud, 256
Castillo, Jorge del, 67
Castillo Castillo, Víctor Raúl, 268, 280
Catholic Church, 169–70
caudillos, 43, 95
Cedras, Raoul, 229
Central America, 295
Central Intelligence Agency (CIA), 237, 239, 273, 292 n. 34
CEPAL (Comisión Económica para América Latina y el Caribe), 187, 188–89
Cerro de Pasco Mining, 230
Chamber of Deputies, 81
charisma, 13, 14, 17, 18; of Fujimori, 21; neopopulism and, 64; opportune issues and, 35; political parties and, 52, 84
Chávez, Hugo, 4, 14, 38 n. 1; authoritarianism and, 295; as classic populist, 79 n. 2; popularity ratings, 17; subnational government and, 79
Chávez, Martha, 111, 115, 117, 165, 285; as advisor on privatization, 153; corruption and, 155, 158, 176 n. 60; as president of Congress, 157–58
Chávez Peñaherrera, Demetrio, 115

"checks and balances," 46–52
Chile, 168, 201; economic growth in, 186,
   189, 219, 220, 224; Gross Domestic
   Product (GDP), 203; macroeconomic indicators in, 202; market reforms in, 206,
   211, 217; OAS meeting in Santiago, 232;
   trade liberalization in, 192, 194–95;
   value-added exports, 222, 224
China, 276
Chinese-Peruvians, 54
cholos, 258
Christian Democratic Party, 4
churches, 57, 90
Cipriani, Bishop Luis, 115
citizenship, 43
civil liberties, 40, 45, 162, 300, 303
civil society, 11, 33, 37, 82, 89, 297; democracy and, 34, 42; downfall of Fujimori and, 99; electoral authoritarianism
   and, 299; feminists and, 165; Fujimori
   legacy and, 314–16; personalistic cliques
   and, 93; political parties and, 85; presidential power and, 39; referendum on
   2000 reelection, 142–43; weakening of,
   43, 57–59, 165, 305, 306–8
class differences, 52–53, 75, 118; Fujimori's
   popularity and, 129–30; market reforms
   and, 141, 142; privatization policies and,
   138–39; votes for Fujimori and, 145
clientelism, 7, 8, 72, 103, 297; as obstacle
   to democratization, 59; oppositional social mobilization and, 99
Clinton, William Jefferson, administration
   of, 228–29, 232–35, 258
Colán, Blanca Nélida, 115, 121, 153, 165,
   281; arrest of, 116; "Vladivideo" and,
   269
Cold War, 22, 227
Collor de Mello, Fernando, 14, 18, 64, 89,
   302, 304
Colombia, 106, 122; economic growth in,
   189; FARC guerrillas in, 237, 238, 239,
   292 n. 34; trade liberalization in, 192;
   U.S. policy toward, 229
Comercio, El (newspaper), 130, 158, 258
Comisión de Promoción de la Inversión Privada (COPRI), 56, 215
Comisión Ejecutiva del Poder Judicial (Executive Judiciary Commission), 110
Committee on Women, 170
communists, 84, 134

Conaghan, Catherine, 8–9, 54, 251,
   285–86
Confederación Nacional de Instituciones
   Empresariales Privadas (CONFIEP), 207
Conferencia Anual de Ejecutivos (CADE),
   207
Congreso Constituyente Democrático
   (CCD), 155, 157, 247, 248
Congress, Peruvian, 1, 21, 24, 104; autogolpe and, 2, 245; "checks and balances"
   and, 46–48; closure of, 2, 69, 113, 295;
   Constitutional Tribunal and, 49; culture
   of cover-up and, 116; explanation for
   corruption and, 118–19; Fujimori electoral vehicles and, 93–95; Fujimori majority in, 31, 33, 236, 248; institutional
   autonomy of, 91; Lima's representation
   in, 70; "midnight" laws enacted, 3; neopopulism and, 22; political parties and,
   84; presidential power and, 44, 45–46,
   308; public opinion and, 128; seats
   bought in, 36; veto and, 46–47; "Vladi-
   deo" and, 279–80; women in, 9, 150,
   152, 154, 161, 165–66, 172
Consejo Transitorio de Administración Regional (CTAR), 51
conspiracy, 4
Constituent Assembly, 24, 45, 69, 94
constitution (1979): "checks and balances"
   and, 47, 48; election of local officials and,
   66; presidential power and, 44; regionalization and, 51; suspension of, 2, 46
constitution (1993), 3, 36; ban on multiple
   reelections, 97, 109; "checks and balances" and, 46, 47; executive power and,
   233; FONCODES and, 217; Law of Authentic Interpretation and, 142; laws benefiting women and, 171; plebiscite and,
   45, 69; Senate abolished by, 24; unicameral legislature and, 32, 46
Constitutional Tribunal, 33, 46, 49, 97,
   236, 271; corruption and, 112; Law of
   Authentic Interpretation and, 251; Montesinos and, 280–81
Contrapunto (news program), 276
Contraloría General de la República (National Comptroller's Office), 51
corporations, multinational, 55, 56
corporatism, 43, 297, 298
corruption, 7, 10, 48, 58, 312; in Brazil, 18;
   clearing remains of, 120–22; as constitutive feature of Fujimori regime, 103; cul-

corruption (*continued*)
ture of cover-up, 113–17; defined, 104–5, 123 n. 7; drug trafficking and, 49; explanation for, 117–20; Fujimori legacy and, 316–17; Fujimori regime's collapse and, 31, 77; "greed rings," 105–9; of journalists, 119; judicial powers and, 49; neopopulism and, 65; of political class, 16; political motivation for, 109–13; of political parties, 88; videotaped, 102

Costa Rica, 169, 183–84; economic growth in, 185, 186, 189, 194; poverty level in, 188; trade liberalization in, 192, 194

Cotler, Julio, 83

coup plotters, 4

cover-up, culture of, 113–17

Crousillat, José Fransisco, 109, 269, 276, 281

Cuba, 167, 230, 294

Cuculiza, Luisa María, 159, 165, 269, 281

currency, value of, 10

Dammert Ego Aguirre, Manuel, 279

death squads, 121, 244, 247

debts, external, 210

decentralization, reversal of, 51–52

Decree Number 25475, 134

Decree 776, 71–72, 73

defector model, 8, 87, 95

"delegative democracy" (DD), 3–5, 6, 45, 288, 300; defined, 13; electoral authoritarianism (EA) and, 301–3; military regimes in contrast to, 295. *See also* democracy

Delgado Aparicio, Luis, 280

Delgado Parker, Manuel, 269, 281

della Porta, Donatella, 120

Dellepiane, José, 49

demagoguery, 171

democracy, 2, 31, 162; "checks and balances," 24, 40–41; civil society and, 57; "delegative," 3–5, 6, 13, 45, 288; electoral authoritarianism and, 242, 253, 255, 299–301; executive power and, 39–40; formal appearance of, 3, 65, 68, 98, 147; plebiscitary dimension of, 147; populism and, 32; promises to restore, 22; regional commitment to, 317–18; restoration of, 34, 44, 91, 210; Santiago Resolution of OAS and, 232; separation of powers, 40–41; subversion of, 6; suspension of, 32; theorists of, 40; transitions to, 79, 84, 98, 224, 289–90, 294–99; U.S.–Peruvian relations and, 235–38. *See also* "delegative democracy" (DD)

Democratic Forum, 251–52

democratization, 7, 52, 59, 299

deregulation, 204

Diamond, Larry, 243

Díaz Velarde, Patricia, 161

Dietz, Henry, 8, 304

Dominican Republic, 254

drug trafficking, 5, 9, 10, 23, 107, 207; Andean Initiative and, 227; in Colombia, 229; by executive branch officials, 48; judicial powers and, 49, 280–81; military and, 114; Peru as "narcostate," 105; U.S.–Latin American relations and, 229; U.S.–Peruvian relations and, 233, 234

due process, 40, 50

Dufour Martinez, Oscar, 269

Duhalde, Eduardo, 32

Durand, Francisco, 106, 284, 285

Duthurburu, Luis, 105

Easterly, William, 197

economy, 103, 118, 223–25; basic structural conditions, 180–82; crisis situation and, 44, 57, 59, 86; Fujimori legacy and, 219–23; growth and structural change, 182–86; informal, 63, 66; liberalization of, 7, 9–10, 56, 178–80, 191–95; paradoxes of recovery, 205–9; poverty and economic growth, 186–88; renewed economic problems, 27–28; structural reforms launched, 211–17. *See also* hyperinflation; market reforms; neoliberalism

Ecuador, 4, 14, 122, 193, 247; economic growth in, 186, 189; hostilities with Peru, 234, 235, 236, 238; poverty level in, 188

educational system, 9, 70, 132, 200; economic growth and, 181; quality of, 195–96; women and, 151

election (1995), 3, 10, 26, 65, 218; counterinsurgency laws and, 248–50; extension of social benefits and, 19; fraud and, 250, 265 n. 25; Fujimori's landslide reelection, 15, 27, 94, 142, 306

election (2000), 9, 11, 19, 33, 98; corruption/fraud and, 58–59, 68, 102, 120, 145; Fujimori's challengers, 74–75; Fujimori's preparation for, 96; public opin-

ion and, 142–46, 286; regime
classification and, 243, 244, 253–55
elections, 79–80 n. 6, 296; 1990 election,
20, 65, 87; "preferential votes," 168–69,
174 n. 25, 249; 2001 election, 77, 88, 89;
U.S.–Peruvian relations and, 258
electoral authoritarianism (EA), 242–45,
255, 288, 289; defined, 299–301; "delegative democracy" (DD) and, 301–4; limits of, 311–13; presidential power and,
309; rise to power in Peru, 305–11
El Niño, 30
El Salvador Peace Accords, 227–28
employment issues, 25, 29; economic
growth and, 178, 181, 197; Fujimori's
approval ratings and, 132; jobs creation,
221; privatization and, 138; trade liberalization and, 193; underemployment, 18.
See also unemployment
Enterprise for the Americas Initiative, 227
environment, degradation of, 66
European countries, 22, 85
exchange rates, 10, 194, 197, 200 n. 2, 209
executive power, 40–45, 209, 308–9
exports, 10, 179, 181; economic growth led
by, 211; foreign exchange and, 184, 185;
mining, 182; raw materials, 218; value-
added, 222
Expreso (daily), 58, 110, 130, 268

federalism, 41
Federalist Papers (Madison), 40, 41
Federicci, María Luisa, 155
Feinberg, Richard, 232
feminism, 151–52, 157, 165, 170, 172. *See
also* women
Fernandini, Anita, 152
Fiscalía de la Nación (Office of Judicial
Oversight), 104, 281
Fish, Steven M., 3, 308
Flores Nano, Lourdes, 87, 161, 166–67,
170, 173
Fondo de Compensación Municipal (FON-
COMUN), 52, 71, 72
Fondo Metropolitano de Inversión (INVER-
MET), 72
Fondo Nacional de Compensación y Desar-
rollo Social (FONCODES), 26, 50, 54, 75,
217
Fondo Nacional de Vivienda (National
Housing Fund [FONAVI]), 50

foreign direct investment (FDI), 211, 226 n.
5
Foreign Investment Promotion Act (1991),
216
France, 230
Frecuencia Latina (TV channel), 109, 276
Freedom House, 242, 245, 253, 263 n. 2
Frente Democrático (FREDEMO), 89, 307
Frente Independiente Moralizador (FIM),
269, 273, 276, 277, 293 n. 48
Frente Independiente Perú 2000, 53, 255,
256, 258, 266 n. 48; creation of, 96; election signatures scandal and, 281, 282
Frente País Solidario (FREPASO), 32
frontpersons, 8, 87–88
Fujimori, Alberto (A.F.), 39, 59–60, 92,
204, 214; approval ratings, 22, 23, 69,
76, 126–28, 129, 131–33, 211, 293 n.
51; authoritarian project of, 2–5, 126,
127; criminal charges against, 121, 123
n. 6; culture of cover-up and, 113–14,
116–17; decline in popularity of, 27–28;
democracy and, 22; economic legacy of,
219–23; electoral authoritarianism and,
305–11; electoral vehicles created by, 50,
53, 74, 93–96, 131; exile in Japan, 1, 76,
104, 122; flight from Peru, 34, 107, 153,
169, 283; Fujimori–Montesinos alliance,
34, 112, 124–25 n. 41, 270, 272–75,
279, 282–83; "greed rings" and, 107–9;
hypocrisy of, 121; international community and, 261; judiciary and, 48; marital
breakup of, 155–57, 163–64; mass support for, 128–35; mayors of Lima and, 8,
61–79; neopopulism and, 16, 18–21, 23–
24, 29–31, 302; paradox of success and,
28, 29; party system and, 52–54, 77, 80
n. 25; political predominance established
by, 21–23; popularity of, 9, 11, 19, 68,
83, 271, 283, 309; reelection campaign,
24–27; Shining Path insurrection and,
19, 21; U.S.–Peruvian relations and,
231–32, 233–39; "Vladivideo" and, 269,
278–79; vote-buying tactics, 143–44
Fujimori, Keiko Sofía (daughter of A.F.),
156, 278
Fujimori, Rosa (sister of A.F.), 108, 114,
156
Fujimori, Santiago (brother of A.F.), 55,
156
Fujimori regime: antiterrorism measures,
22, 131; arbitrary power of, 120; author-

Fujimori regime (*continued*)
  itarian tradition and, 45; classification of,
  242–43, 245, 252–53; collapse of, 1, 11,
  31, 33–36, 102, 121, 239–40; criminal
  investigations of, 8, 104–5; economic restructuring program, 135; executive bureaucracy, 50; legacy of, 313–18;
  partisan void under, 92–99; political
  scandals and, 83; regionalization and,
  51–52; technocrats and, 56–57; "Vladivideo" and, 268–90, 289; women and,
  150–73
Fujimorismo, 2, 9, 88, 90; authoritarianism
  of, 98; culture of cover-up and, 113;
  democratic accountability and, 92, 95;
  feminine face of, 152, 165; "Vladivideo"
  and, 278; without Fujimori, 93

García Pérez, Alan, 22, 32, 75, 79 n. 2; approval ratings, 17–18, 128; *autogolpe*
  and, 246; bank nationalization scheme,
  44, 53, 57, 87–88; Congress and, 44, 46;
  corruption charges against, 93, 113, 124
  n. 24, 316; covert support for Fujimori,
  90, 100; credit expansion under, 182;
  economic stagnation under, 211, 213; executive power and, 308; legislative authority and, 48; Lima's mayoral elections
  and, 67; local autonomy and, 51; neopopulism and, 35, 303–4; personalistic
  leadership of, 100; political parties and,
  53, 90–91; resurrected political fortune
  of, 99; taxation under, 196; in 2001 election, 77; U.S.–Peruvian relations and,
  230–31, 234; "Vladivideo" and, 269;
  women in government of, 152
Gaviria, César, 237, 250, 261
Geddes, Barbara, 55
"geishas," 164, 175 n. 39
gender equity, 9, 158, 166
Germany, 79 n. 4
Glass of Milk (Vaso de Leche) program, 50,
  52, 58, 72, 73
Goldenberg, Sonia, 162
governance, 7, 64, 92
"greed rings," 8, 54, 115, 117, 310
Grupo Colina (Colina Group), 121, 123 n.
  6, 247–48, 275
Grupo Especial de Inteligencia (GEIN), 234
Guatemala, 229, 247, 289
guerrilla insurgency, 14–15, 18, 25, 30, 59;
  authoritarian response to, 44–45; in Co-

lombia, 106, 229; Fujimori's popular
  support and, 127, 128; hostage situation
  in Lima, 116; military abuses and,
  134–35; "New Left" and, 84; political
  parties and, 86; receding threat of, 97,
  131, 133. *See also* Movimiento Revolucionario Tupac Amaru (MRTA); Revolutionary Armed Forces of Colombia
  (FARC); Shining Path (Sendero Luminoso)
Gutierrez, Lucio, 4
Gutiérrez, Pablo, 69
Guzmán Reynoso, Abimael, 131, 160, 234

Haiti, 229, 254, 289
Hamilton, John, 237, 239, 257, 261
hard-liners, 289–90, 298
Haya de la Torre, Víctor Raúl, 16, 84
health, public, 132, 133
Helfer, Gloria, 153
Herminia Drago, María, 155
Hermoza, Carlos, 115
Hermoza Ríos, Gen. Nicolás de Bari, 105,
  106, 115, 121, 285
Higa, Alejandro Afuso, 54
Higaonna, Carmen, 153
Higuchi, Susana (wife of A.F.), 54, 108,
  123 n. 14, 164; construction company
  owned by, 166; imprisoned by intelligence service, 124 n. 29, 156; marital
  breakup with Fujimori, 155–57; *ropa donada* scandal and, 114, 157
Hildebrandt, César, 80 n. 22, 269, 273
Hildebrandt, Martha, 158, 166, 167
Hokama, Daniel, 54
human development and resources, 179,
  180, 199
human rights, 3, 48; amnesty law for military officers and, 49–50, 95, 135; campaign to extradite Fujimori, 122; civil
  society and, 57; Fujimori's approval ratings and, 132; García regime and, 93; intelligence agency and violations of, 288;
  military campaigns against guerrillas
  and, 134–35, 233, 236; public opinion
  and, 127, 146; U.S. government monitoring of, 257; U.S.–Peruvian relations and,
  232–33; women in human rights movement, 162
Hurtado Miller, Juan Carlos, 74
hyperinflation, 14, 18, 19, 21, 25, 30, 97,
  118; annual rate of, 131; crisis situation

and, 201, 305; defeat of, 92, 131, 160; economic measures to combat, 135, 202, 209; fiscal shock treatment and, 214; political parties and, 86. *See also* inflation

Ibárcena, Adm. Antonio, 269, 281
Iberico, Luis, 276
illiteracy, 71, 188, 295
impeachment, 48
imports, 184
income growth, 142
indigenous population, 35, 43
industrialization, 297
infant mortality, 72
inflation, 10, 69, 126; economic growth and, 178; exchange rate and, 197; Fujimori's approval ratings and, 131–33. *See also* hyperinflation
infrastructure, 50, 66, 70, 217
institutionalization, 17, 18, 34, 62; corruption and, 103, 104; Fujimori regime's collapse and, 34; of neopopulism, 36; rejection of, 37, 95, 98
Instituto Cuánto, 187
Instituto Nacional de Infraestructura Educativa y de Salud (National Educational and Health Infrastructure [INFES]), 26, 75
insurrection. *See* guerrilla insurgency
intelligence services, 93, 96, 116, 162, 244. *See also* Servicio de Inteligencia Nacional (SIN)
Inter-American Development Bank (IDB), 120, 136, 192, 199, 210
interest groups, 29, 30
international community, 4–5, 6, 122, 130; *autogolpe* and, 109, 246; decomposition of Fujimori regime and, 289; election monitoring by, 256–57; elections under authoritarian regimes and, 10–11; Fujimori's legitimacy as president and, 244, 262; Fujimori's popular support and, 146–47; permissiveness of, 310–11
International Financial Institutions (IFIs), 232, 233, 234
International Monetary Fund (IMF), 136, 210, 216
International Petroleum Company (IPC), 230
investments, foreign, 230
Italy, 119
Ivcher, Baruch, 58, 236, 252, 269, 276

Izquierda Unida (IU), 84, 85, 87, 100–101 n. 5, 307; *autogolpe* and, 246; women in, 152

Japan, 22, 96, 107; charitable donations of clothes from, 114, 156; electoral observation funds provided by, 257; Fujimori's exile in, 1, 104, 122, 201
Japanese-Peruvians, 54, 153, 284
Jett, Dennis, 234, 236, 239
journalists, 3, 58, 114, 162, 244, 271. *See also* media
Journal of Democracy, 242, 243
Joy Way, Victor, 54, 106, 285; corruption of journalists and, 119; criminal conviction of, 121; "greed rings" and, 115; Montesinos and, 281; "Vladivideo" and, 269, 276
judiciary, 1, 22, 45–46, 271; "checks and balances" and, 48–50; corruption of, 3, 110–11, 316; crimes of Fujimori regime and, 104; dismissed by Fujimori, 2, 113; electoral authoritarianism and, 300; "greed rings" and, 9; Montesinos and, 273, 280–81; separation of powers and, 40; women in, 153, 162
Jurado de Elecciones (JNE), 2, 3, 97, 110; corruption and, 112; Higuchi banned from political candidacy, 114, 157; Montesinos and, 272, 281

Keefer, Philip, 208
Kennedy, John F., administration of, 230
Kobashigawa, Víctor, 54
Kouri, Alberto, 117, 119, 275, 276, 279, 280; bribed to defect from Perú Posible, 269; as "emblematic" corrupted figure, 277
Kouri, Alex, 74, 120
Kuchma, Leonid, 304

Labor Code, 58
labor markets, 194, 210
labor movements, 85
land reform, 143–44, 294
La Rosa Bustamante, Leonor, 162, 175 n. 45, 244
Latin America, 39, 196, 254; classical populism in, 36; corruption in, 118, 122; democracy in, 2, 4, 5, 103, 294–99, 317–18; economic growth in, 178, 180, 183, 186; gender-equity legislation in,

Latin America (*continued*)
167, 172; "lost decade," 6; market reforms in, 127, 135, 205, 218; military governments in, 296–98; neopopulist leadership in, 14; political parties in, 84; relations with United States, 227–30; technocrats in, 55–57. *See also specific countries*
Lauer, Mirko, 71
law, rule of, 96, 243, 263, 275
Law for Protection from Family Violence, 170
Law of Authentic Interpretation, 142, 251, 281
legislation, targeted, 7
legislative power, 40–41
Levitsky, Steven, 242, 300
Liberación (newspaper), 117
Lima, 27, 28, 161; gender quotas in, 168, 169; hostage rescue mission in, 116; importance of, 65–66; political parties in, 43, 67; public opinion polls in, 137–38, 139, 149 n. 4; squatters on outskirts of, 143–44
Lima, mayors of, 5, 8, 33, 54, 66–68, 308; Fujimori and, 68–80; neopopulism and, 61–62; populist outsiders as, 88
Lima stock exchange, 216
Linz, Juan, 254, 298
Luna, Ricardo, 235

Macher, Sofía, 162
McCaffrey, Gen. Barry, 125 n. 41, 236, 237, 239, 259
McClintock, Cynthia, 3, 11, 301
Madison, James, 40, 41
Magallanes, Ana Cecilia, 162
Mahuad, Jamil, 122, 235
Malco Villanueva, Gen. Víctor, 105
Manzetti, Luigi, 118
Maoism, 84, 134
Marcenaro, Ricardo, 95
Marcha de las Cuatro Suyos (March of the Four Suyos), 146, 277, 287, 315
Marchand, Luis, 232
Marcona Mining Company, 230
Mariátegui, José Carlos, 84
market reforms, 9, 23, 127, 217–19; business-military coalition and, 206–7; executive power and, 209–11; Fujimori legacy and, 313–14; inequality and, 223; neopopulism and, 302; popular economic demands and, 25–26; public opinion and, 127, 135–42, 146; social class and, 130; timing and sequence of, 205. *See also* economy; neoliberalism; privatization
mass support, 16, 37, 61, 63, 64
Mauceri, Philip, 8, 24, 306
media, 8, 82, 252; *autogolpe* aftermath and, 245–46; civil society and, 57; corruption of, 1, 109–10, 118, 256; demise of party system and, 86; demobilization of civil society and, 58; electoral publicity, 74–75; "greed rings" and, 9; harassment of, 2–3; scrutiny of corruption scandals, 117. *See also* journalists; television
Menem, Carlos, 14, 17, 63; constraints on power of, 31–32; economic policies, 204; market reforms and, 208; neopopulism and, 302, 304; popularity of, 130; subnational government and, 78–79
Merino, Beatriz, 170–71, 173
Merino, Rafael, 274
Mexico, 16, 60 n. 2, 122, 183–84, 201; economic growth in, 185, 186, 189, 194, 224; electoral authoritarianism (EA) in, 300; Gross Domestic Product (GDP), 203; macroeconomic indicators in, 202; market reforms in, 192, 206, 211, 217; value-added exports, 222, 224
middle class, 31, 37, 129; in Argentina, 130; corruption and, 118; feminists from, 165; Lima's mayoral elections and, 69; market reforms and, 142, 314; military regimes and, 297; privatization policies and, 139; votes for Fujimori, 145. *See also* class differences
"midnight" laws, 3
military, Peruvian: authoritarian rule and, 44; *autogolpe* and, 248; civilian control over, 34; coalition with business class, 10, 206–7; corruption scams involving, 105, 111; "countercoup" of, 247; drug trafficking scandals and, 114; emergency powers against insurgency and, 44–45; Fujimori backed by, 23; "greed rings" and, 9; "Green Book" plan of, 207, 274; human rights violations by, 3, 134–35; Montesinos and, 34, 55, 274–75, 278, 281, 286; personalistic regimes and, 93; in power, 66, 84, 294, 298; repression by, 14; return to civilian rule and, 204;

United States' assistance to, 230; weakening of civil society and, 57; women in, 159

Minaya, Greta, 162

Ministry for the Promotion of Women and Human Development (PROMUDEH), 158, 159, 164, 165

Ministry of Defense, 110, 111, 274

Ministry of Economy and Finance (MEF), 52, 71, 106, 203, 284

Ministry of the Interior, 111

Ministry of the Presidency, 26, 50, 51, 80 n. 23; corruption and, 107; Glass of Milk program and, 52; as slush fund, 219; social programs and, 271, 315; women at head of, 155; Yoshiyama as director, 54

Miyagusuku, Augusto, 116

Mohme, Gustavo, 244

money laundering, 105–6

Montes de Oca, Alipio, 269, 280

Montesinos, Vladimiro, 3, 5–6, 32, 93, 220, 306; arrest of, 96, 104; bribery and, 31, 89; C90-NM and, 94; challenge to Fujimori's authority, 15; criminal charges against, 104, 112, 123 n. 12; culture of cover-up and, 115–17; drug trafficking and, 49, 106, 115, 281, 288; elections and, 256, 261; exile in Panama, 237; first lady and, 156; flight from Peru, 1; Fujimori-Montesinos alliance, 34, 112, 124–25 n. 41, 270, 272–75, 279, 282–83; "greed rings" and, 8, 105; Grupo Colina and, 248; lack of checks on power of, 95, 120; Lima's mayors and, 74; personalistic network of Fujimori and, 55; politically motivated corruption and, 109–12; prison sentence, 121; Swiss bank accounts of, 106–7; television channels and, 236; testimony about corruption, 102, 103, 112, 117; U.S.–Peruvian relations and, 236, 237, 238, 239; weakness of political parties and, 98; women in Fujimori regime and, 153, 159, 174 n. 22. See also "Vladivideos" (Montesino videotapes)

Movimiento Revolucionario Tupac Amaru (MRTA), 30, 133, 134, 234–35, 238. See also guerrilla insurgency

Mugabe, Robert, 304

Mulder, Mauricio, 104

Municipal Compensation Fund. See Fondo de Compensación Municipal (FONCOMUN)

municipalities, 8, 51–52, 71, 75

Muñoz Arce, Rómulo, 114, 269, 281

Murray, Santiago, 250

narcotrafficking. See drug trafficking

National Council of Magistrates (Consejo Nacional de la Magistratura), 49

National Democratic Institute (NDI), 257, 258, 262

National Election Board. See Jurado de Elecciones (JNE)

National Fund for Social Compensation and Development. See Fondo Nacional de Compensación y Desarrollo Social (FONCODES)

National Institute for the Defense of Competition and Intellectual Property Protection (INDECOPI), 159, 225 n. 4

National Intelligence Service. See Servicio de Inteligencia Nacional (SIN)

National Office of Electoral Processes. See Oficina de Procesos Electorales (ONPE)

National Organization of Electoral Processes. See Oficina de Procesos Electorales (ONPE)

National Statistics Institute (INEI), 187

National University of Education, 49

natural catastrophes, 30

Needler, Martin, 301

neoliberalism, 2, 26–28, 63, 79. See also market reforms; privatization

neopopulism, 7, 13–15, 38 n. 1, 225, 300; classical populism contrasted with, 36–37, 61, 63; democracy and, 3–4; disappearance of opportune issues for, 29–31; electoral authoritarianism (EA) and, 302–3; expectations of, 62–65; fragility of populist leaders, 64; Fujimori regime's collapse and, 33–36; imposed continuation of, 31–33; leadership and, 8; Lima mayoralty and, 78; recurrence of, 35–36; rise of Fujimori's leadership, 20–21; strengths and weaknesses of, 15–19

New Spain, viceroyalty of, 65

newspapers, 74–75

Nixon, Richard, administration of, 102

nongovernmental organizations (NGOs), 151, 170, 172

normality, restoration of, 30

North American Free Trade Agreement (NAFTA), 194, 228, 229
Nueva Mayoría (NM), 53, 74; after fall of Fujimori, 89; Cambio 90 in congressional bloc with, 32, 94, 97, 131, 249; corruption and, 111, 114–15; majority in Congress and, 248; rejection of institutionalization, 95; women in, 169

O'Donnell, Guillermo, 3, 6, 103, 298, 304
Oficina de Control de la Magistratura (Office of Judicial Oversight [OCMA]), 104, 110
Oficina de Procesos Electorales (ONPE), 144, 258, 259, 261, 272
oligarchy, traditional, 84
Olivera, Fernando "Popi," 269, 273, 276–77, 279
Ombudsman's Office (Defensoría del Pueblo), 48, 158, 159, 170
Operation Recruitment, 111
opposition, political, 6, 40, 156, 272; *autogolpe* and, 246–47; electoral authoritarianism and, 299; electoral legitimation and, 256, 263, 265 n. 31; intelligence service operations against, 162; party system and, 81; *prensa chicha* and, 58; regime classification and, 244; at subnational level, 64–65, 78; unification of, 145–46; "Vladivideo" and, 285–86; women in, 160, 162
Organization of American States (OAS), 2, 11, 109, 144, 262, 307; *autogolpe* and, 246, 310–11; Election Observation Mission, 250, 257, 260, 263, 293 n. 52; Inter-American Democratic Charter, 317–18; monitoring of democracy in Peru, 147; Peru's ambassador to, 159; Santiago Resolution, 227, 232; U.S.–Peruvian relations and, 27, 239; "Vladivideo" and, 277, 280, 289
Orrego, Eduardo, 67
Ottaway, Marina, 312
Ovando, Alfredo, 298
Oviedo, Lino, 4

Palmer, David Scott, 10, 23, 310, 311
Pampa Bonita, 273
Panama, 237, 298
Pandolfini, Adolfo, 116
Paniagua, Valentín, 34, 76–77, 91, 100; corruption and, 316; remains of corruption and, 121; "Vladivideo" and, 269, 289
Paraguay, 4, 289
paramilitary groups, 48, 229
Pareja Paz-Soldán, José, 43
Paris Club, 136, 210, 216, 233
partidocracia ("party-archy"), 94
Partido Popular Cristiano (PPC), 84, 87, 88; *autogolpe* and, 246; Fujimori regime and, 94; "Vladivideo" and, 277; woman as leader of, 161
parties, political, 2, 5, 7, 15, 81–83; in Argentina, 32; civil society and, 57; collapse of party system, 52–57; democracy and, 41–42; discredited, 37; electoral dispensability and, 83–92; fragmentation of, 13; Fujimori legacy and, 314–16; market reforms and, 205; in 1990 election, 20; partisan void and political autocracy, 92–99; popular aversion to, 16–17; weakening of, 14, 16, 43–44, 59, 307–8; women and, 160
Passage, David, 232
patronage, state, 97, 218
Peace Corps, 230
peasants, 57, 58
Pease García, Henry, 73
Peres, Wilson, 221
Pérez de Cuéllar, Javier, 65, 88, 248–49
Perón, Juan, 16
Peronist Party, 32
personalism, 44, 60; corruption and, 312–13; institutional fragility of, 93; neopopulism and, 63; as substitute for political parties, 53–54; women in Fujimori regime and, 161, 162
Peru, 8, 11, 15, 22; Argentina compared with, 31–32; civil society in, 57–58; colonial history of, 65; crisis situation in, 7, 223; democracy in, 31, 99–100, 127–28; *departamentos* of, 67; economic liberalization in, 178–80, 184; electoral authoritarianism in, 305–11; extradition request for Fujimori, 104; foreign loans and investment in, 136, 140, 141; Gross Domestic Product (GDP), 185, 195–96, 203, 213, 221; history of authoritarianism in, 44; hostilities with Ecuador, 234, 235, 236, 238; "liberal revolution," 127; macroeconomic indicators in, 202, 212; military rule in, 66, 84, 294, 298; neoliberalism in, 192, 193; political parties in,

52–53, 83–92; populism in, 16; presidential power in, 39, 40–41, 42–45; "reengineering" of, 2; relations with United States, 230–40
Perú Posible, 89, 262, 276, 315
Perú 2000. *See* Frente Independiente Perú 2000
Peruvian Communist Party, 84, 134
Petróleros del Perú (PETROPERU), 215
Petrosian, Ter, 304
Phelps-Dodge, 230
Pinchi Pinchi, Matilde, 107, 112, 269, 275, 276
Pizzorno, Alessandro, 119
plebiscites, 33, 45, 63, 304
Pocock, J.G.A., 305
political class, 14, 16, 317; "checks and balances" and, 59; culture of cover-up and, 113; neopopulism and, 37; neopopulist leaders and, 17; party system and, 77; popular rejection of, 24
Polity, 242, 245, 253, 263 n. 2
polls, 7, 16, 53, 148 n. 1; antiterror legislation and, 136; on criminal charges against Fujimori regime, 121; Lima's mayors and, 70; on market reforms, 141; on Montesino's criminal activity, 115; multiple reelections and, 251; as political weapons, 127; reliability of, 252; *ropa donada* scandal and, 114. *See also* public opinion
polyarchy, 301
Popular Kitchen Committee, 58
Popular y Porvenir, 116
populism, classic, 16, 79 n. 2, 318 n. 3; class-oriented appeals and, 53; neopopulism contrasted with, 36–37, 61, 63
populist outsiders, 8, 88–91
poverty, 18, 25, 28, 178, 180, 183; degrees of, 186–88, 200 n. 1; Fujimori's populism and, 35; in Lima, 66; social benefit programs and, 26–27, 216–17, 309; U.S.–Latin American relations and, 227
Prado, Manuel, 80 n. 6
prensa chicha, 58, 74–75, 109
prices, 141, 209
prison massacre (1986), 48
privatization, 50, 56–57, 107, 204, 214–16; economic reform indexes and, 192; inequality and, 222–23; public opinion and, 136–39; slowing of, 218. *See also* market reforms; neoliberalism

Procuraduría Ad Hoc (Special Prosecutor's Office), 104, 107
Programa de Lotes Familiares (PROFAM), 143–44
Programa Nacional de Asistencia Alimentaria (National Program of Food Assistance [PRONAA]), 26, 50
PromPerú, 159
Przeworski, Adam, 4, 298, 303
public opinion, 1, 5, 9; authoritarian rule and, 45; civil society and, 57; cover-ups and, 117; "defector" candidates and, 87; elections and, 33; fluctuations of, 63; human rights violations and, 127; ignored by Fujimori regime, 115–16; legislators and, 101 n. 14; limits of, 146–48; market reforms and, 135–42; mobilization of, 58. *See also* polls
public-works programs, 27, 50
Puente, Susana de la, 155, 162

racism, 43, 59, 291 n. 19
Ramacciotti, Beatriz, 159
regionalization, 51–52, 77
Report on Human Rights Practices for Peru (U.S. Department of State), 257
República, La (newspaper), 71, 73, 117, 278
Revolutionary Armed Forces of Colombia (FARC), 237, 238, 239, 292 n. 34. *See also* guerrilla insurgency
Revoredo, Delia, 162
Rio Protocol (1942), 235
Rio Summit (1992), 229
Roberts, Kenneth, 8, 52, 63, 302
Robles, Rodolfo, 269, 282
Roca, Leoni, 159
Rodríguez Medrano, Alejandro, 269, 280
Romero, Dionisio, 110, 120
ropa donada (donated clothes) scandal, 114, 156, 157
Rúa, Fernando de la, 31
Rubin, James P., 258
Russia, military aircraft from, 105
Rustow, Dankwart A., 299

Salas, Federico, 256, 269, 279
Salazar, Fabián, 244
Salgado, Luz, 94, 111, 155, 166, 167, 170
Salinas de Gortari, Carlos, 63, 64, 122, 208, 284
Salinas Sedó, Jaime, 247

Samper, Ernesto, 122
San Román, Máximo, 246, 247
Santiago Summit (1998), 229
Saquicuray, Antonia, 162
Sartori, Giovanni, 82
Schedler, Andreas, 244, 296, 299
Schenone, Miriam, 158–59
Schmidt, Gregory, 9
Schmitter, Philippe C., 298
Schutz, Ernesto, 109, 269, 281
security apparatus, 10, 55
Sendero Luminoso. *See* Shining Path (Sendero Luminoso)
Servicio de Inteligencia Nacional (SIN), 55, 102, 116; corruption and, 110, 111, 117, 120; first lady and, 124 n. 29, 156, 157; Fujimori's political campaigns and, 111, 122, 277; Grupo Colina and, 275; human rights violations by, 244, 288; as pillar of Fujimori regime, 285; public opinion research of, 161; slush fund of, 108; violence against opposition by, 287; "Vladivideo" and, 186, 279. *See also* intelligence services
Sheahan, John, 9–10, 312, 314
Shining Path (Sendero Luminoso), 19, 21, 30, 69; beginning of insurgency, 134; capture of leadership of, 23, 24, 25, 131; defeat of, 28, 70, 92, 252; economic growth and, 198; expansion of insurgency, 44; Fujimori's success against, 133; Peruvian military and, 207; political class and, 20; social base and leadership of, 274; U.S.–Peruvian relations and, 232, 233; weakening of civil society and, 57; women's movement and, 152, 160. *See also* guerrilla insurgency; terrorism
Shinsato, Lucila, 155
social programs, 50, 97, 99, 164, 179, 309
soft-liners, 289–90, 298
Solidaridad Nacional, 255
Somos Perú, 85, 87, 100 n. 1, 255
Soto, Hernando de, 56
Soviet Union, 230
Spain, 79 n. 4
Stallings, Barbara, 221
Standard Oil, 230
state apparatus, 54, 141–42, 191, 289, 297
"state capture," 122, 125 n. 47
State Department, U.S., 228, 231, 232–33, 239; Fujimori deemed legitimate by, 260, 262; human rights monitoring and, 257,

315; Peruvian elections and, 250; third term for Fujimori and, 284
state-owned enterprises (SOES), 210, 215–16
Stein, Eduardo, 11, 237, 250, 259; lost confidence in Fujimori regime, 260–61, 262; OAS election monitoring mission and, 257
sterilization program, 170, 176 n. 62
students, 58, 82
success, paradox of, 19, 25, 28, 29, 34, 37
Summit of the Americas (1994), 229
Superintendencia Nacional de Administración Tributaria (SUNAT), 56, 80 n. 22, 153, 196, 214
Supreme Court, 2, 3, 246, 269; "checks and balances" and, 48; dismissal of, 295; of Ecuador, 4; Montesino and, 280. *See also* judiciary

Tanaka, Martín, 82, 84
taxation, 47, 52, 56, 179; categories of, 214; emergency, 209; Export Process Zones and, 194; Fujimori's tax evasion, 273, 291 n. 10; harassment of journalists and, 58; Lima mayoralty and, 71, 72, 75, 76; Montesino's income tax declarations, 116; tax code, 210; tax collection improvements, 196
technocrats, 55–57, 94, 103, 106, 310
television, 16, 37, 80 n. 22, 114, 198; *Buenos Días* program, 70; electoral publicity on, 4, 82, 255–56; financial woes of stations, 118; Fujimori's election campaign and, 90; ownership of channels, 236, 252, 276; political corruption and, 109, 110; "populist outsiders" and, 89; in United States, 200 n. 4
terrorism, 29, 118, 274; defeat of, 172; Fujimori's approval ratings and, 132; of Montesinos, 288; trials of suspected terrorists, 50
Toledo, Alejandro, 32, 33, 100, 144, 261, 287; approval ratings, 149 n. 3; character issue and, 284; corruption charges against, 121, 317; election of, 77; market reforms and, 225; neopopulism and, 35, 36; as opponent of Fujimori, 96; Perú Posible and, 315; as "populist outsider," 88, 89, 90; remains of corruption and, 121; U.S. officials and, 259–60; as victim of electoral fraud, 256, 258–59; "Vladi-

video" and, 270; withdrawal as presidential candidate, 164, 175 n. 41, 237, 260, 262, 286
Torres, Juan José, 298
Torrijos, Omar, 298
Townsend, Anel, 104, 161, 293 n. 46
Townsend Commission, 106
trade unions. *See* unions
tránsfugas (turncoats), 111, 119, 276, 280, 288
Transparencia, 74, 248, 249, 256, 259, 264 n. 15
transportation, 66, 75
Tribunal Constitucional (TC), 49
Tuesta Soldevilla, Fernando, 46, 250
Tupac Amaru Revolutionary Movement. *See* Movimiento Revolucionario Tupac Amaru (MRTA)

Ukraine, 304, 312
Ulloa, Manuel, 110
unemployment, 18, 19, 28, 126; civil society and, 306; crisis situation and, 305; economic markers of, 190–91. *See also* employment issues
Unidad Nacional, 67
Unión Cívica Radical (UCR), 32
unions, 16, 37, 57, 63, 86
United Left. *See* Izquierda Unida (IU)
United Nations (UN), 158, 170, 188, 237, 248
United States, 6, 55, 200 n. 4; aid to Peru, 79 n. 4; *autogolpe* and, 310–11; drug trafficking in Peru and, 116; international community and, 4, 5; Peru's relations with, 5, 9–11, 230–40, 246, 250; political parties in, 85; presidential power in, 47, 48; relations with Latin America, 294; threat of sanctions and, 22
United States Agency for International Development (USAID), 121, 233, 256–57
upper class, 129; in Argentina, 130; market reforms and, 142; privatization policies and, 139; votes for Fujimori, 145. *See also* class differences
urbanization, 151
Urízar, Ilda, 152
Uruguay, 186, 188, 189, 192, 194–95, 310

Valdivia, Luis, 123 n. 12
Valencia, Juan, 105
Valenzuela, Cecilia, 162

Valladolid, Flor de María, 161
value-added tax (VAT), 214
Vamos Vecino (Let's Go, Neighbor), 53, 74, 95
Vannucci, Alberto, 120
Vara Ochoa, Manuel, 115
Vargas, Getúlio, 16
Vargas Llosa, Mario, 20, 65, 90, 93; election standing of, 272; Frente Democrático of, 89; as "frontperson" candidate, 87–88; gender difference in support for, 163; structural adjustments advocated by, 97; "Vladivideo" and, 270
Vaso de Leche. *See* Glass of Milk (Vaso de Leche) program
Vásquez, Absalon, 74, 95
Velasco Alvarado, Juan, 182, 230, 298
Venero, Víctor, 105
Venezuela, 1, 193; Chávez government, 4, 14, 17, 38 n. 1; economic growth in, 186, 189; erosion of democracy in, 289; market reforms abandoned in, 206; Montesinos arrested in, 96; political polarization in, 130; subnational government in, 79
Vera Abad, Julio, 109, 270, 281
veto, presidential, 46–47
viceroyalty, Spanish colonial, 42–43
Villalobos, Mónica, 253
Villanueva Ruesta, Gen. José, 270, 281
Villarán, Susana, 162
"Vladivideos" (Montesinos videotapes), 11–12, 68, 76, 96, 102–3, 287–90; fall of Fujimori regime and, 270–72, 275–90; figures associated with, 110, 268–70; Fujimori regime already in decline before, 283–87; politically motivated corruption and, 109

wages, 25, 29, 180, 191
Waisman, David, 104
Waisman Commission, 105–7
Washington Consensus, 204, 218
Washington Office on Latin America (WOLA), 233
Watergate scandal, 102
Way, Lucan A., 242, 300
Weyland, Kurt, 7–8, 63, 92, 302, 305
"white mafia," 106
Winter, Méndel, 109, 236, 276
Winter, Samuel, 109, 236, 276
Wise, Carol, 10, 179, 195, 312

women, 5, 150–51, 171–73; "bull market" for women in politics, 160–62; electoral strategy and, 162–64; Fujimori's political tactics and, 164–66; gender quotas and, 7, 9, 150, 159–60, 166–69; political parties and, 82; social progress in Peru and, 151–52. *See also* feminism

working class, 37, 82, 139, 297, 299, 314. *See also* class differences

World Bank, 26, 74, 120, 121, 258; corruption and, 122; "Country Assistance Strat-egy" of, 199; education spending and, 195; Peru's external debts and, 210; poverty indicators in Peru and, 188

Yanukovich, Viktor, 304
Yoshiyama, Jaime, 33, 54, 73, 285

Zanabria, Luzmila, 155
Zanata, Luisa, 162, 249
Zimbabwe, 304